YAKUZA
— REINCARNATION —

02

ART BY **HIROKI MIYASHITA**
STORY BY **TAKESHI NATSUHARA**

D1291166

CONTENTS

CHAPTER 5: WALKING DISASTER

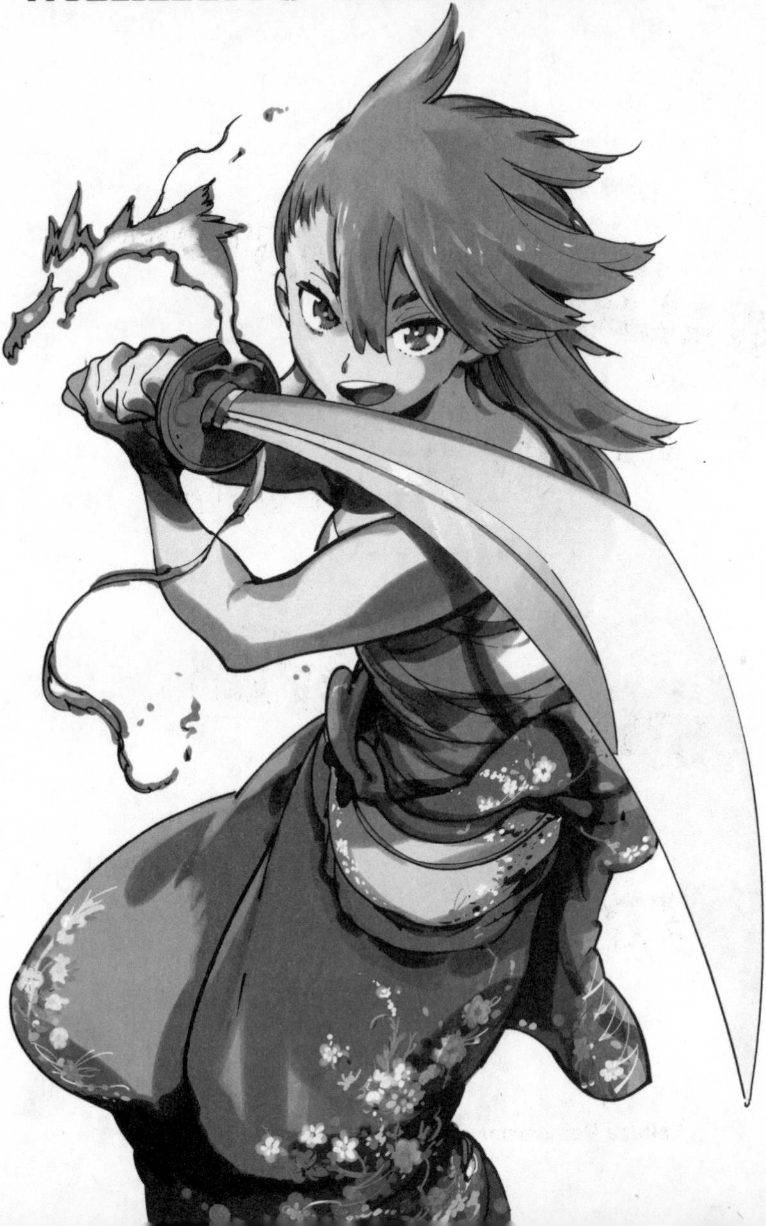

YAKUZA

REINCARNATION

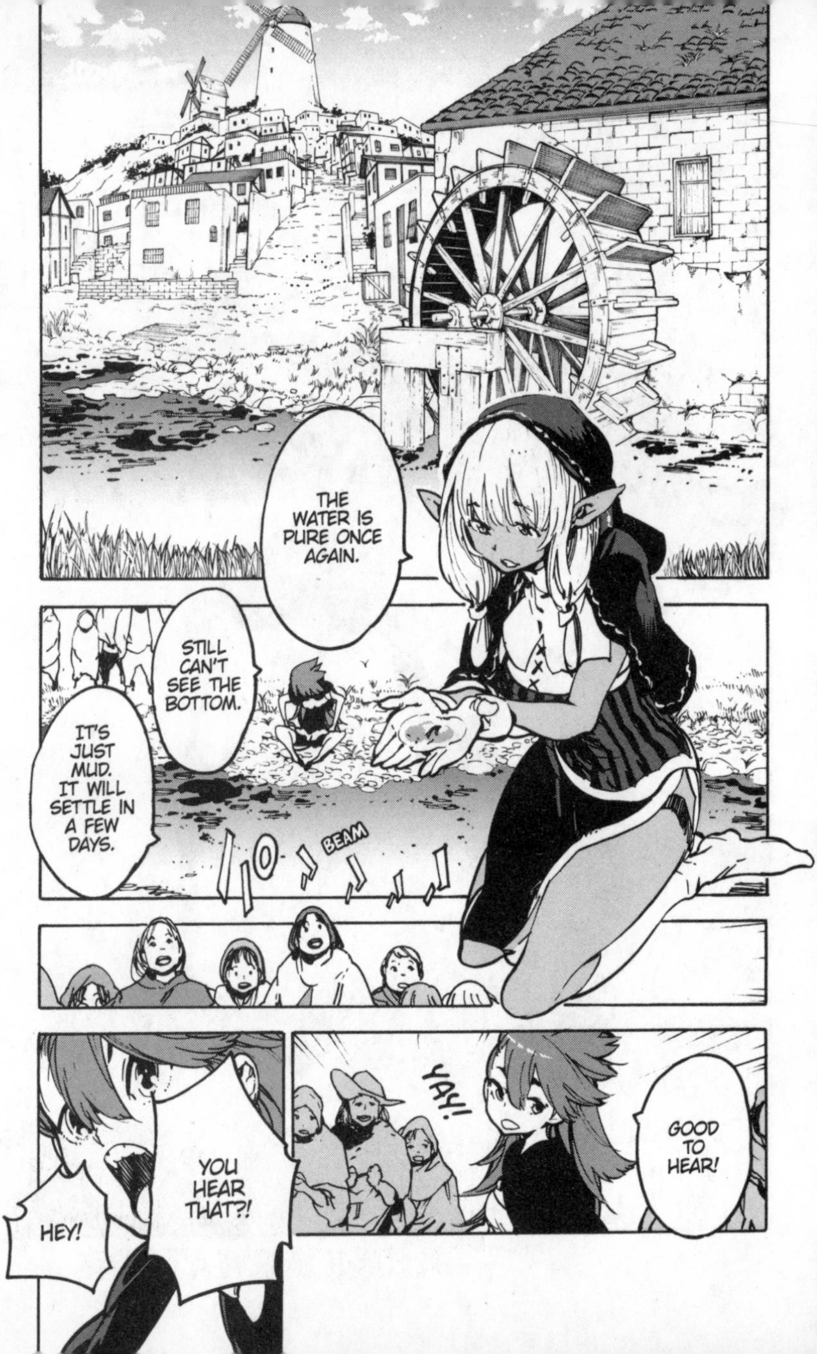
THE WATER IS PURE ONCE AGAIN.
STILL CAN'T SEE THE BOTTOM.
IT'S JUST MUD. IT WILL SETTLE IN A FEW DAYS.
BEAM
GOOD TO HEAR!
YAY!
YOU HEAR THAT?!
HEY!

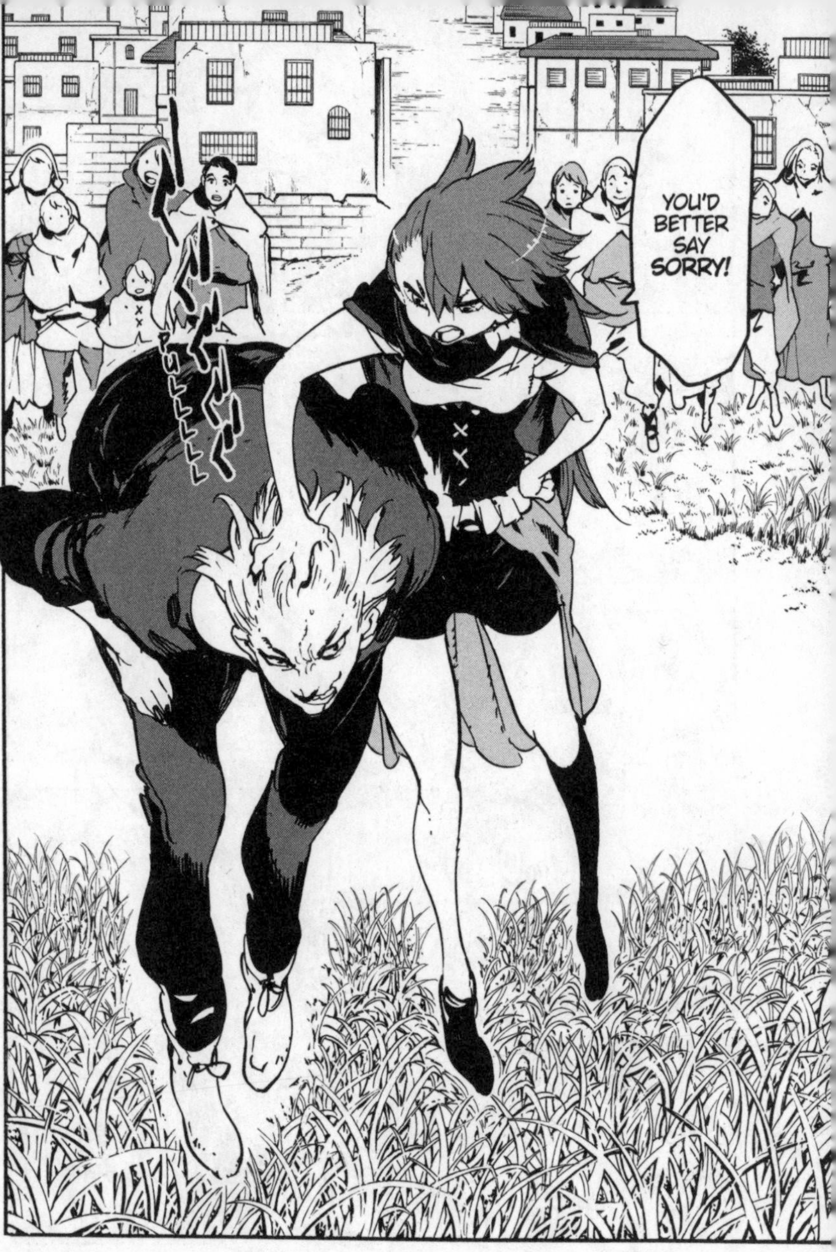
YOU'D BETTER SAY SORRY!
PULLLLLL

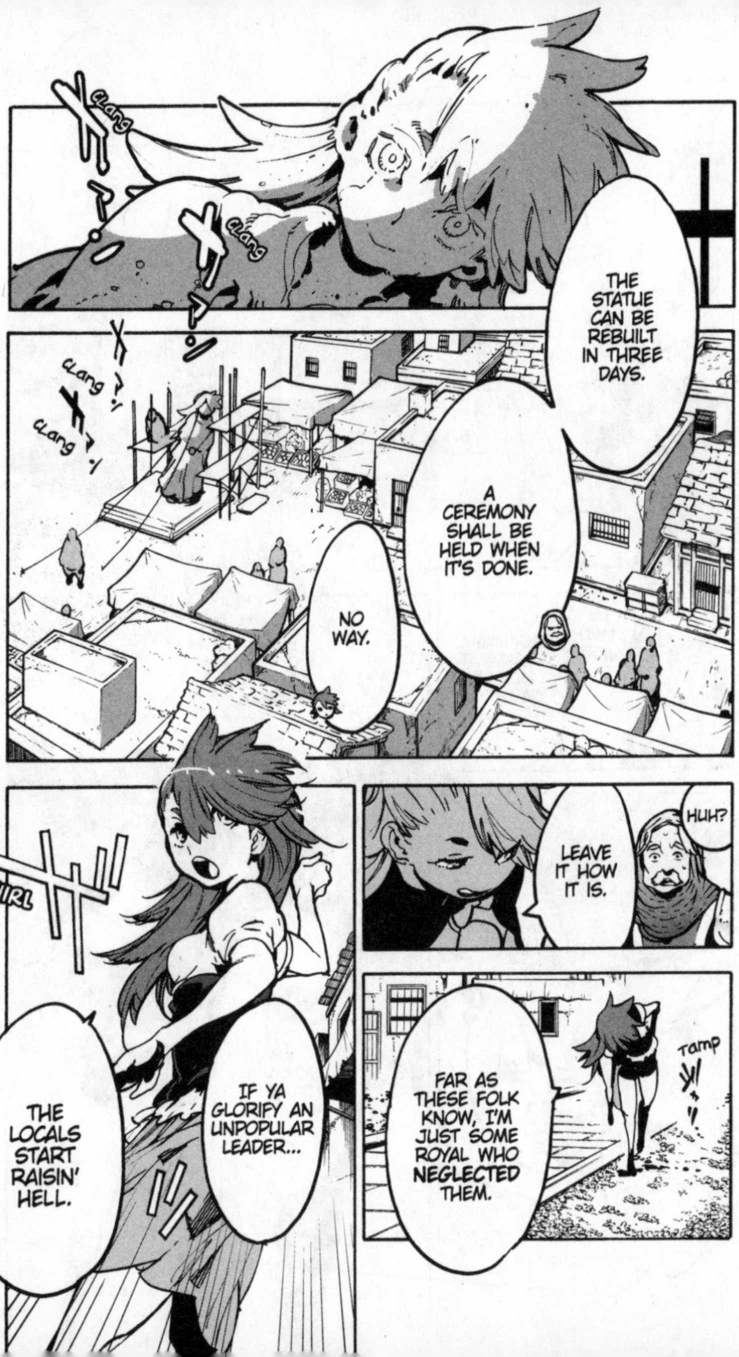

CLang
CLang
THE STATUE CAN BE REBUILT IN THREE DAYS.
CLang
CLang
A CEREMONY SHALL BE HELD WHEN IT'S DONE.
NO WAY.
HUH?
LEAVE IT HOW IT IS.
FAR AS THESE FOLK KNOW, I'M JUST SOME ROYAL WHO NEGLECTED THEM.
Tamp
WHIRL
IF YA GLORIFY AN UNPOPULAR LEADER...
THE LOCALS START RAISIN' HELL.

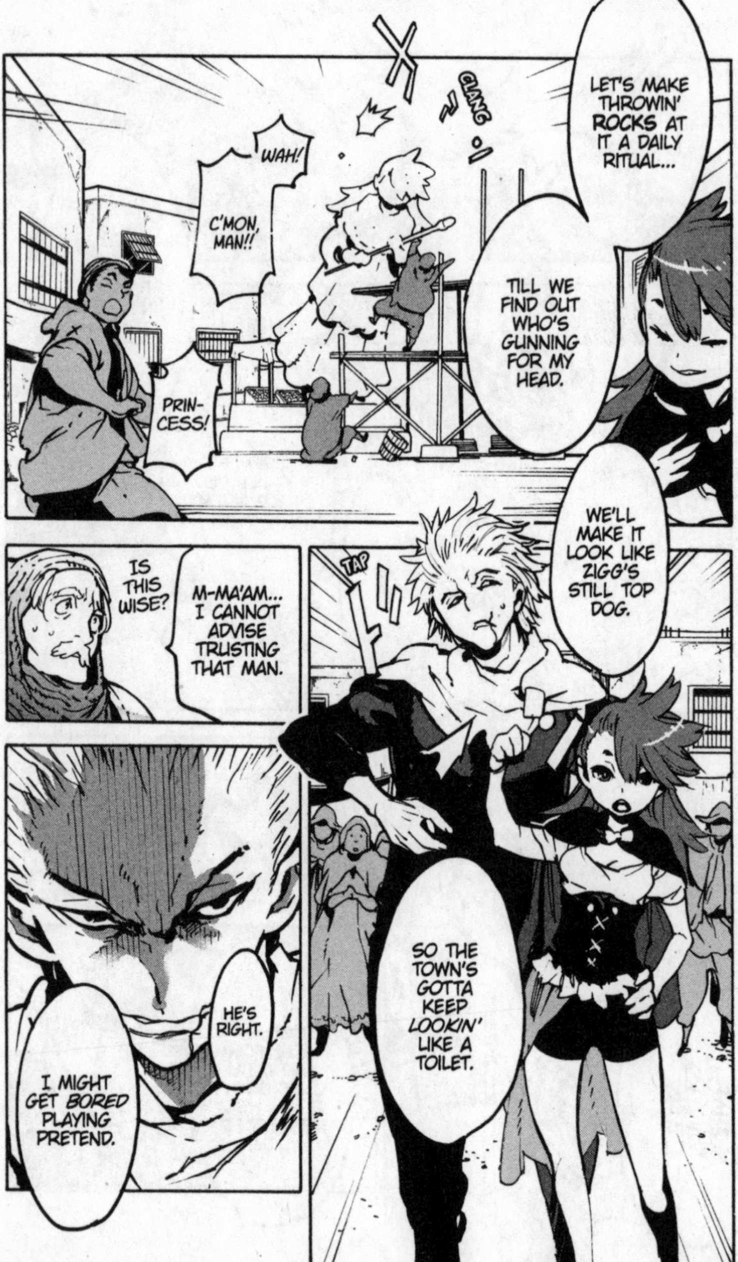
LET'S MAKE THROWIN' ROCKS AT IT A DAILY RITUAL...
TILL WE FIND OUT WHO'S GUNNING FOR MY HEAD.
CLANG
WAH!
C'MON, MAN!!
PRIN-CESS!
WE'LL MAKE IT LOOK LIKE ZIGG'S STILL TOP DOG.
TAP
SO THE TOWN'S GOTTA KEEP *LOOKIN'* LIKE A TOILET.
M-MA'AM... I CANNOT ADVISE TRUSTING THAT MAN.
IS THIS WISE?
HE'S RIGHT.
I MIGHT GET *BORED* PLAYING PRETEND.

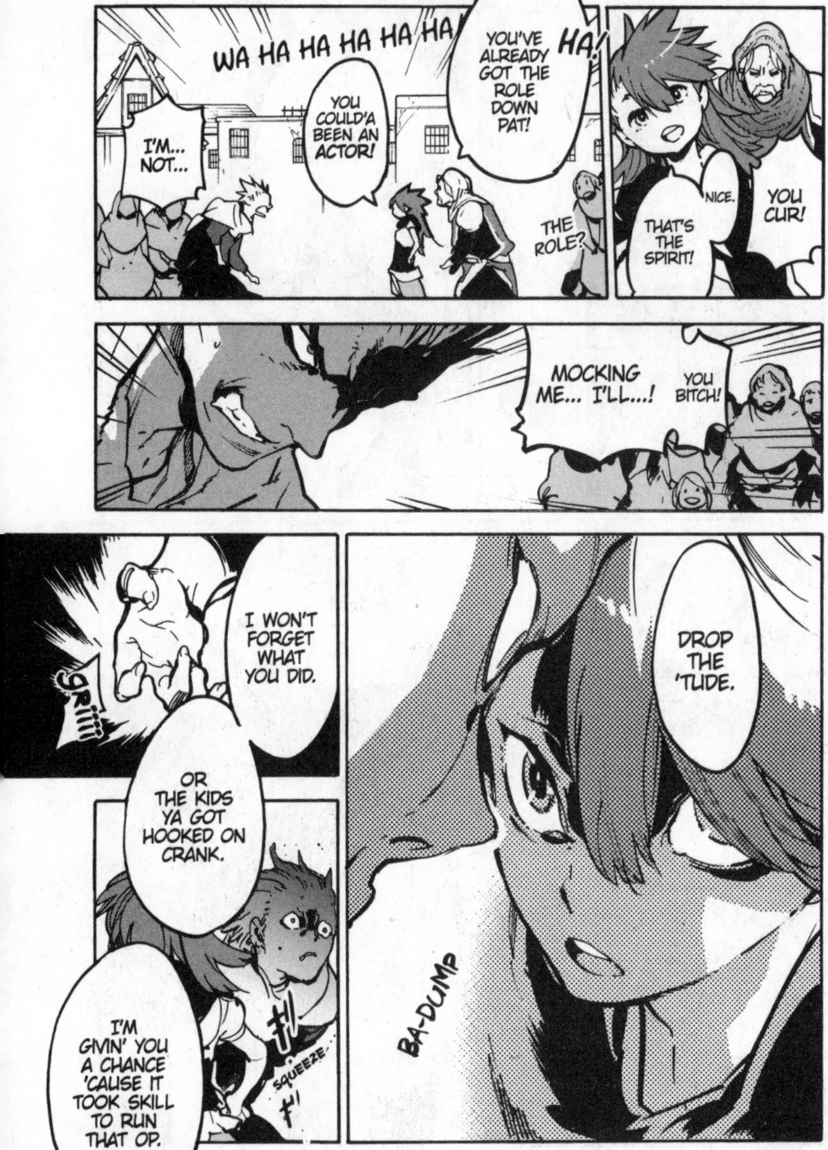
YOU CUR!
NICE.
THAT'S THE SPIRIT!
YOU'VE ALREADY GOT THE ROLE DOWN PAT!
WA HA HA HA HA HA HA!
YOU COULD'A BEEN AN ACTOR!
THE ROLE?
I'M... NOT...
YOU BITCH!
MOCKING ME... I'LL...!
DROP THE 'TUDE.
BA-DUMP
I WON'T FORGET WHAT YOU DID.
GRIIII
OR THE KIDS YA GOT HOOKED ON CRANK.
I'M GIVIN' YOU A CHANCE 'CAUSE IT TOOK SKILL TO RUN THAT OP.
SQUEEZE

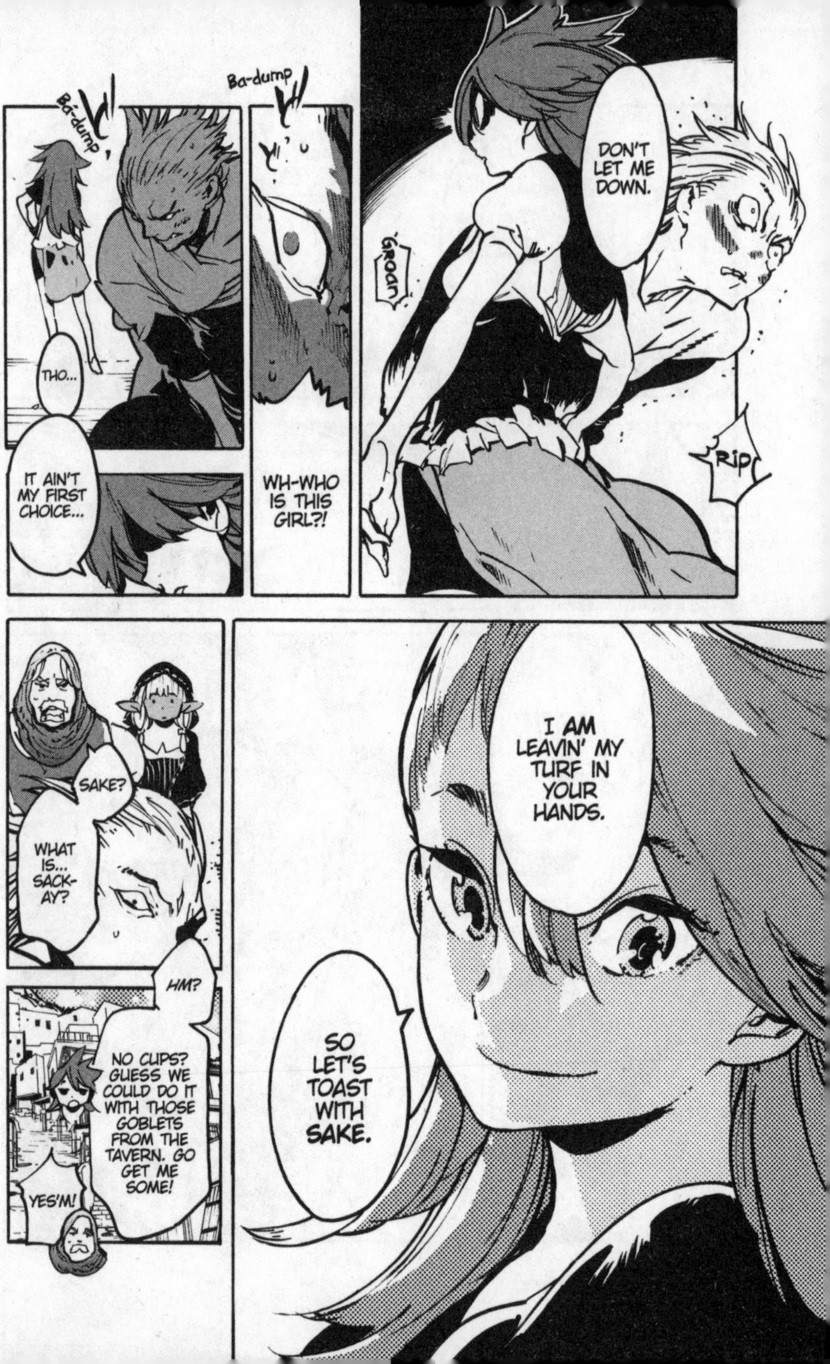
DON'T LET ME DOWN.
Groan
Rip
Ba-dump
Ba-dump
THO...
WH-WHO IS THIS GIRL?!
IT AIN'T MY FIRST CHOICE...
I AM LEAVIN' MY TURF IN YOUR HANDS.
SO LET'S TOAST WITH SAKE.
SAKE?
WHAT IS... SACK-AY?
HM?
NO CUPS? GUESS WE COULD DO IT WITH THOSE GOBLETS FROM THE TAVERN. GO GET ME SOME!
YES'M!

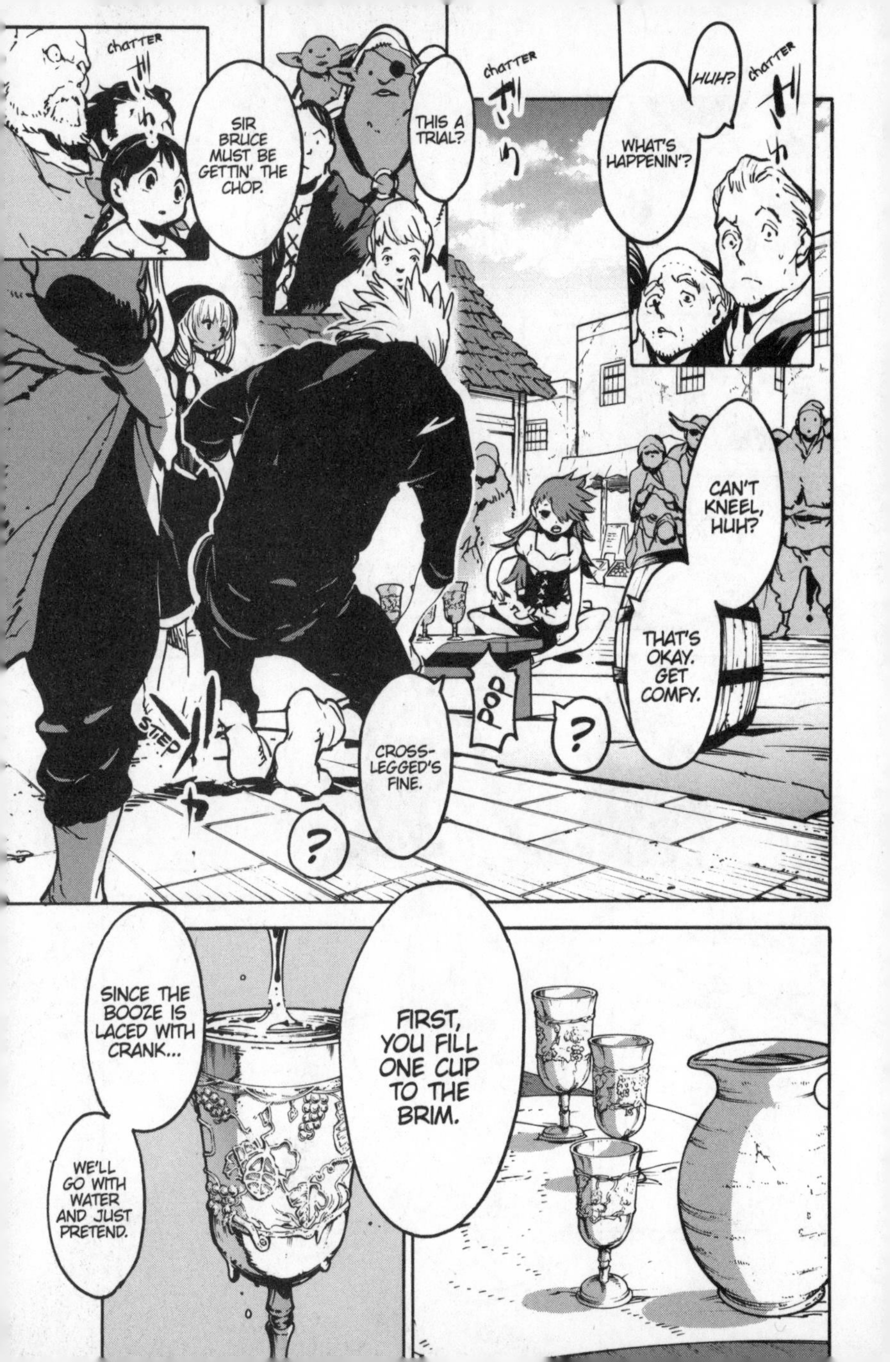

CHATTER
HUH?
WHAT'S HAPPENIN'?
CHATTER
THIS A TRIAL?
CHATTER
SIR BRUCE MUST BE GETTIN' THE CHOP.
CAN'T KNEEL, HUH?
THAT'S OKAY. GET COMFY.
?
POP
CROSS-LEGGED'S FINE.
?
STEP
FIRST, YOU FILL ONE CUP TO THE BRIM.
SINCE THE BOOZE IS LACED WITH CRANK...
WE'LL GO WITH WATER AND JUST PRETEND.

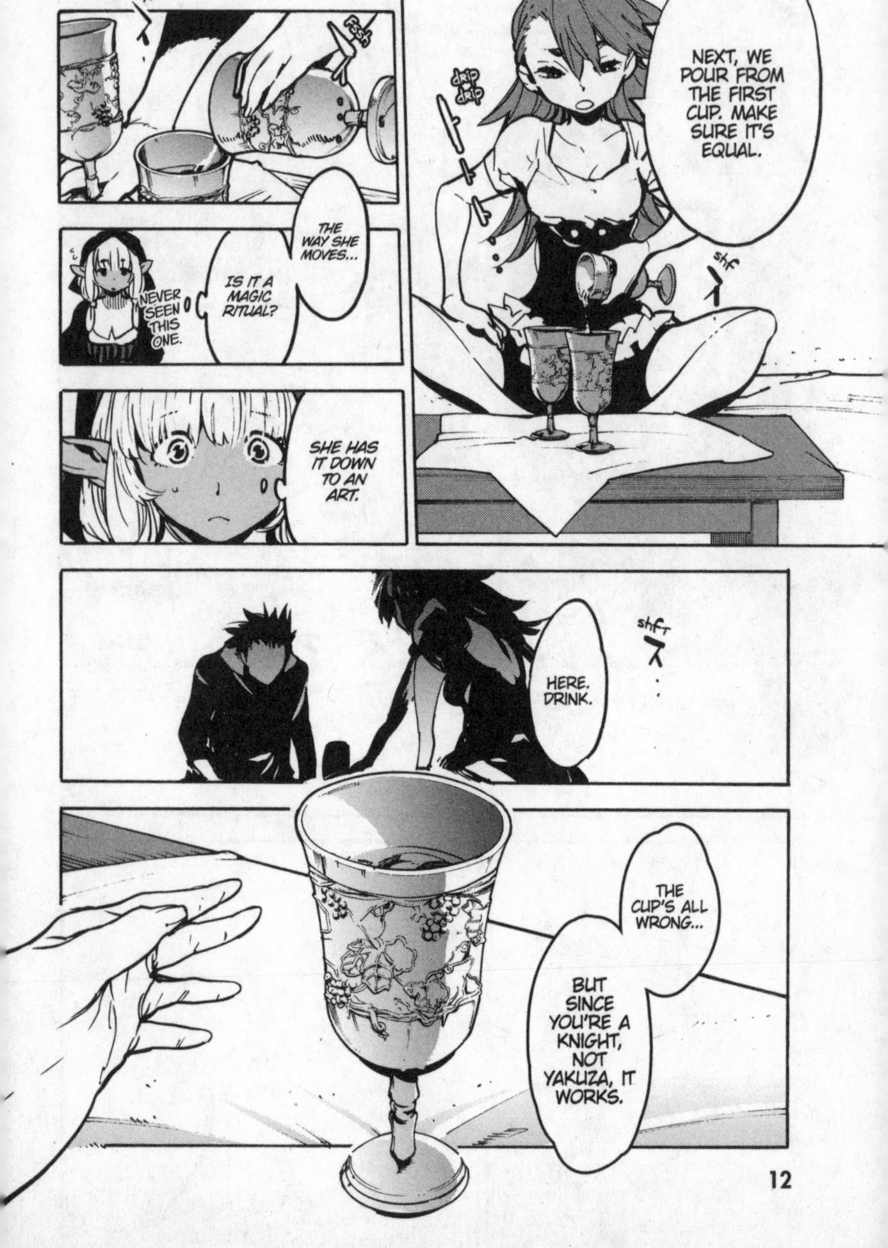
drip drip
NEXT, WE POUR FROM THE FIRST CUP. MAKE SURE IT'S EQUAL.
shf
shff
THE WAY SHE MOVES...
IS IT A MAGIC RITUAL?
NEVER SEEN THIS ONE.
SHE HAS IT DOWN TO AN ART.
shfr
HERE. DRINK.
THE CUP'S ALL WRONG...
BUT SINCE YOU'RE A KNIGHT, NOT YAKUZA, IT WORKS.

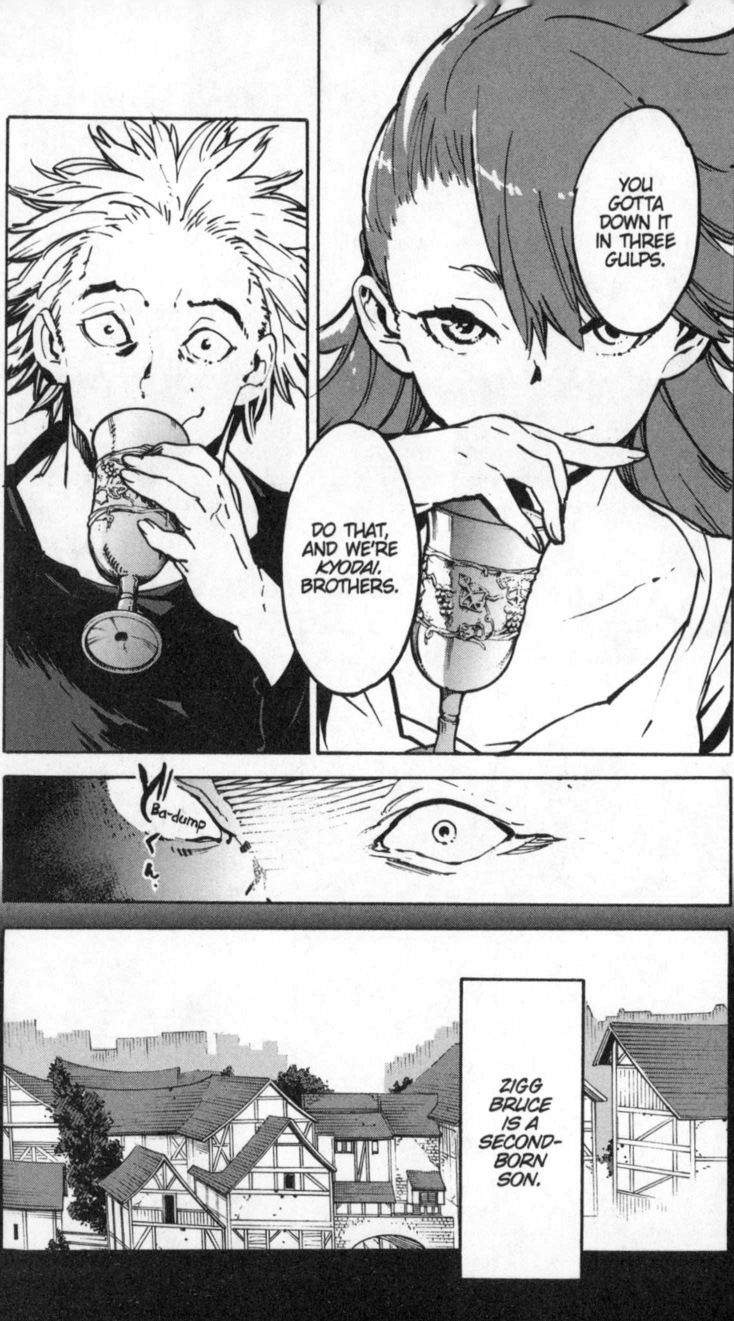
YOU GOTTA DOWN IT IN THREE GULPS.
DO THAT, AND WE'RE *KYODAI*. BROTHERS.
Ba-dump
ZIGG BRUCE IS A SECOND-BORN SON.

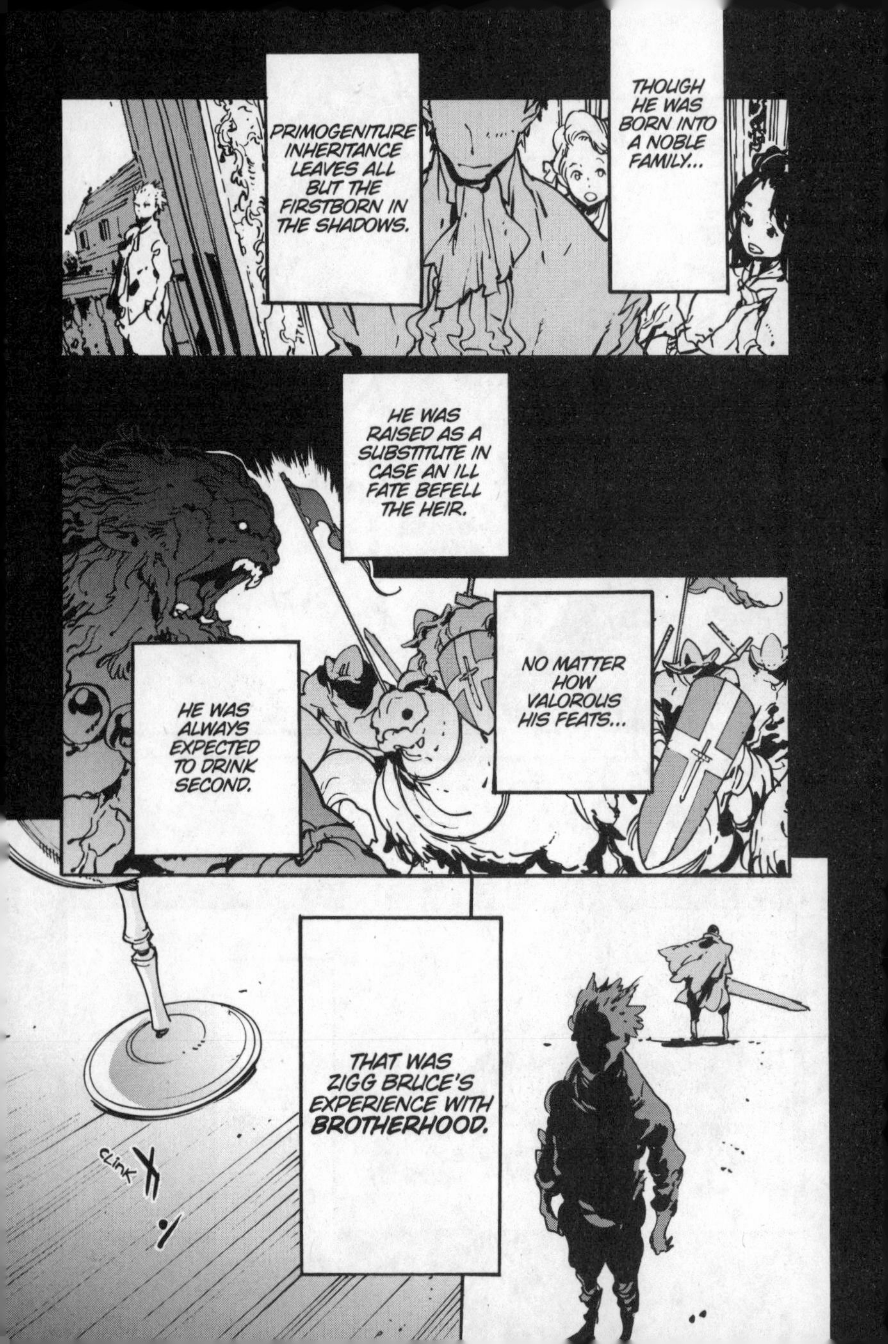
THOUGH HE WAS BORN INTO A NOBLE FAMILY...
PRIMOGENITURE INHERITANCE LEAVES ALL BUT THE FIRSTBORN IN THE SHADOWS.
HE WAS RAISED AS A SUBSTITUTE IN CASE AN ILL FATE BEFELL THE HEIR.
NO MATTER HOW VALOROUS HIS FEATS...
HE WAS ALWAYS EXPECTED TO DRINK SECOND.
THAT WAS ZIGG BRUCE'S EXPERIENCE WITH BROTHERHOOD.
CLINK

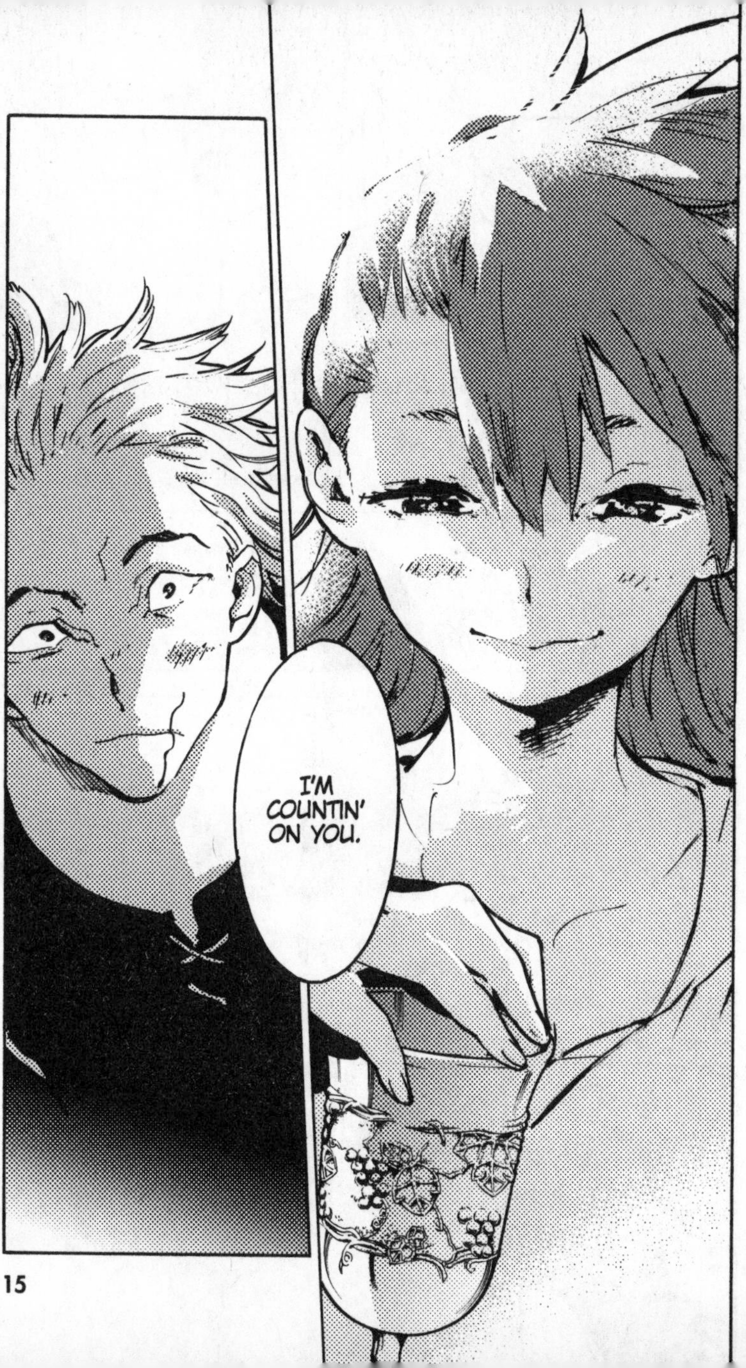
I'M COUNTIN' ON YOU.

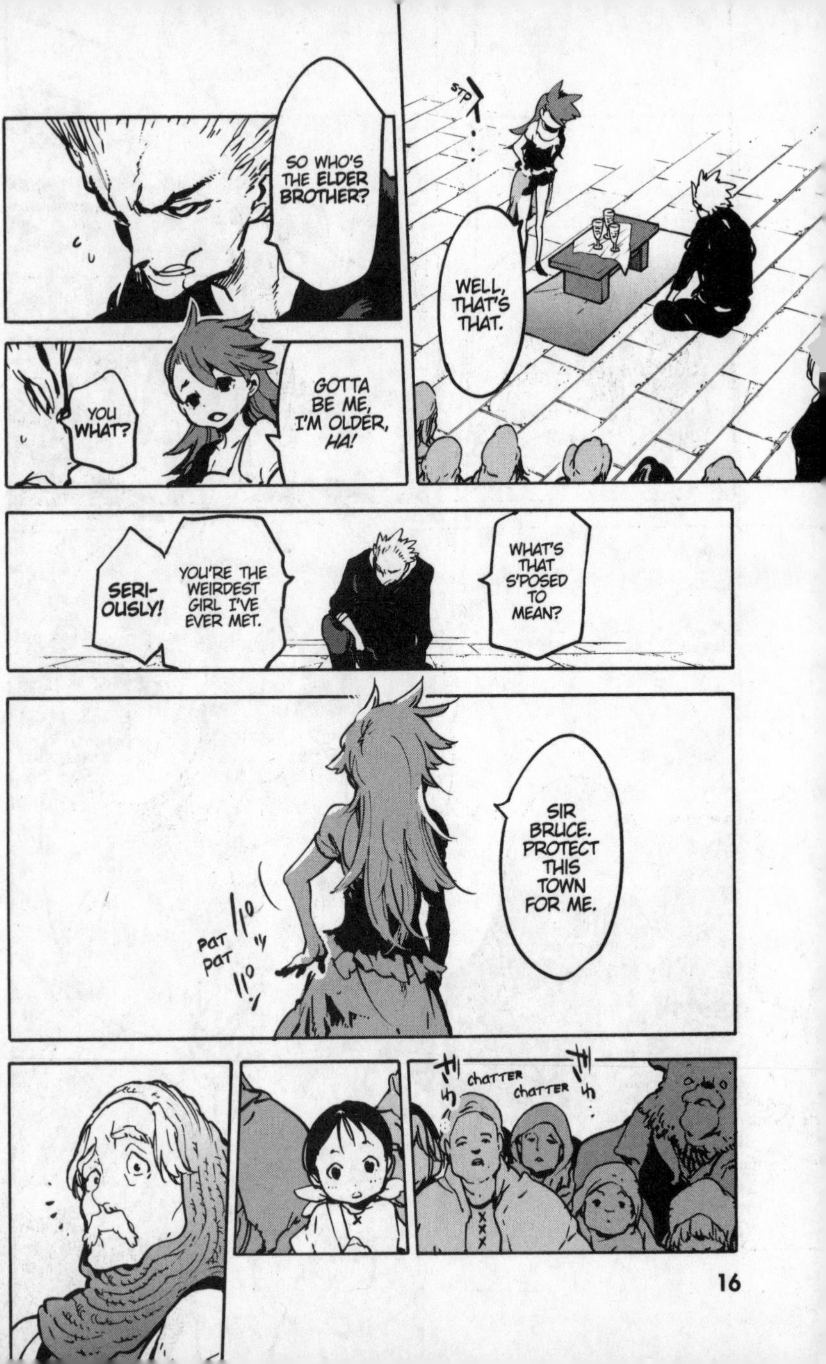
STP
WELL, THAT'S THAT.
SO WHO'S THE ELDER BROTHER?
GOTTA BE ME, I'M OLDER, HA!
YOU WHAT?
WHAT'S THAT S'POSED TO MEAN?
YOU'RE THE WEIRDEST GIRL I'VE EVER MET.
SERI-OUSLY!
SIR BRUCE. PROTECT THIS TOWN FOR ME.
pat pat
chatter chatter

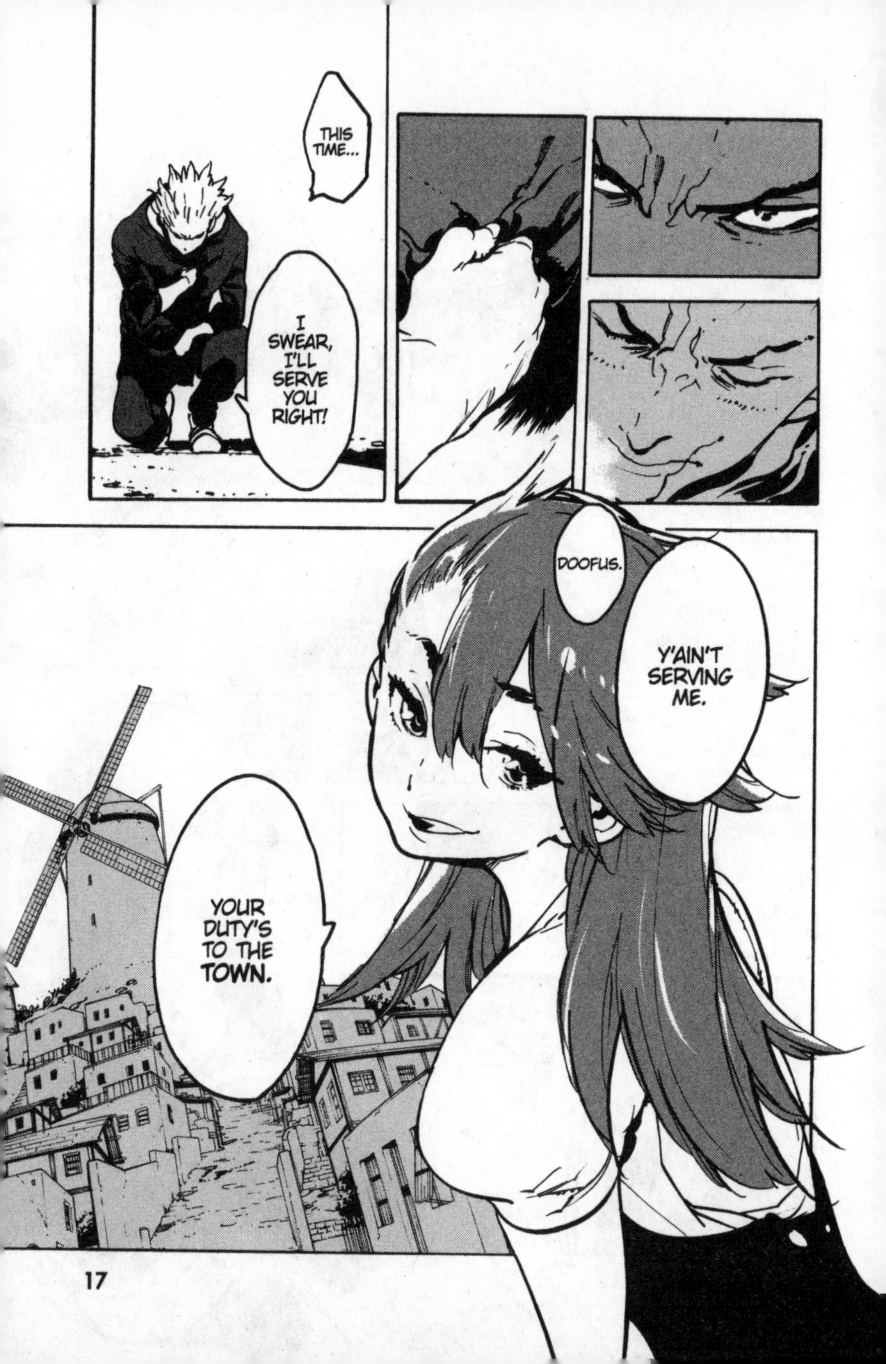
THIS TIME...
I SWEAR, I'LL SERVE YOU RIGHT!
DOOFUS.
Y'AIN'T SERVING ME.
YOUR DUTY'S TO THE TOWN.

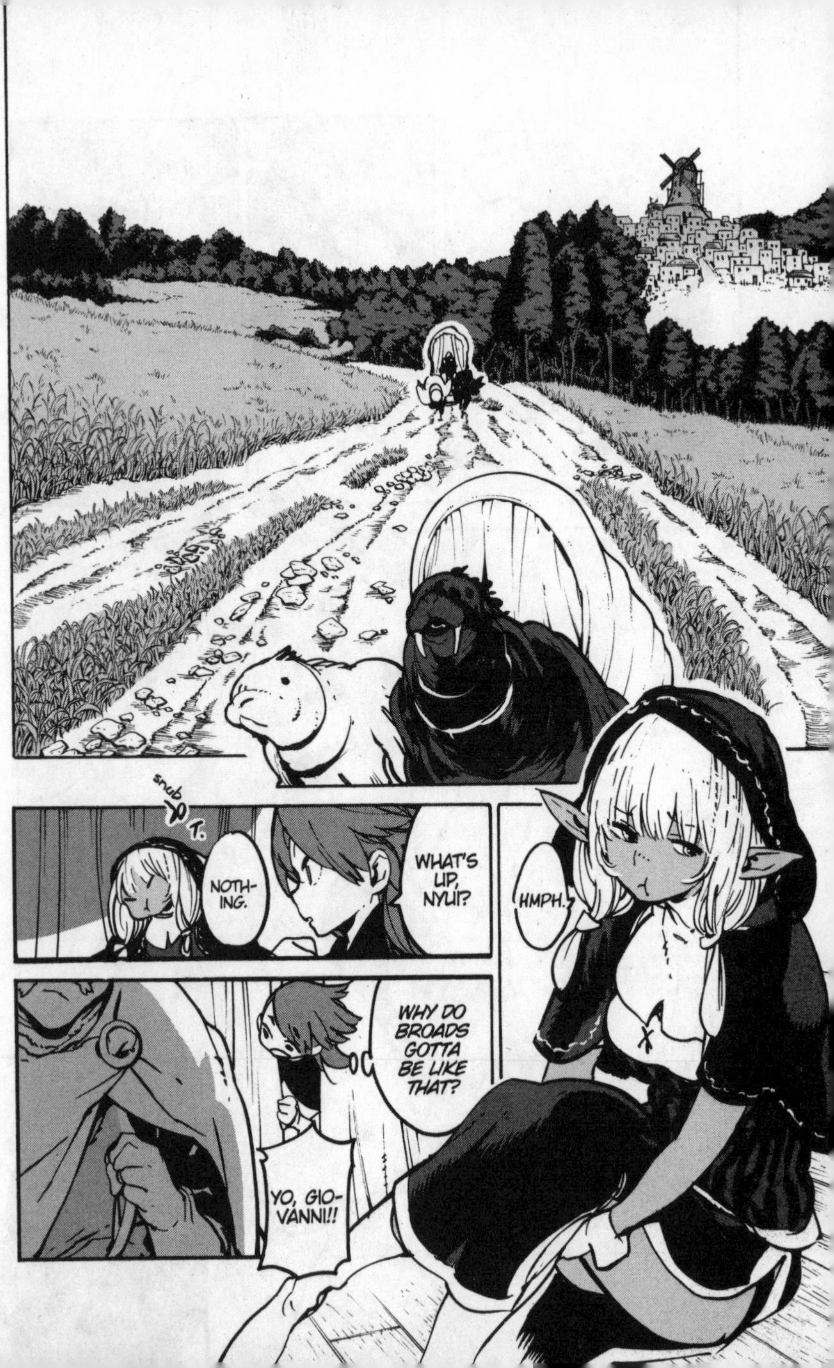
HMPH.
WHAT'S UP, NYUI?
NOTH-ING.
snub
T.
WHY DO BROADS GOTTA BE LIKE THAT?
YO, GIO-VANNI!!

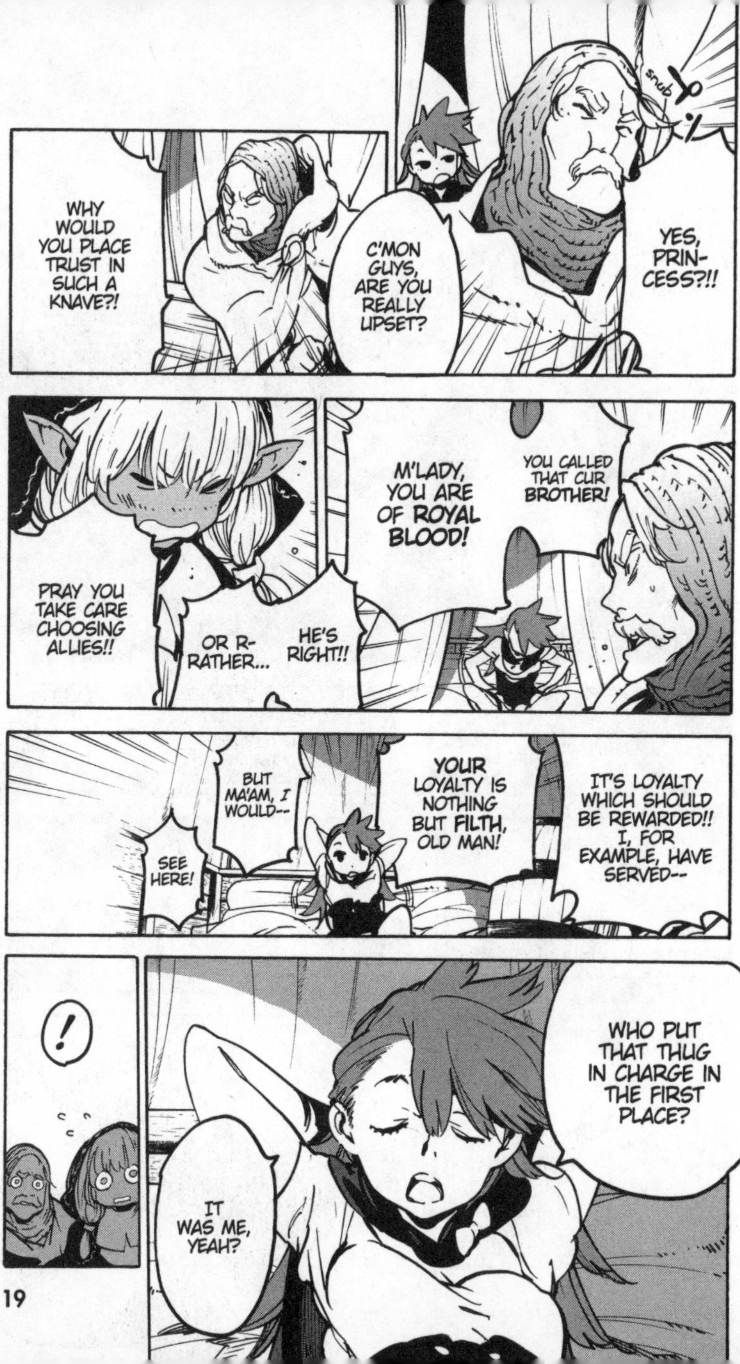
snub
YES, PRIN-CESS?!!
C'MON GUYS, ARE YOU REALLY UPSET?
WHY WOULD YOU PLACE TRUST IN SUCH A KNAVE?!
YOU CALLED THAT CUR BROTHER!
M'LADY, YOU ARE OF ROYAL BLOOD!
HE'S RIGHT!!
OR R-RATHER...
PRAY YOU TAKE CARE CHOOSING ALLIES!!
IT'S LOYALTY WHICH SHOULD BE REWARDED!! I, FOR EXAMPLE, HAVE SERVED--
YOUR LOYALTY IS NOTHING BUT FILTH, OLD MAN!
BUT MA'AM, I WOULD--
SEE HERE!
WHO PUT THAT THUG IN CHARGE IN THE FIRST PLACE?
IT WAS ME, YEAH?
!

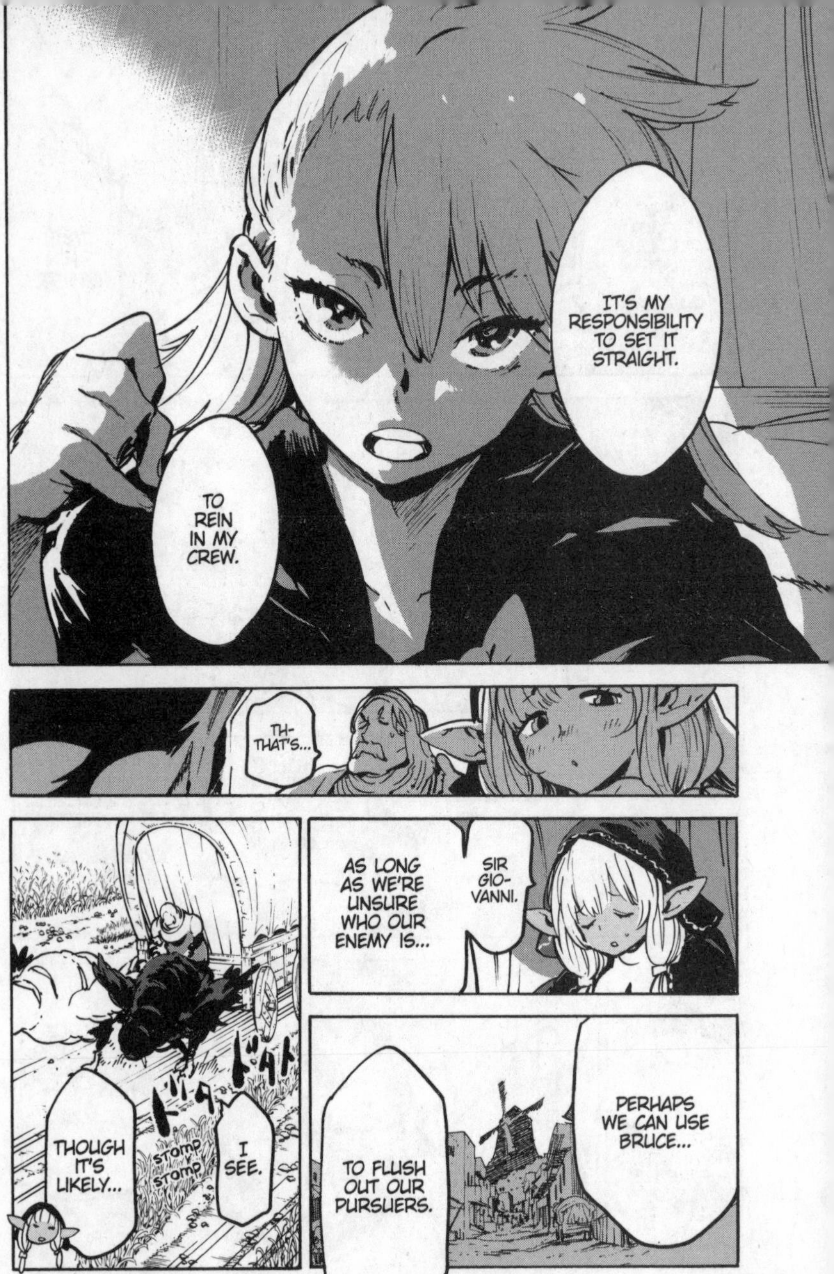
IT'S MY RESPONSIBILITY TO SET IT STRAIGHT.
TO REIN IN MY CREW.
TH- THAT'S...
SIR GIO-VANNI.
AS LONG AS WE'RE UNSURE WHO OUR ENEMY IS...
PERHAPS WE CAN USE BRUCE...
TO FLUSH OUT OUR PURSUERS.
I SEE.
stomp stomp
THOUGH IT'S LIKELY...

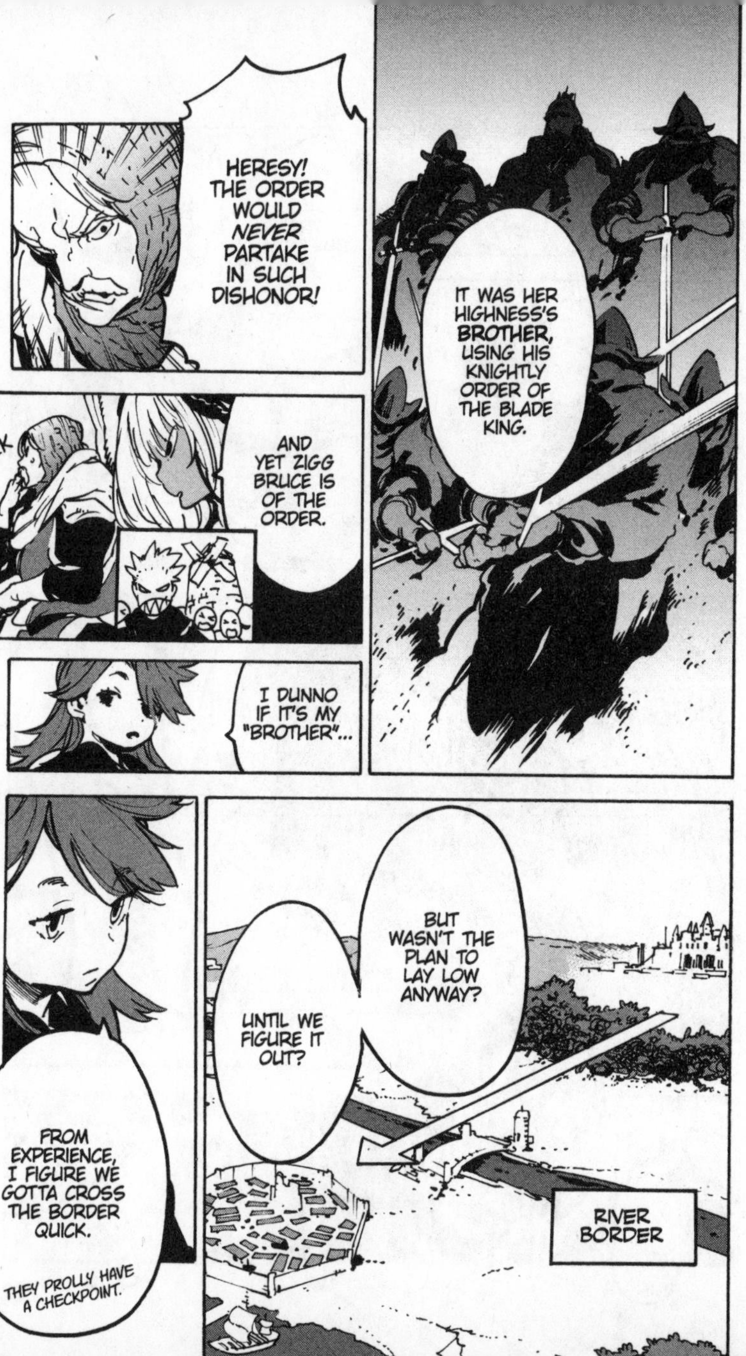
IT WAS HER HIGHNESS'S BROTHER, USING HIS KNIGHTLY ORDER OF THE BLADE KING.
HERESY! THE ORDER WOULD *NEVER* PARTAKE IN SUCH DISHONOR!
AND YET ZIGG BRUCE IS OF THE ORDER.
URK
UGH...
I DUNNO IF IT'S MY "BROTHER"...
BUT WASN'T THE PLAN TO LAY LOW ANYWAY?
UNTIL WE FIGURE IT OUT?
RIVER BORDER
FROM EXPERIENCE, I FIGURE WE GOTTA CROSS THE BORDER QUICK.
THEY PROLLY HAVE A CHECKPOINT.

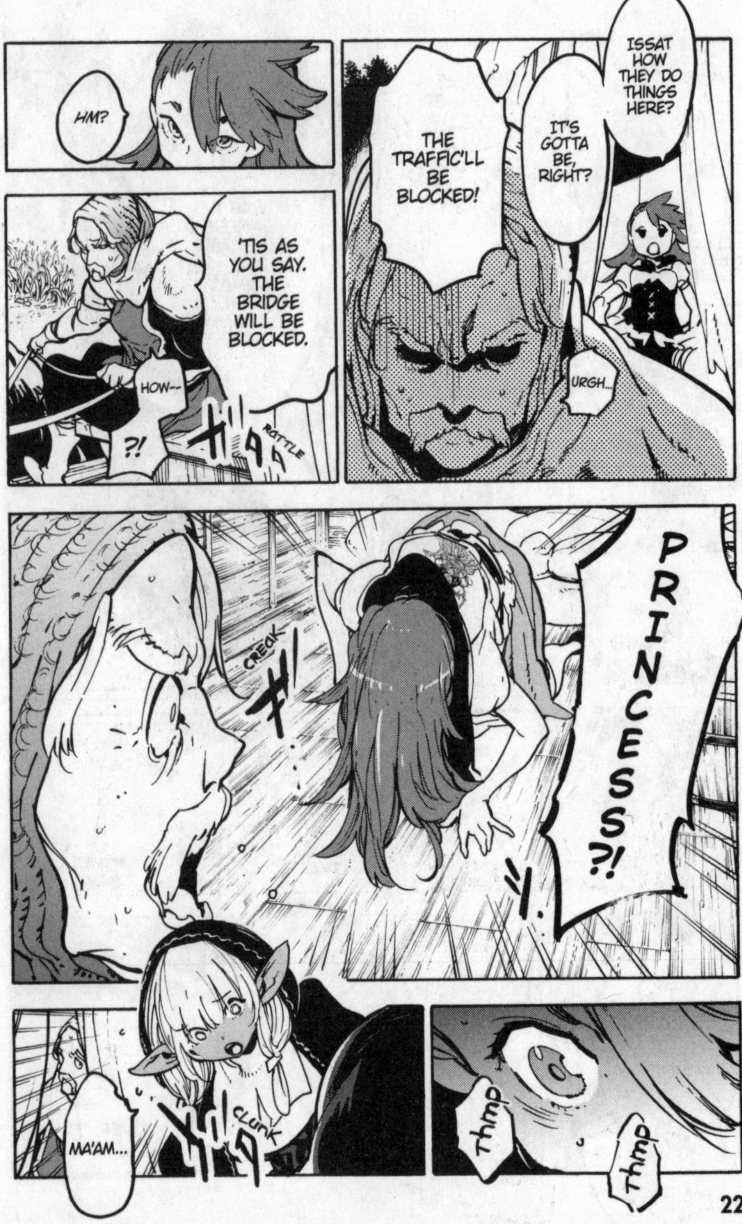
ISSAT HOW THEY DO THINGS HERE?
IT'S GOTTA BE, RIGHT?
THE TRAFFIC'LL BE BLOCKED!
URGH...
HM?
'TIS AS YOU SAY. THE BRIDGE WILL BE BLOCKED.
RATTLE
HOW--
?!
PRINCESS?!
CREAK
Thmp
Thmp
CLUNK
MA'AM...

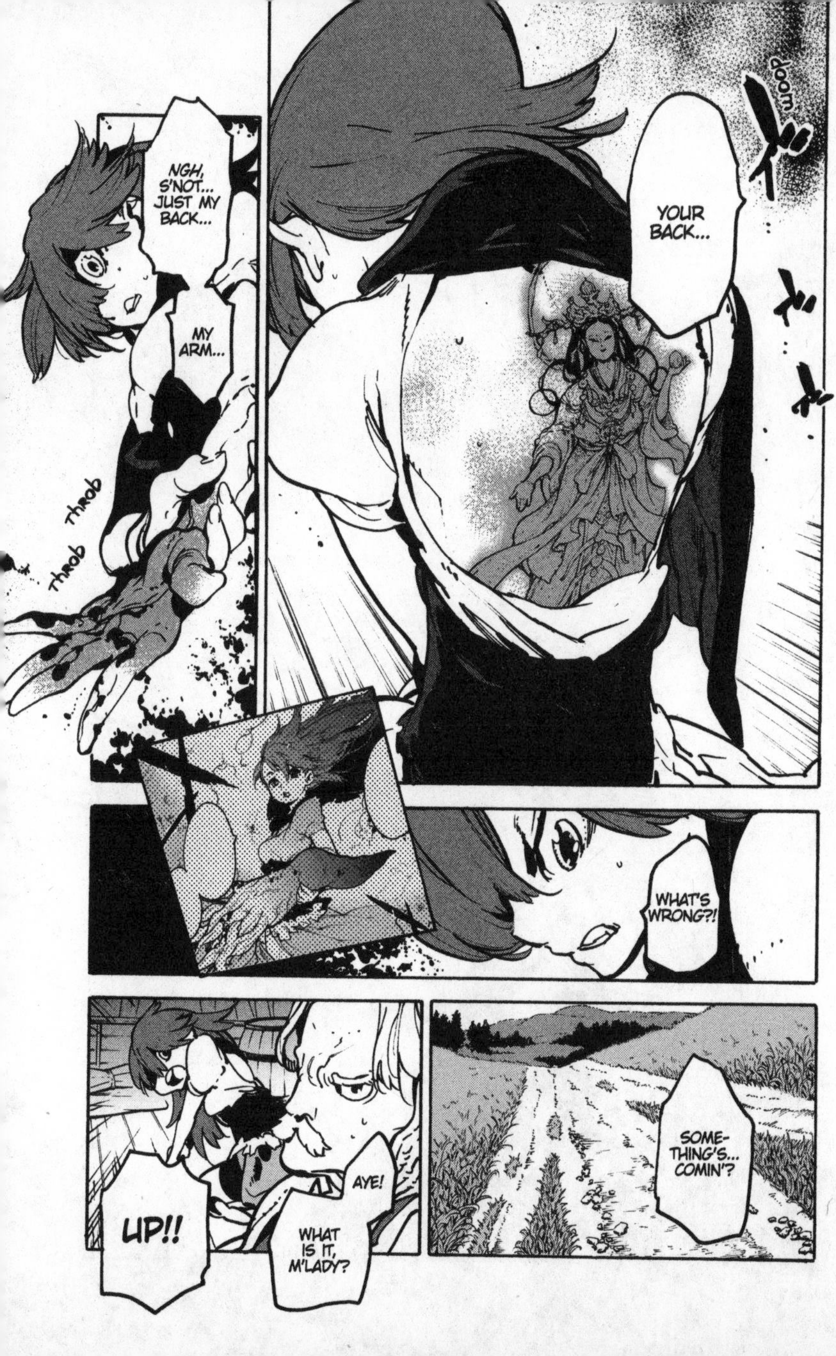
doom
YOUR BACK...
NGH, S'NOT... JUST MY BACK...
MY ARM...
throb throb
WHAT'S WRONG?!
SOME-THING'S... COMIN'?
AYE!
WHAT IS IT, M'LADY?
UP!!

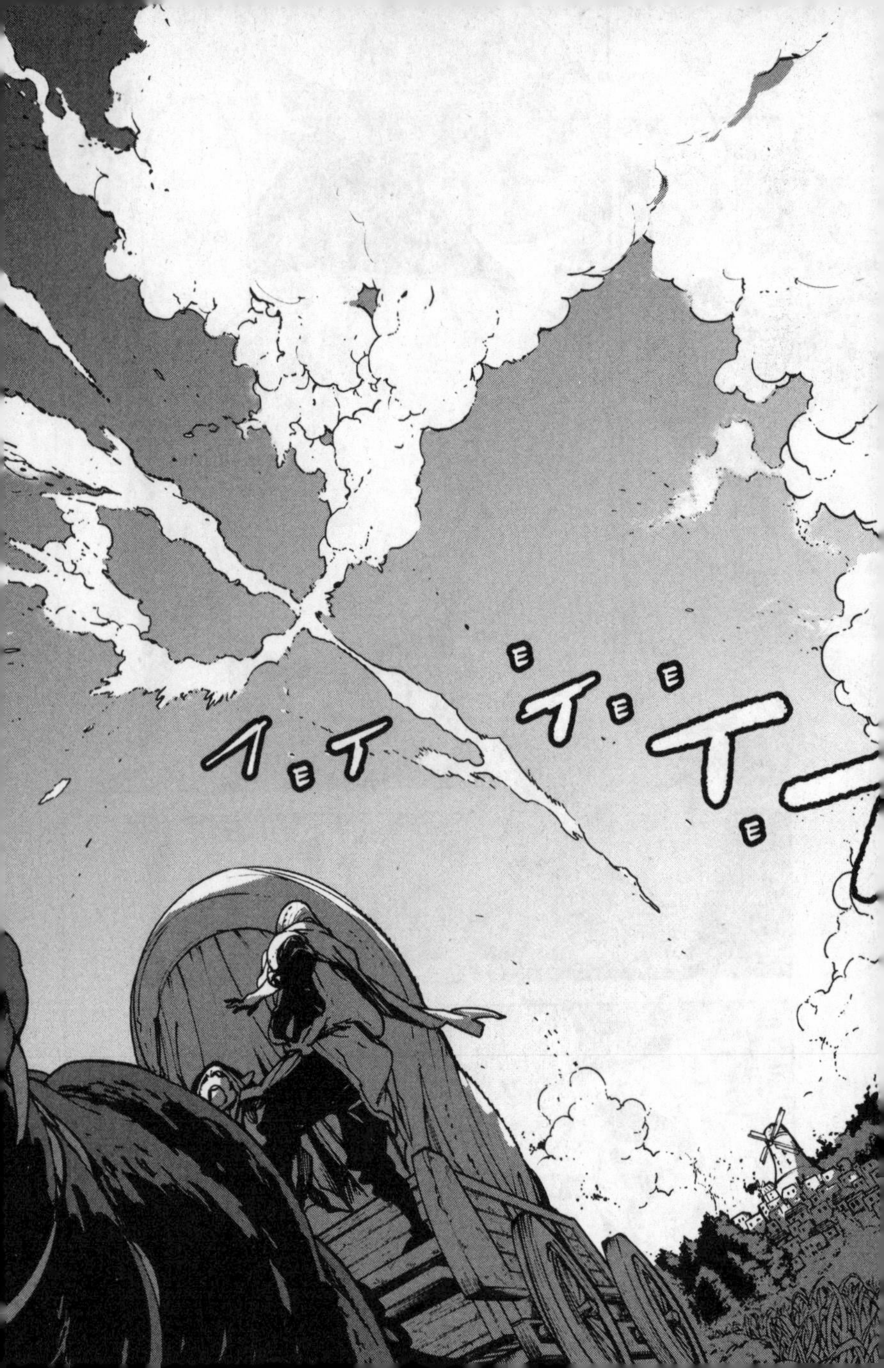
イEイ
EイEEイEー

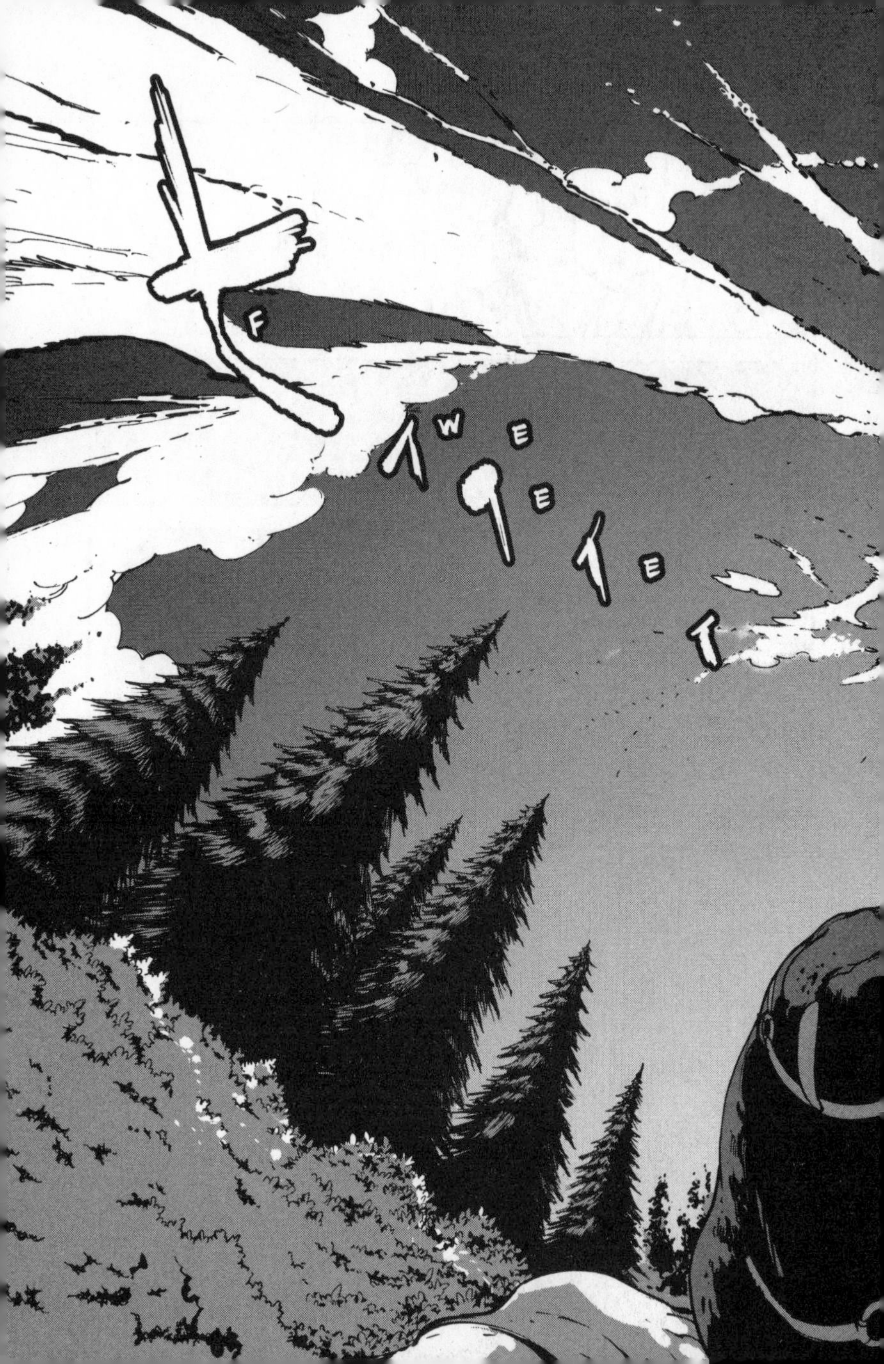
FWEEEET

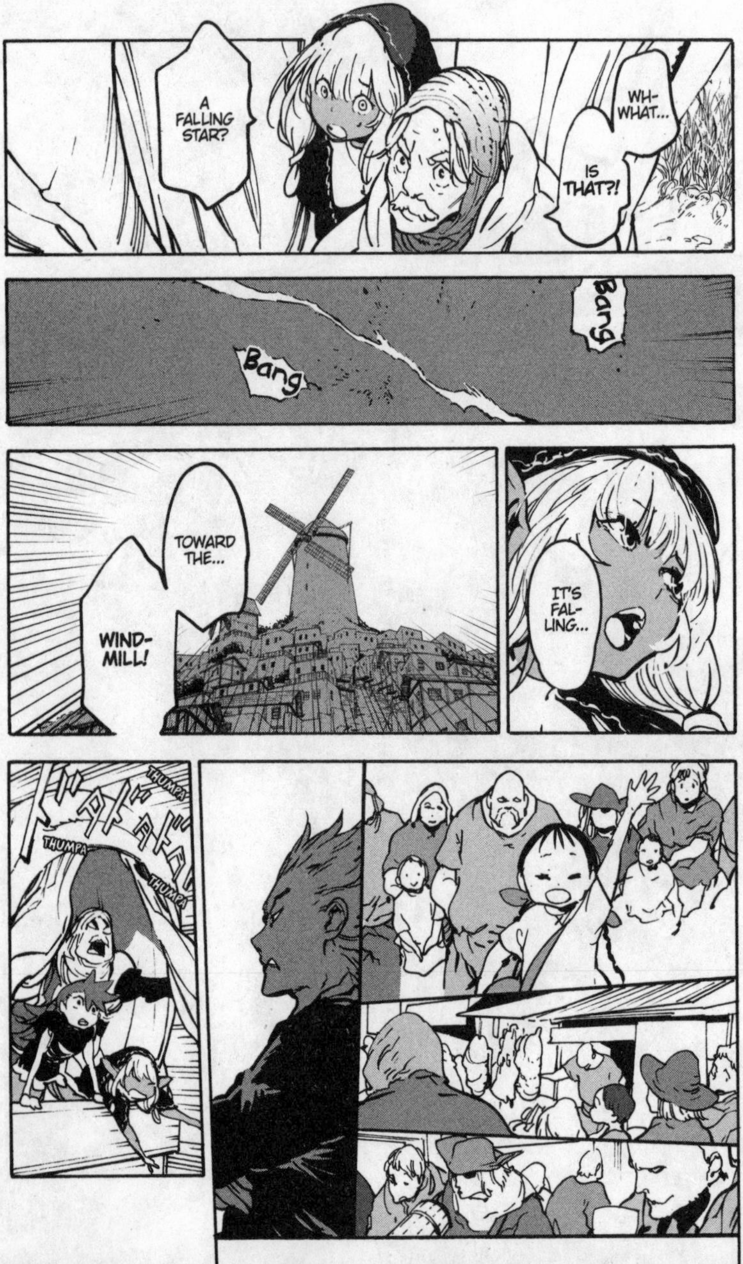
WH- WHAT...
IS THAT?!
A FALLING STAR?
Bang
Bang
IT'S FAL- LING...
TOWARD THE...
WIND- MILL!
THUMPA
THUMPA
THUMPA

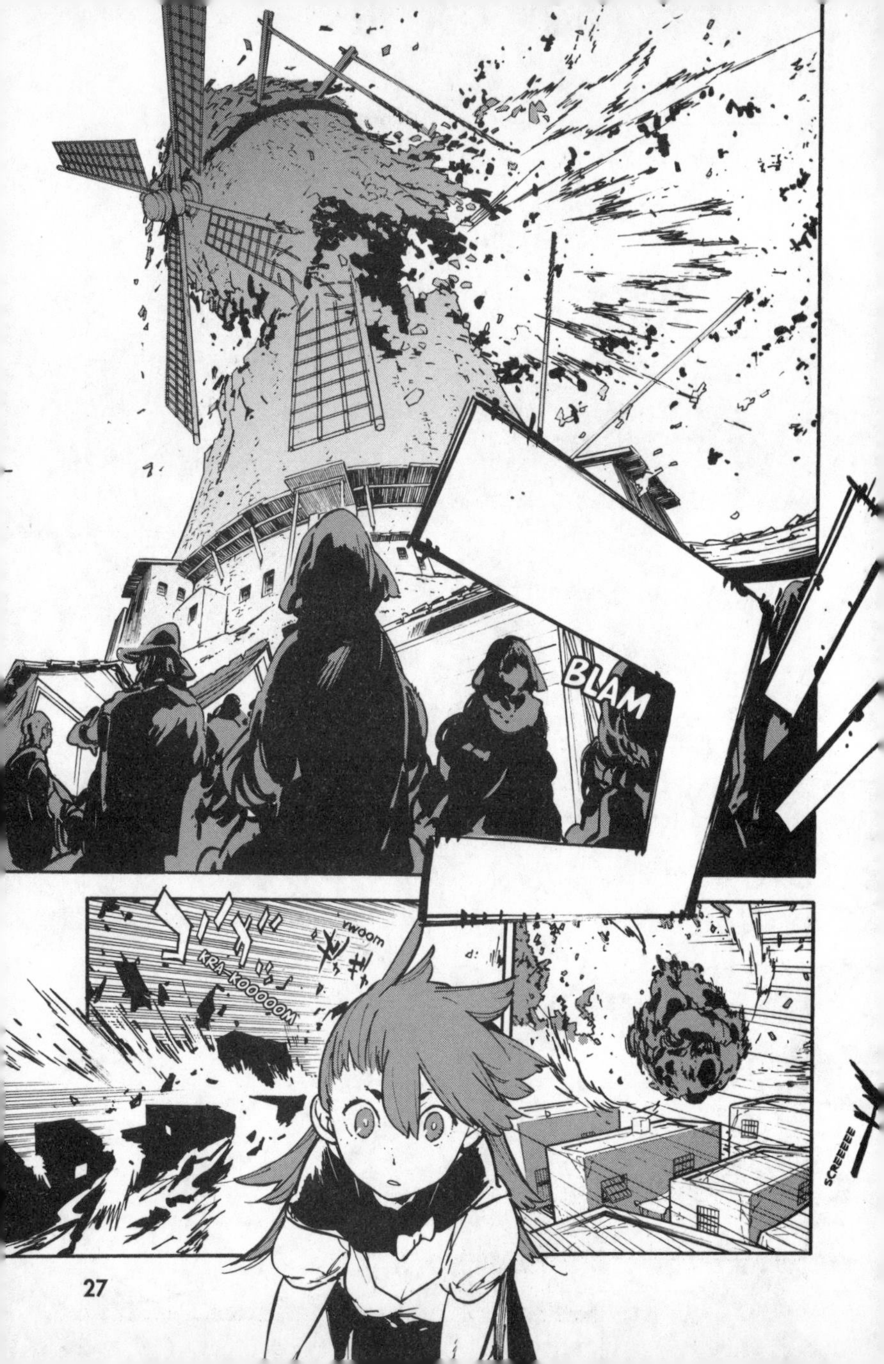
BLAM
SCREEEEE
rwoom
KRA-KOOOOOM

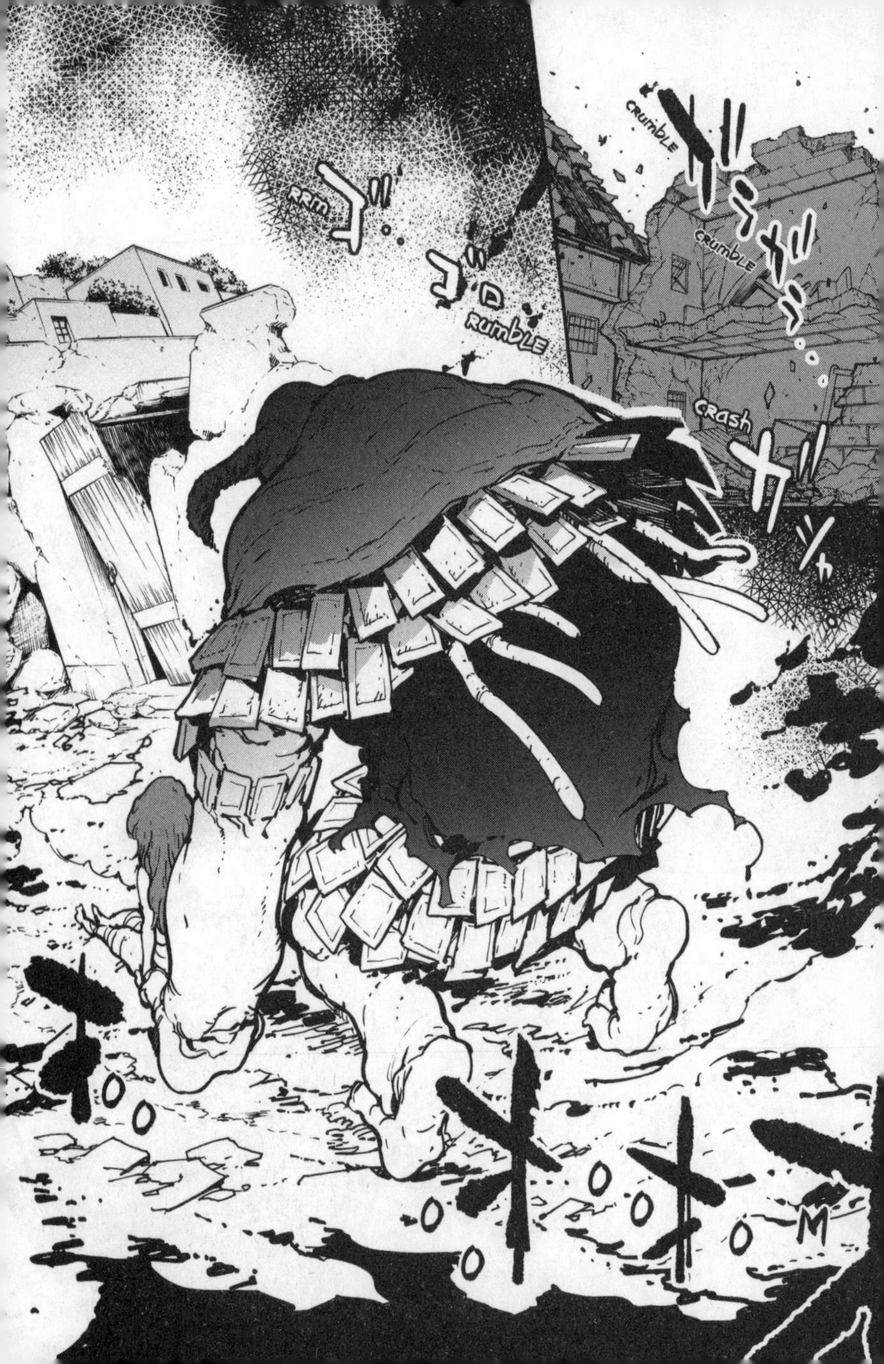
CRUMBLE
CRUMBLE
CRASH
RRM
RUMBLE

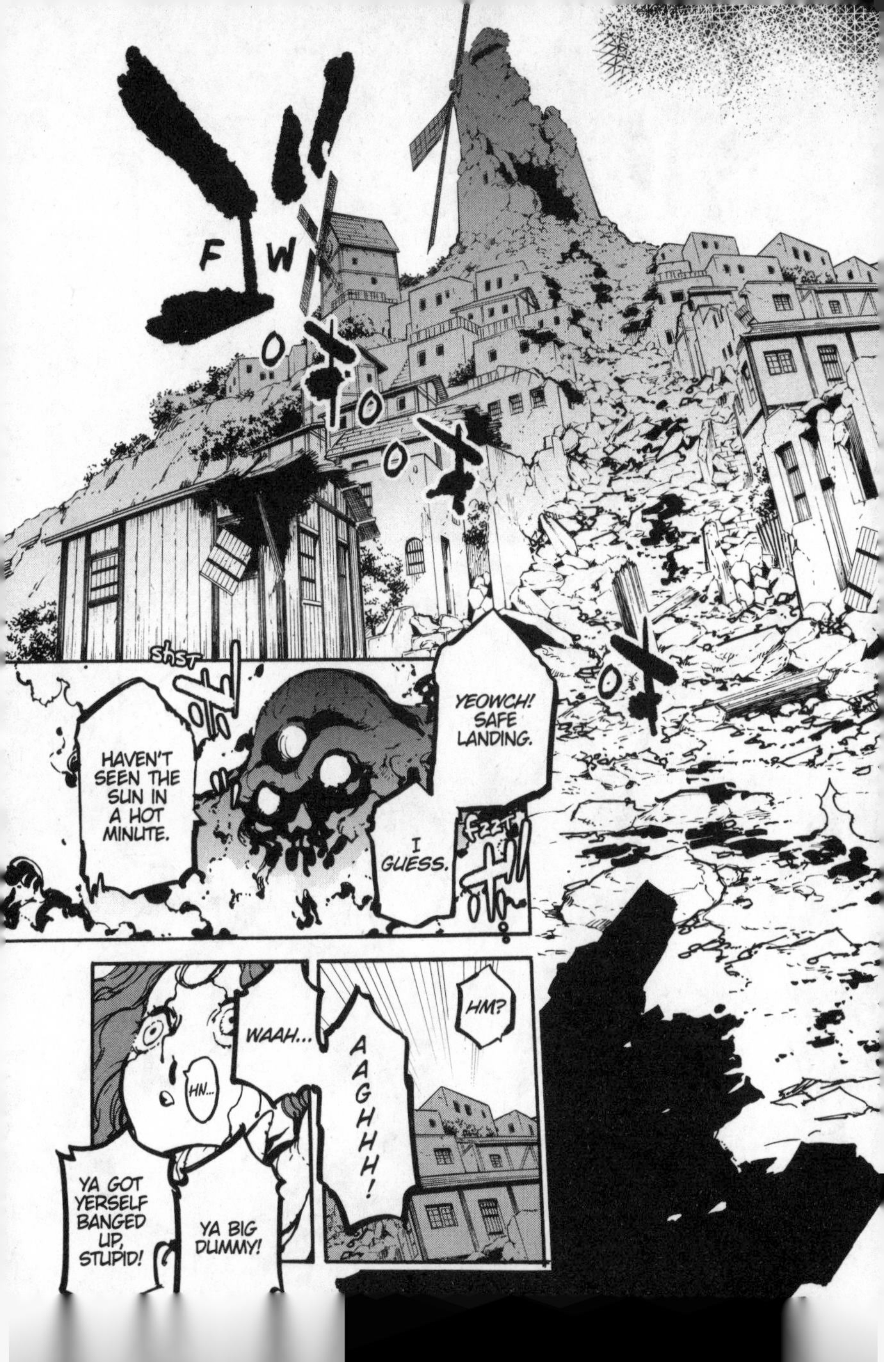

YEOWCH! SAFE LANDING.
I GUESS.
fzzt
shst
HAVEN'T SEEN THE SUN IN A HOT MINUTE.
HM?
WAAH...
AAGHHH!
HN...
YA GOT YERSELF BANGED UP, STUPID!
YA BIG DUMMY!

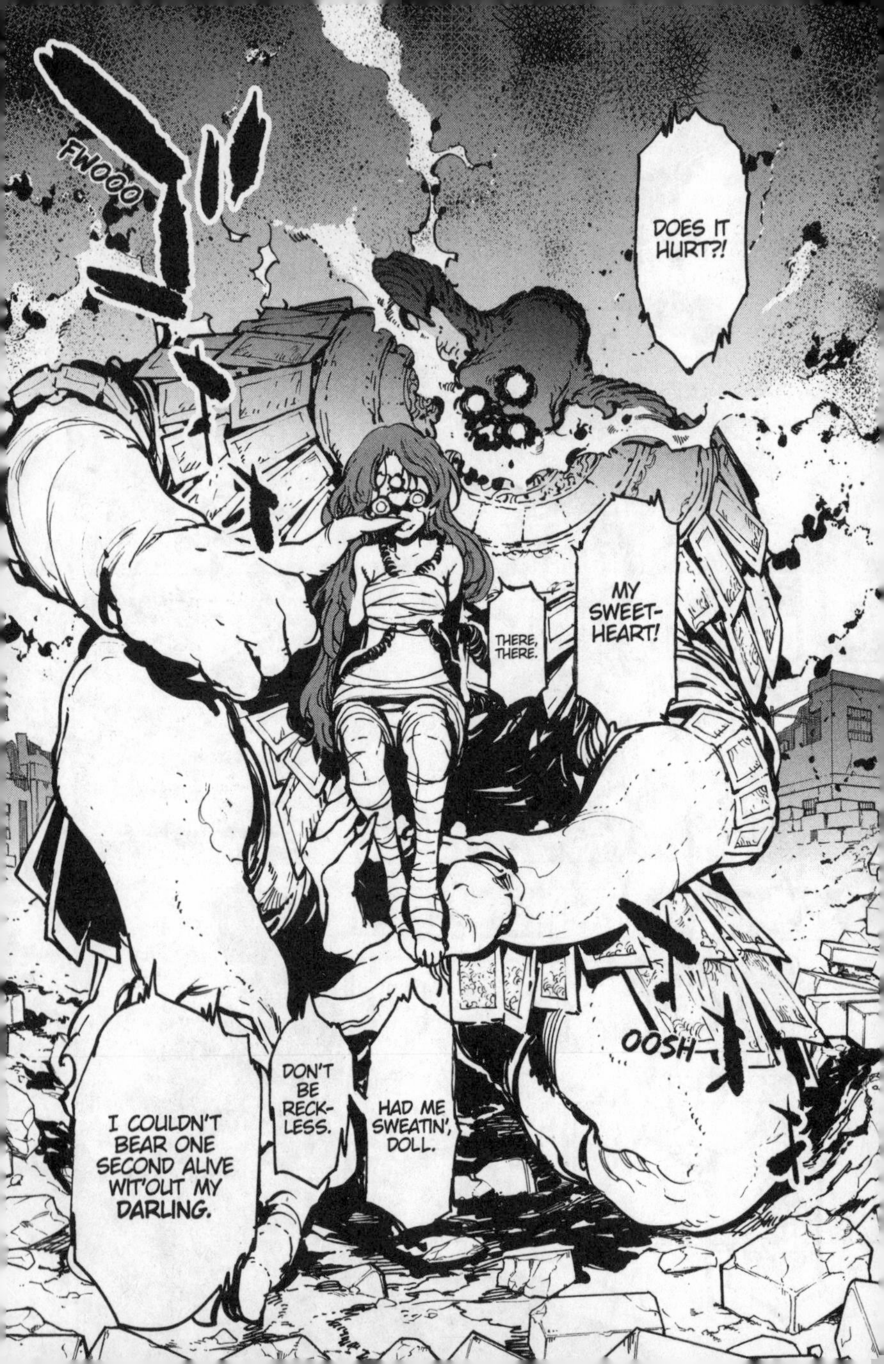
DOES IT HURT?!
FWOOOO
MY SWEET-HEART!
THERE, THERE.
OOSH
HAD ME SWEATIN', DOLL.
DON'T BE RECK-LESS.
I COULDN'T BEAR ONE SECOND ALIVE WIT'OUT MY DARLING.

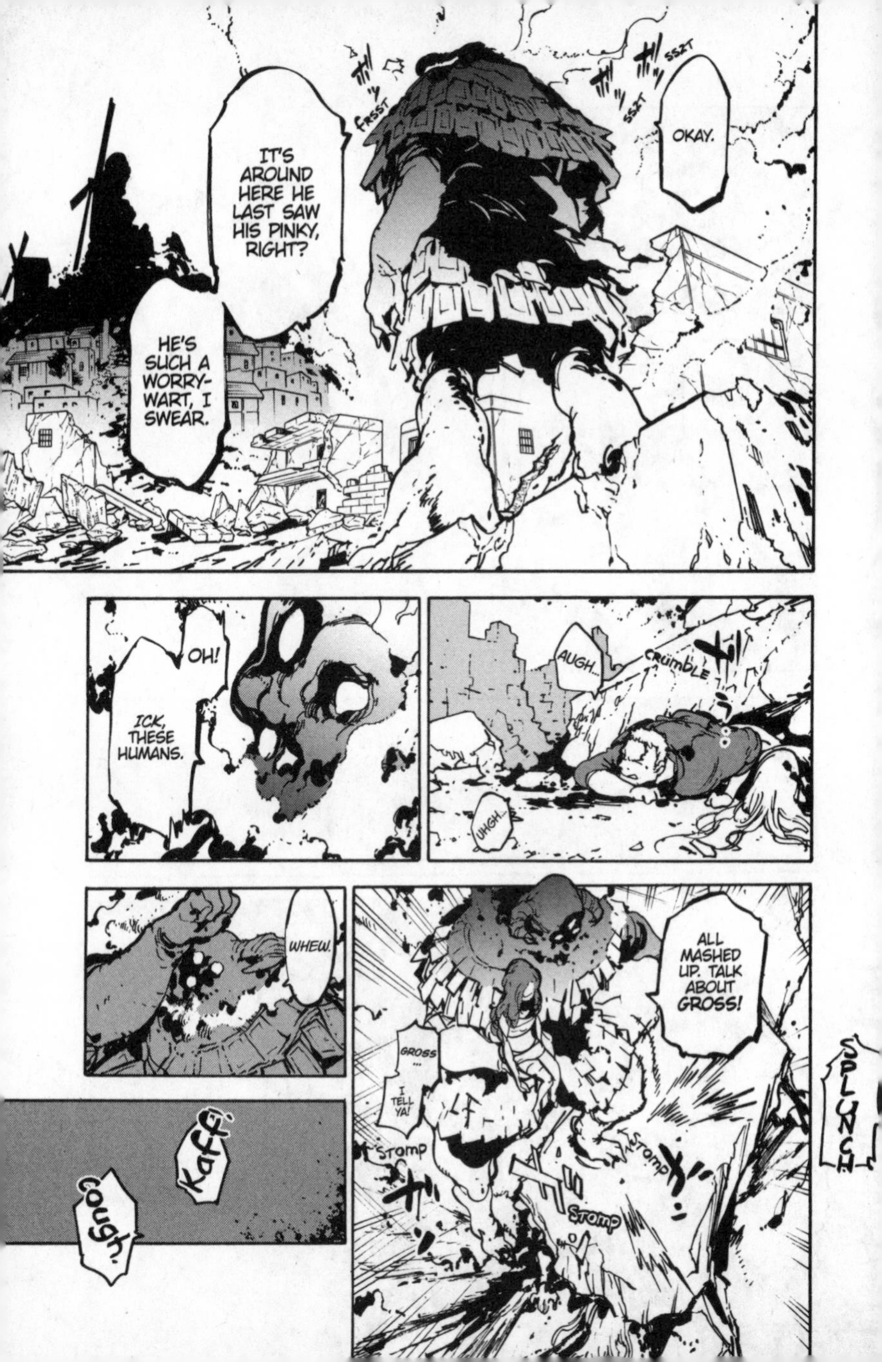
SSZT
SSZT
FRSST
IT'S AROUND HERE HE LAST SAW HIS PINKY, RIGHT?
OKAY.
HE'S SUCH A WORRY-WART, I SWEAR.
AUGH...
CRUMBLE
UHGH...
OH!
ICK, THESE HUMANS.
SPLUNCH
ALL MASHED UP. TALK ABOUT GROSS!
GROSS... I TELL YA!
STOMP
STOMP
STOMP
WHEW.
KAFF!
COUGH.

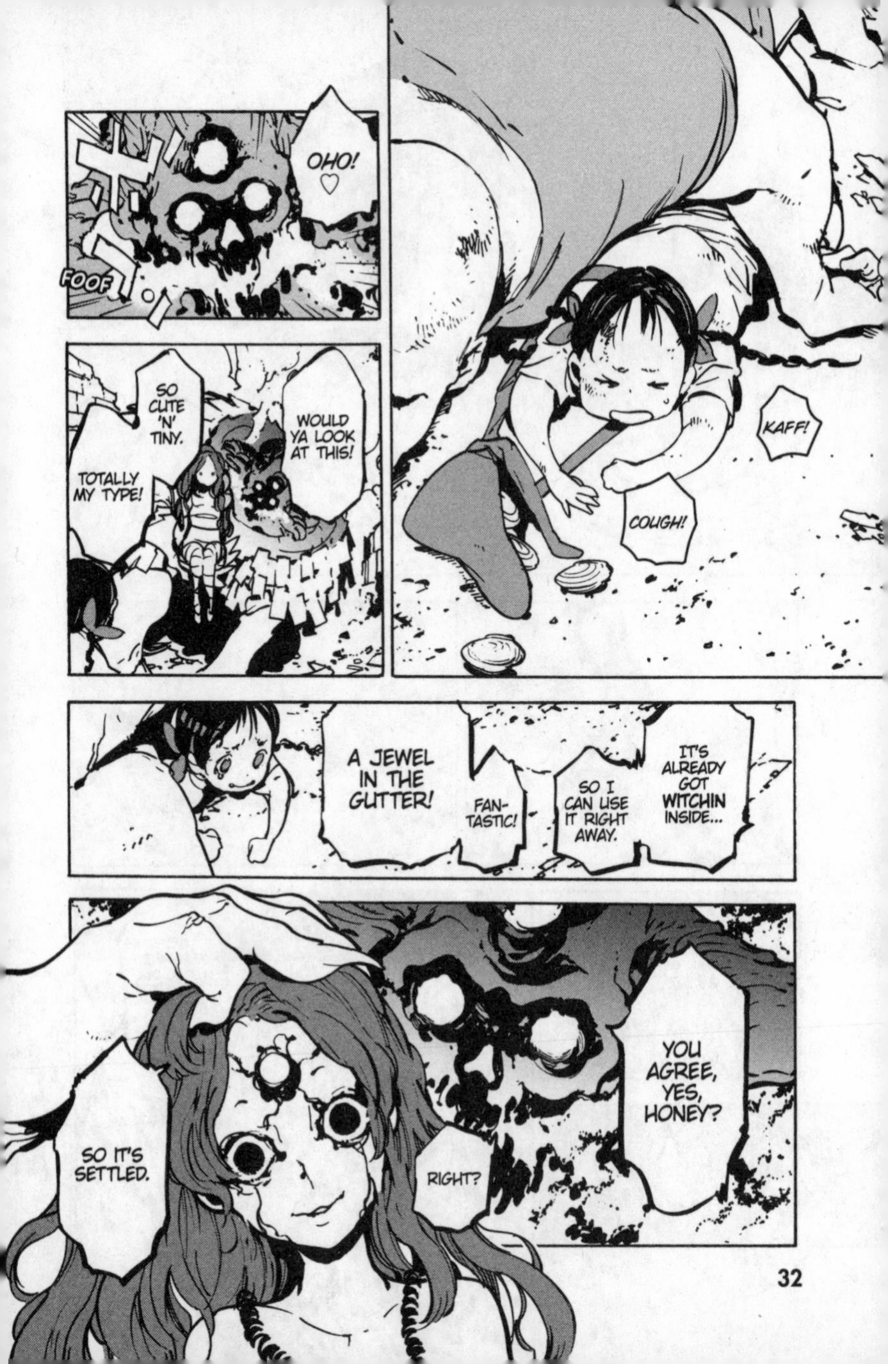
KAFF!
COUGH!
OHO! ♡
FOOF
WOULD YA LOOK AT THIS!
SO CUTE 'N' TINY.
TOTALLY MY TYPE!
IT'S ALREADY GOT WITCHIN INSIDE...
SO I CAN USE IT RIGHT AWAY.
FAN-TASTIC!
A JEWEL IN THE GUTTER!
YOU AGREE, YES, HONEY?
RIGHT?
SO IT'S SETTLED.

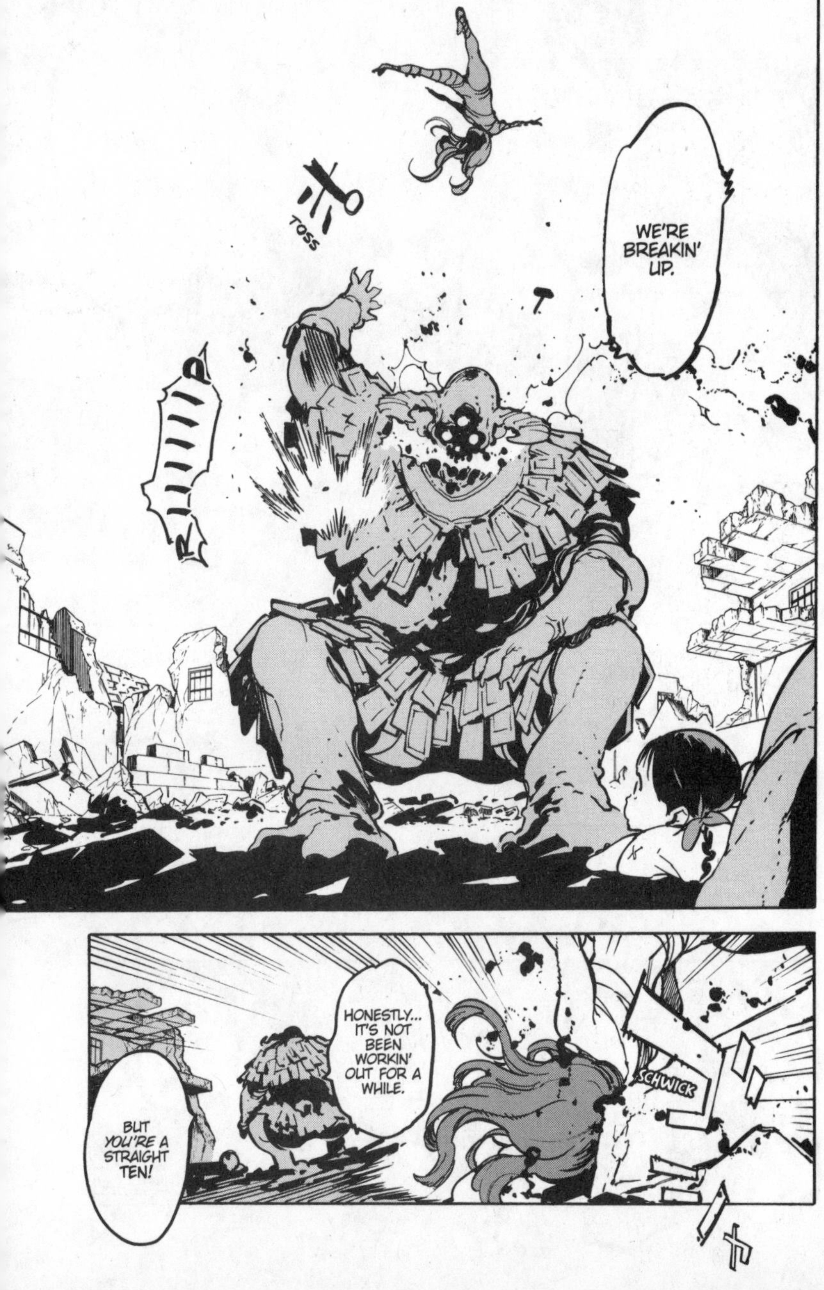
WE'RE BREAKIN' UP.
TOSS
RIIIIIP
SCHWICK
HONESTLY... IT'S NOT BEEN WORKIN' OUT FOR A WHILE.
BUT YOU'RE A STRAIGHT TEN!

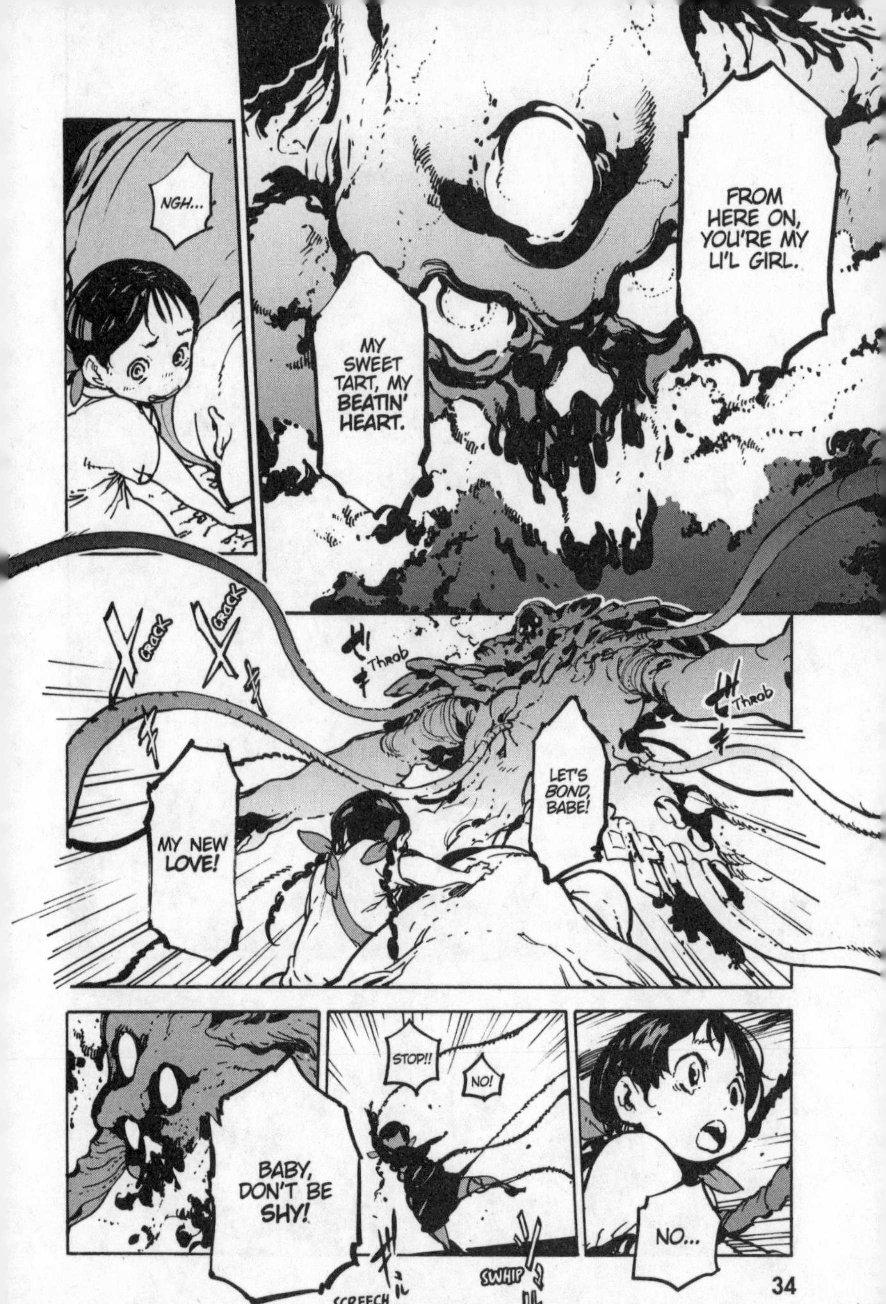
FROM HERE ON, YOU'RE MY LI'L GIRL.
MY SWEET TART, MY BEATIN' HEART.
NGH...
Throb
LET'S BOND, BABE!
Throb
CRACK
CRACK
MY NEW LOVE!
NO...
STOP!!
NO!
SWHIP
BABY, DON'T BE SHY!
SCREECH

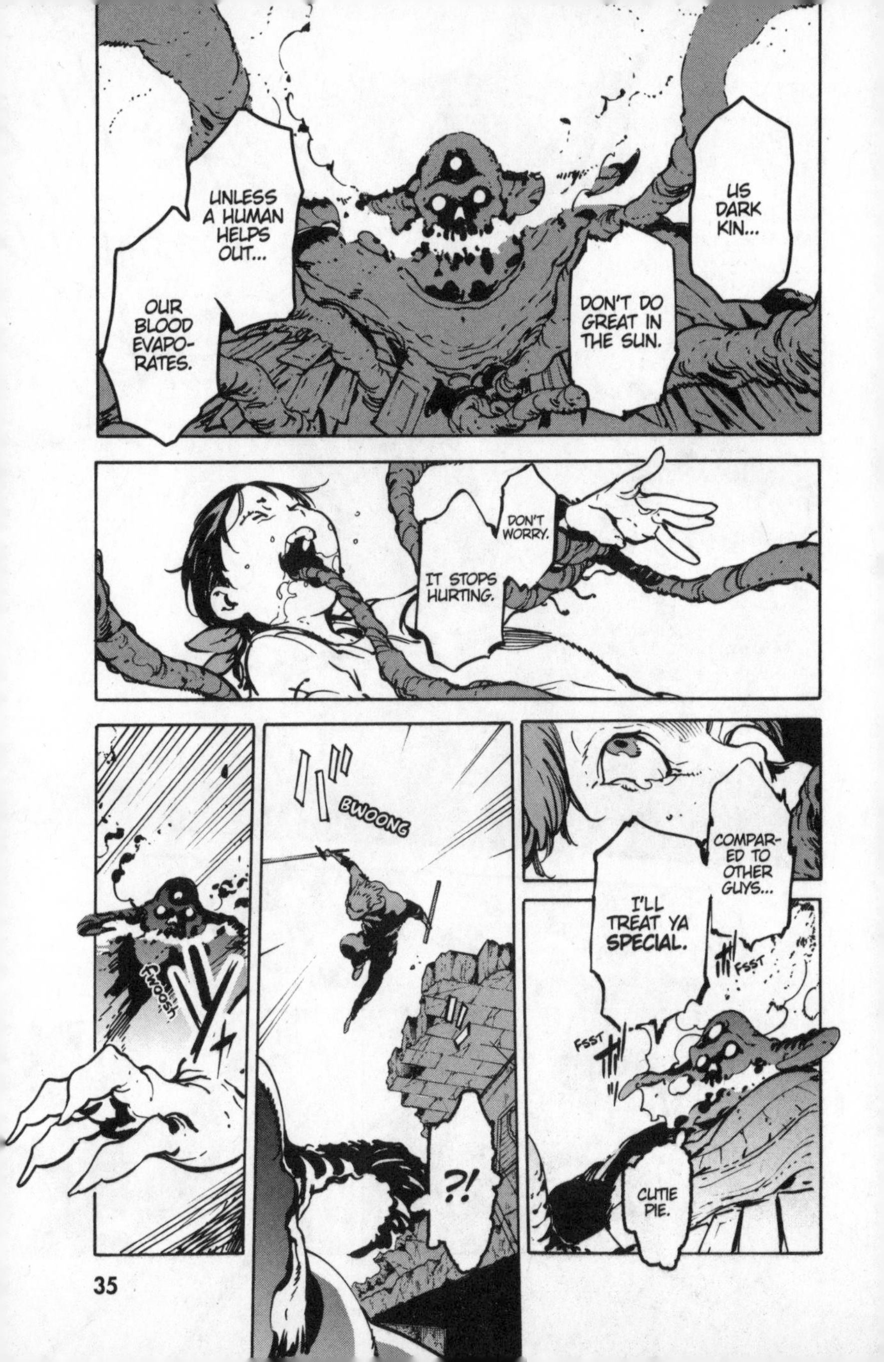
US DARK KIN...
DON'T DO GREAT IN THE SUN.
UNLESS A HUMAN HELPS OUT...
OUR BLOOD EVAPORATES.
DON'T WORRY.
IT STOPS HURTING.
COMPARED TO OTHER GUYS...
I'LL TREAT YA SPECIAL.
FSST
FSST
CUTIE PIE.
BWOONG
?!
FWOOSH

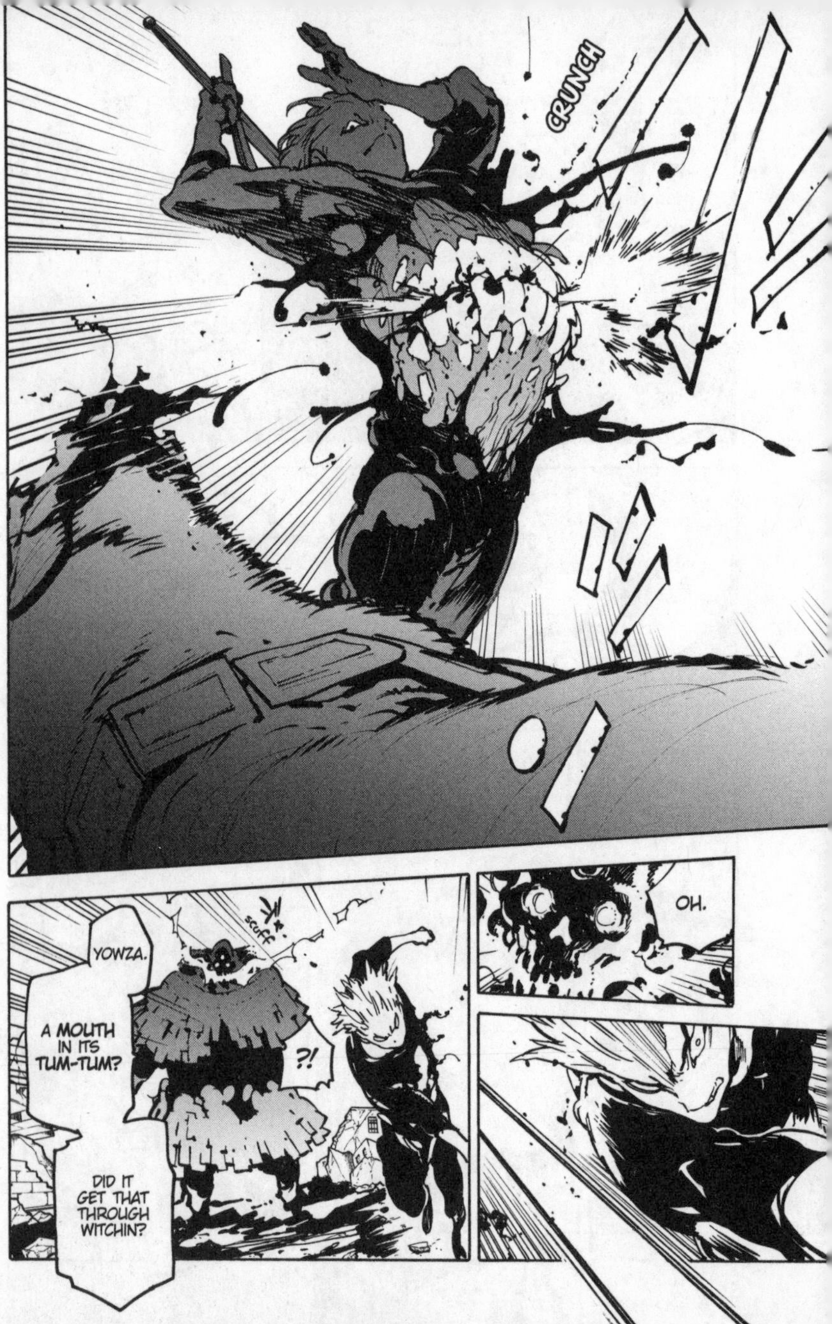
CRUNCH
OH.
scuff
?!
YOWZA.
A MOUTH IN ITS TUM-TUM?
DID IT GET THAT THROUGH WITCHIN?

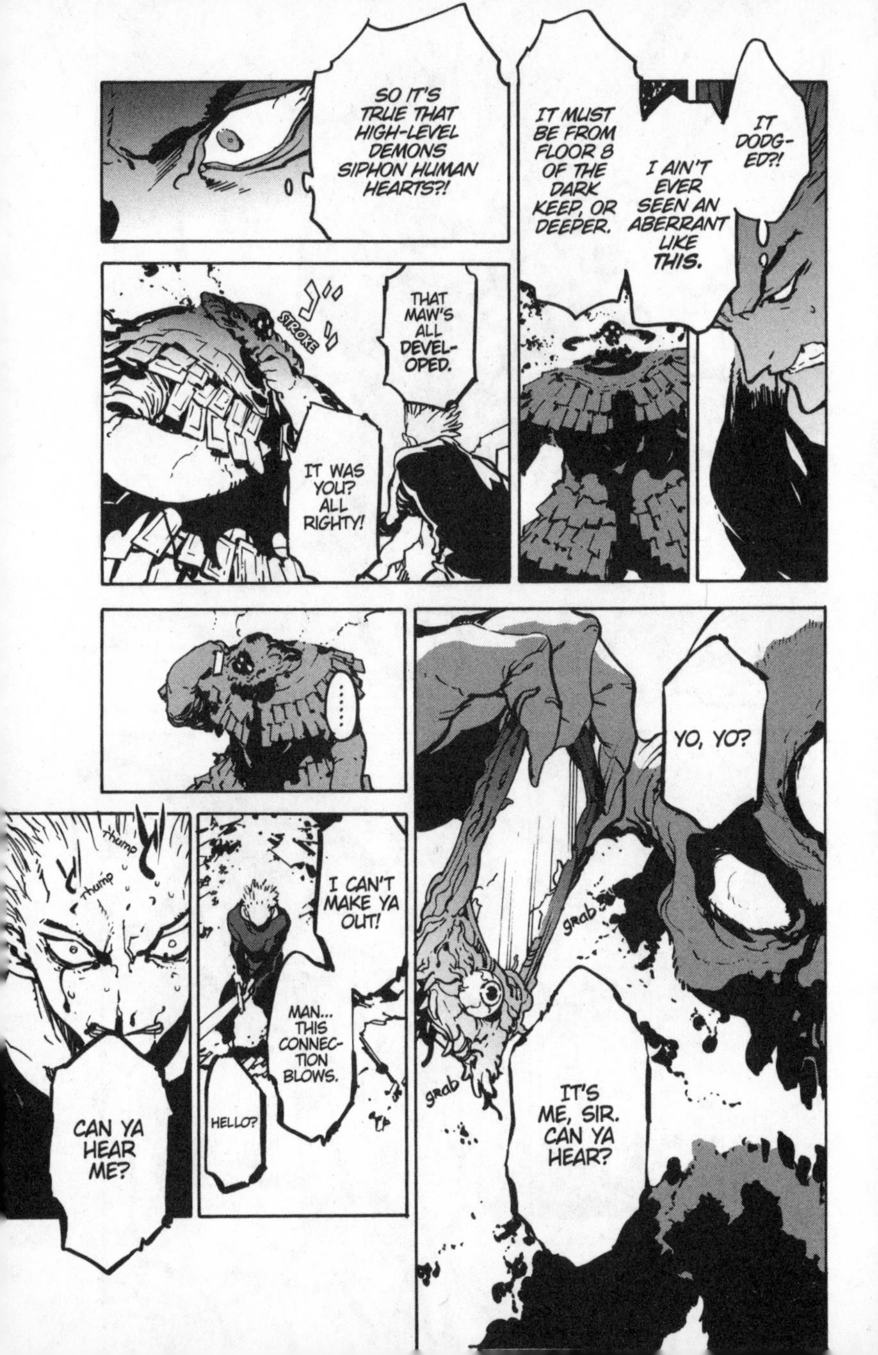
IT DODGED?!
I AIN'T EVER SEEN AN ABERRANT LIKE THIS.
IT MUST BE FROM FLOOR 8 OF THE DARK KEEP, OR DEEPER.
SO IT'S TRUE THAT HIGH-LEVEL DEMONS SIPHON HUMAN HEARTS?!
THAT MAW'S ALL DEVEL-OPED.
STROKE
IT WAS YOU? ALL RIGHTY!
YO, YO?
grab
grab
IT'S ME, SIR. CAN YA HEAR?
......
I CAN'T MAKE YA OUT!
MAN... THIS CONNECTION BLOWS.
HELLO?
thump
thump
CAN YA HEAR ME?

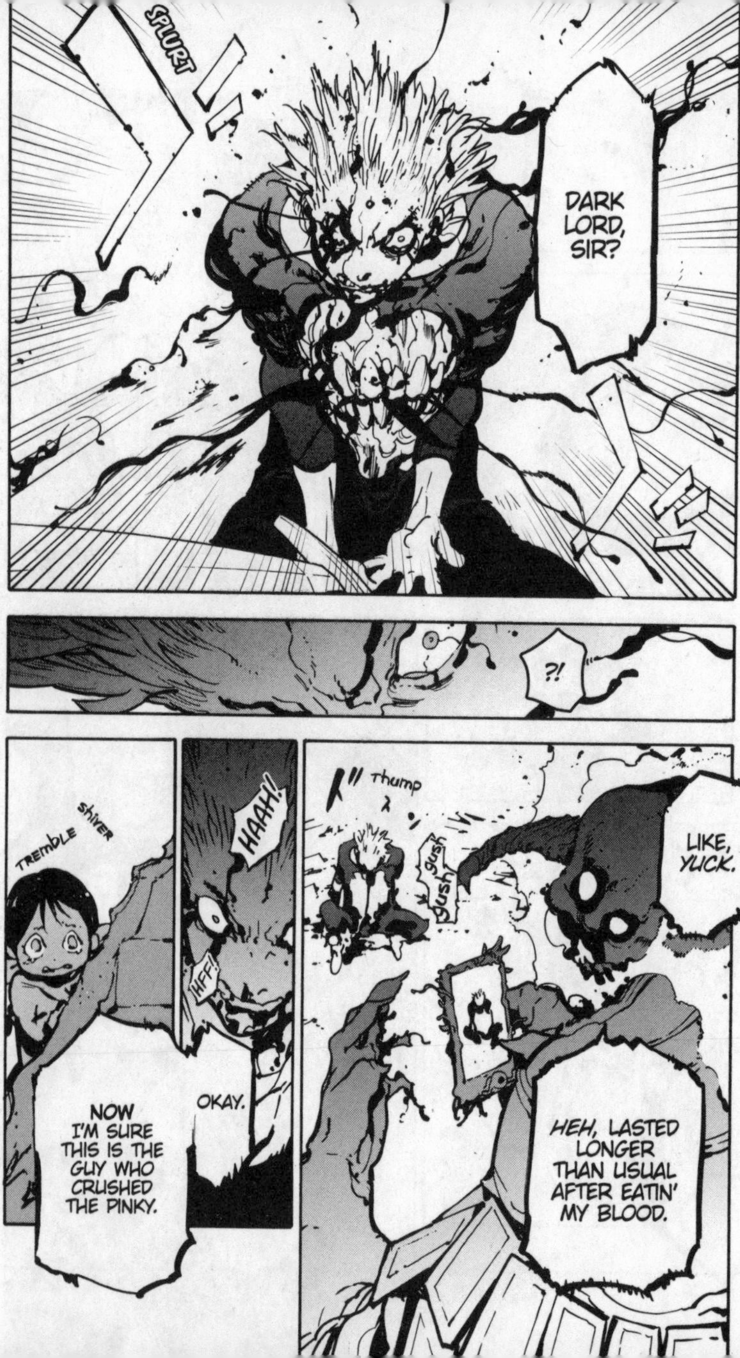

DARK LORD, SIR?
SPLURT
?!
LIKE, YUCK.
Thump
gush gush
HEH, LASTED LONGER THAN USUAL AFTER EATIN' MY BLOOD.
HAAAH!
HFF!
OKAY.
shiver
TREMBLE
NOW I'M SURE THIS IS THE GUY WHO CRUSHED THE PINKY.

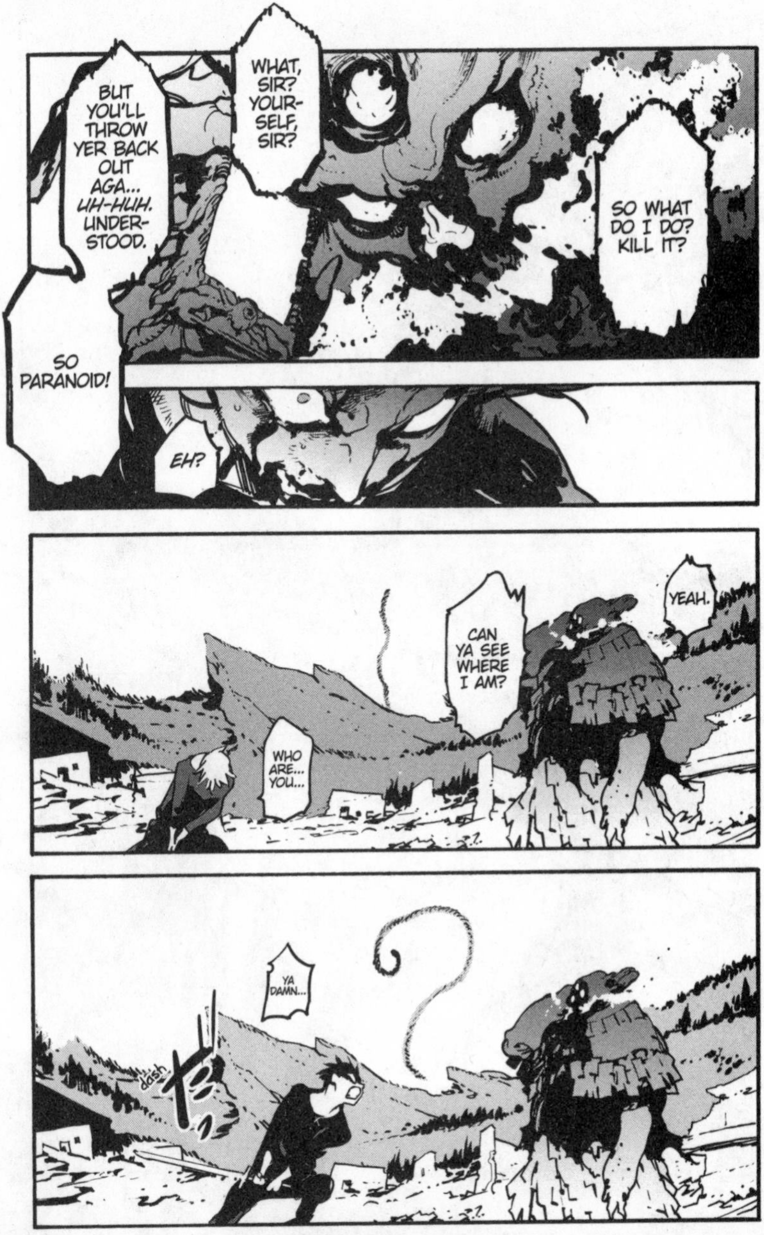
SO WHAT DO I DO? KILL IT?
WHAT, SIR? YOUR-SELF, SIR?
BUT YOU'LL THROW YER BACK OUT AGA... UH-HUH. UNDER-STOOD.
SO PARANOID!
EH?
YEAH.
CAN YA SEE WHERE I AM?
WHO ARE... YOU...
YA DAMN...
dash

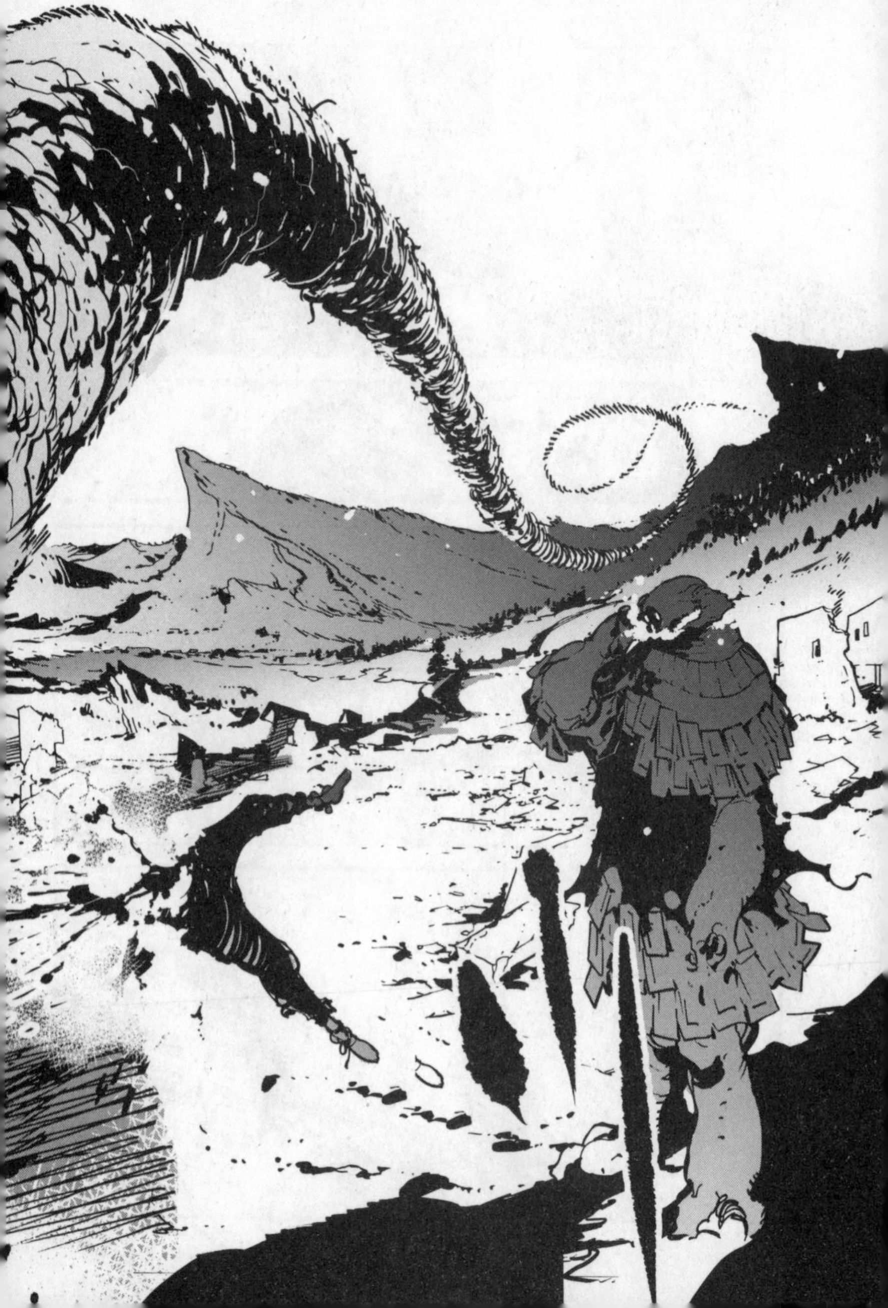

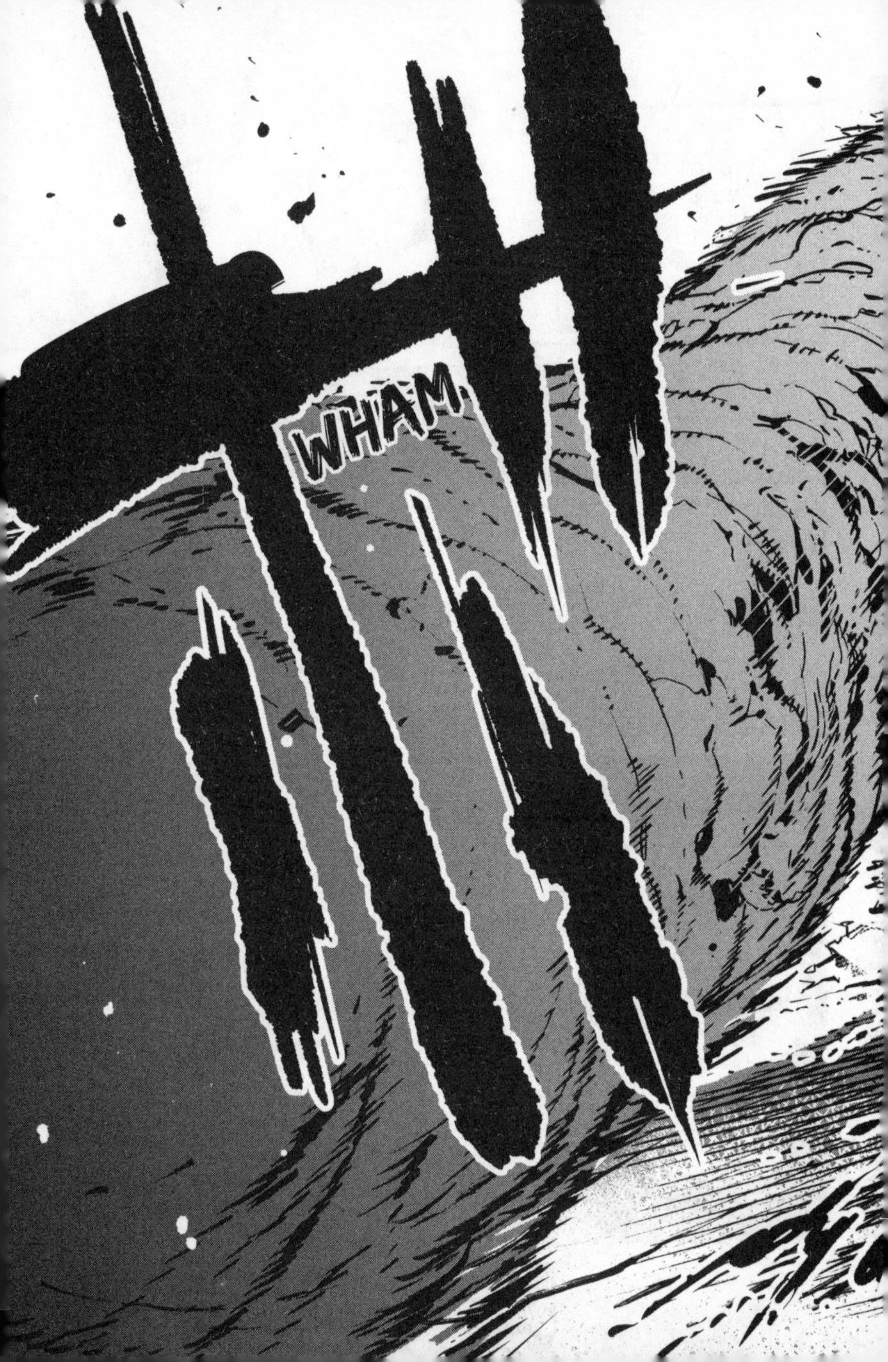
WHAM

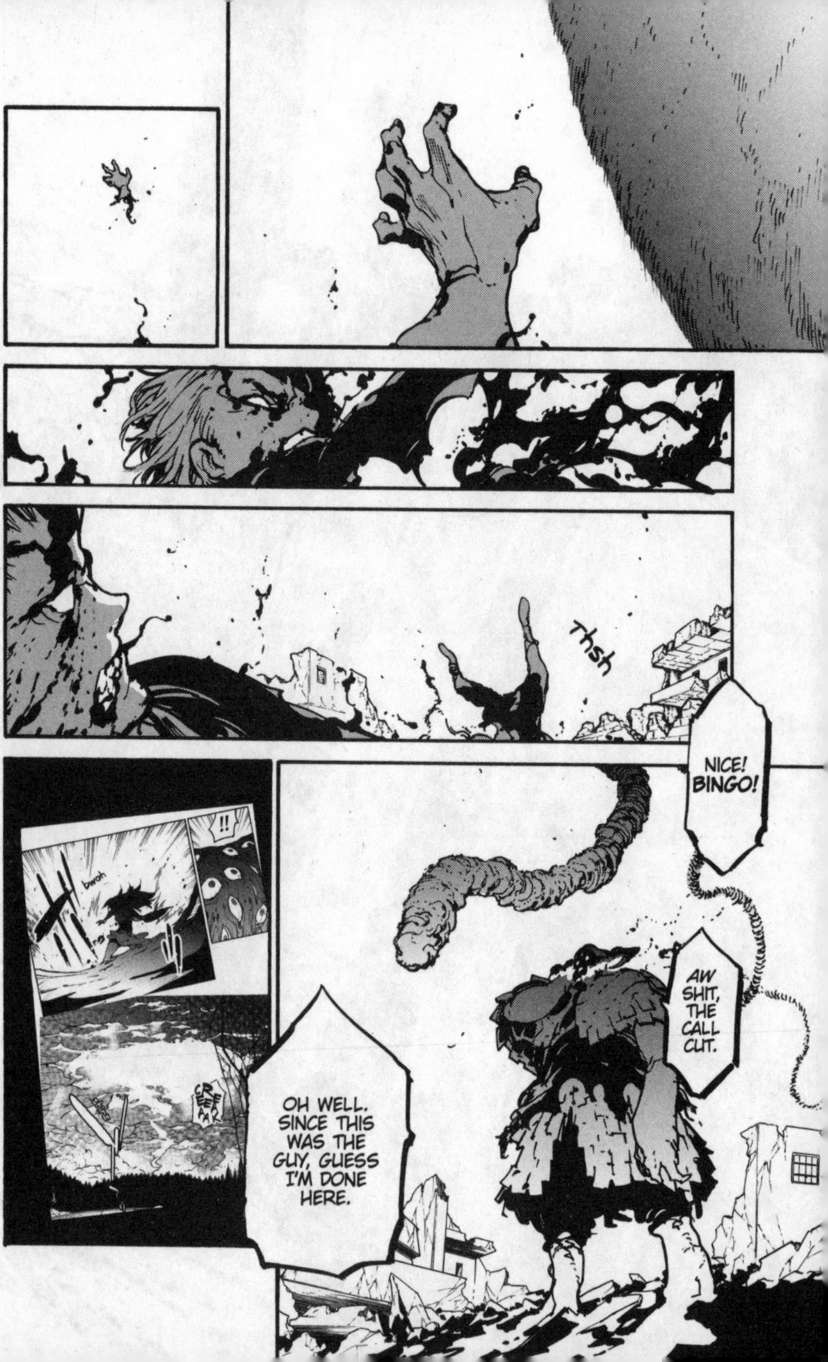
Thsh
NICE! BINGO!
AW SHIT, THE CALL CUT.
OH WELL. SINCE THIS WAS THE GUY, GUESS I'M DONE HERE.
!!
bwoh
CREEEAAK
SHINE

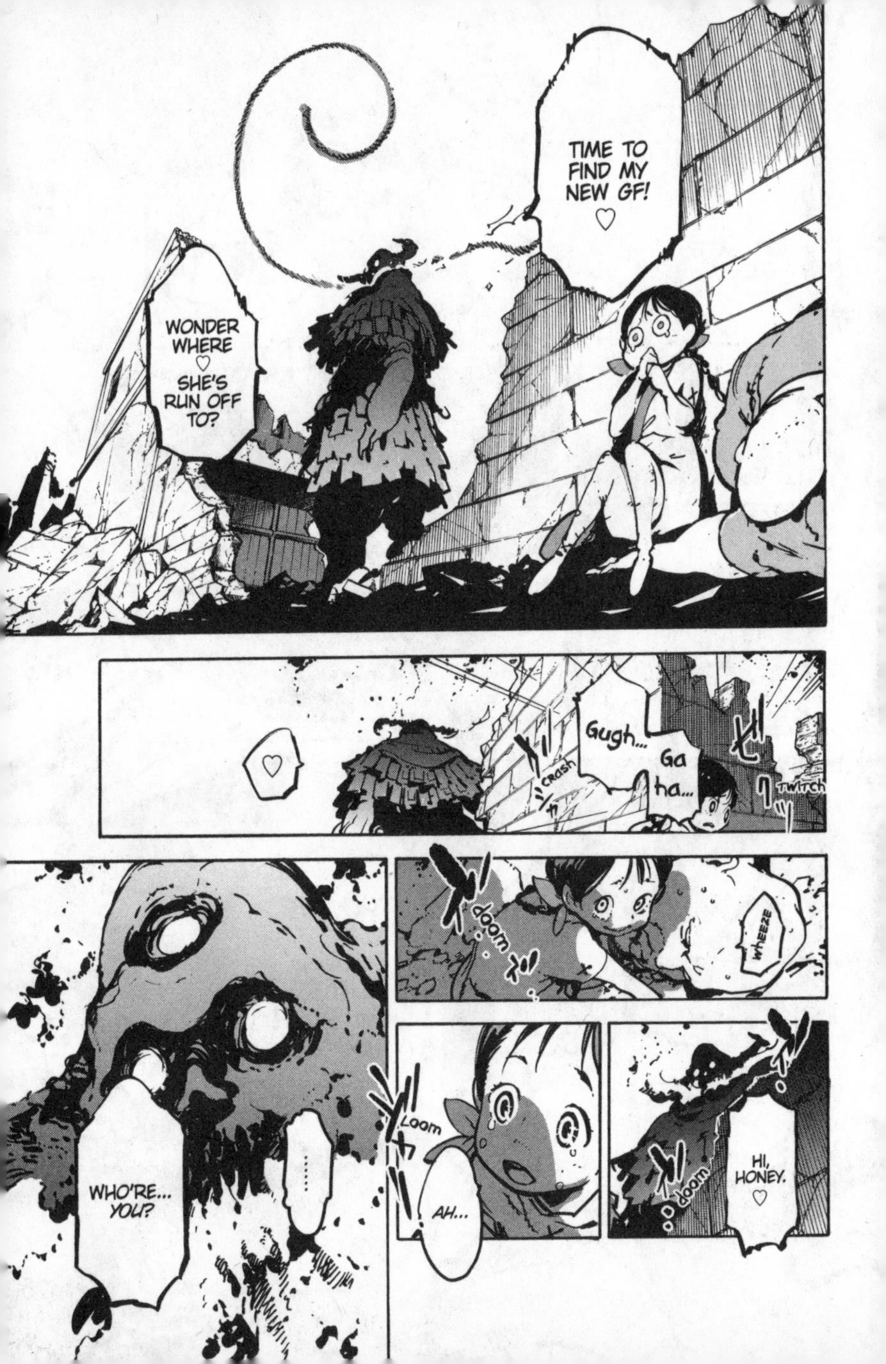

TIME TO FIND MY NEW GF! ♡
WONDER WHERE ♡ SHE'S RUN OFF TO?
Twitch
Gugh... Ga ha...
CRASH
♡
wheeze
doom
HI, HONEY. ♡
doom
Loom
AH...
......
WHO'RE... YOU?

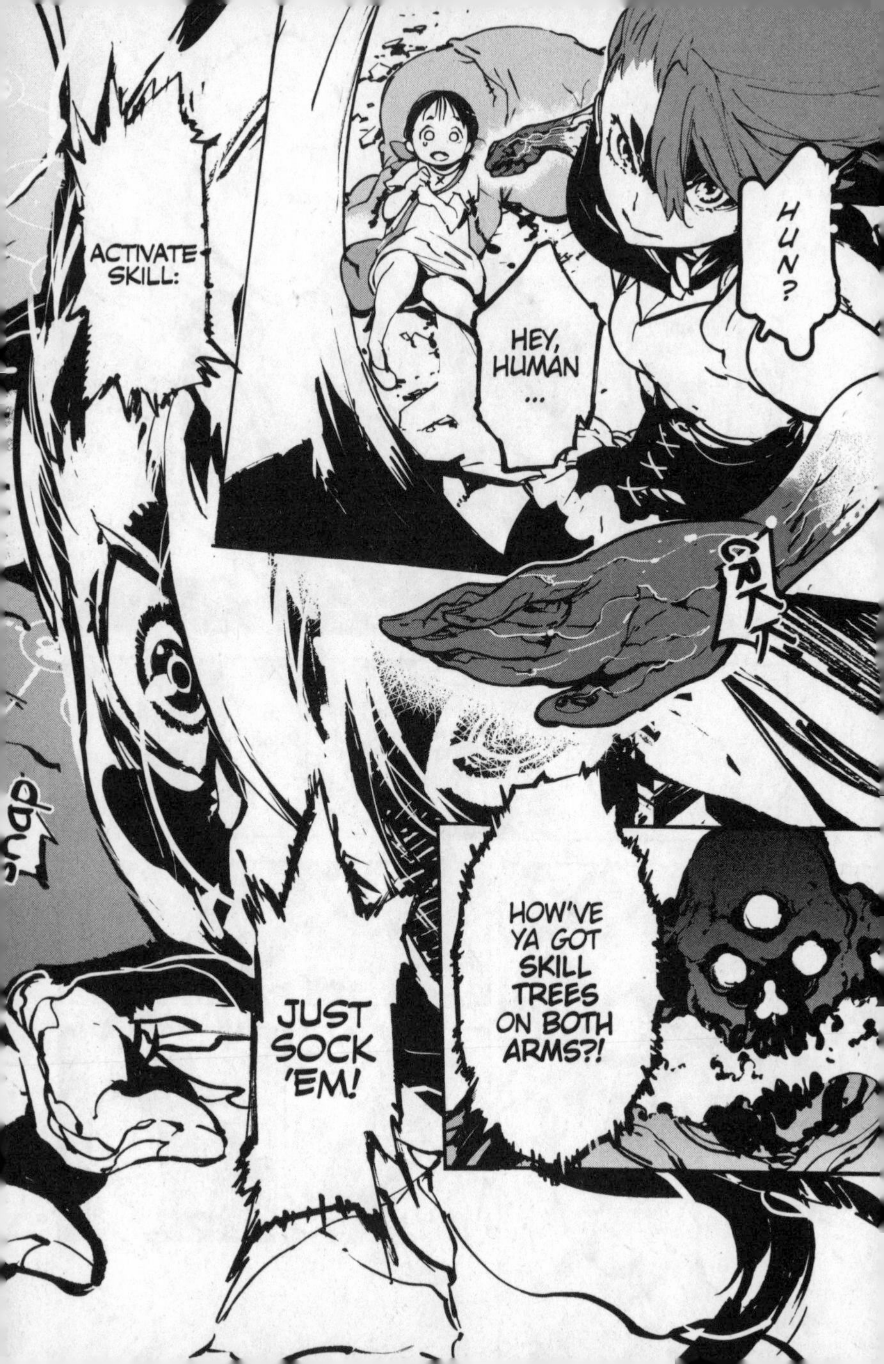
HUN?
HEY, HUMAN ...
CRK
HOW'VE YA GOT SKILL TREES ON BOTH ARMS?!
ACTIVATE SKILL:
JUST SOCK 'EM!

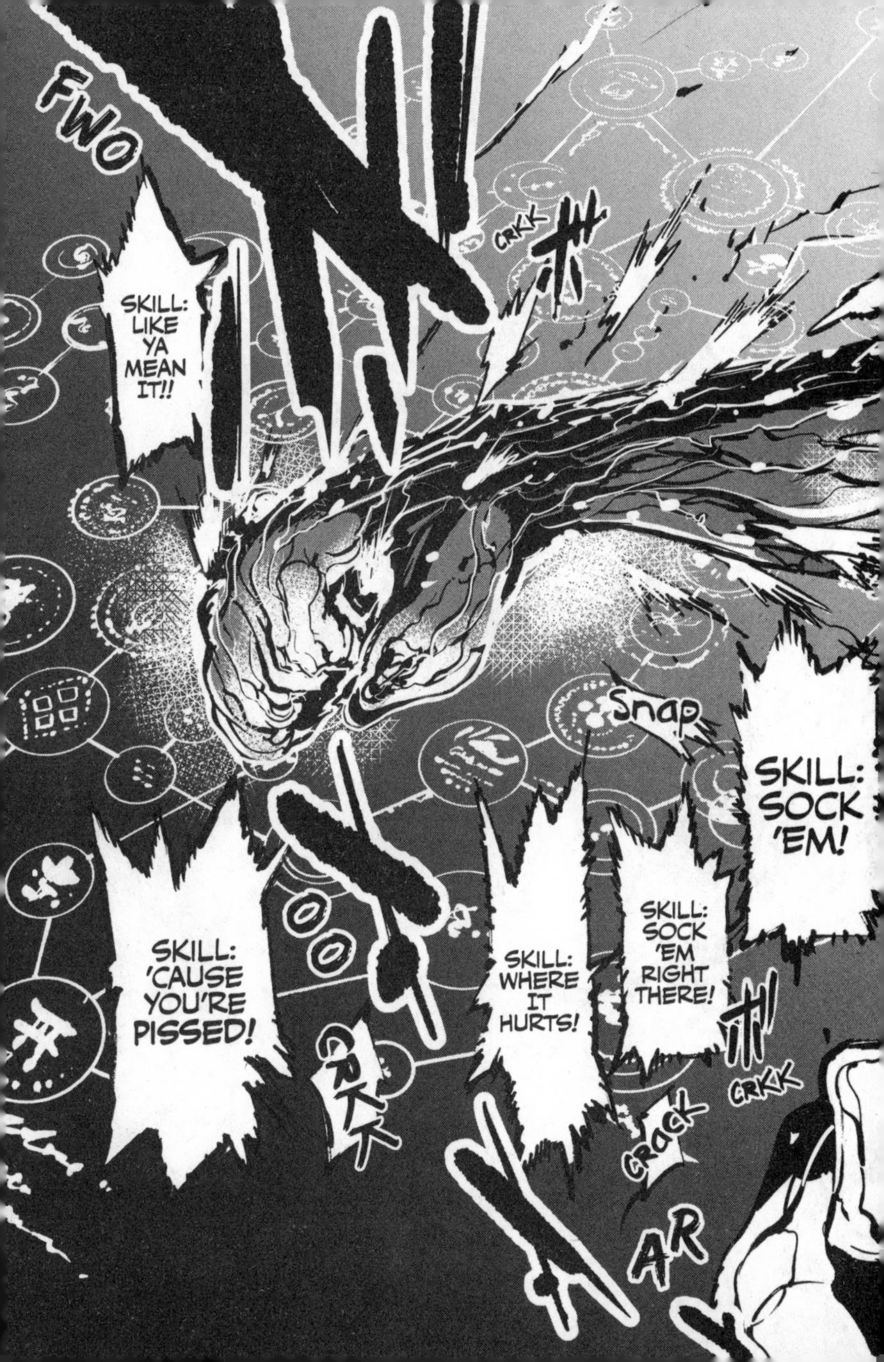
CRKK
FWO
SKILL: LIKE YA MEAN IT!!
SKILL: SOCK 'EM!
Snap
SKILL: SOCK 'EM RIGHT THERE!
CRKK
CRACK
SKILL: WHERE IT HURTS!
AR
CRKK
OO
SKILL: 'CAUSE YOU'RE PISSED!

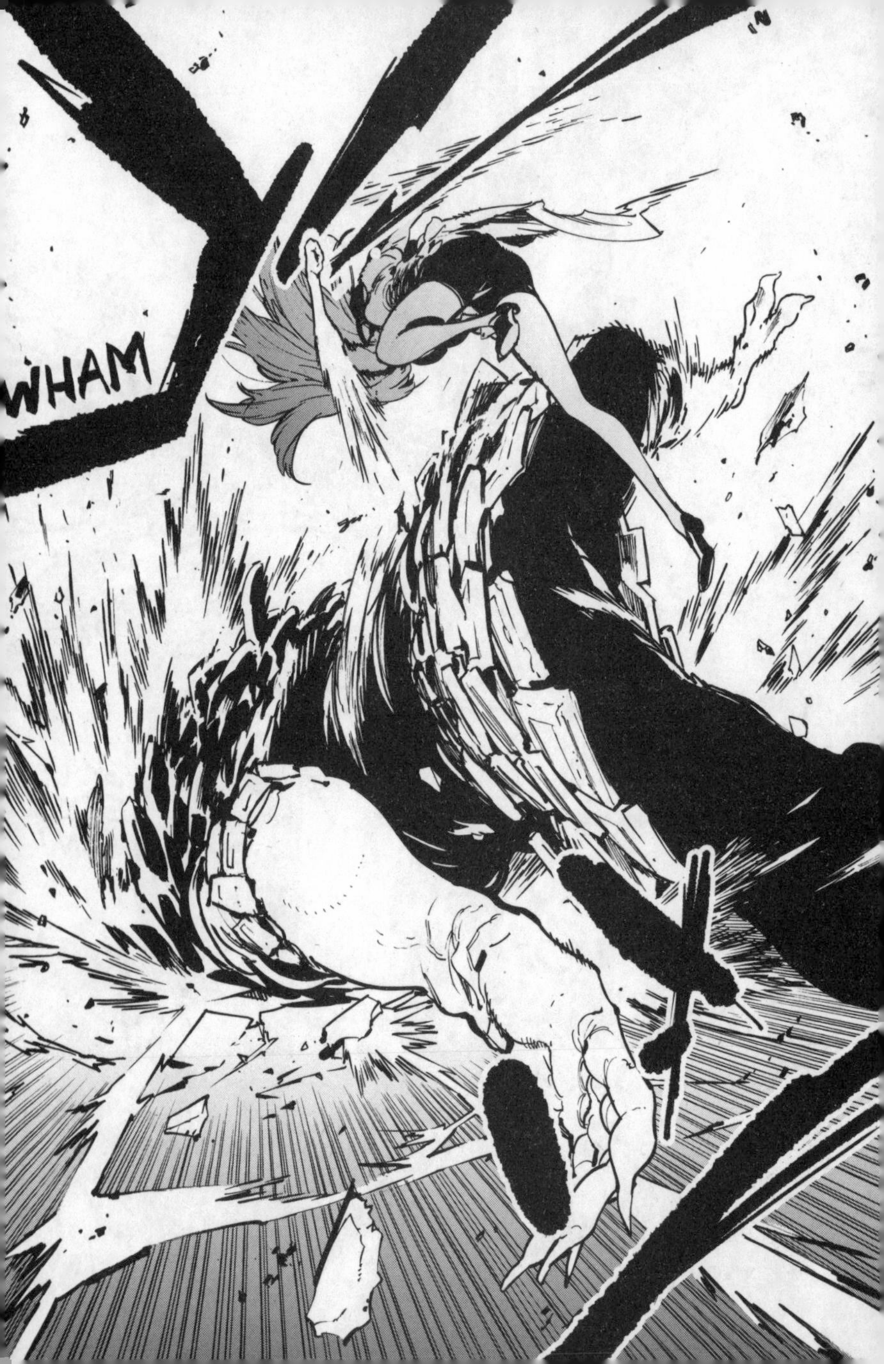
WHAM

YAKUZA
REINCARNATION

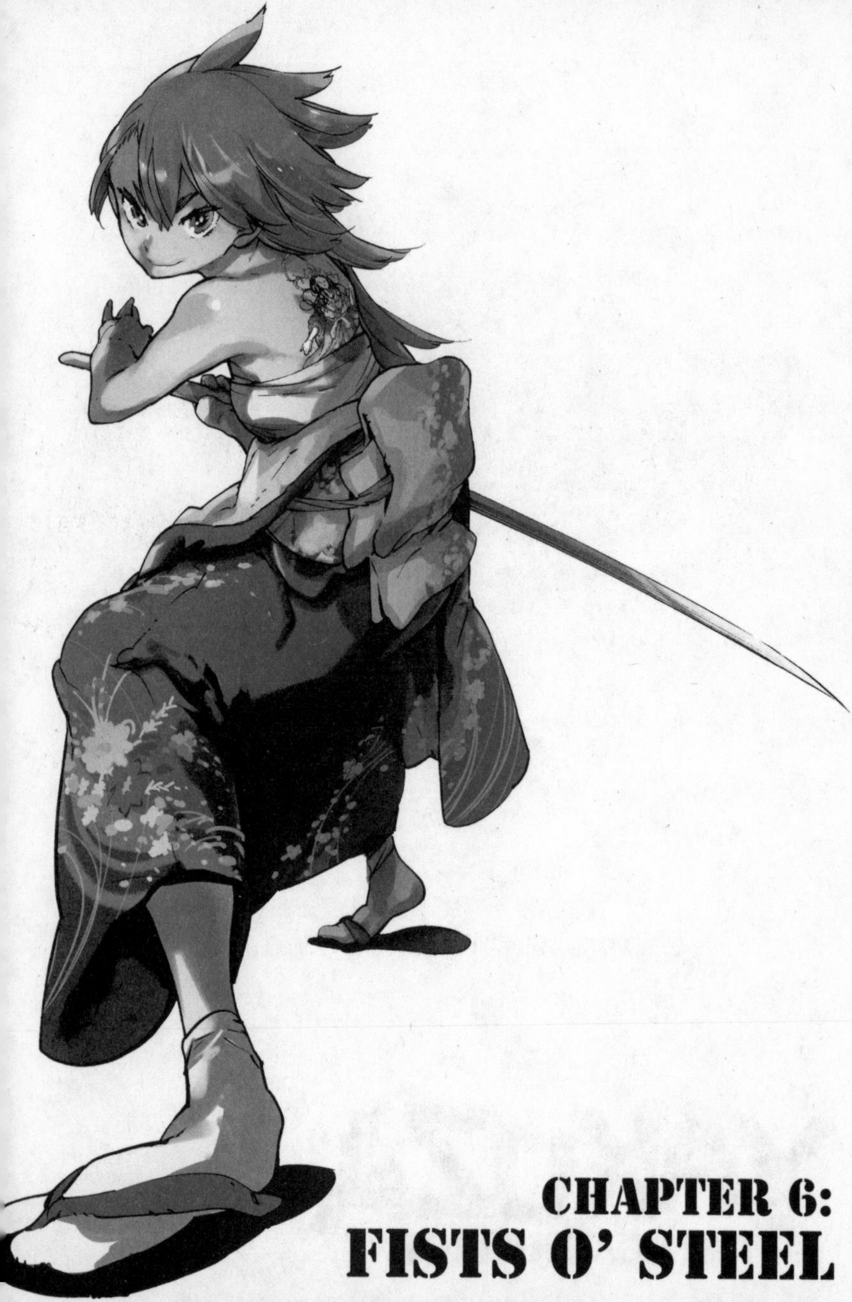

CHAPTER 6: FISTS O' STEEL

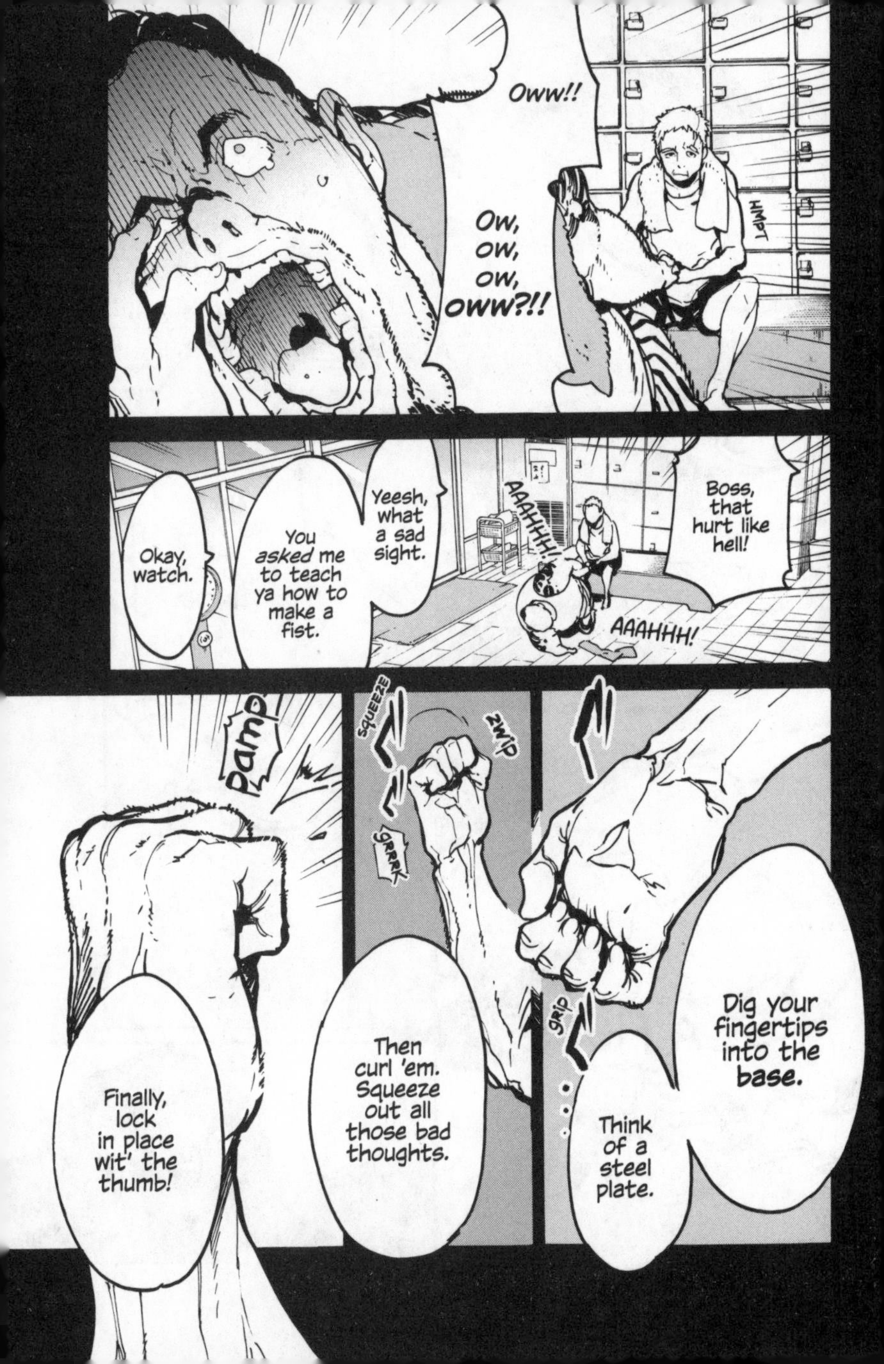
Oww!!
HMPT
Ow, ow, ow, OWW?!!
Boss, that hurt like hell!
AAAHHHH!
AAAHHH!
Yeesh, what a sad sight.
You *asked* me to teach ya how to make a fist.
Okay, watch.
Dig your fingertips into the **base.**
grip
Think of a steel plate.
zwip
squeeze
grrrk
Then curl 'em. Squeeze out all those bad thoughts.
pamp
Finally, lock in place wit' the thumb!

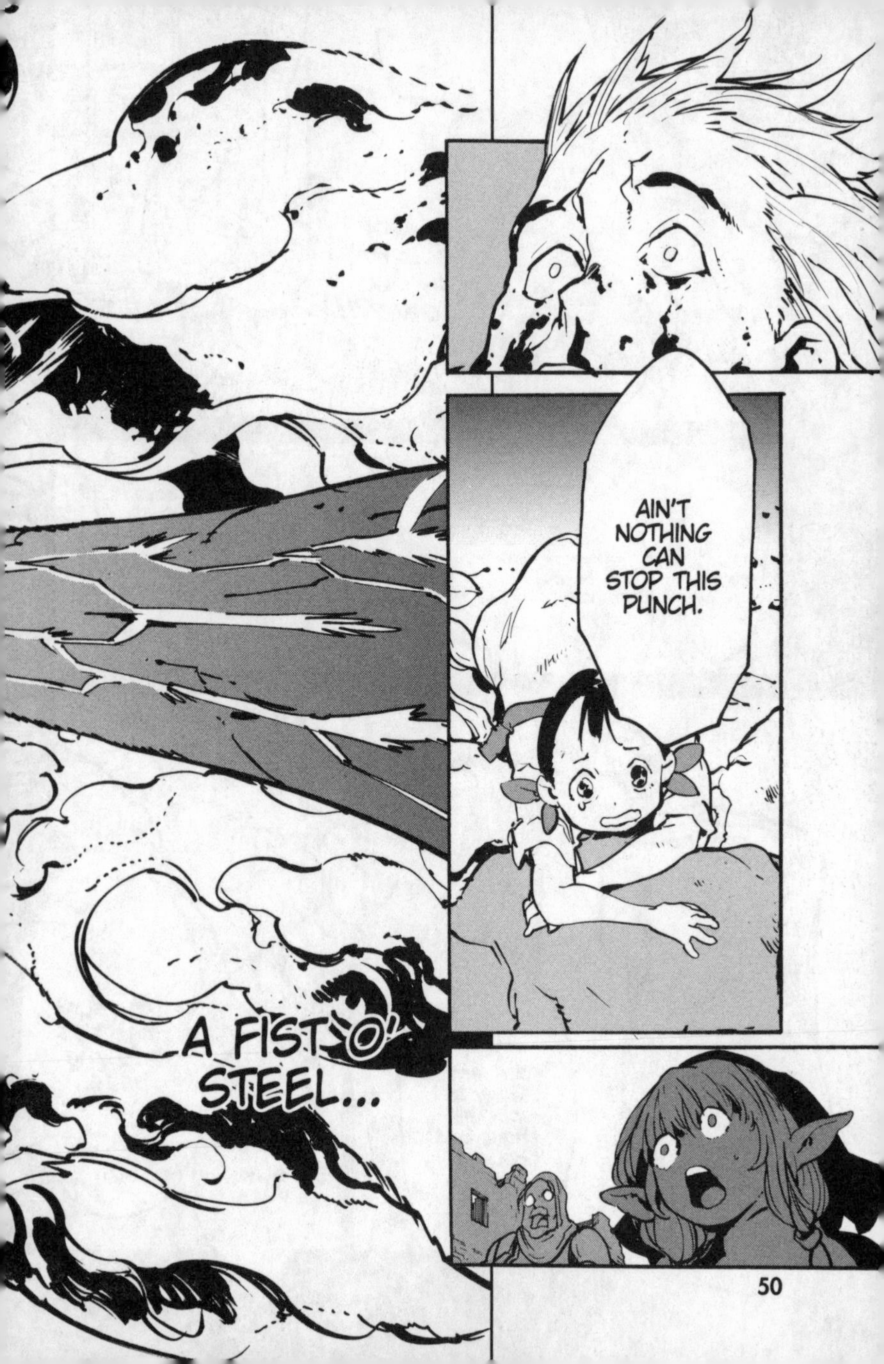
AIN'T NOTHING CAN STOP THIS PUNCH.
A FIST O' STEEL...

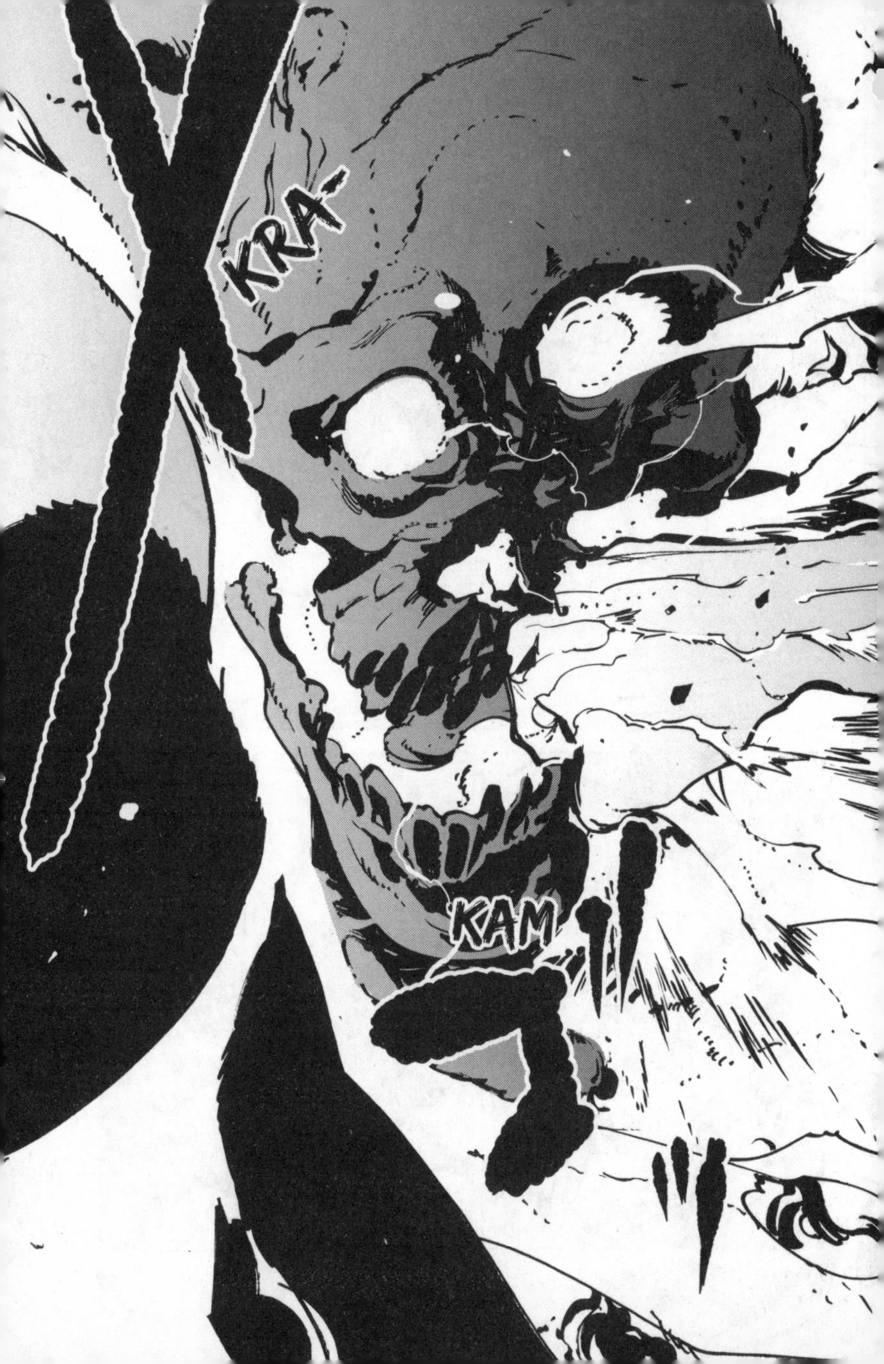
KRA-
KAM

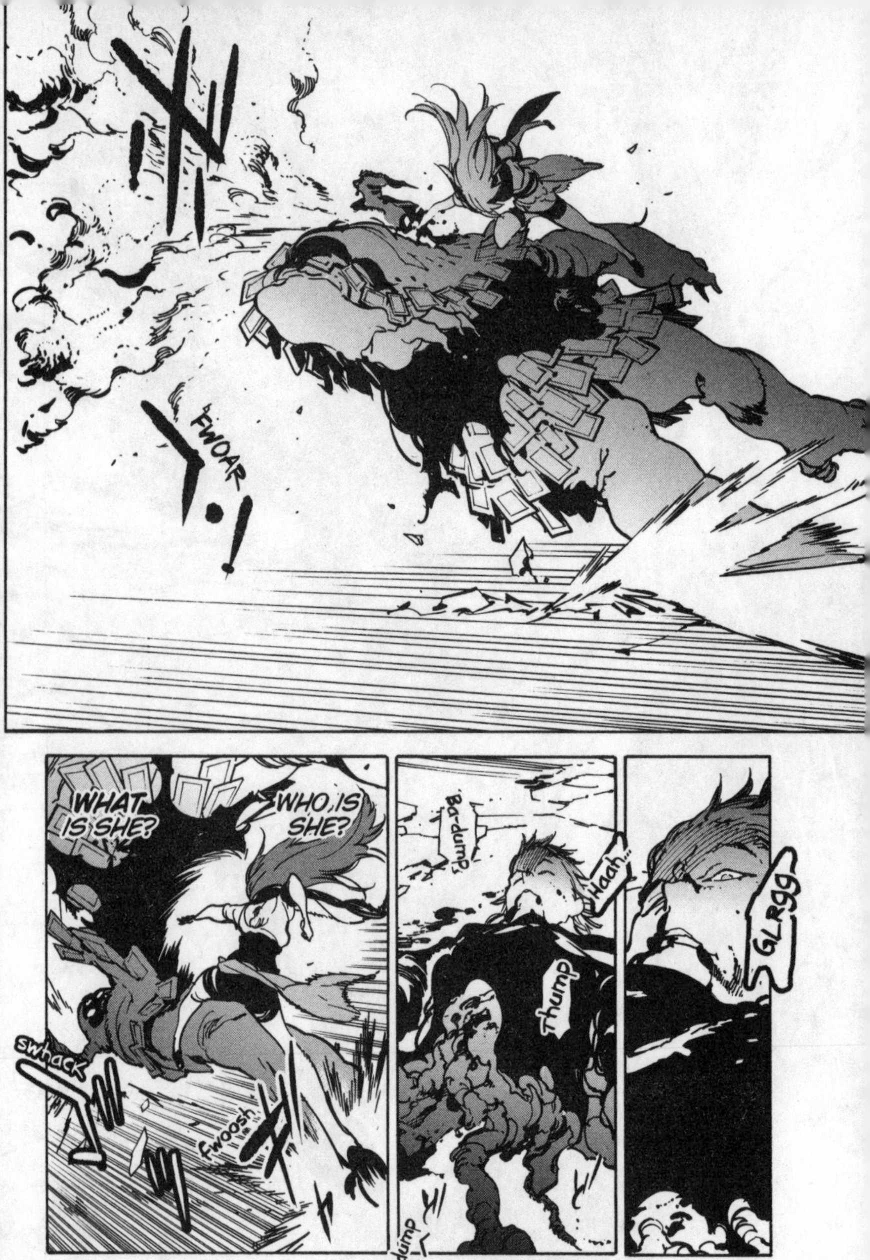
FWOAR
GLRGG
Ba-dump
Haah...
Thump
Ba-dump
WHO IS SHE?
WHAT IS SHE?
swhack
fwoosh

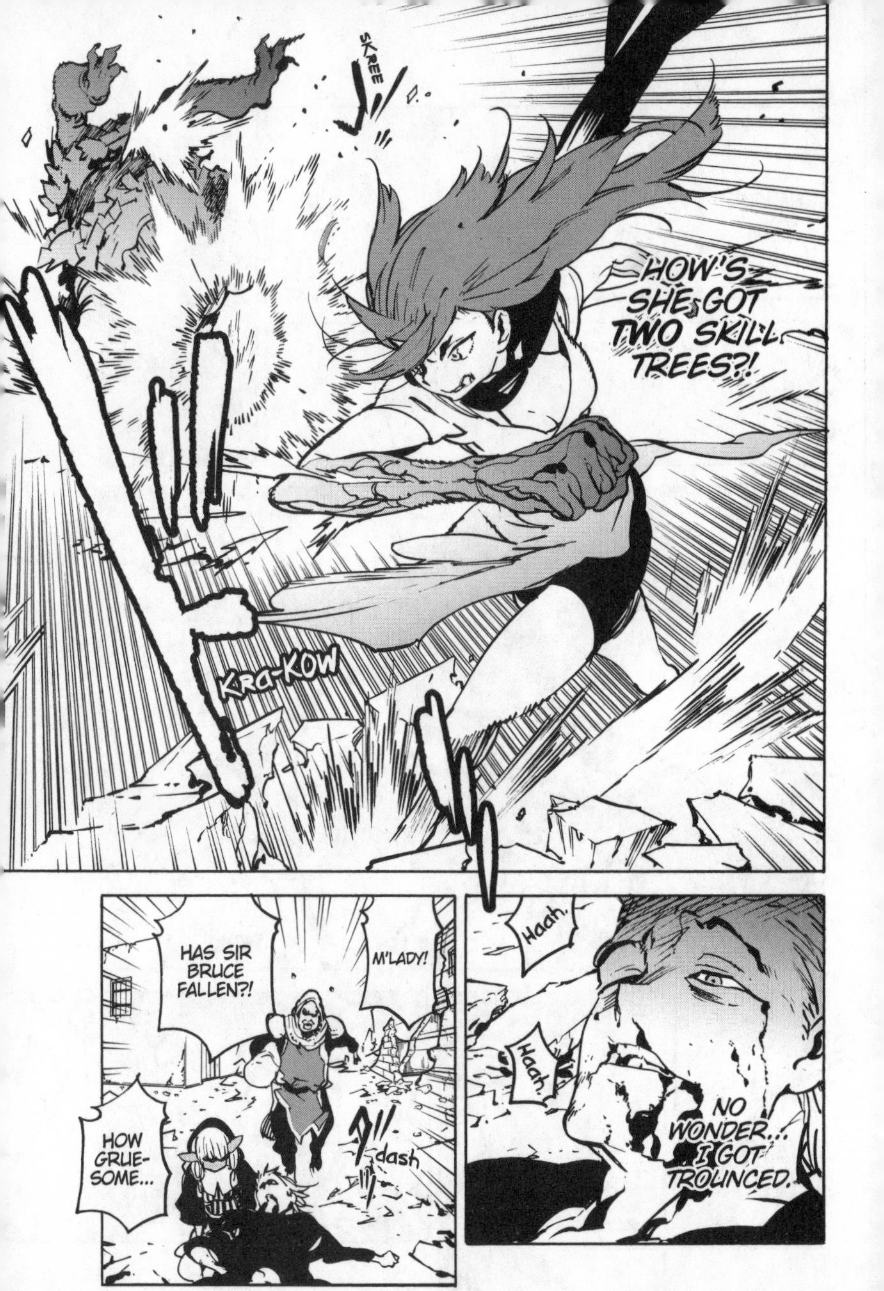
SKREE
HOW'S SHE GOT TWO SKILL TREES?!
Kra-KOW
Haah.
Haah.
NO WONDER... I GOT TROUNCED.
M'LADY!
HAS SIR BRUCE FALLEN?!
dash
HOW GRUE-SOME...

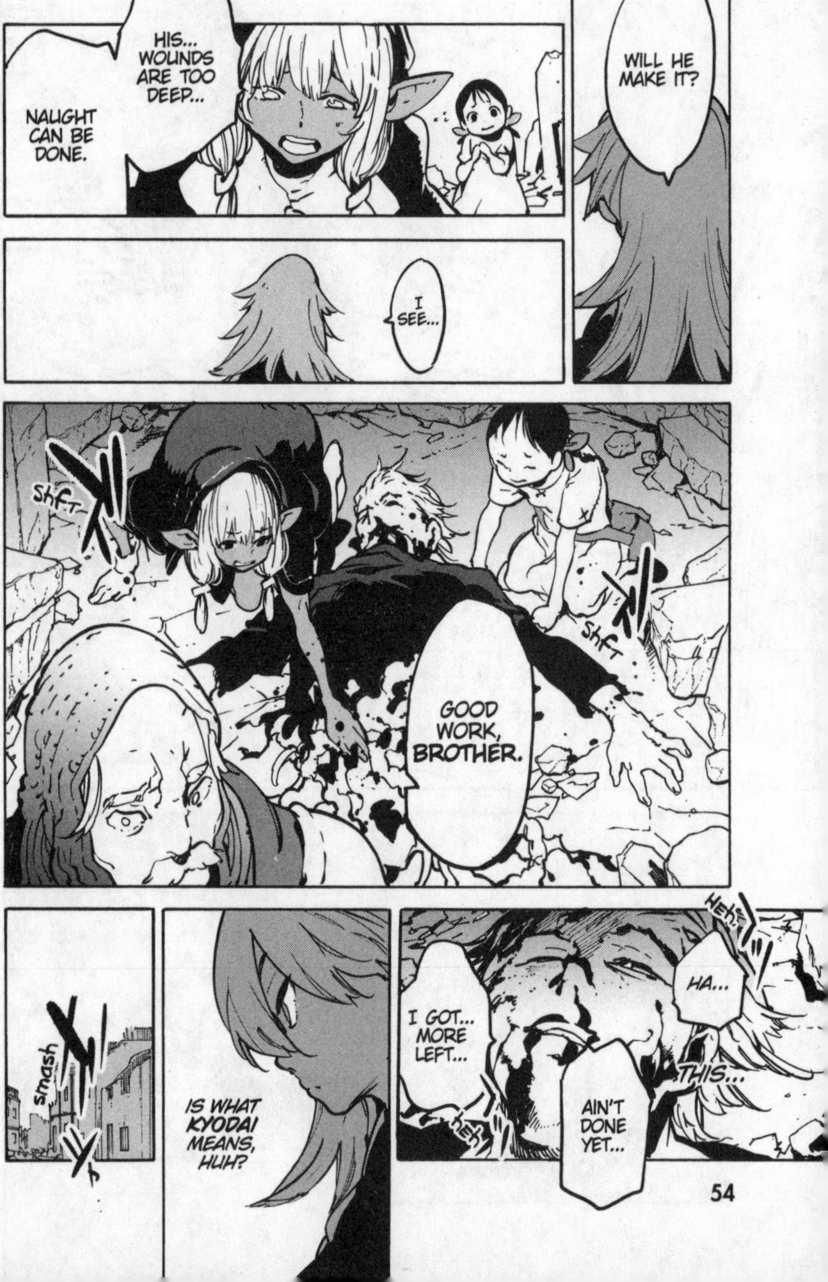
WILL HE MAKE IT?
HIS... WOUNDS ARE TOO DEEP...
NAUGHT CAN BE DONE.
I SEE...
shft
shft
GOOD WORK, BROTHER.
Heh
HA...
THIS...
AIN'T DONE YET...
I GOT... MORE LEFT...
heh
IS WHAT KYODAI MEANS, HUH?
smash

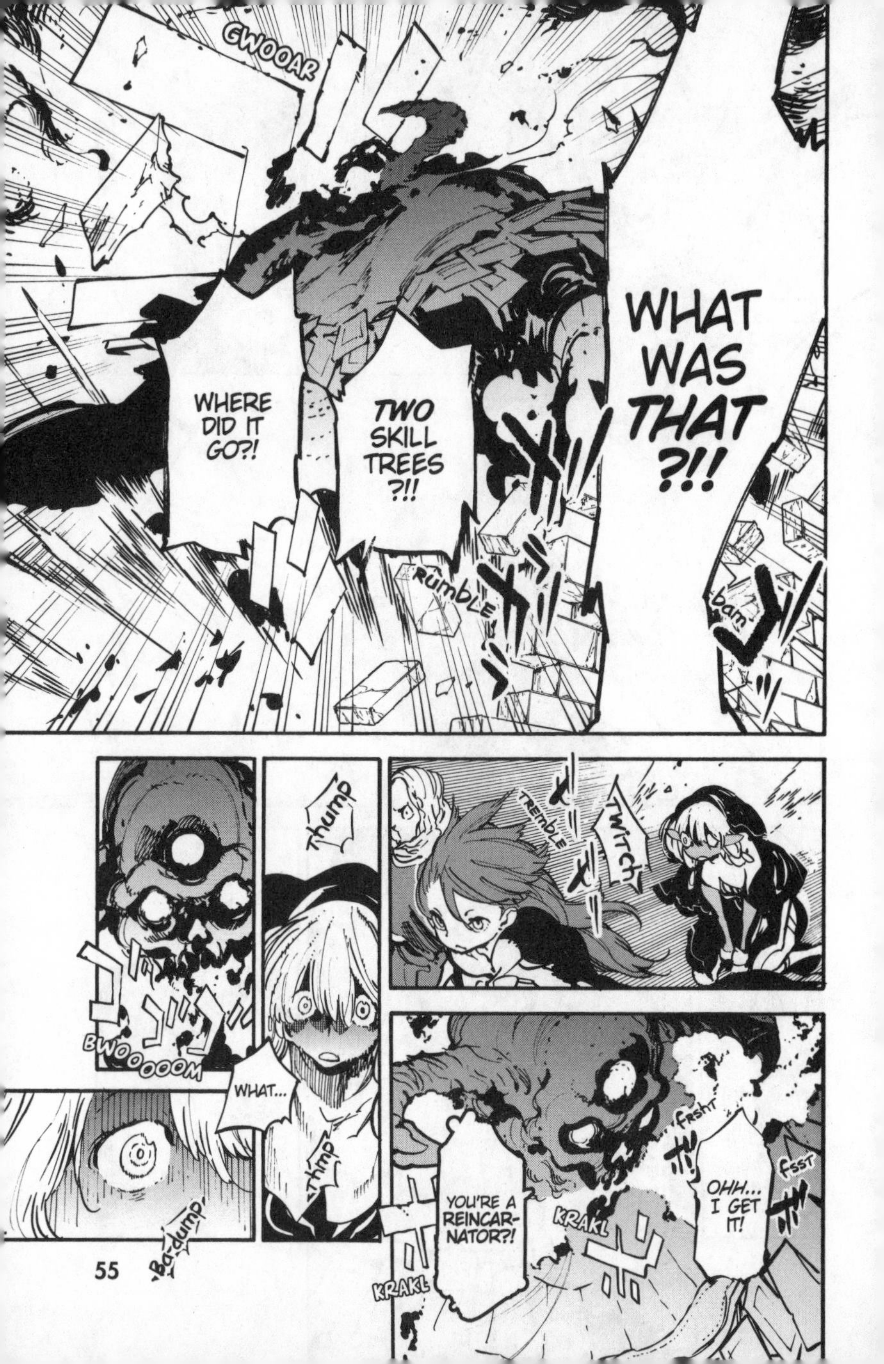
GWOOAR
WHAT WAS THAT?!!
TWO SKILL TREES?!!
WHERE DID IT GO?!
bam
rumble
TWITCH
TREMBLE
Thump
BWOOOOOM
frshht
fsst
OHH... I GET IT!
YOU'RE A REINCARNATOR?!
KRAKL
KRAKL
WHAT...
Thmp
Ba-dump

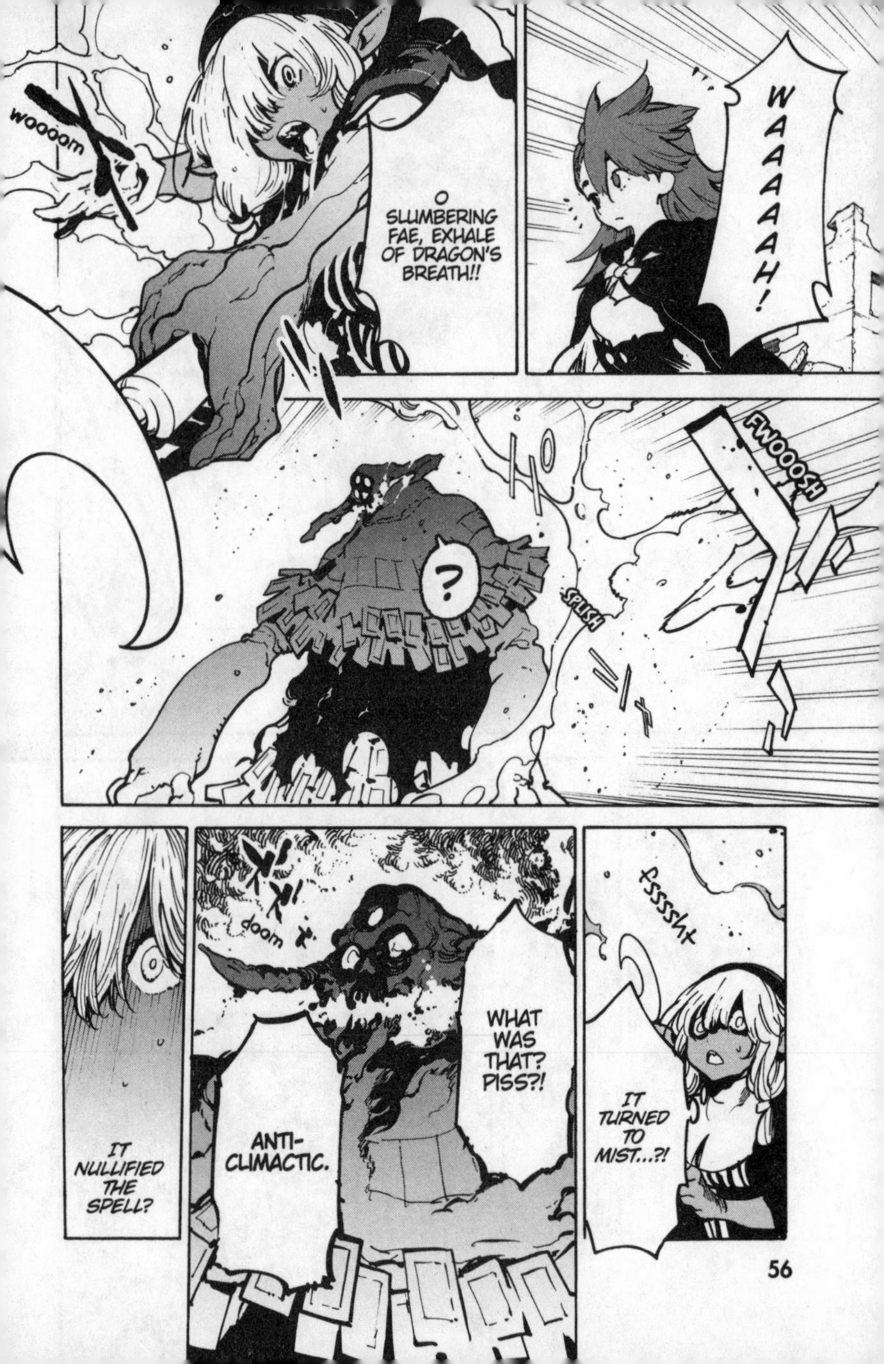

WAAAAAH!
wooooom
O SLUMBERING FAE, EXHALE OF DRAGON'S BREATH!!
FWOOOSH
?
SPLISH
fssssht
IT TURNED TO MIST...?!
doom
WHAT WAS THAT? PISS?!
ANTI-CLIMACTIC.
IT NULLIFIED THE SPELL?

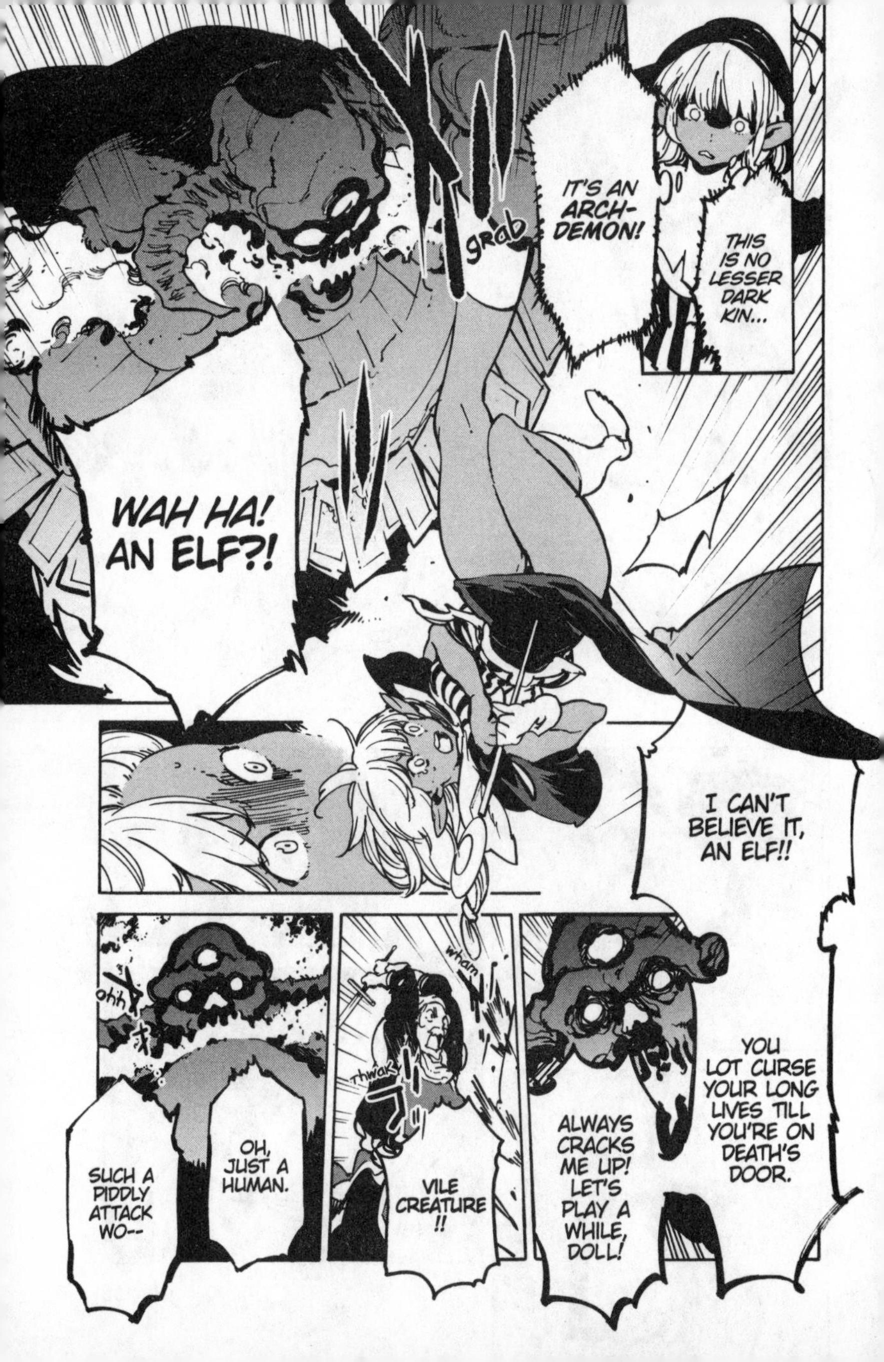
THIS IS NO LESSER DARK KIN...
IT'S AN ARCH-DEMON!
grab
WAH HA! AN ELF?!
I CAN'T BELIEVE IT, AN ELF!!
YOU LOT CURSE YOUR LONG LIVES TILL YOU'RE ON DEATH'S DOOR.
ALWAYS CRACKS ME UP! LET'S PLAY A WHILE, DOLL!
wham
thwak
VILE CREATURE!!
ohh
OH, JUST A HUMAN.
SUCH A PIDDLY ATTACK WO--

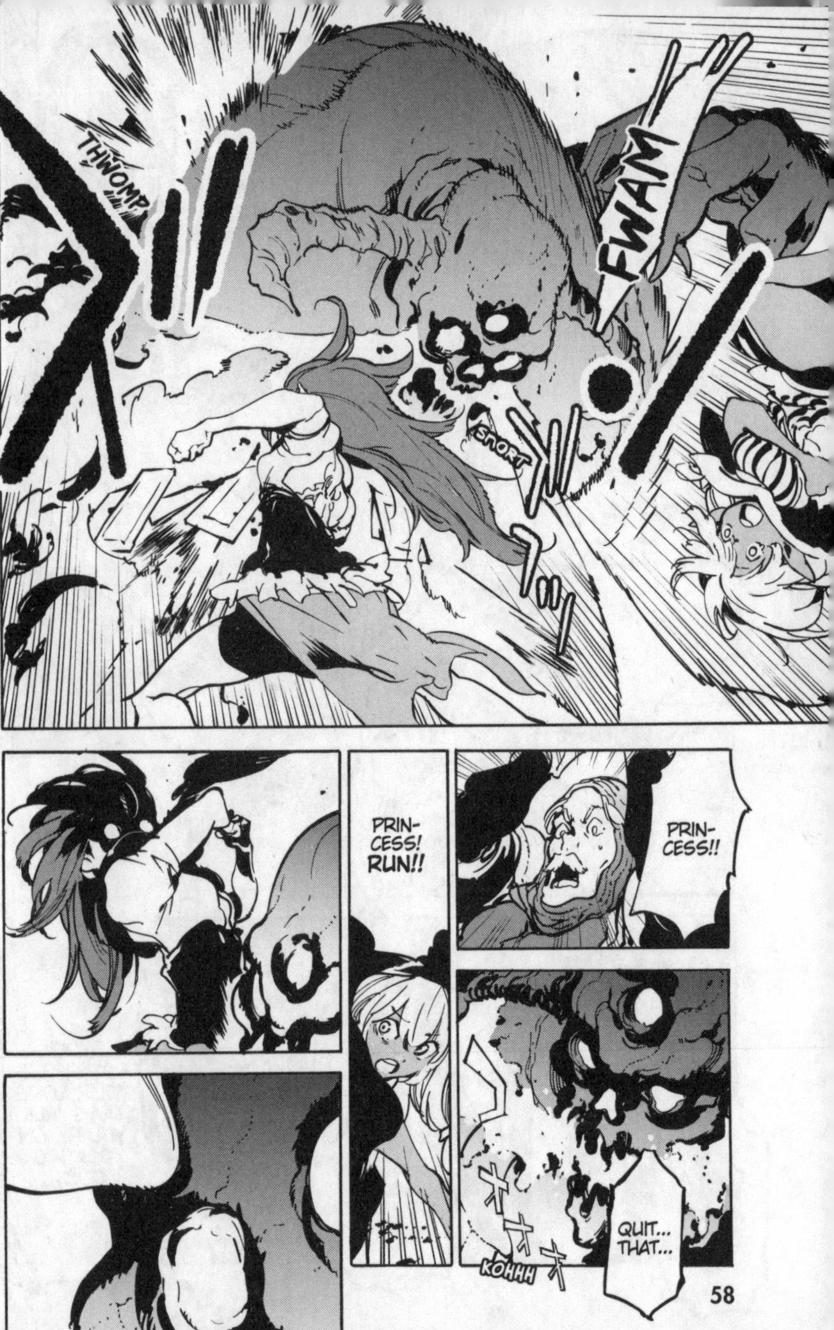
FWAM
THWOMP
SNORT
PRIN-
CESS!!
KOHHH
QUIT...
THAT...
PRIN-
CESS!
RUN!!

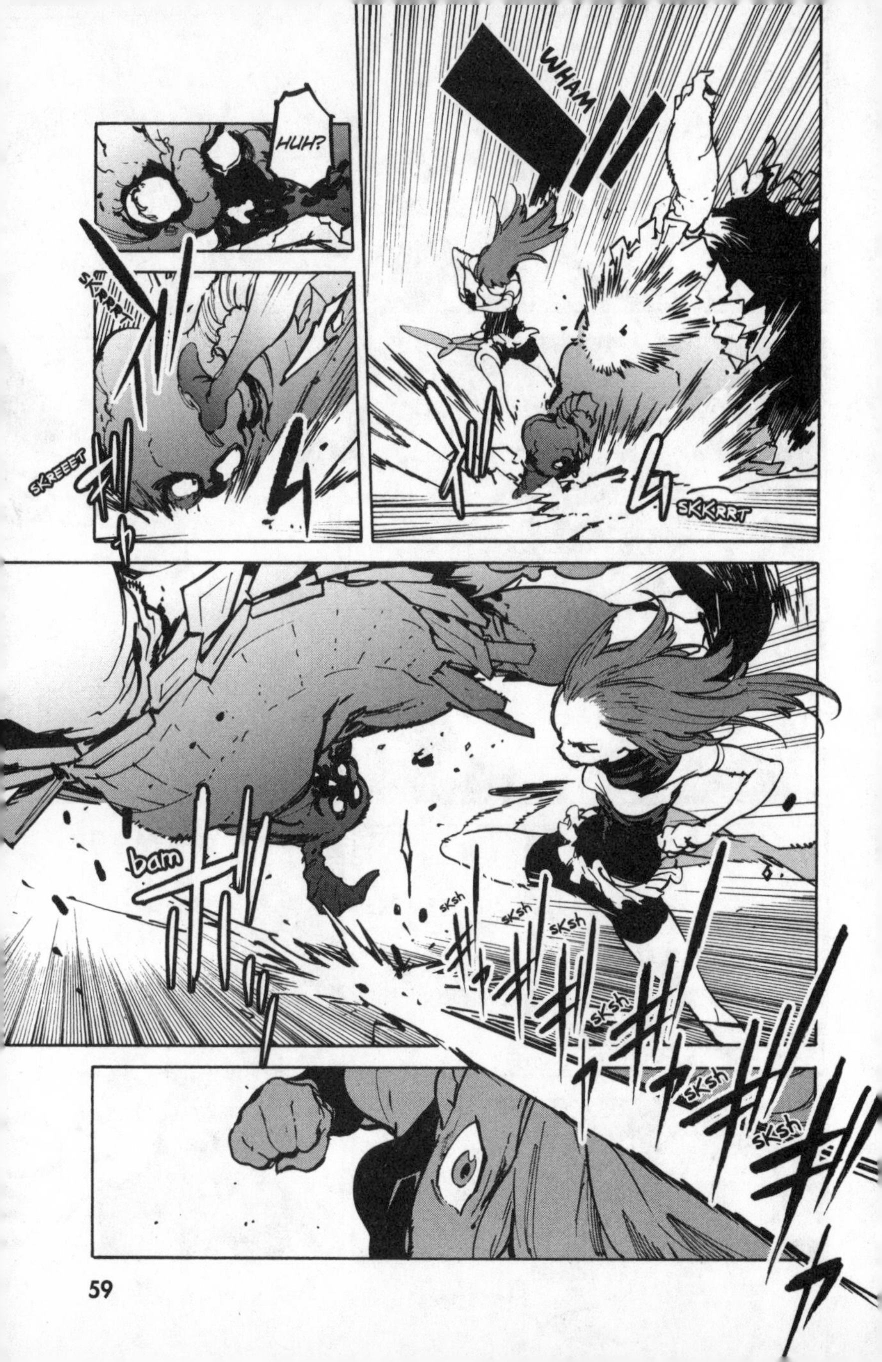
WHAM
SKKRRT
HUH?
SKRRRT
SKREEET
bam
sksh
sksh
sksh
sksh
sksh
sksh

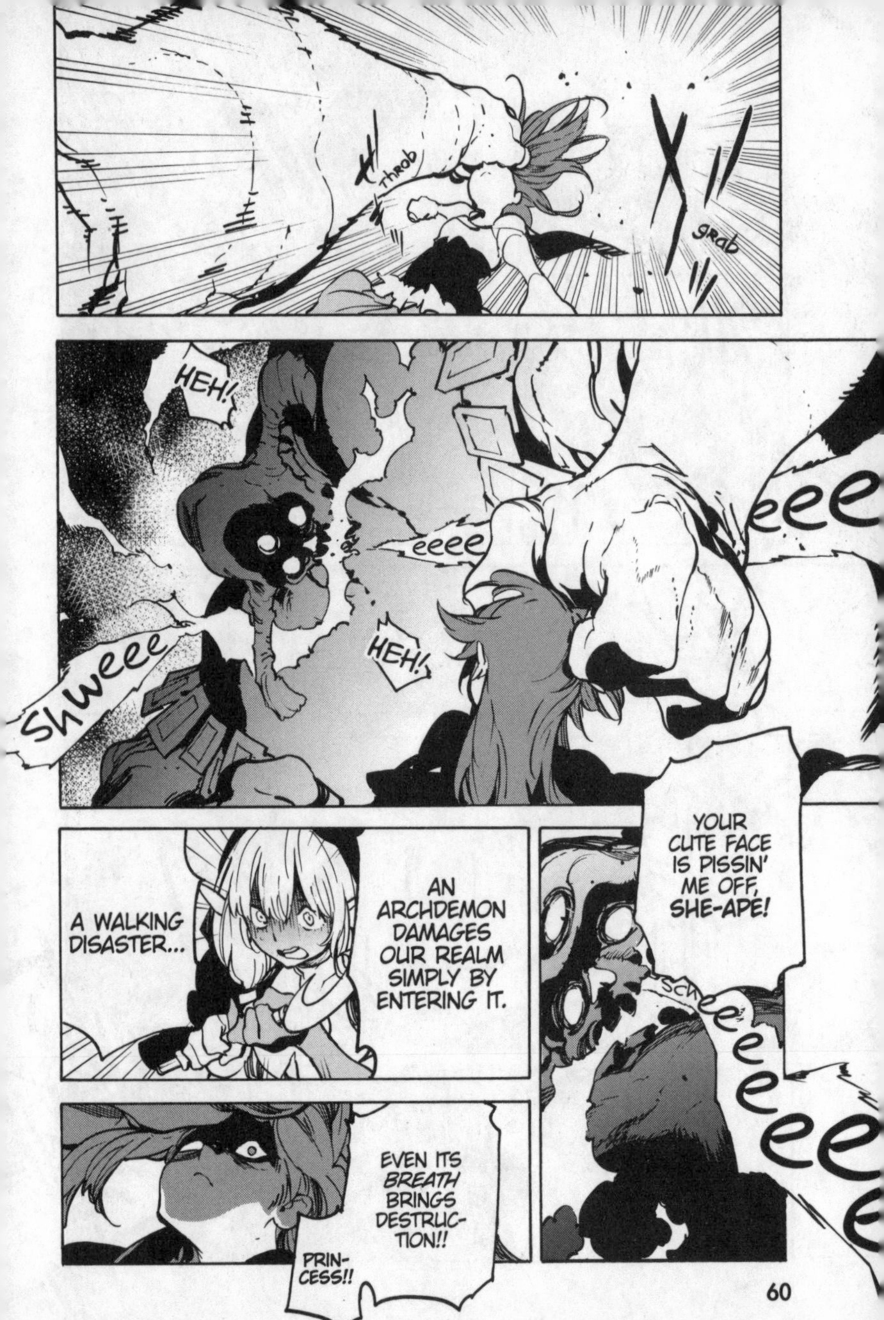
grab
throb
eee
HEH!
eeee
HEH!
Shweee
YOUR CUTE FACE IS PISSIN' ME OFF, SHE-APE!
Scheeeeeeee
AN ARCHDEMON DAMAGES OUR REALM SIMPLY BY ENTERING IT.
A WALKING DISASTER...
EVEN ITS *BREATH* BRINGS DESTRUCTION!!
PRINCESS!!

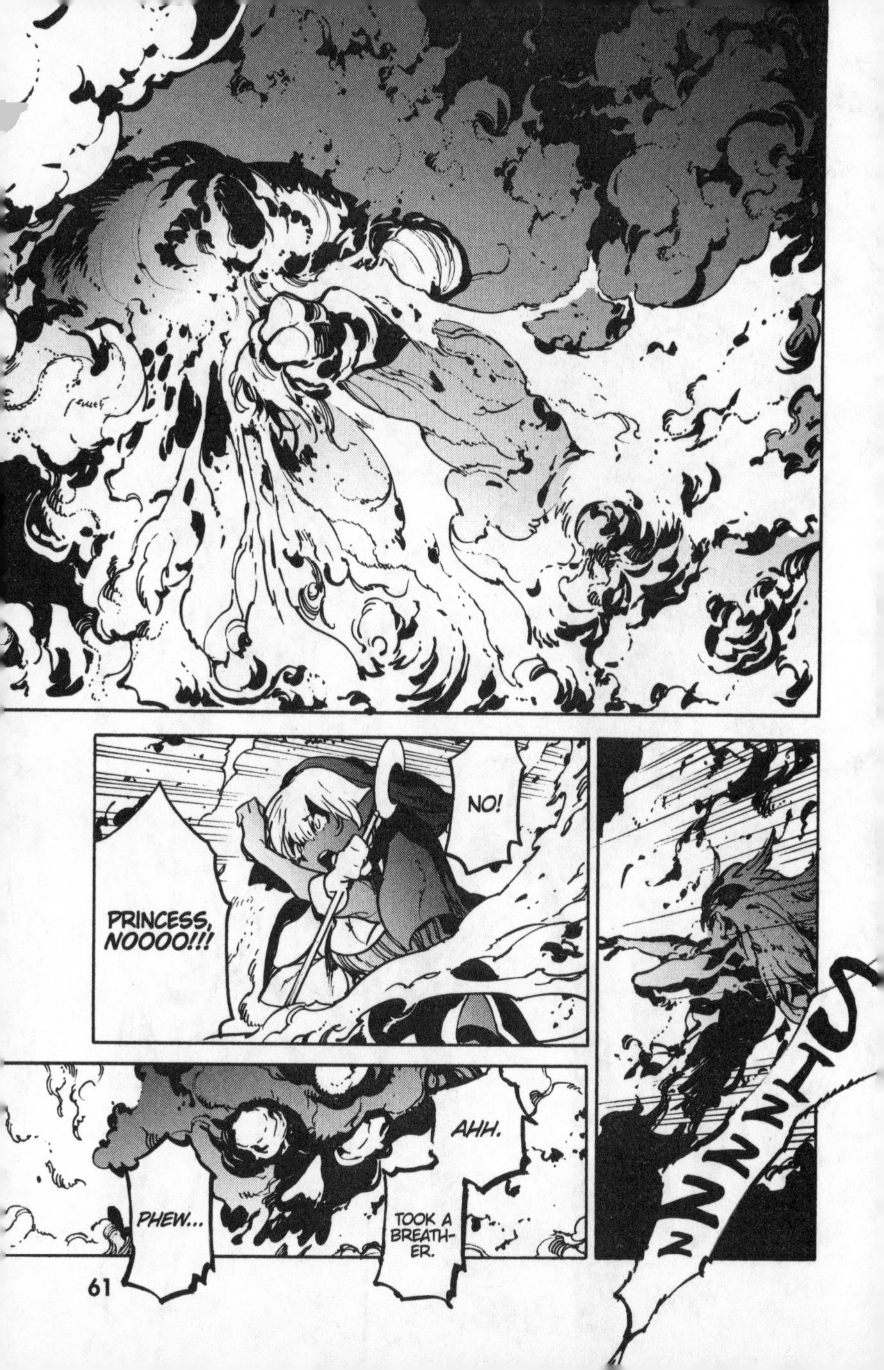
SHNNNN
NO!
PRINCESS, NOOOO!!!
AHH.
TOOK A BREATHER.
PHEW...

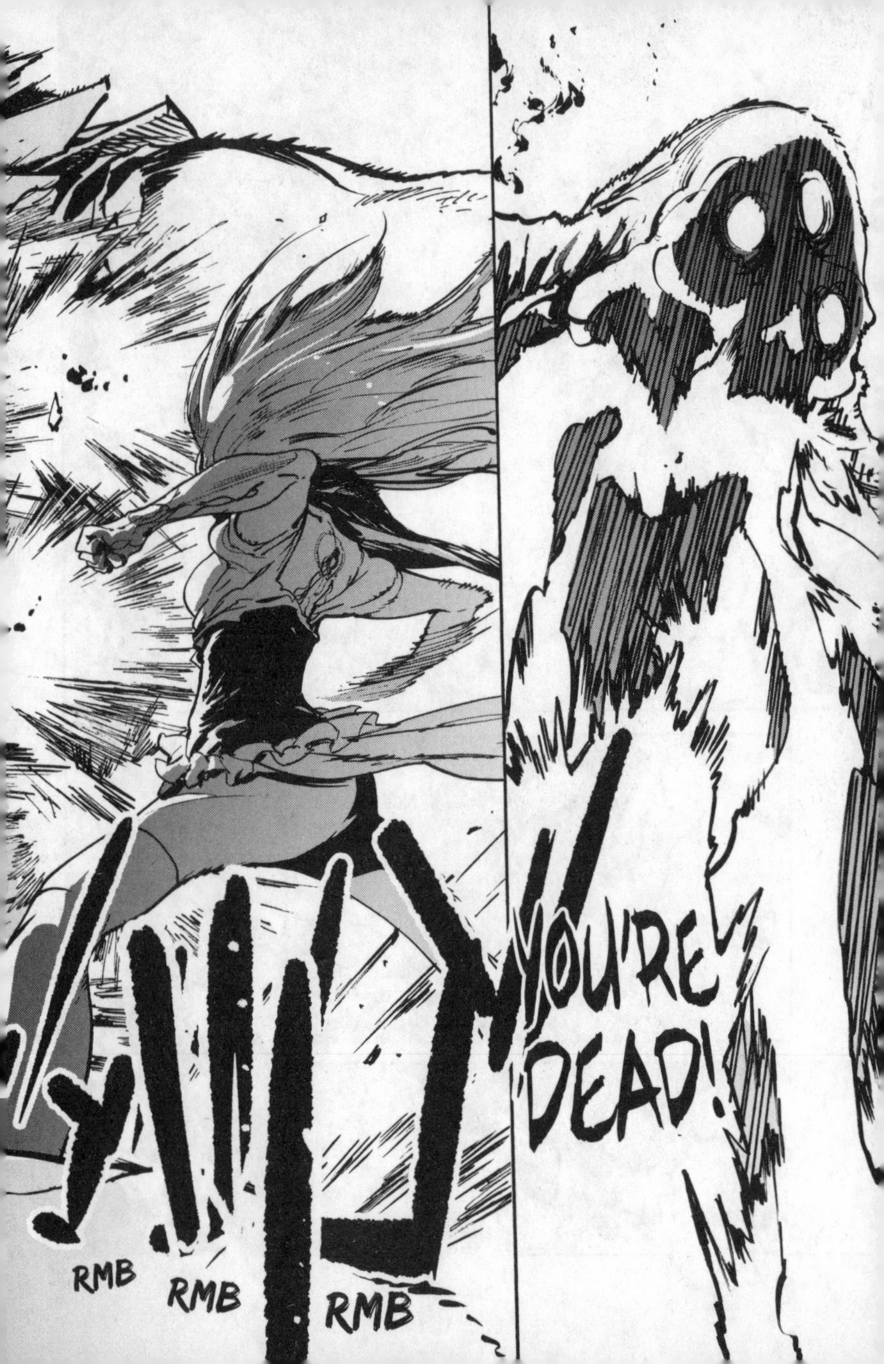
YOU'RE DEAD!
RMB
RMB
RMB

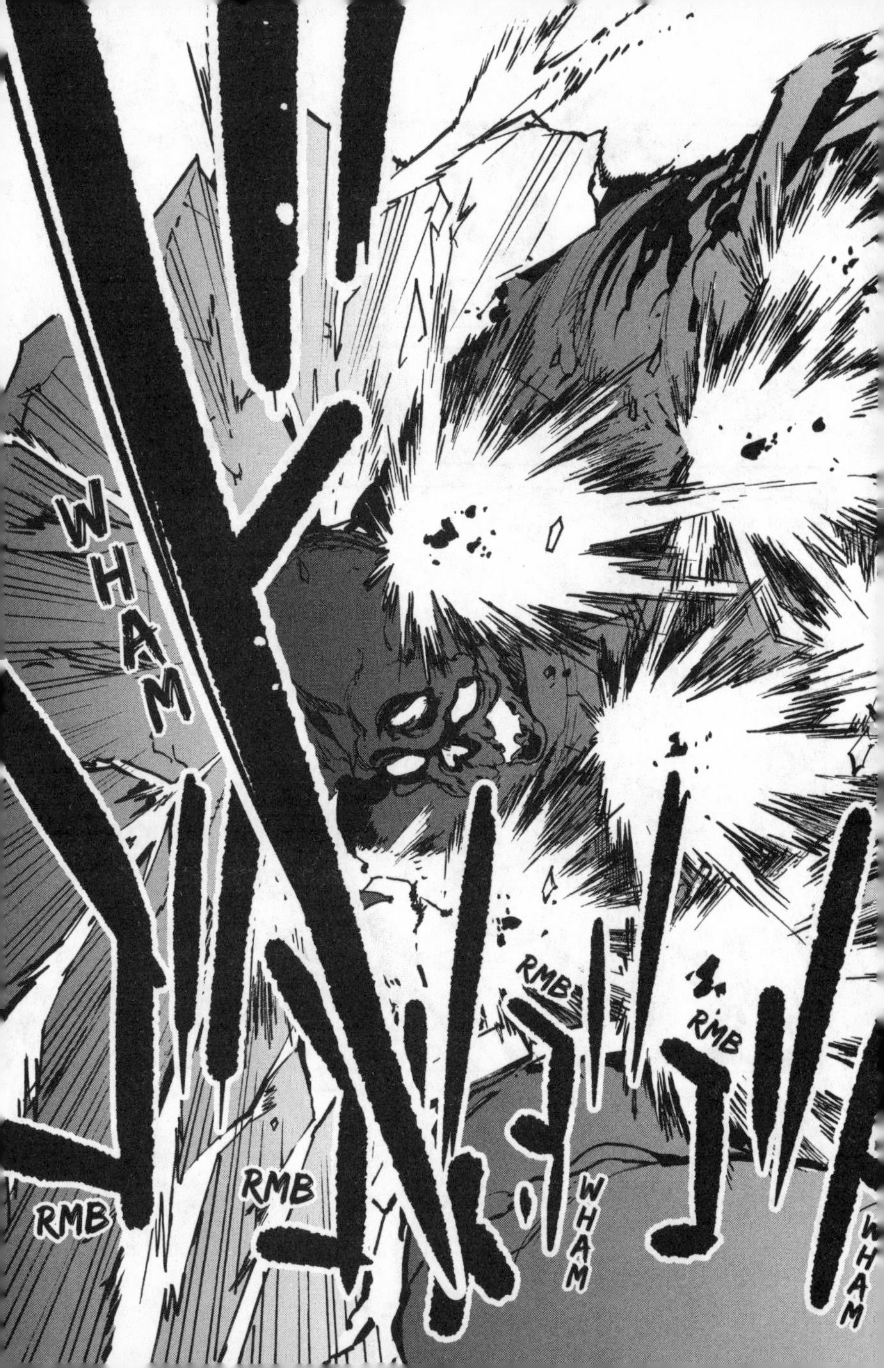
RMB
WHAM
RMB
WHAM
WHAM
RMB
RMB

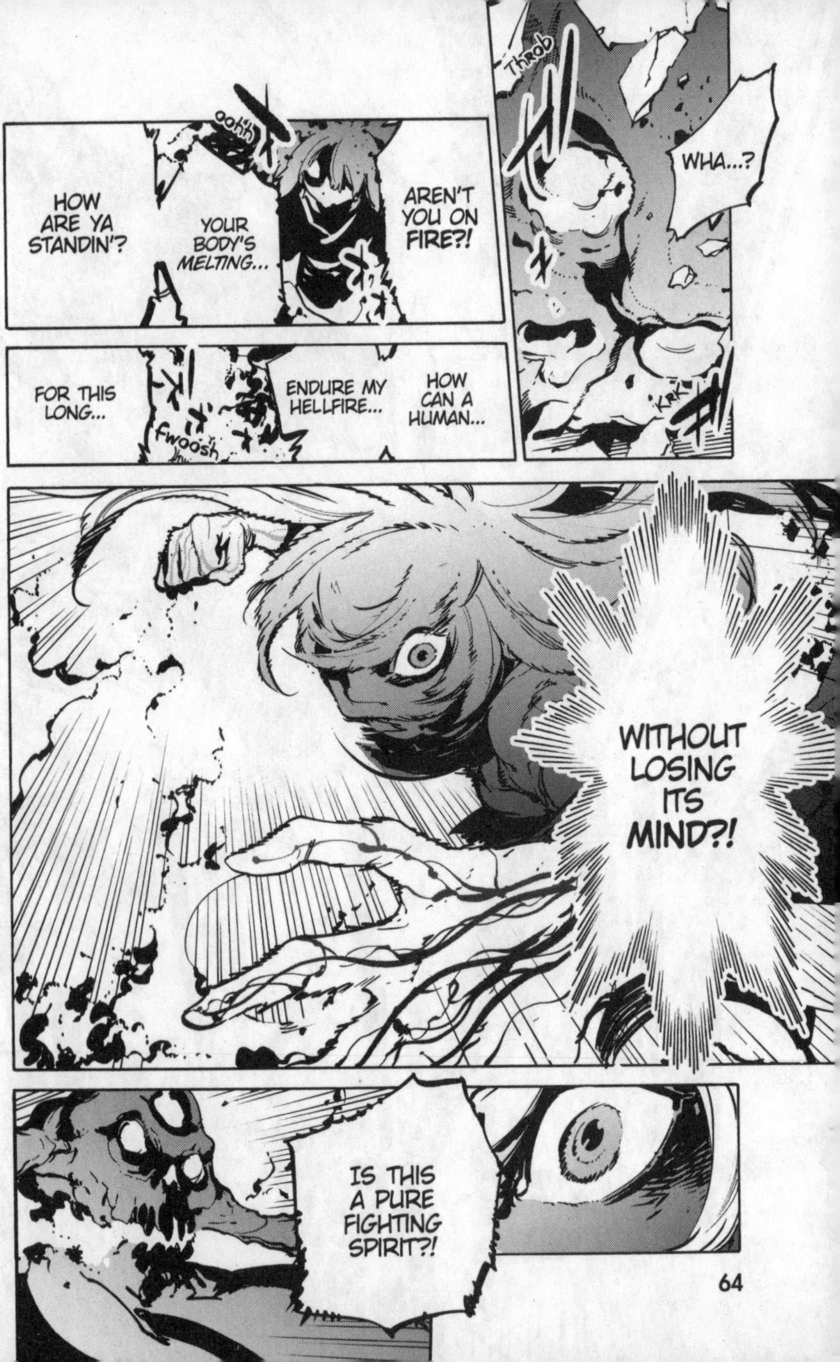
Throb
WHA...?
Krk
AREN'T YOU ON FIRE?!
YOUR BODY'S MELTING...
HOW ARE YA STANDIN'?
HOW CAN A HUMAN...
ENDURE MY HELLFIRE...
FOR THIS LONG...
fwoosh
WITHOUT LOSING ITS MIND?!
IS THIS A PURE FIGHTING SPIRIT?!

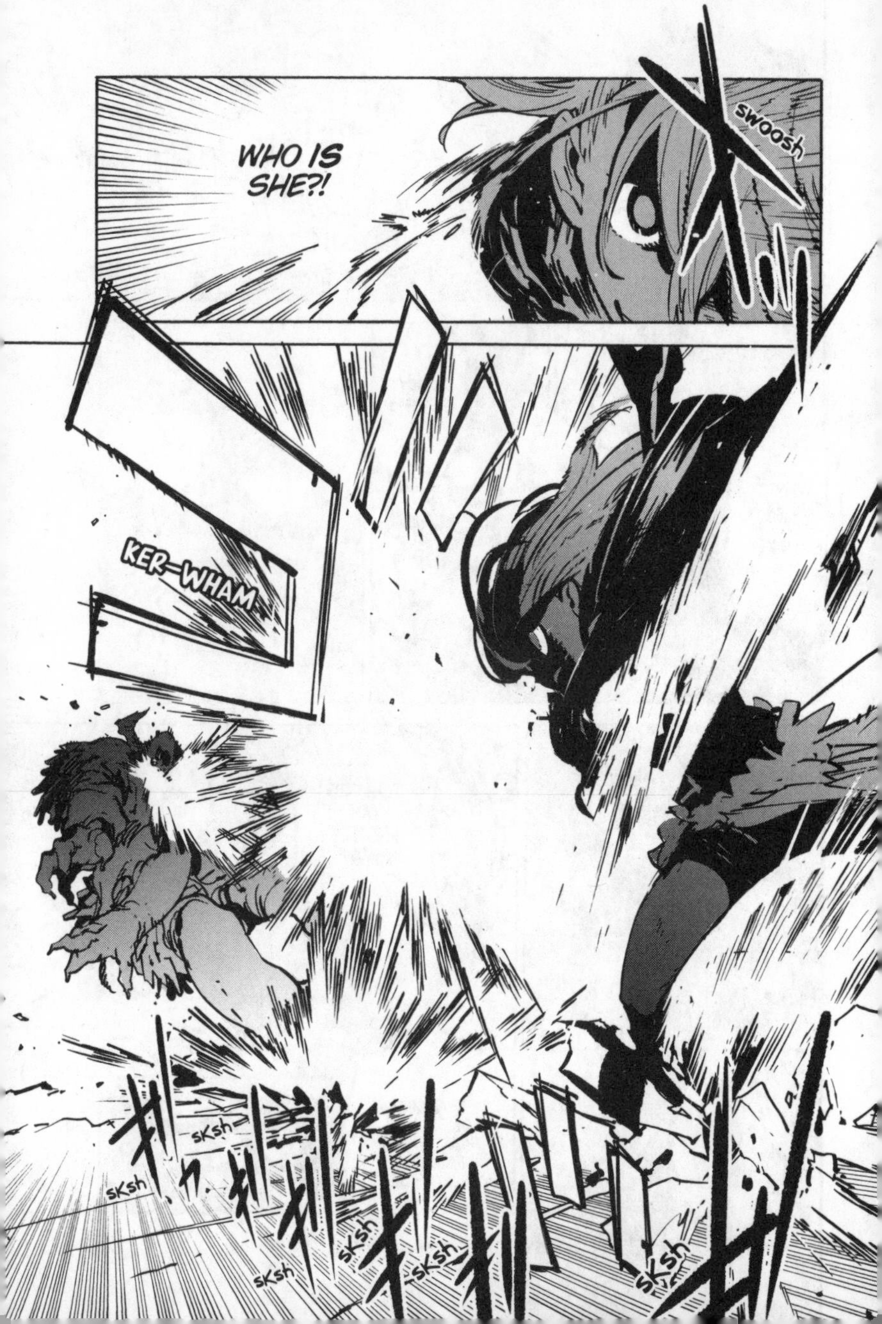
swoosh
WHO IS
SHE?!
KER-WHAM
sKsh
sKsh
sKsh
sKsh
sKsh
sKsh

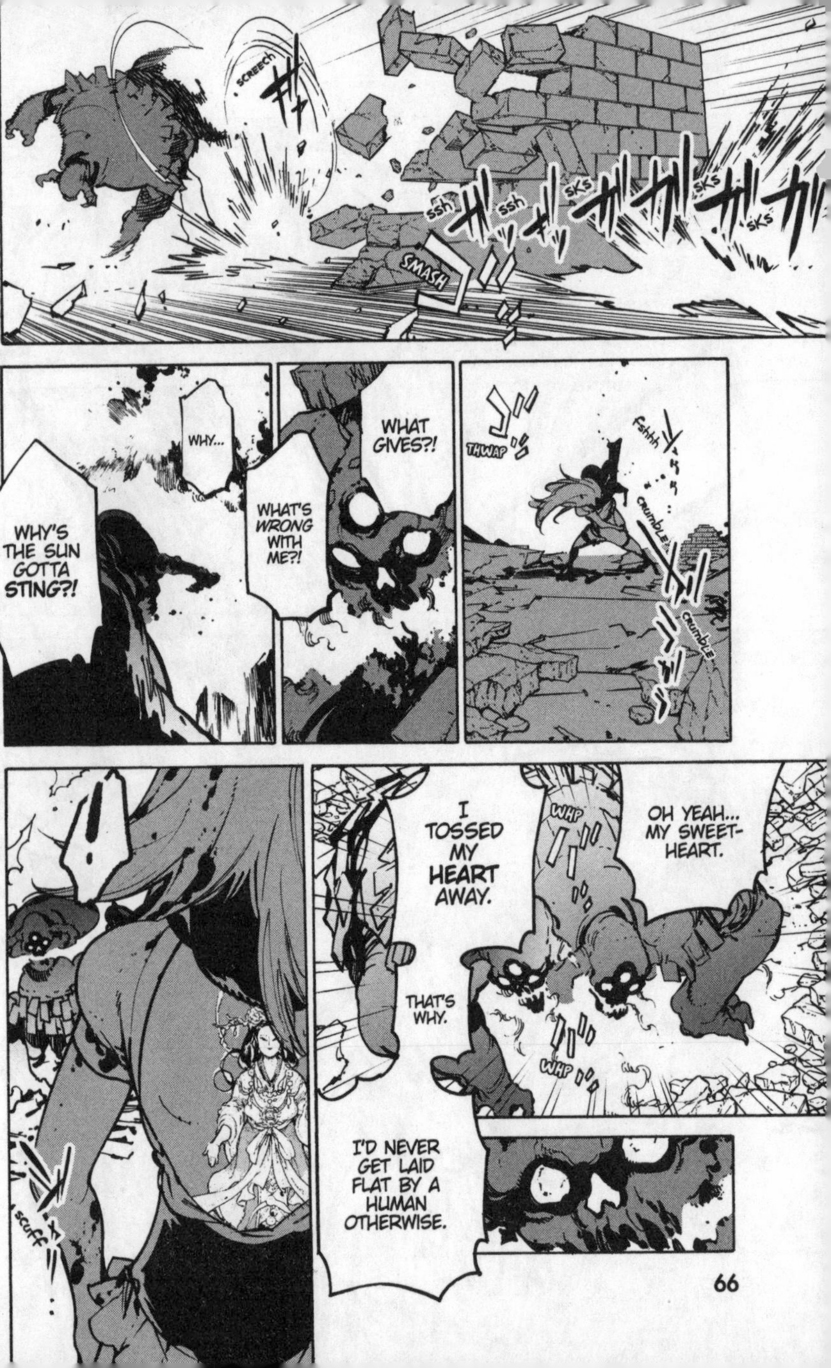
SCREECH
SKS
SKS
SKS
ssh
ssh
SMASH
fshhh
CRUMBLE
CRUMBLE
THWAP
WHAT GIVES?!
WHAT'S WRONG WITH ME?!
WHY...
WHY'S THE SUN GOTTA STING?!
OH YEAH... MY SWEET-HEART.
I TOSSED MY HEART AWAY.
WHP
THAT'S WHY.
WHP
I'D NEVER GET LAID FLAT BY A HUMAN OTHERWISE.
!
scuff

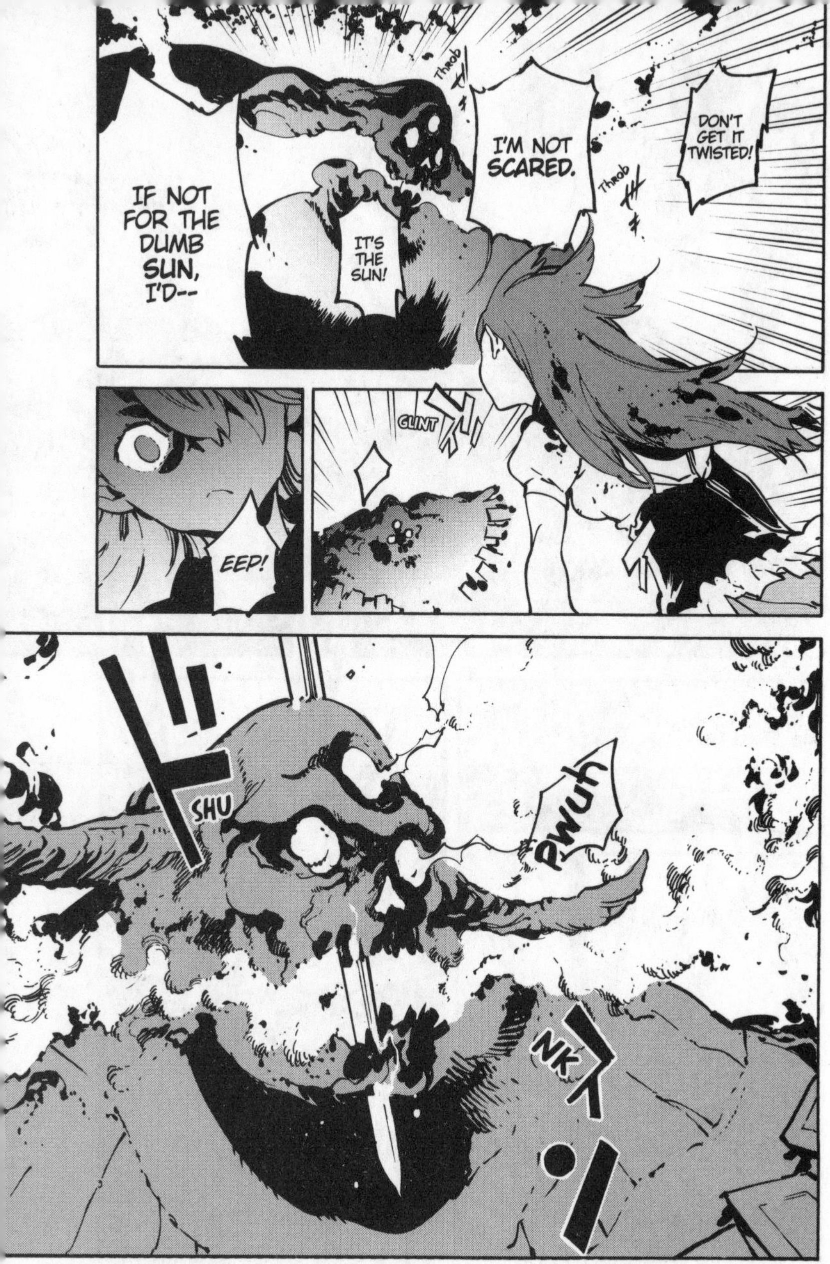
DON'T GET IT TWISTED!
Throb
I'M NOT SCARED.
Throb
IT'S THE SUN!
IF NOT FOR THE DUMB SUN, I'D--
GLINT
EEP!
PWUH
SHU
NK

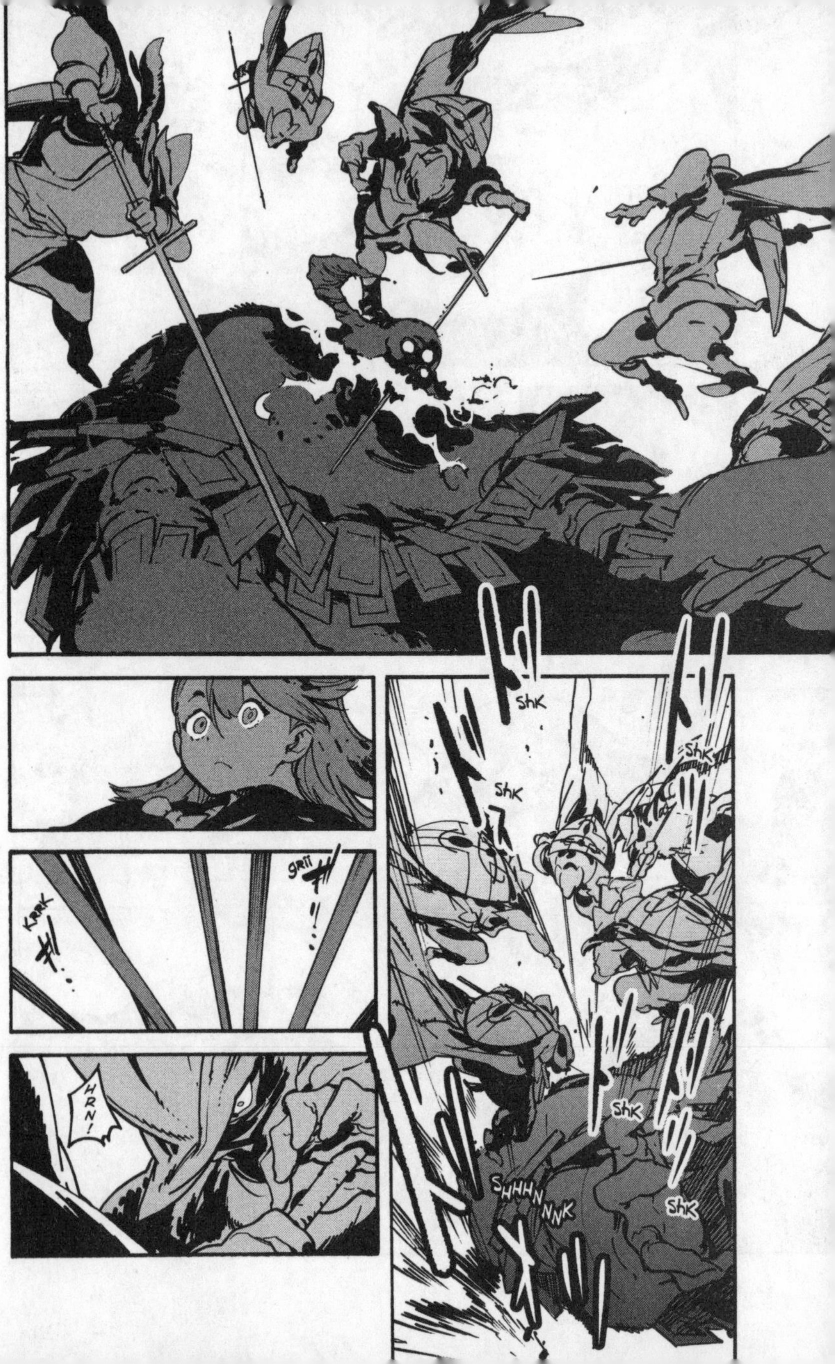
SHK
SHK
SHK
SHK
SHHHNNNK
SHK
GRII
KRRK
HRN!

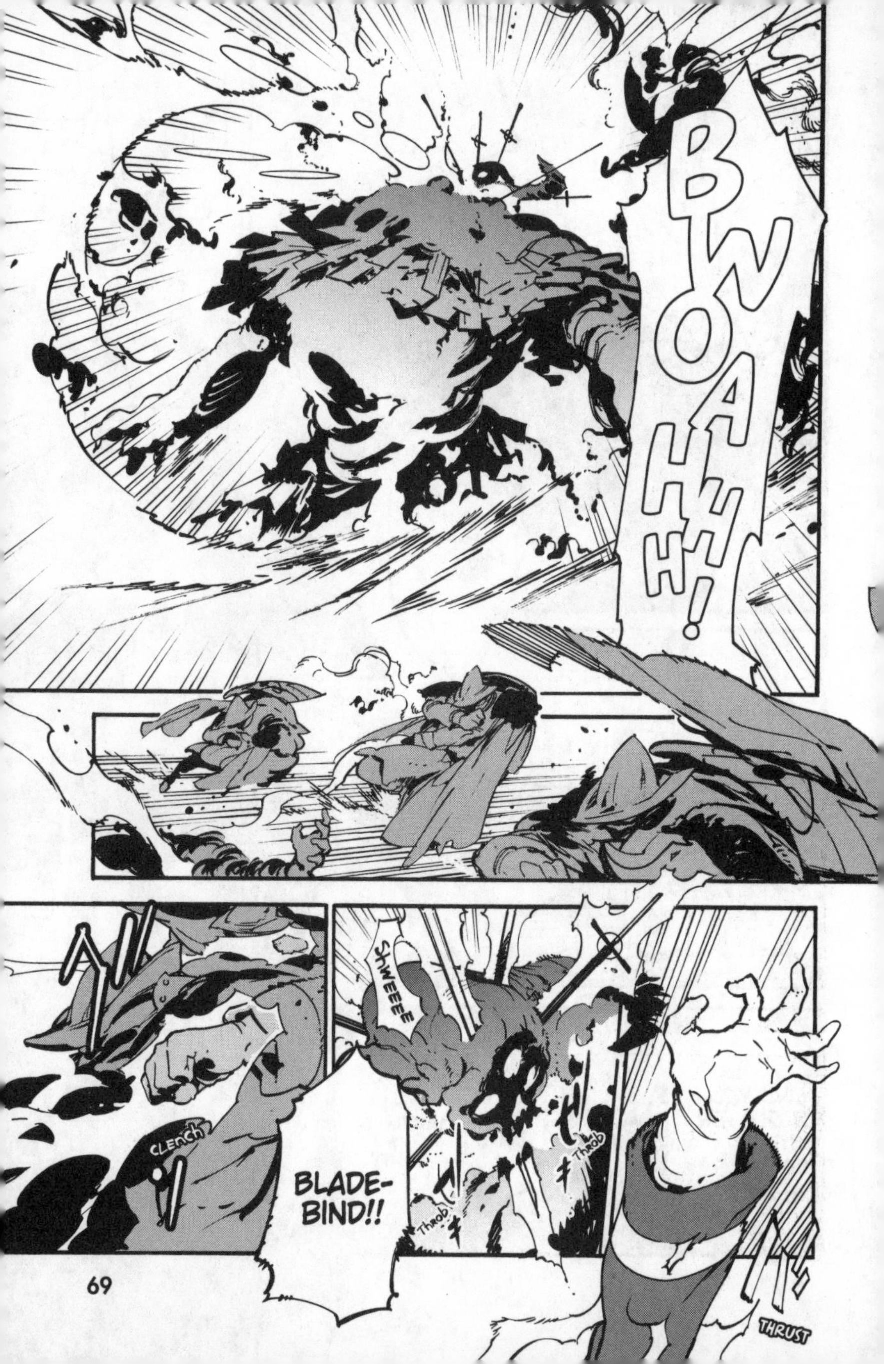
BWOAHHHHH!
SHWEEEE
Throb
Throb
THRUST
BLADE-BIND!!
CLENCH

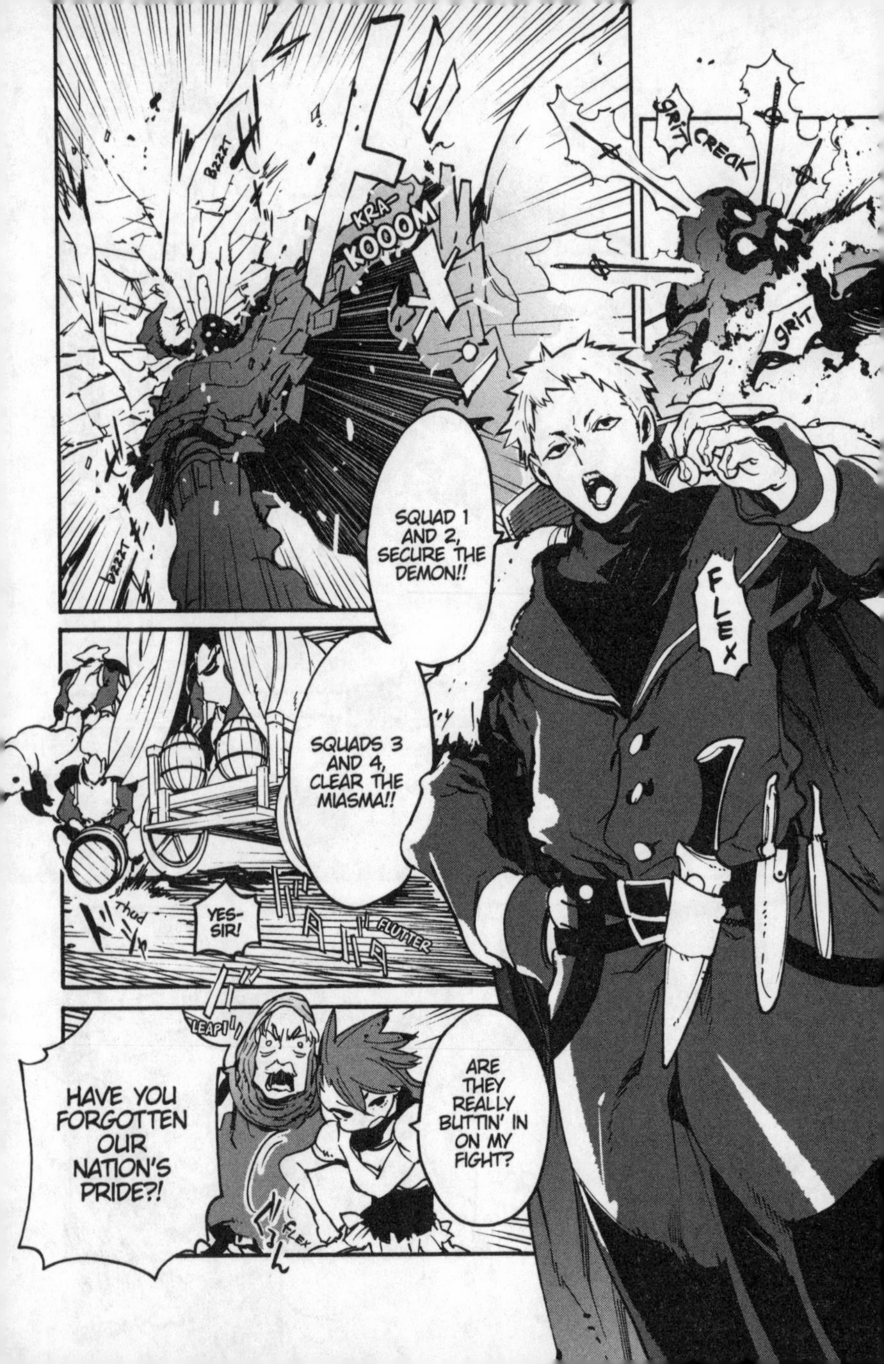
GRIT
CREAK
GRIT
KRA-KOOOM
BZZZT
BZZZT
SQUAD 1 AND 2, SECURE THE DEMON!!
FLEX
SQUADS 3 AND 4, CLEAR THE MIASMA!!
FLUTTER
YES-SIR!
THUD
ARE THEY REALLY BUTTIN' IN ON MY FIGHT?
LEAP!
HAVE YOU FORGOTTEN OUR NATION'S PRIDE?!
FLEX

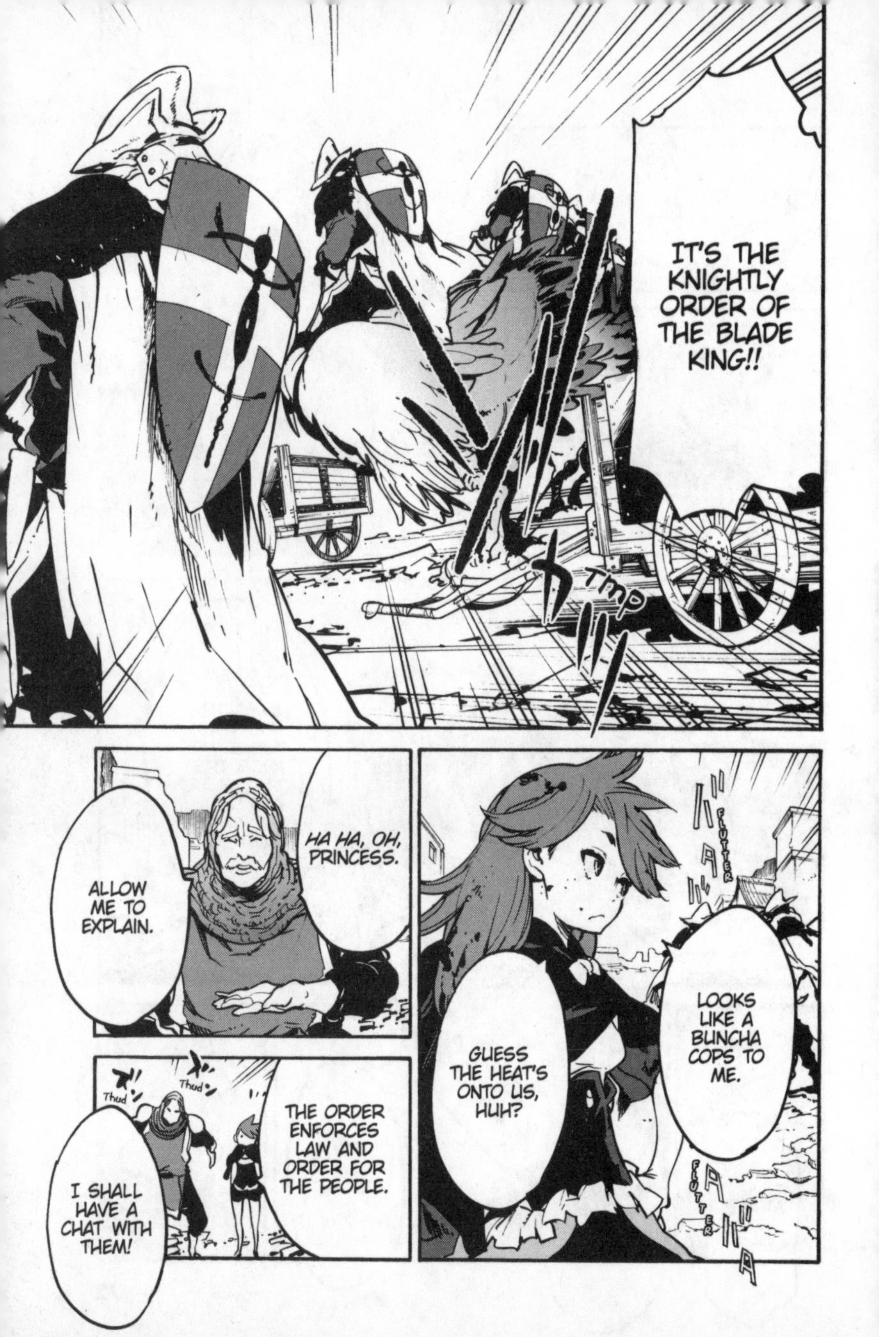
IT'S THE KNIGHTLY ORDER OF THE BLADE KING!!
Tmp
FLUTTER
LOOKS LIKE A BUNCHA COPS TO ME.
GUESS THE HEAT'S ONTO US, HUH?
FLUTTER
HA HA, OH, PRINCESS.
ALLOW ME TO EXPLAIN.
Thud
Thud
THE ORDER ENFORCES LAW AND ORDER FOR THE PEOPLE.
I SHALL HAVE A CHAT WITH THEM!

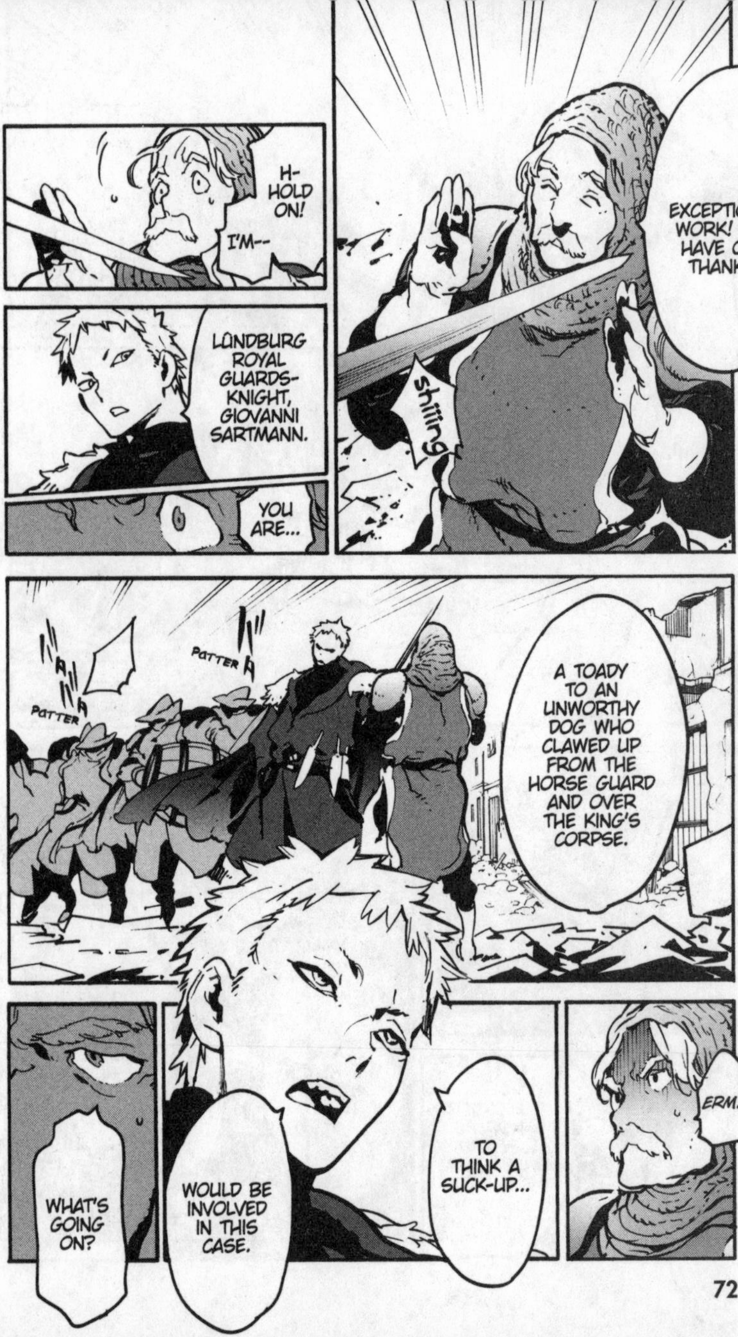
EXCEPTIONAL WORK! YOU HAVE OUR THANKS!
shiiing
H-HOLD ON!
I'M--
LŪNDBURG ROYAL GUARDS-KNIGHT, GIOVANNI SARTMANN.
YOU ARE...
A TOADY TO AN UNWORTHY DOG WHO CLAWED UP FROM THE HORSE GUARD AND OVER THE KING'S CORPSE.
PATTER
PATTER
ERM...
TO THINK A SUCK-UP...
WOULD BE INVOLVED IN THIS CASE.
WHAT'S GOING ON?

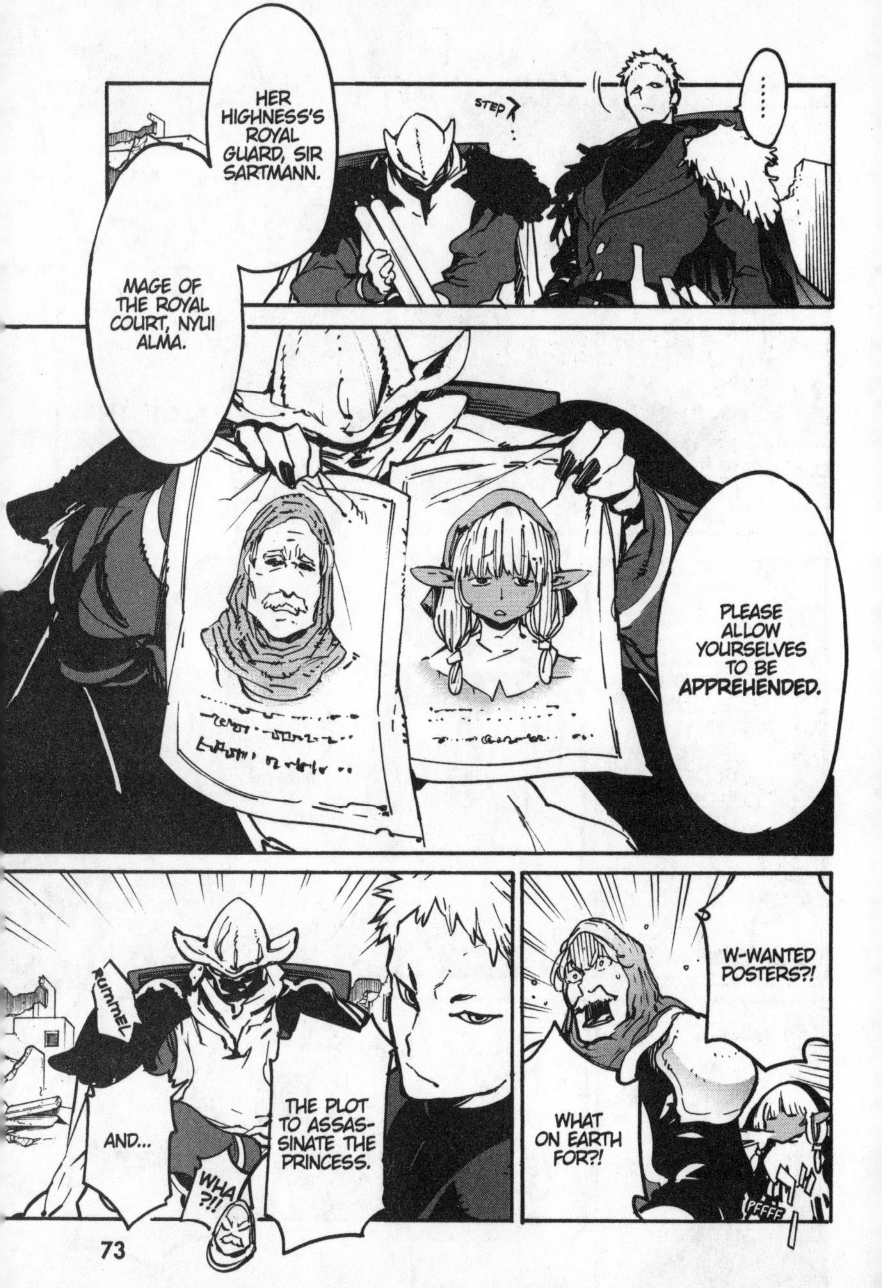
......
STEP
HER HIGHNESS'S ROYAL GUARD, SIR SARTMANN.
MAGE OF THE ROYAL COURT, NYUI ALMA.
PLEASE ALLOW YOURSELVES TO BE **APPREHENDED.**
W-WANTED POSTERS?!
WHAT ON EARTH FOR?!
PFFFF
RUMMEL
AND...
THE PLOT TO ASSAS-SINATE THE PRINCESS.
WHA ?!!

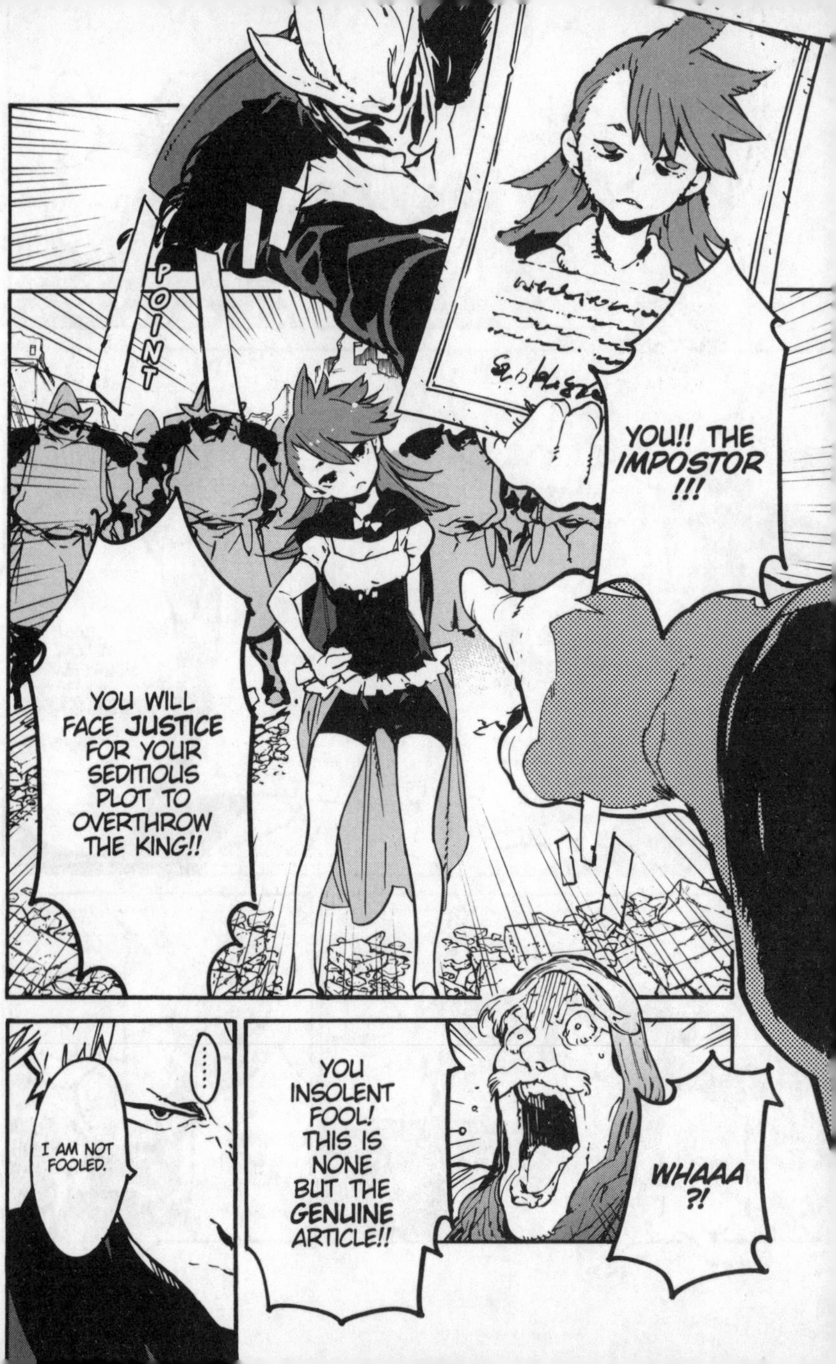
YOU!! THE IMPOSTOR !!!
POINT
YOU WILL FACE JUSTICE FOR YOUR SEDITIOUS PLOT TO OVERTHROW THE KING!!
WHAAA ?!
YOU INSOLENT FOOL! THIS IS NONE BUT THE GENUINE ARTICLE!!
......
I AM NOT FOOLED.

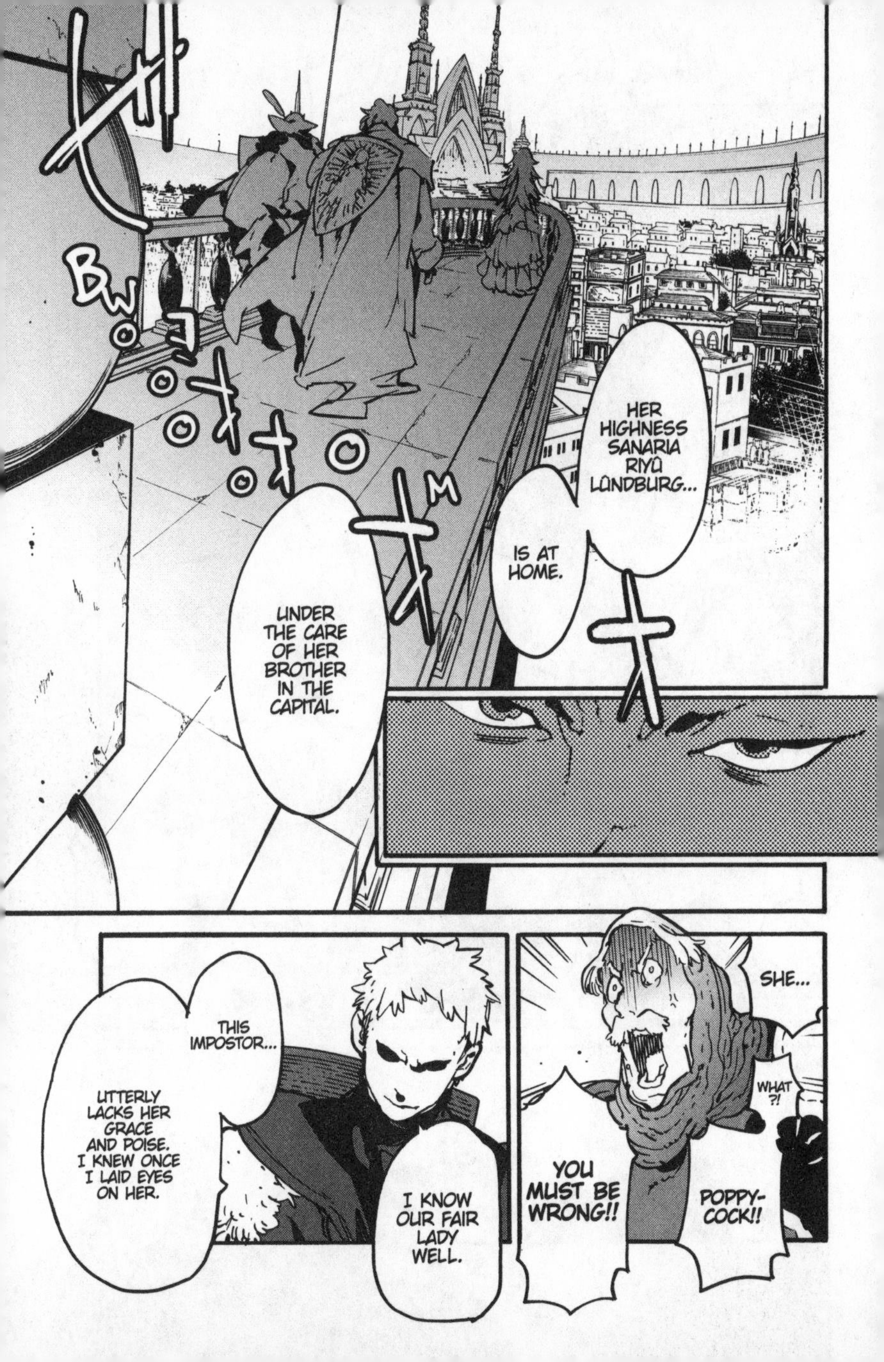
HER HIGHNESS SANARIA RIYÛ LÛNDBURG...
IS AT HOME.
UNDER THE CARE OF HER BROTHER IN THE CAPITAL.
SHE...
WHAT?!
POPPY-COCK!!
YOU MUST BE WRONG!!
THIS IMPOSTOR...
UTTERLY LACKS HER GRACE AND POISE. I KNEW ONCE I LAID EYES ON HER.
I KNOW OUR FAIR LADY WELL.

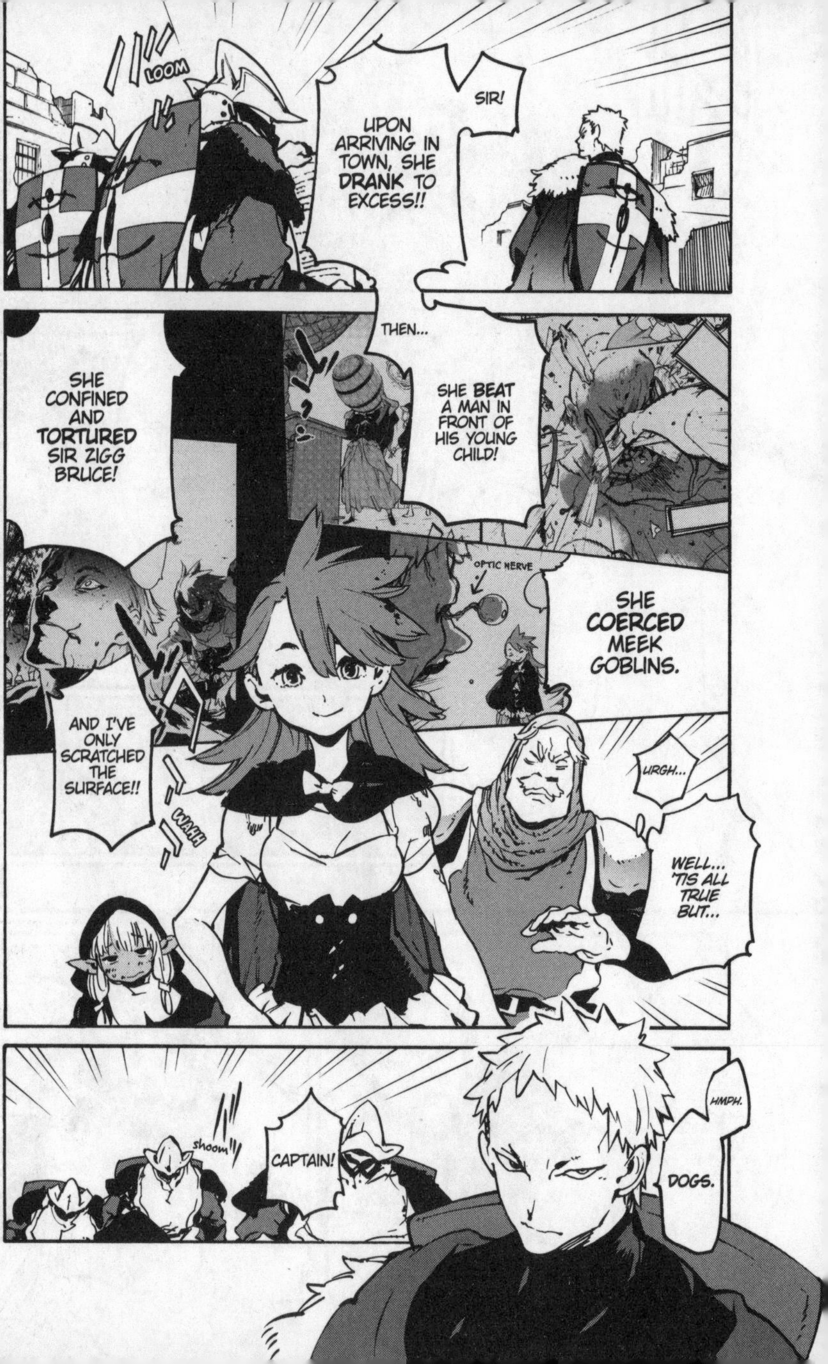
SIR!
UPON ARRIVING IN TOWN, SHE DRANK TO EXCESS!!
LOOM
THEN...
SHE BEAT A MAN IN FRONT OF HIS YOUNG CHILD!
SHE CONFINED AND TORTURED SIR ZIGG BRUCE!
OPTIC NERVE
SHE COERCED MEEK GOBLINS.
AND I'VE ONLY SCRATCHED THE SURFACE!!
WAAH
URGH...
WELL... 'TIS ALL TRUE BUT...
HMPH.
DOGS.
CAPTAIN!
shoom

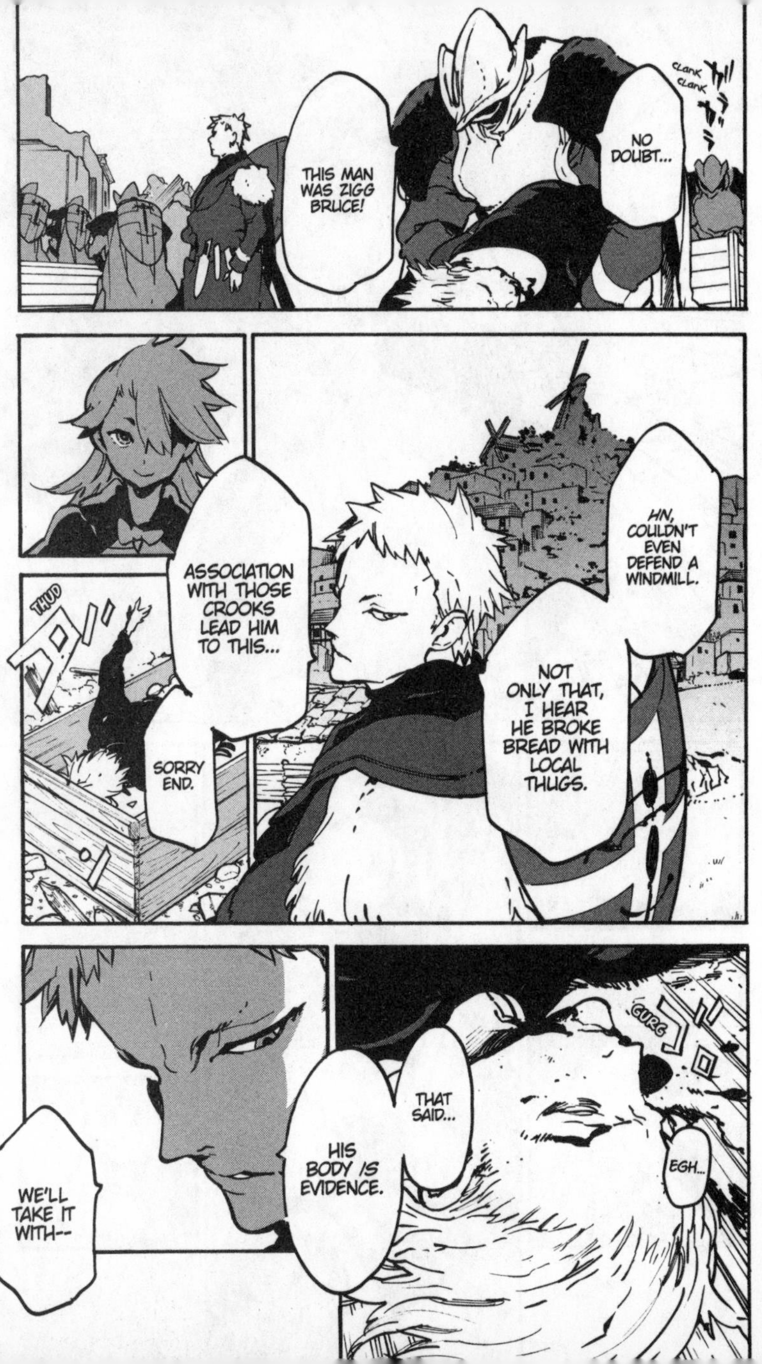
CLANK CLANK
NO DOUBT...
THIS MAN WAS ZIGG BRUCE!
HN, COULDN'T EVEN DEFEND A WINDMILL.
NOT ONLY THAT, I HEAR HE BROKE BREAD WITH LOCAL THUGS.
ASSOCIATION WITH THOSE CROOKS LEAD HIM TO THIS...
THUD
SORRY END.
GURG
EGH...
THAT SAID...
HIS BODY IS EVIDENCE.
WE'LL TAKE IT WITH--

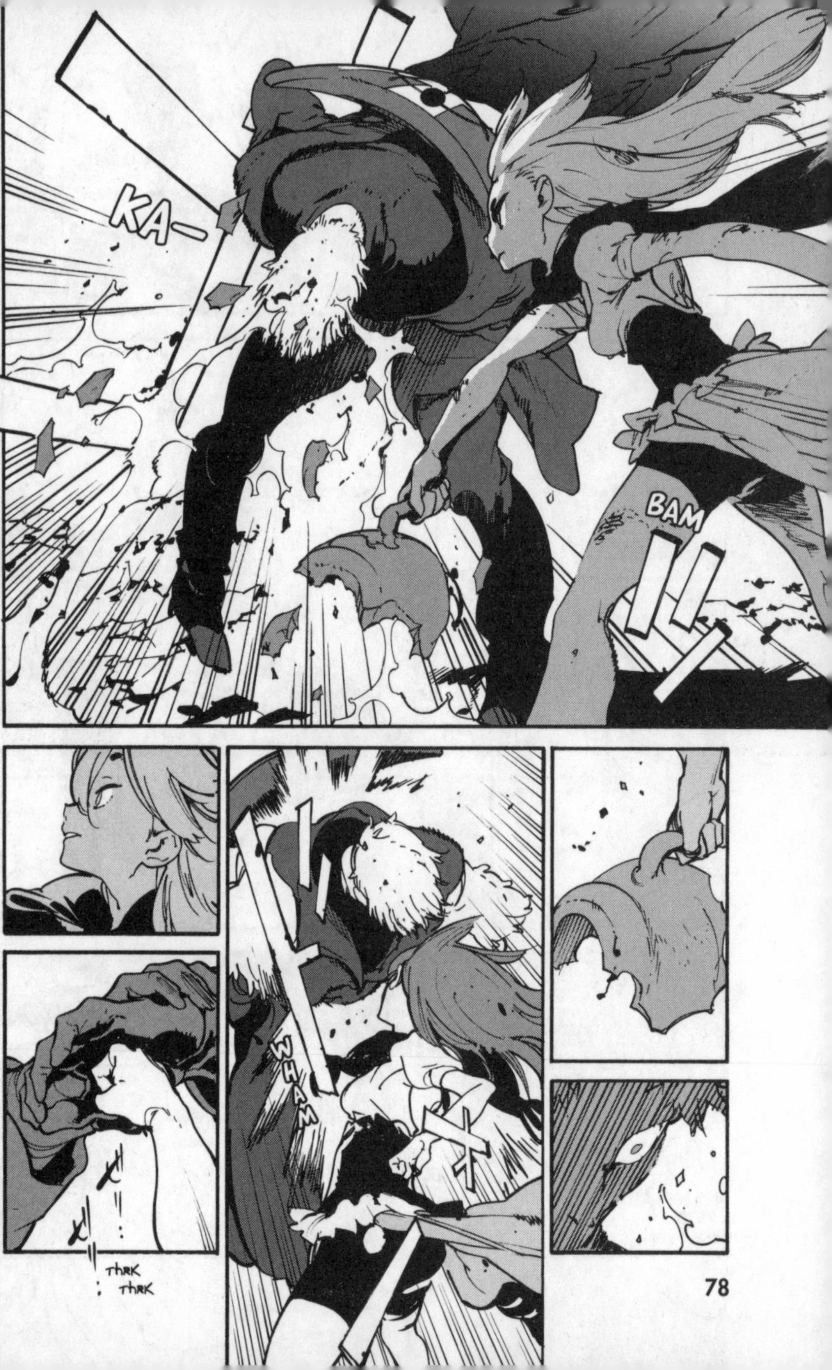
KA–
BAM
WHAM
THRK
THRK

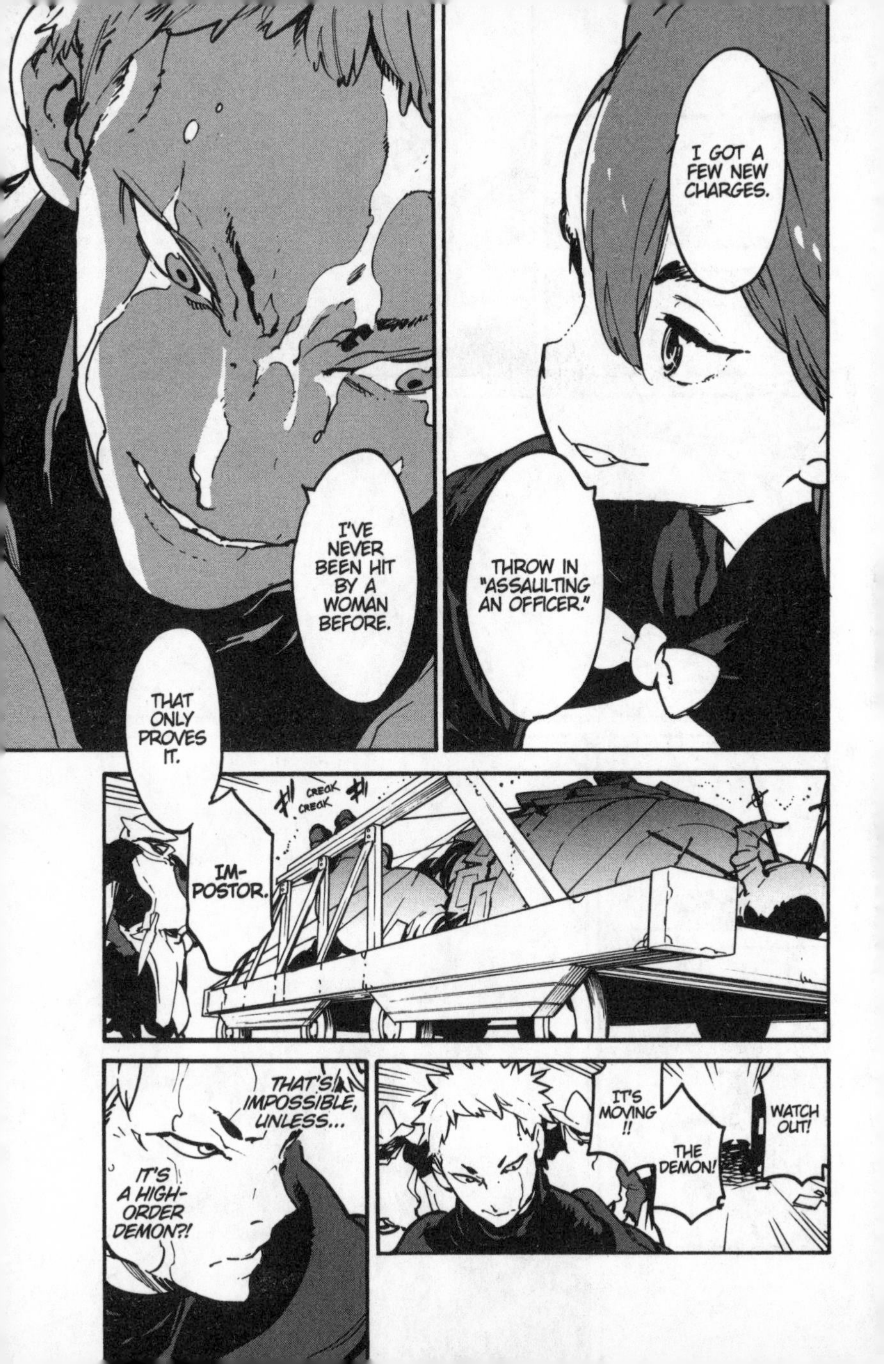
I GOT A FEW NEW CHARGES.
THROW IN "ASSAULTING AN OFFICER."
I'VE NEVER BEEN HIT BY A WOMAN BEFORE.
THAT ONLY PROVES IT.
CREAK CREAK
IM-POSTOR.
WATCH OUT!
IT'S MOVING !!
THE DEMON!
THAT'S IMPOSSIBLE, UNLESS...
IT'S A HIGH-ORDER DEMON?!

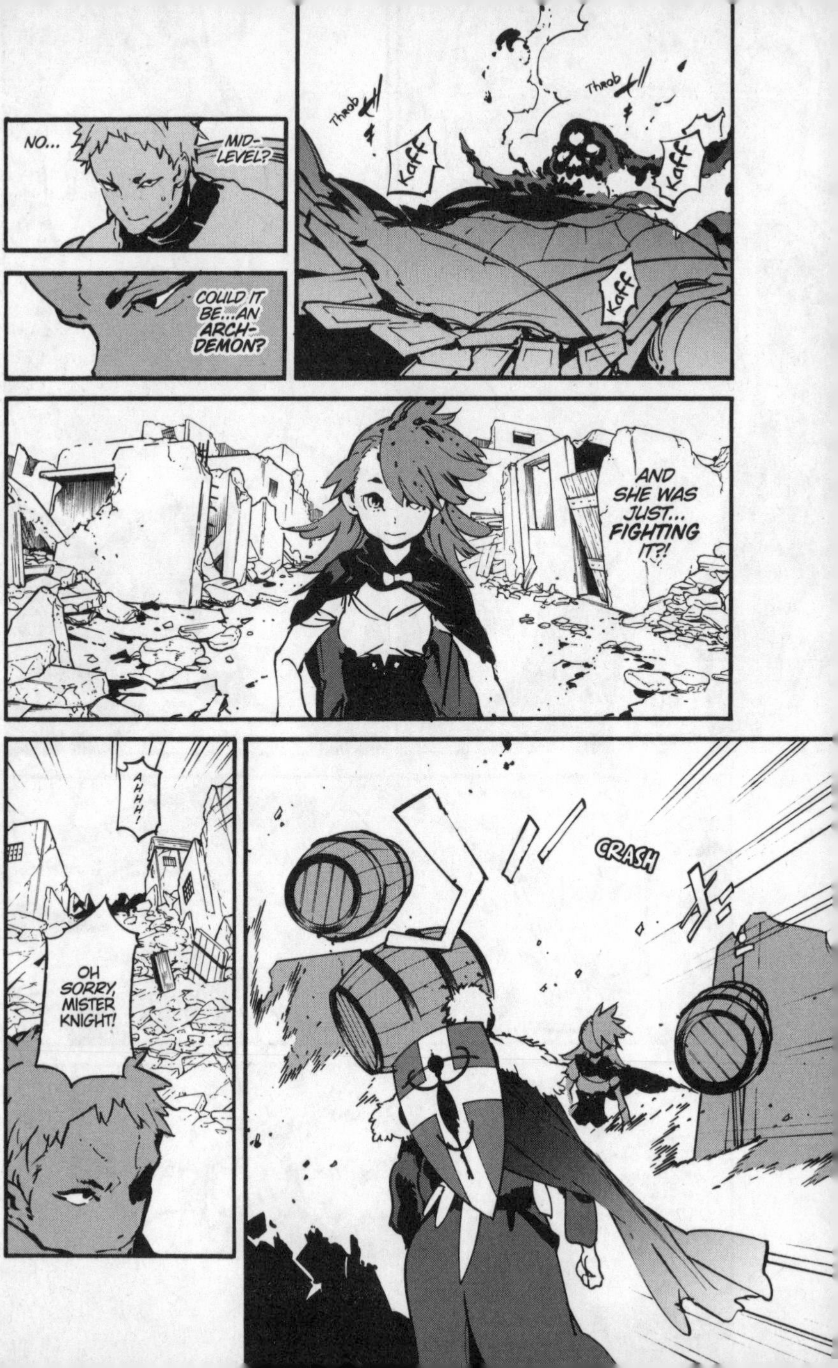
Throb
Throb
Kaff
Kaff
Kaff
NO...
MID-LEVEL?
COULD IT BE...AN ARCH-DEMON?
AND SHE WAS JUST... FIGHTING IT?!
CRASH
AHHH!
OH SORRY, MISTER KNIGHT!

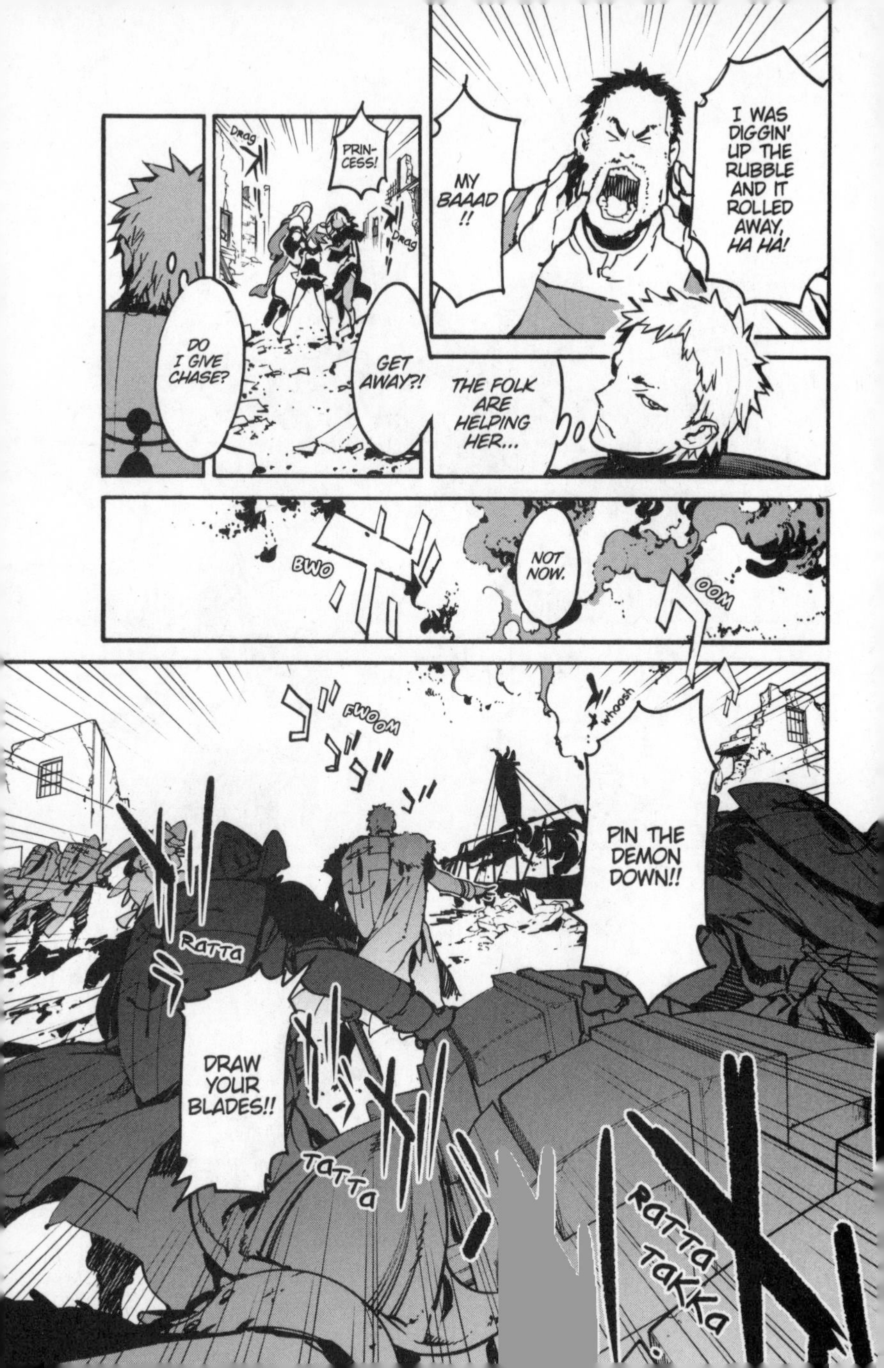
I WAS DIGGIN' UP THE RUBBLE AND IT ROLLED AWAY, HA HA!
MY BAAAD!!
THE FOLK ARE HELPING HER...
PRIN-CESS!
Drag
Drag
GET AWAY?!
DO I GIVE CHASE?
BWO
OOM
NOT NOW.
whoosh
FWOOM
PIN THE DEMON DOWN!!
RATTA TAKKA
DRAW YOUR BLADES!!
TATTA
RATTA

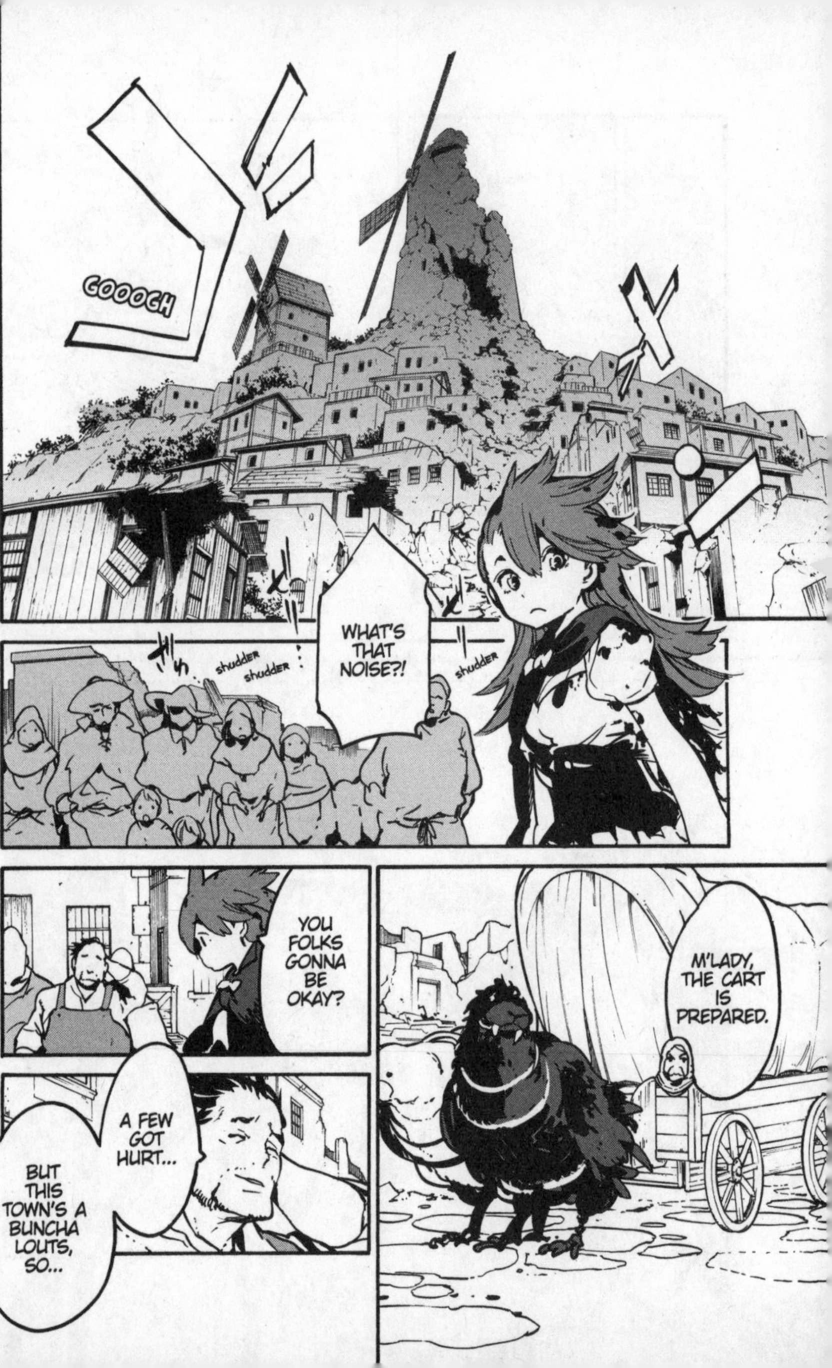
GOOOCH
shudder
WHAT'S THAT NOISE?!
shudder
shudder
M'LADY, THE CART IS PREPARED.
YOU FOLKS GONNA BE OKAY?
A FEW GOT HURT...
BUT THIS TOWN'S A BUNCHA LOUTS, SO...

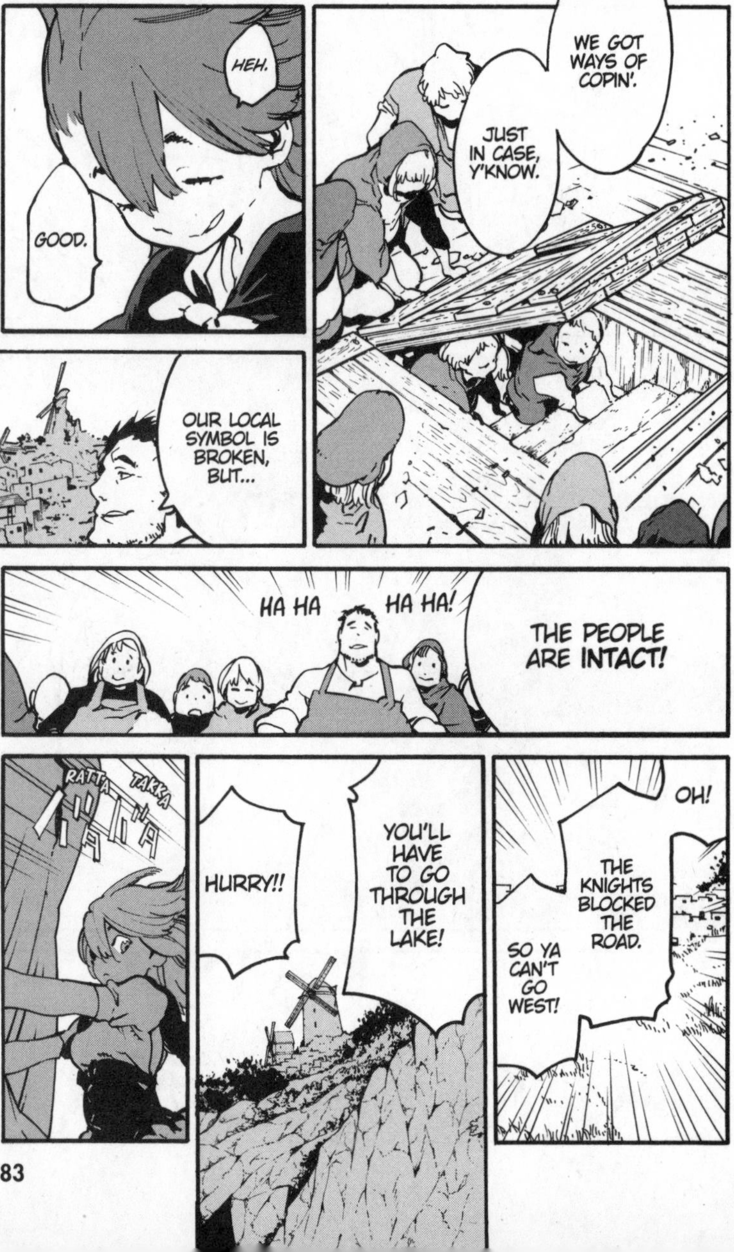
WE GOT WAYS OF COPIN'.
JUST IN CASE, Y'KNOW.
HEH.
GOOD.
OUR LOCAL SYMBOL IS BROKEN, BUT...
HA HA
HA HA!
THE PEOPLE ARE INTACT!
OH!
THE KNIGHTS BLOCKED THE ROAD.
SO YA CAN'T GO WEST!
YOU'LL HAVE TO GO THROUGH THE LAKE!
HURRY!!
RATTA
TAKKA

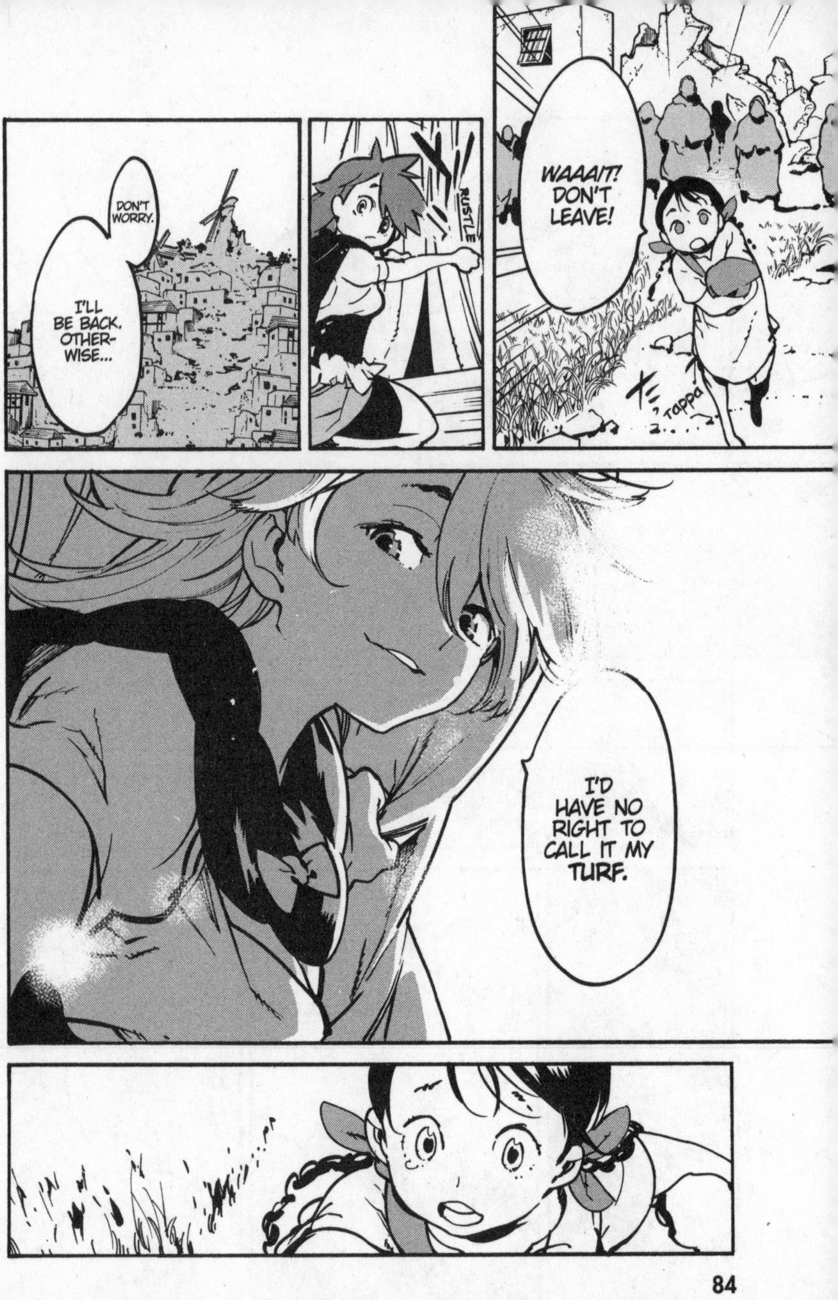
WAAAIT! DON'T LEAVE!
Tappa
RUSTLE
DON'T WORRY.
I'LL BE BACK. OTHERWISE...
I'D HAVE NO RIGHT TO CALL IT MY TURF.

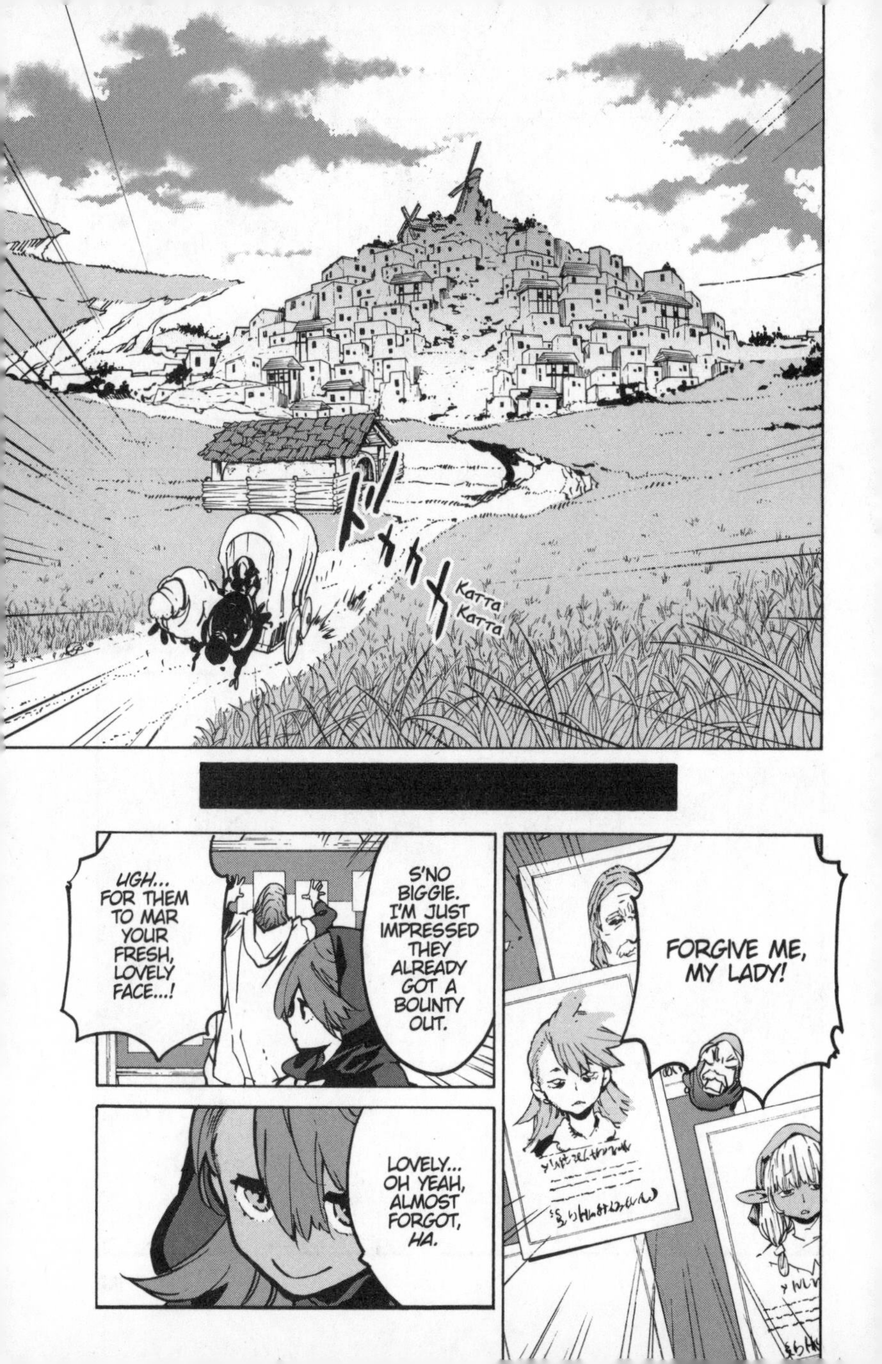
Katta Katta
[redacted]
FORGIVE ME, MY LADY!
UGH... FOR THEM TO MAR YOUR FRESH, LOVELY FACE...!
S'NO BIGGIE. I'M JUST IMPRESSED THEY ALREADY GOT A BOUNTY OUT.
LOVELY... OH YEAH, ALMOST FORGOT, HA.

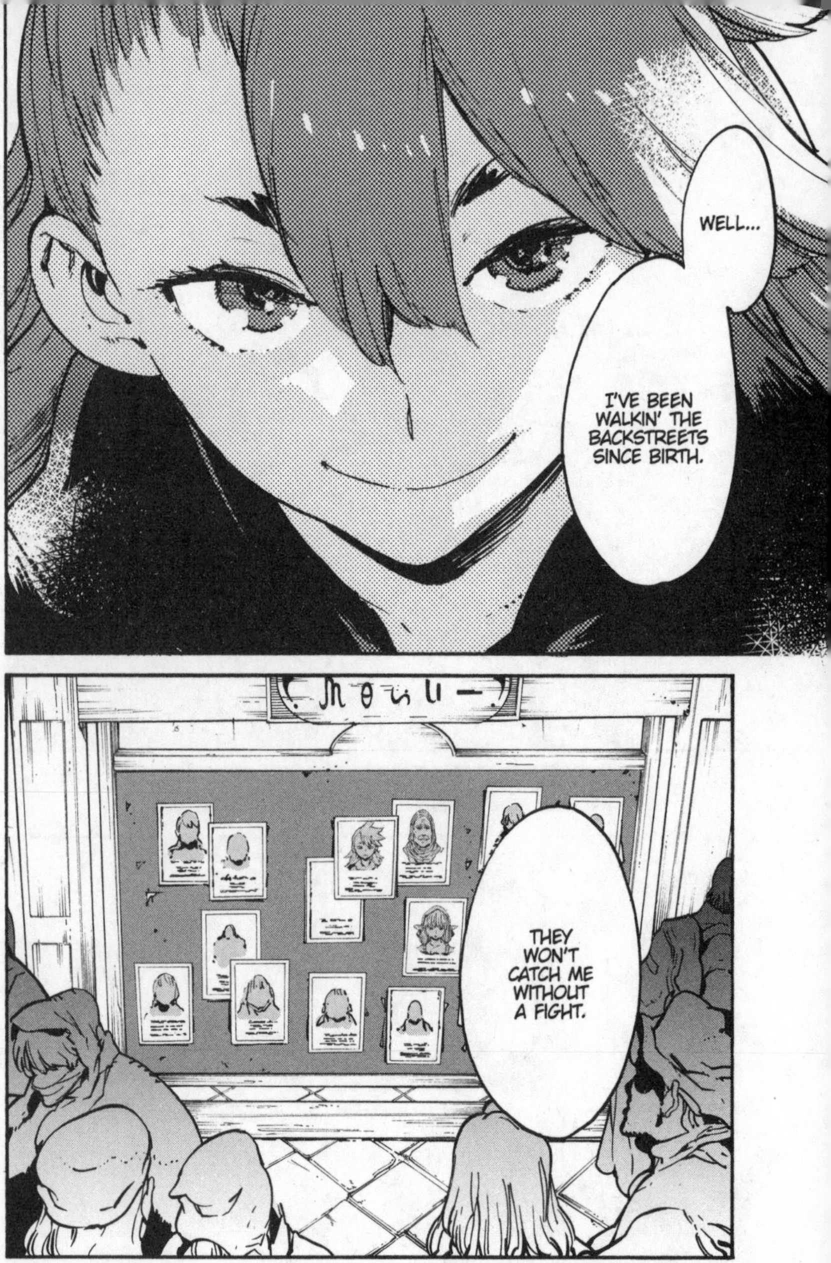
WELL...
I'VE BEEN WALKIN' THE BACKSTREETS SINCE BIRTH.
THEY WON'T CATCH ME WITHOUT A FIGHT.

YAKUZA
REINCARNATION

YAKUZA
REINCARNATION

CHAPTER 7:
SHIT STIRRERS

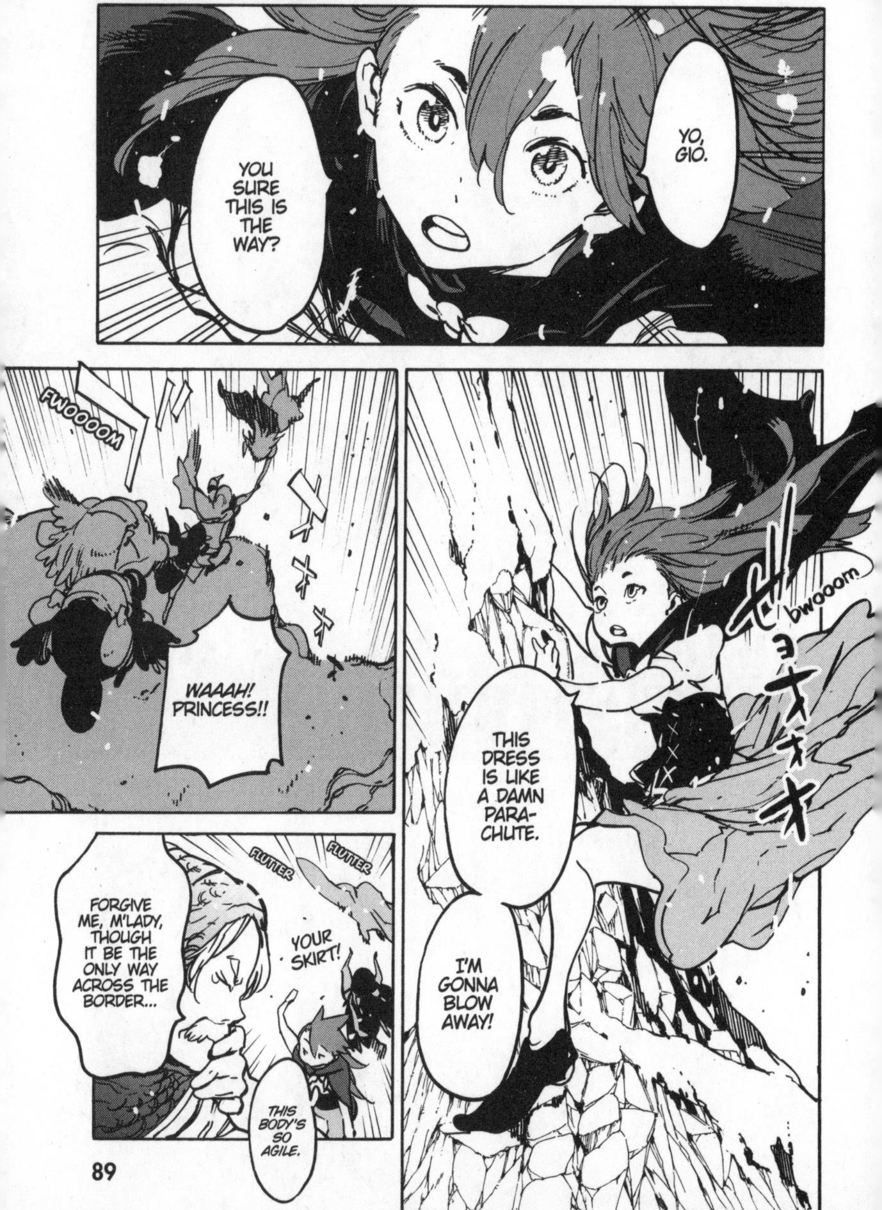
YO, GIO.
YOU SURE THIS IS THE WAY?
bwooom
THIS DRESS IS LIKE A DAMN PARA-CHUTE.
I'M GONNA BLOW AWAY!
FWOOOOM
WAAAH! PRINCESS!!
FLUTTER
FLUTTER
YOUR SKIRT!
FORGIVE ME, M'LADY, THOUGH IT BE THE ONLY WAY ACROSS THE BORDER...
THIS BODY'S SO AGILE.

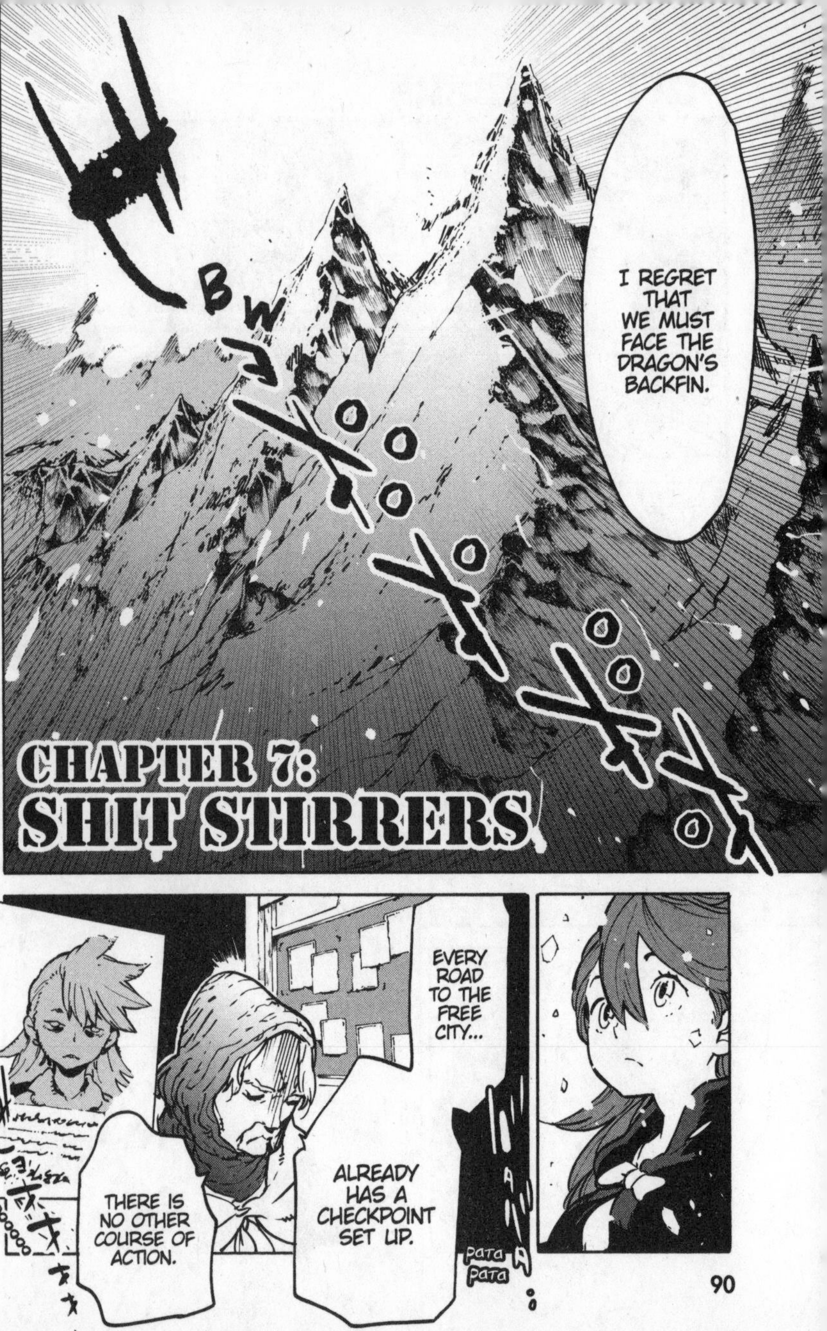
I REGRET THAT WE MUST FACE THE DRAGON'S BACKFIN.
CHAPTER 7: SHIT STIRRERS
pata pata
EVERY ROAD TO THE FREE CITY...
ALREADY HAS A CHECKPOINT SET UP.
THERE IS NO OTHER COURSE OF ACTION.
bwoooooo

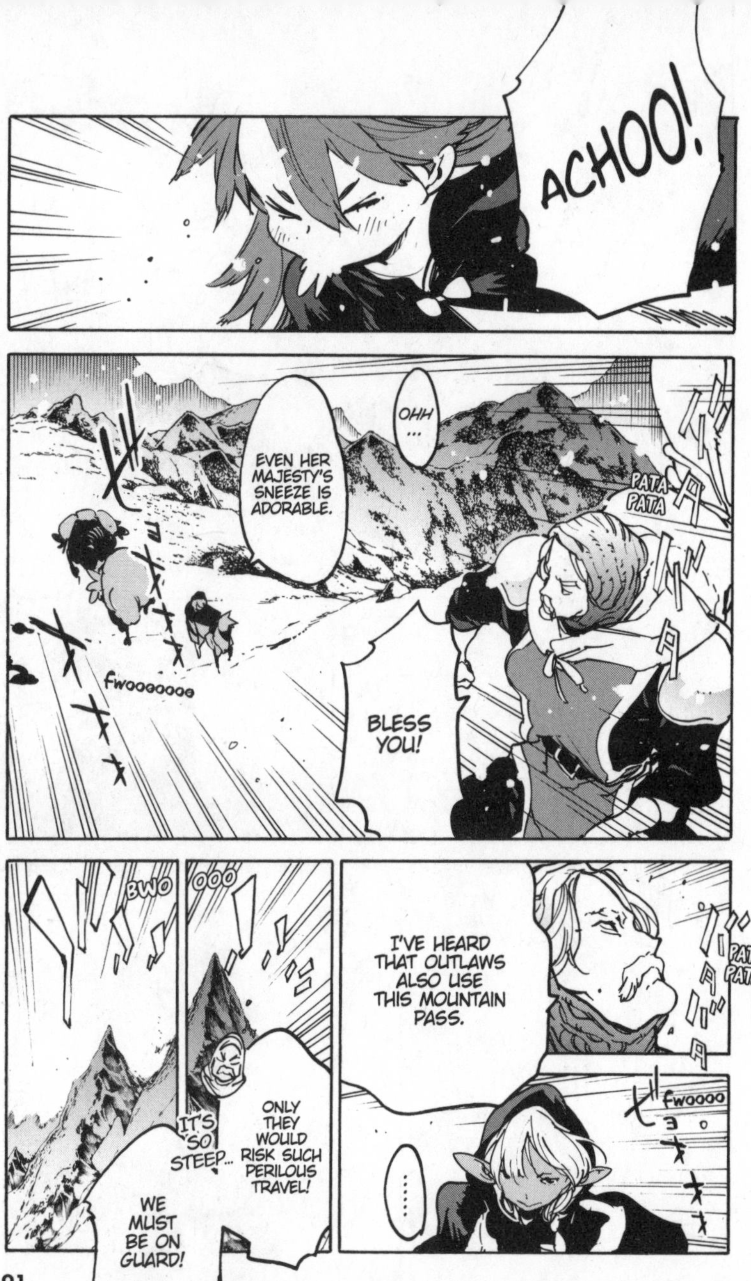
ACHOO!
OHH...
PATA PATA
EVEN HER MAJESTY'S SNEEZE IS ADORABLE.
BLESS YOU!
fwooooooo
I'VE HEARD THAT OUTLAWS ALSO USE THIS MOUNTAIN PASS.
PATA PATA
fwoooo
......
BWO OOO
ONLY THEY WOULD RISK SUCH PERILOUS TRAVEL!
IT'S SO STEEP...
WE MUST BE ON GUARD!

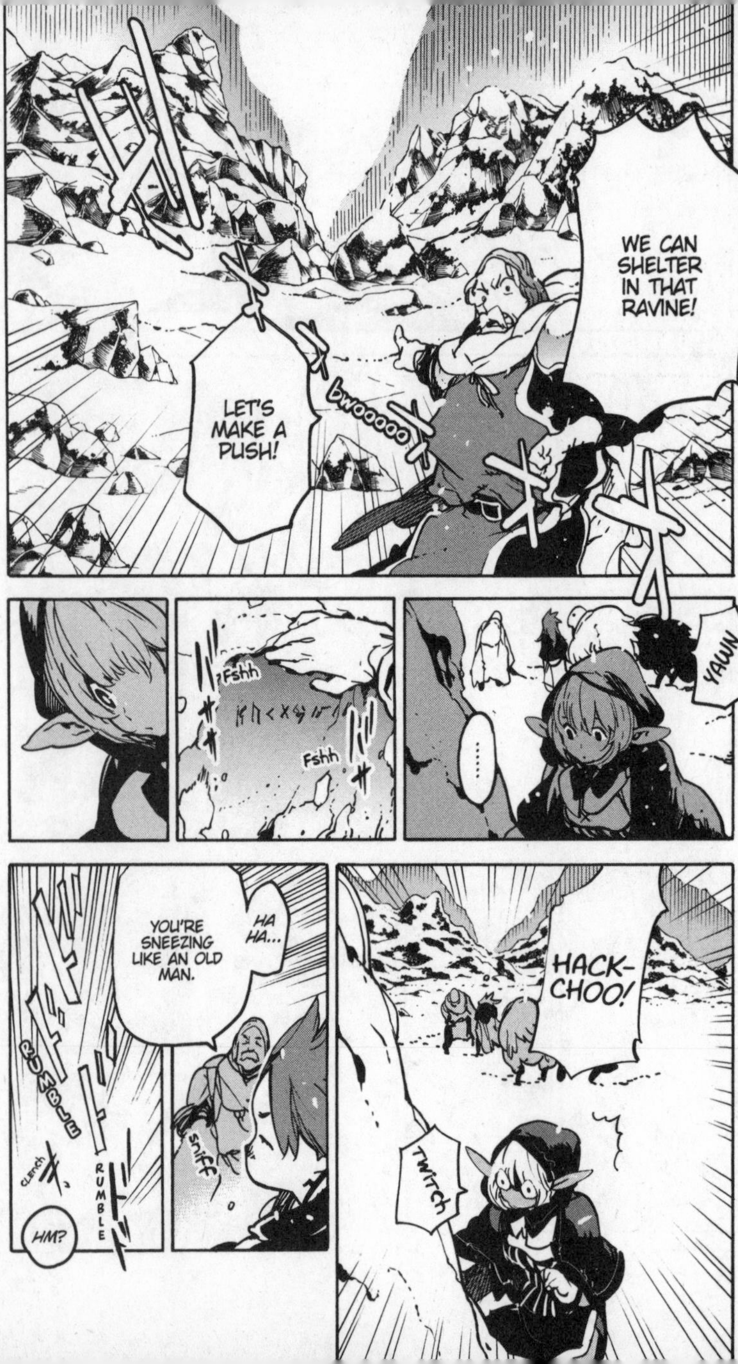
WE CAN SHELTER IN THAT RAVINE!
bwoooooo
LET'S MAKE A PUSH!
YAWN
......
Fshh
Fshh
HACK-CHOO!
TWITCH
HA HA...
YOU'RE SNEEZING LIKE AN OLD MAN.
sniff
RUMBLE
RUMBLE
CLENCH
HM?

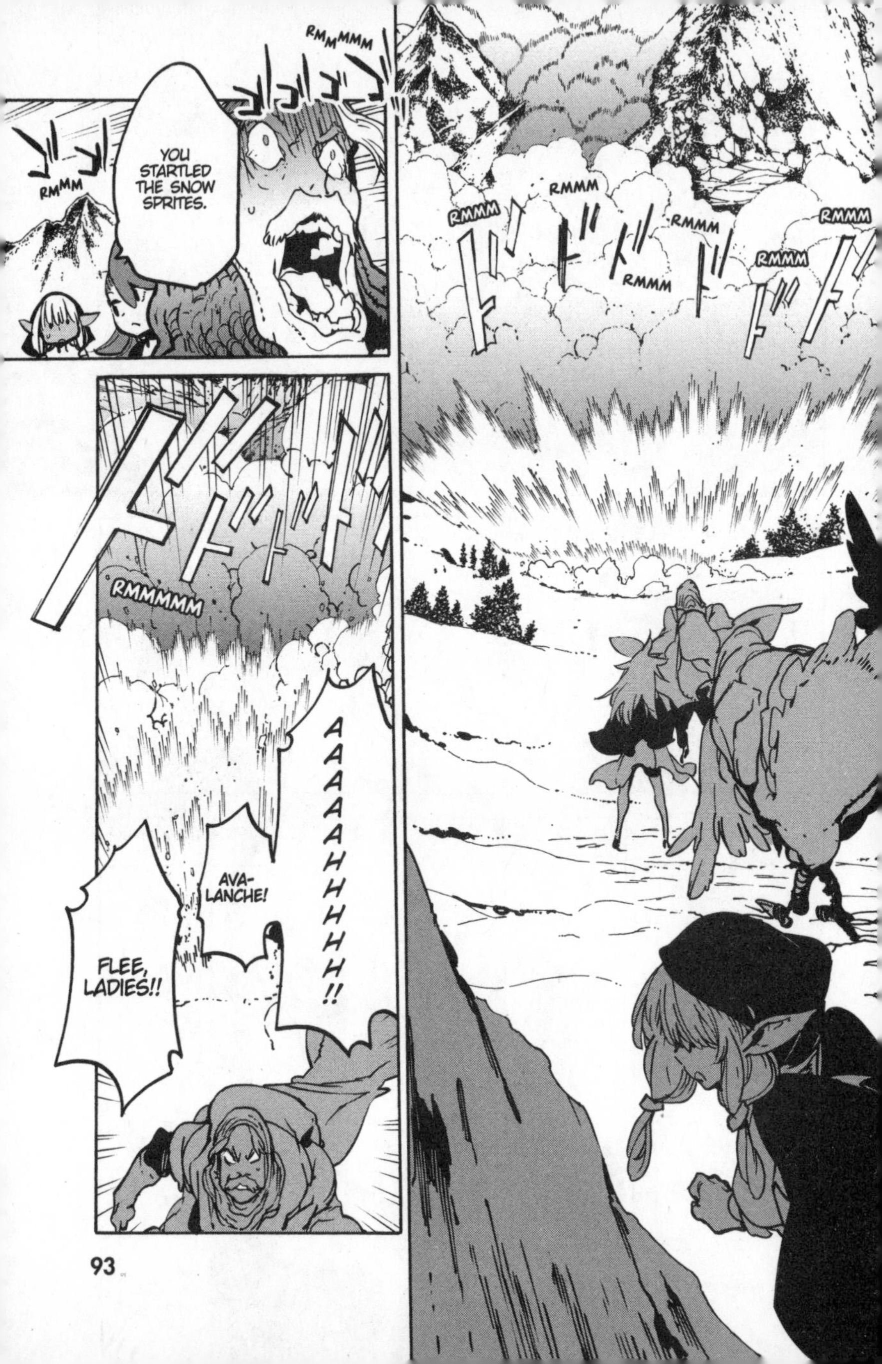
RMMM
RMMM
RMMM
RMMM
RMMM
RMMM
RMMMMM
YOU STARTLED THE SNOW SPRITES.
RMMM
RMMMMM
AAAAAAHHHHHHH!!
AVA-LANCHE!
FLEE, LADIES!!

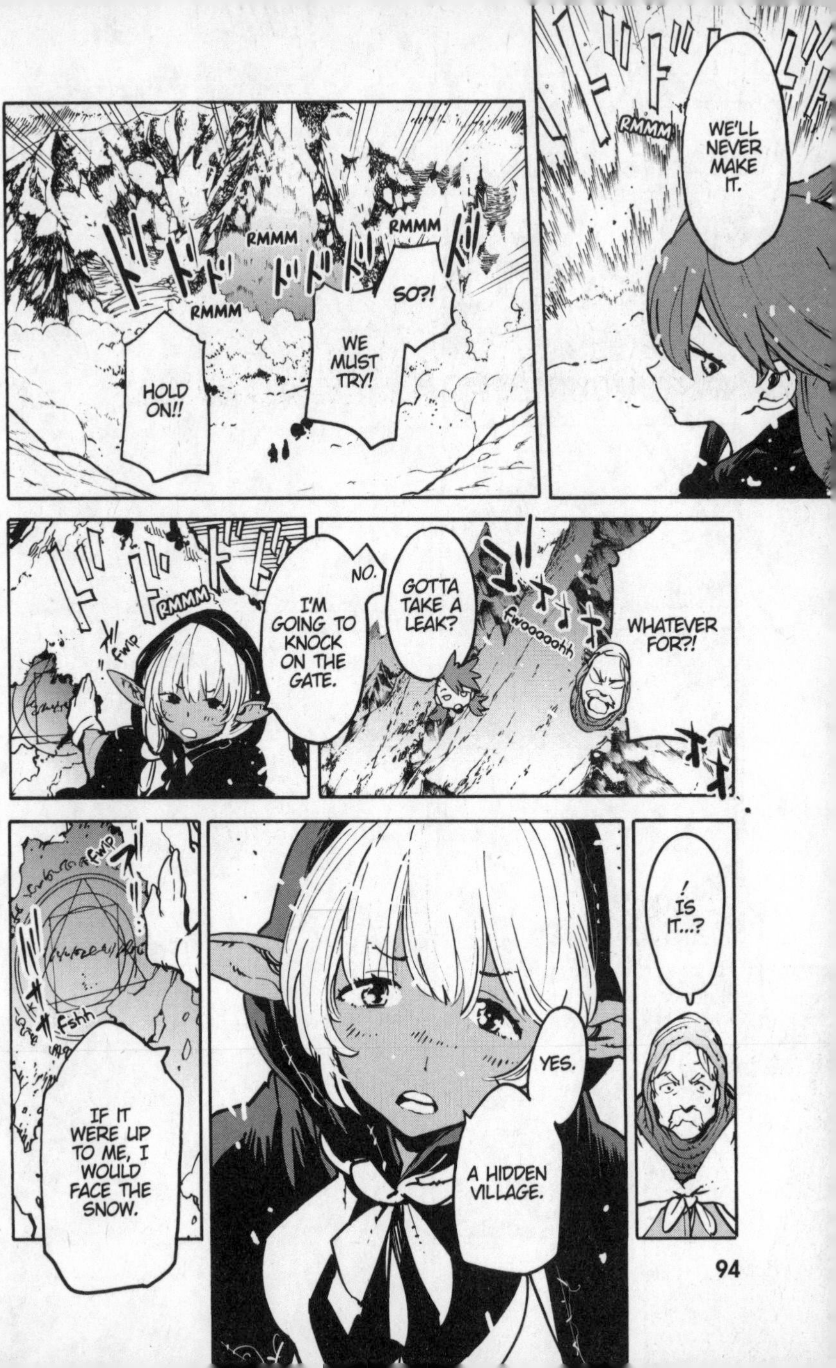
RMMM
WE'LL NEVER MAKE IT.
RMMM
SO?!
RMMM
WE MUST TRY!
RMMM
HOLD ON!!
WHATEVER FOR?!
fwooooohh
GOTTA TAKE A LEAK?
NO.
I'M GOING TO KNOCK ON THE GATE.
RMMM
fwip
! IS IT...?
YES.
A HIDDEN VILLAGE.
fwip
fshh
IF IT WERE UP TO ME, I WOULD FACE THE SNOW.

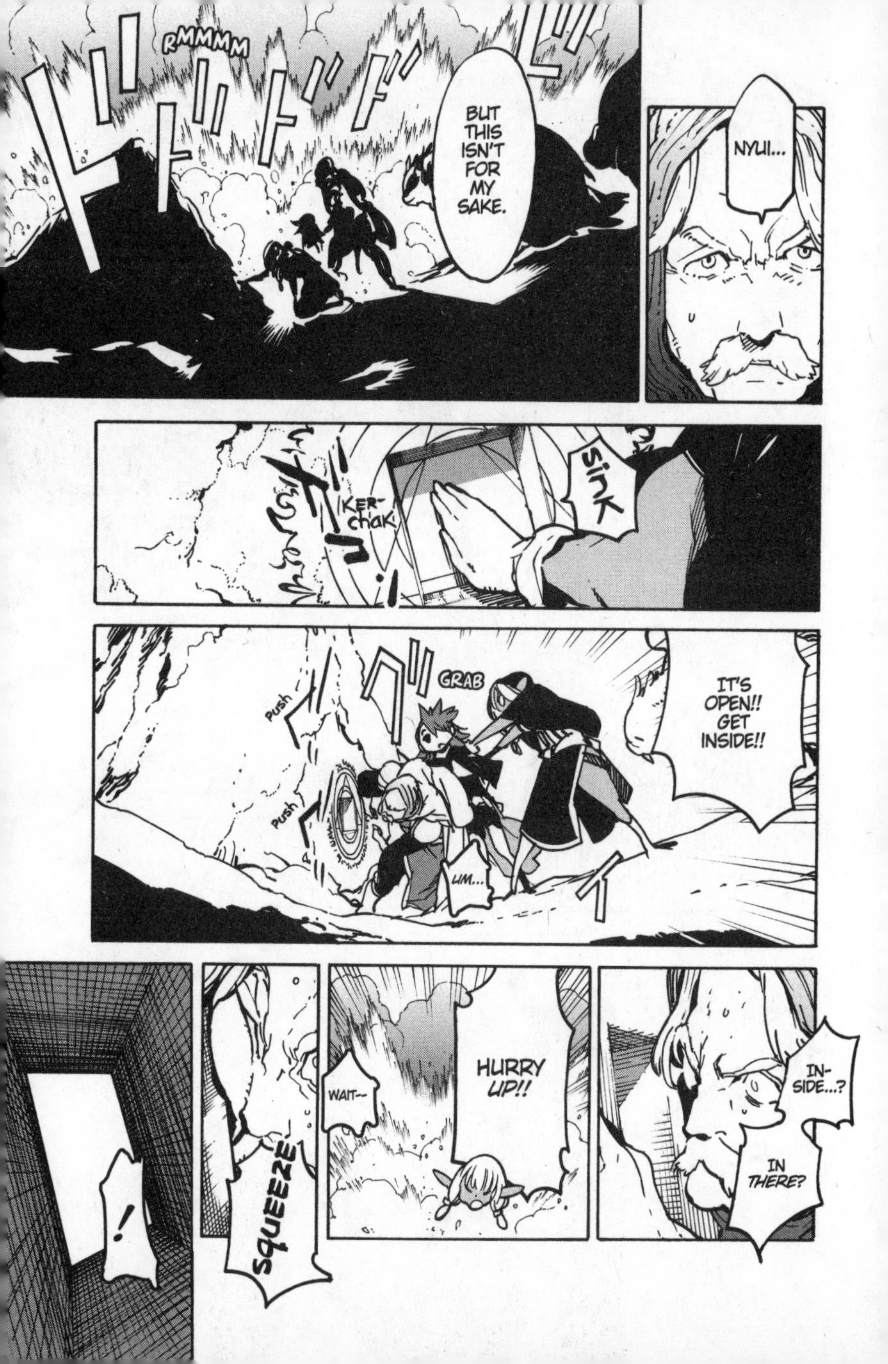
NYUI...
RMMMM
BUT THIS ISN'T FOR MY SAKE.
SINK
KER-CHAK
IT'S OPEN!! GET INSIDE!!
GRAB
Push
Push
UM...
IN-SIDE...?
IN THERE?
HURRY UP!!
WAIT--
SQUEEZE
!

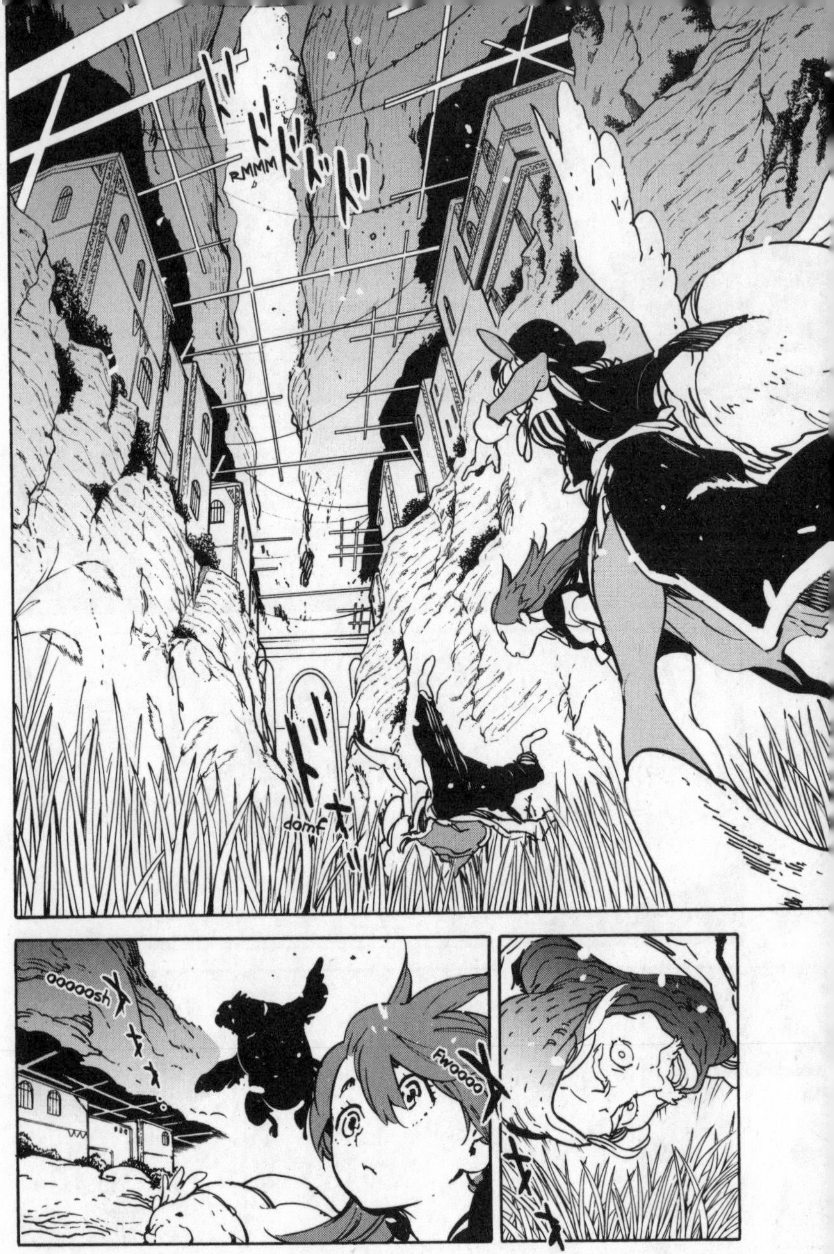
RMMMM
domf
Fwoooo
oooooosh

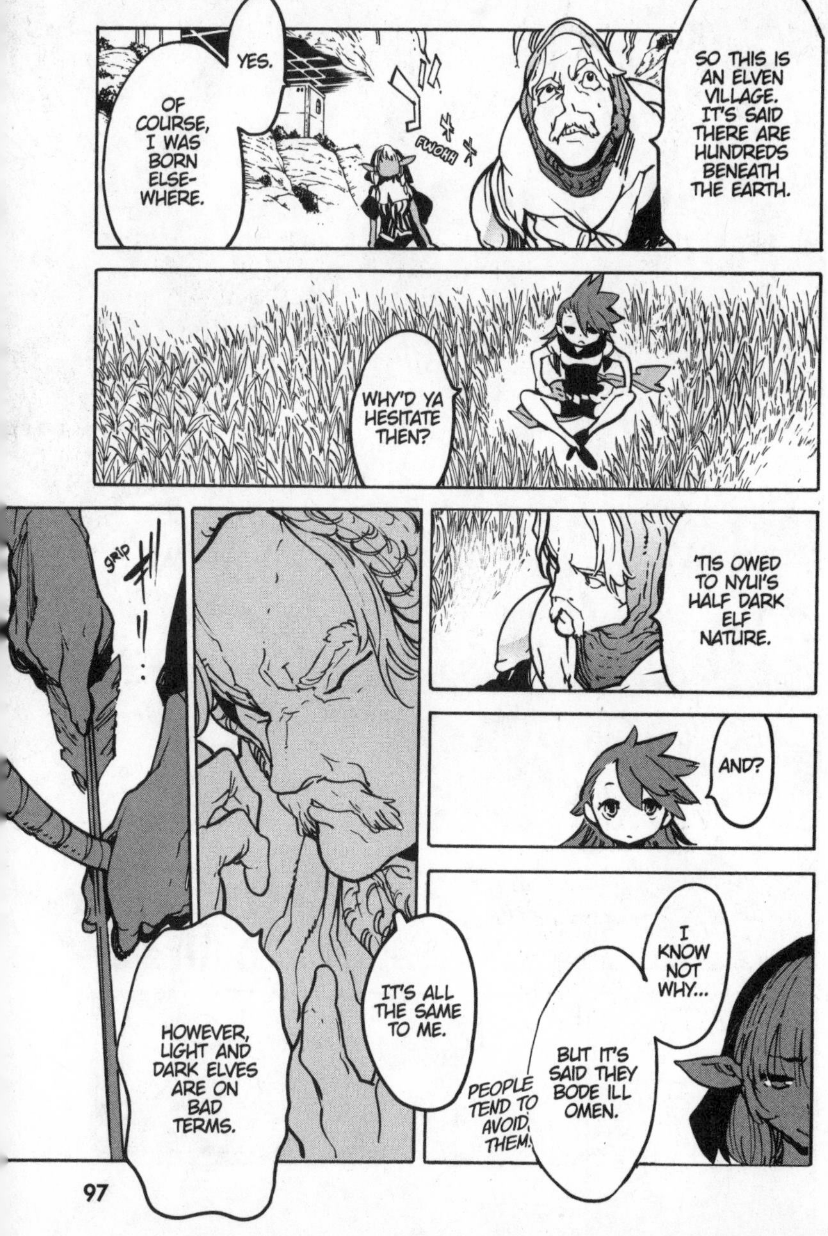
SO THIS IS AN ELVEN VILLAGE. IT'S SAID THERE ARE HUNDREDS BENEATH THE EARTH.
YES.
OF COURSE, I WAS BORN ELSE-WHERE.
FWOHH
WHY'D YA HESITATE THEN?
'TIS OWED TO NYUI'S HALF DARK ELF NATURE.
AND?
I KNOW NOT WHY...
BUT IT'S SAID THEY BODE ILL OMEN.
PEOPLE TEND TO AVOID THEM.
IT'S ALL THE SAME TO ME.
HOWEVER, LIGHT AND DARK ELVES ARE ON BAD TERMS.
grip

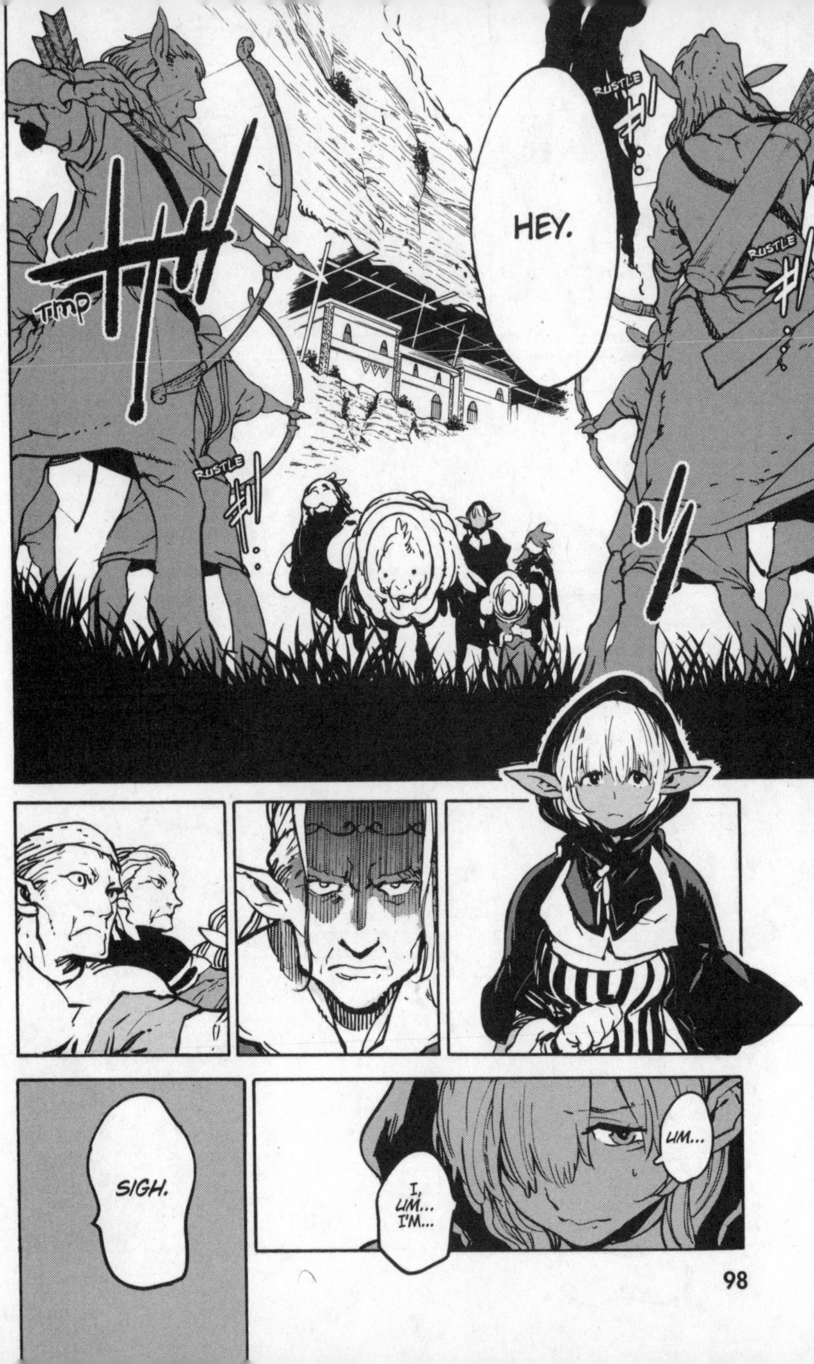
RUSTLE
HEY.
RUSTLE
TMP
RUSTLE
UM...
I, UM... I'M...
SIGH.

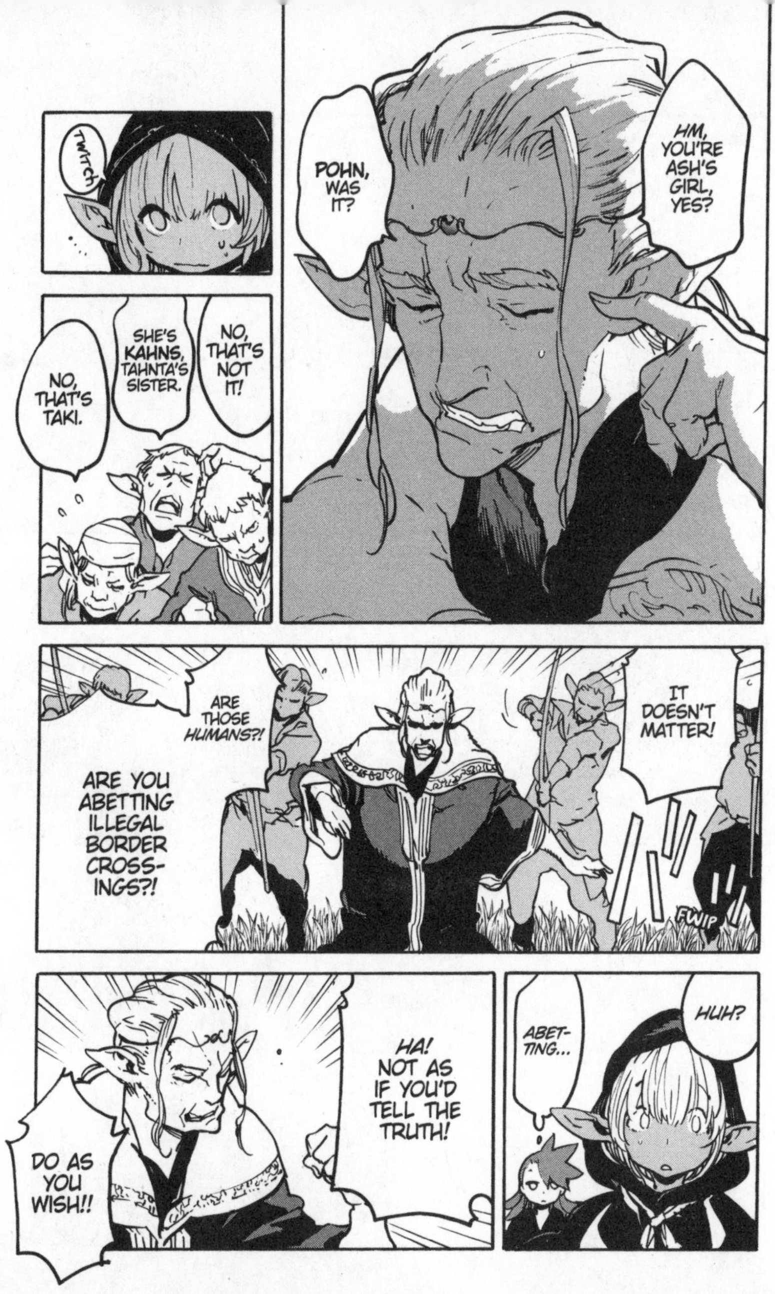
HM, YOU'RE ASH'S GIRL, YES?
POHN, WAS IT?
TWITCH
NO, THAT'S NOT IT!
SHE'S KAHNS, TAHNTA'S SISTER.
NO, THAT'S TAKI.
IT DOESN'T MATTER!
FWIP
ARE THOSE HUMANS?!
ARE YOU ABETTING ILLEGAL BORDER CROSSINGS?!
HUH?
ABETTING...
HA! NOT AS IF YOU'D TELL THE TRUTH!
DO AS YOU WISH!!

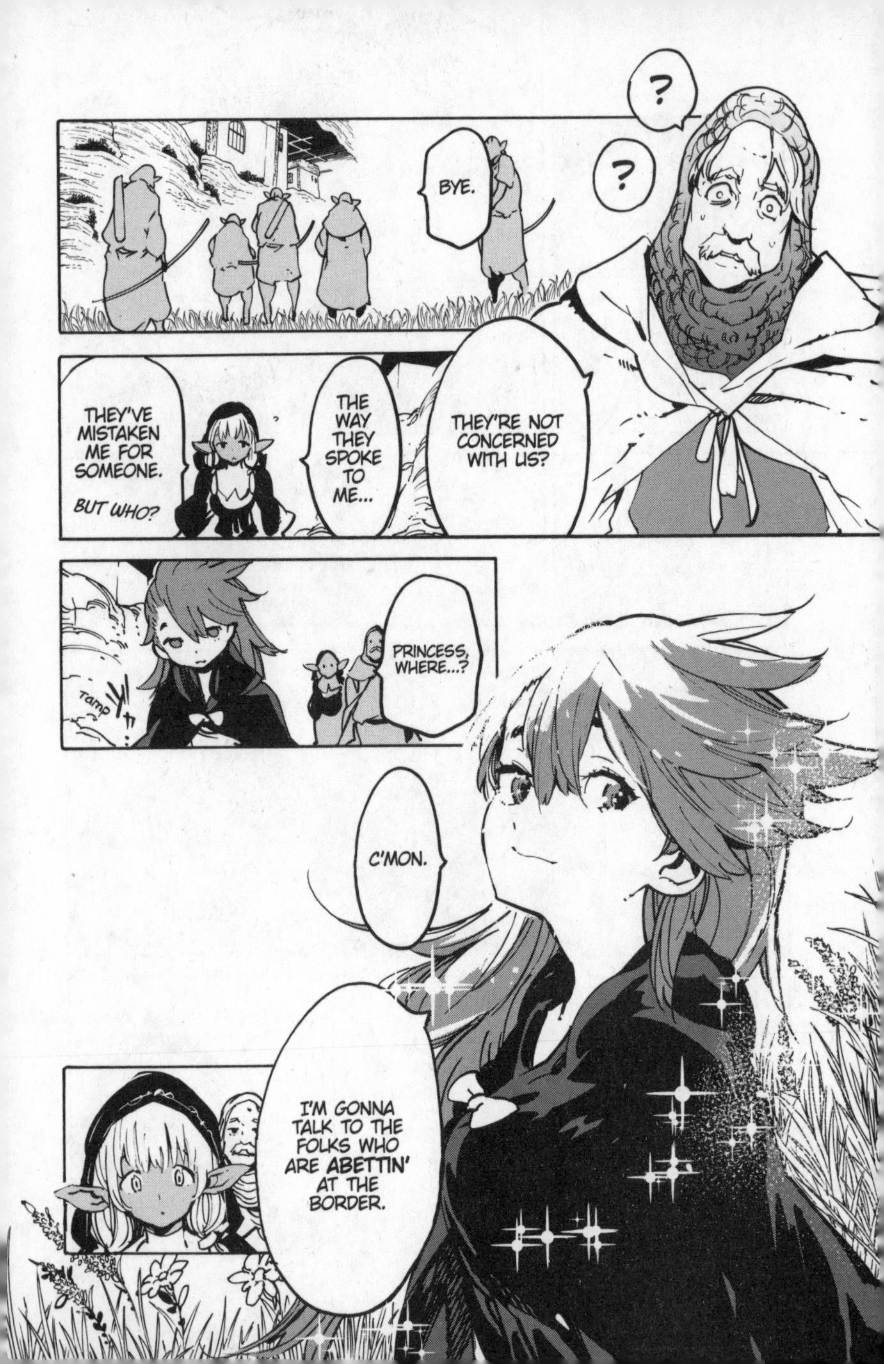

BYE.
?
?
THEY'RE NOT CONCERNED WITH US?
THE WAY THEY SPOKE TO ME...
THEY'VE MISTAKEN ME FOR SOMEONE.
BUT WHO?
PRINCESS, WHERE...?
TAMP
C'MON.
I'M GONNA TALK TO THE FOLKS WHO ARE ABETTIN' AT THE BORDER.

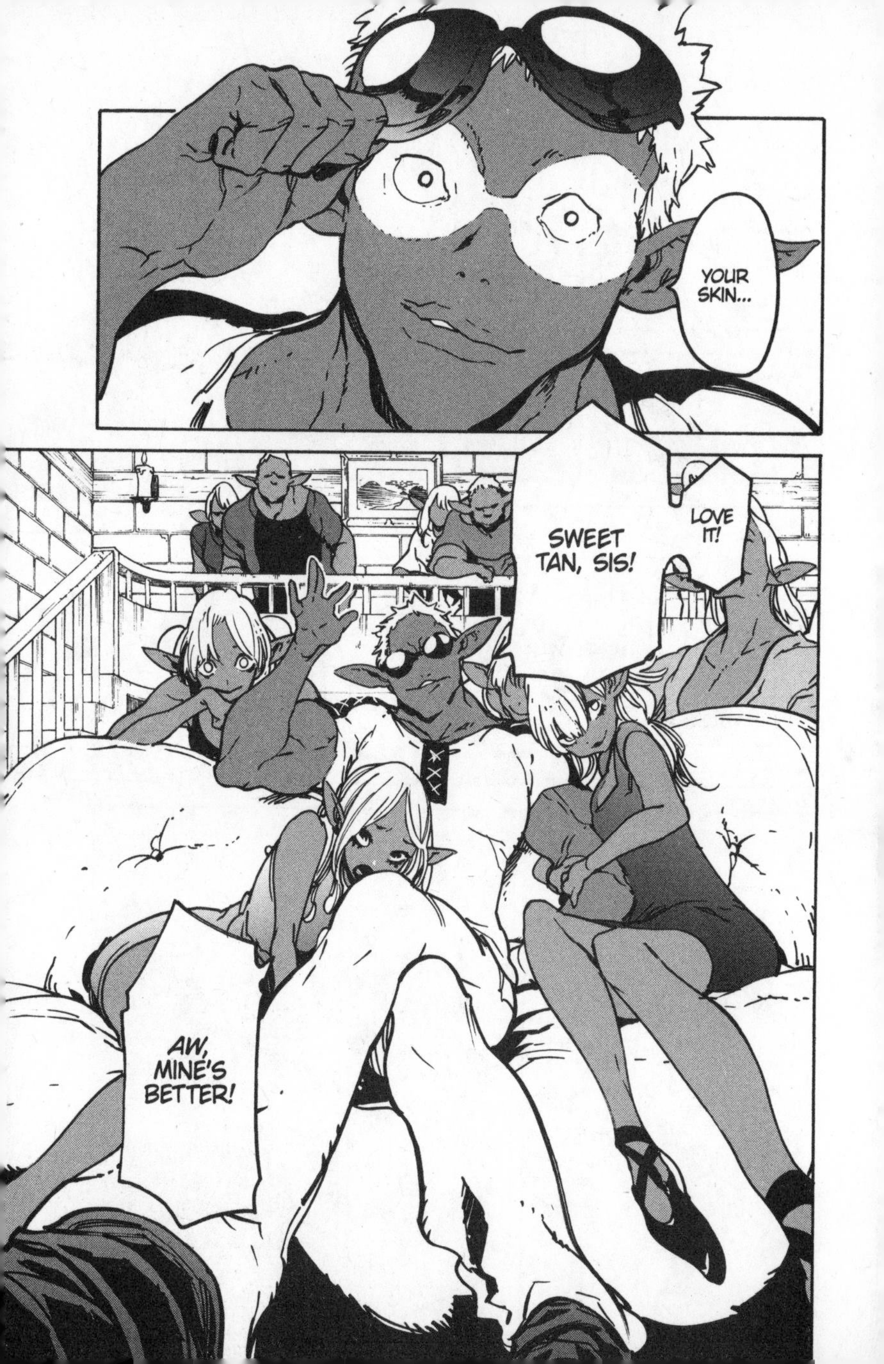
YOUR SKIN...
LOVE IT!
SWEET TAN, SIS!
AW, MINE'S BETTER!

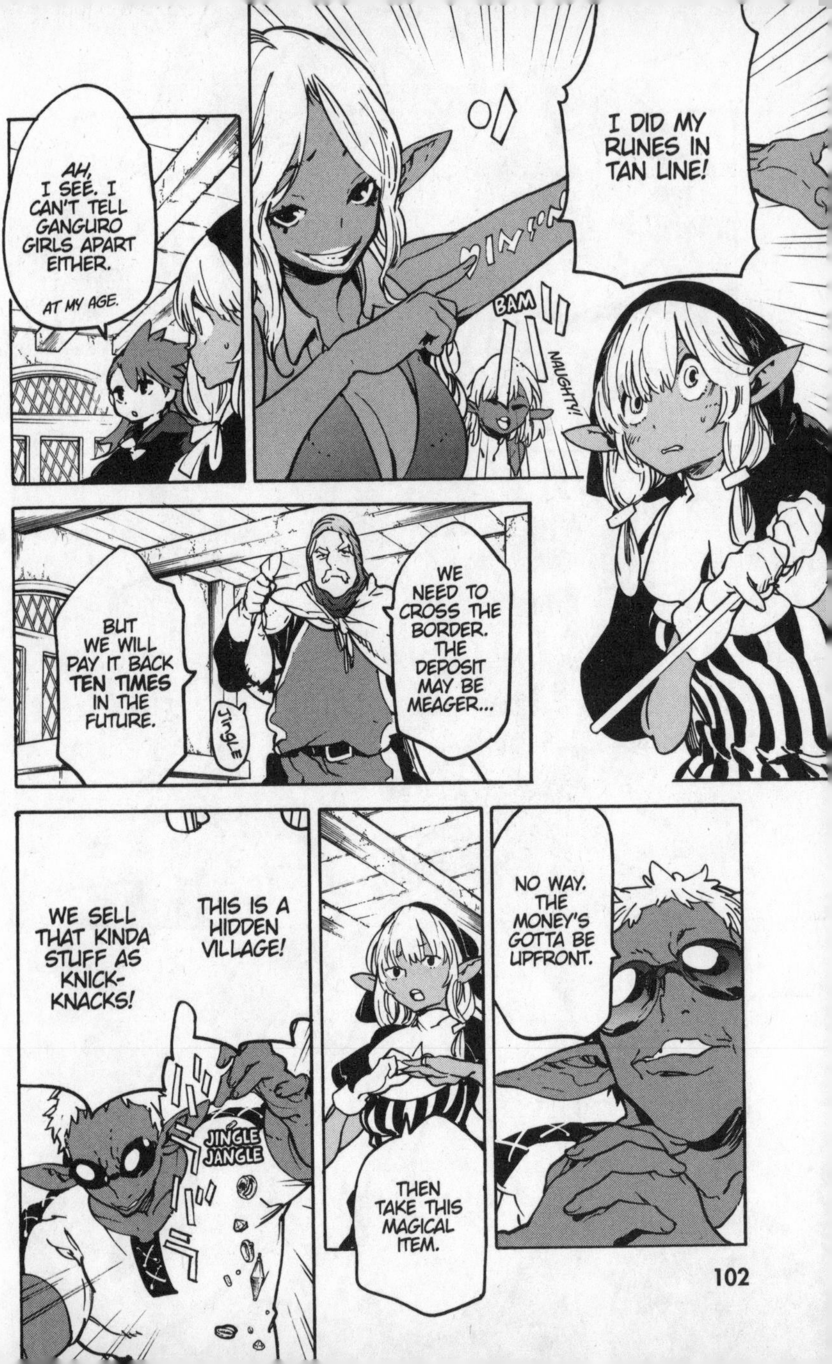
I DID MY RUNES IN TAN LINE!
BAM
NAUGHTY!
AH, I SEE. I CAN'T TELL GANGURO GIRLS APART EITHER.
AT MY AGE.
WE NEED TO CROSS THE BORDER. THE DEPOSIT MAY BE MEAGER...
BUT WE WILL PAY IT BACK TEN TIMES IN THE FUTURE.
JINGLE
NO WAY. THE MONEY'S GOTTA BE UPFRONT.
THEN TAKE THIS MAGICAL ITEM.
THIS IS A HIDDEN VILLAGE!
WE SELL THAT KINDA STUFF AS KNICK-KNACKS!
JINGLE JANGLE

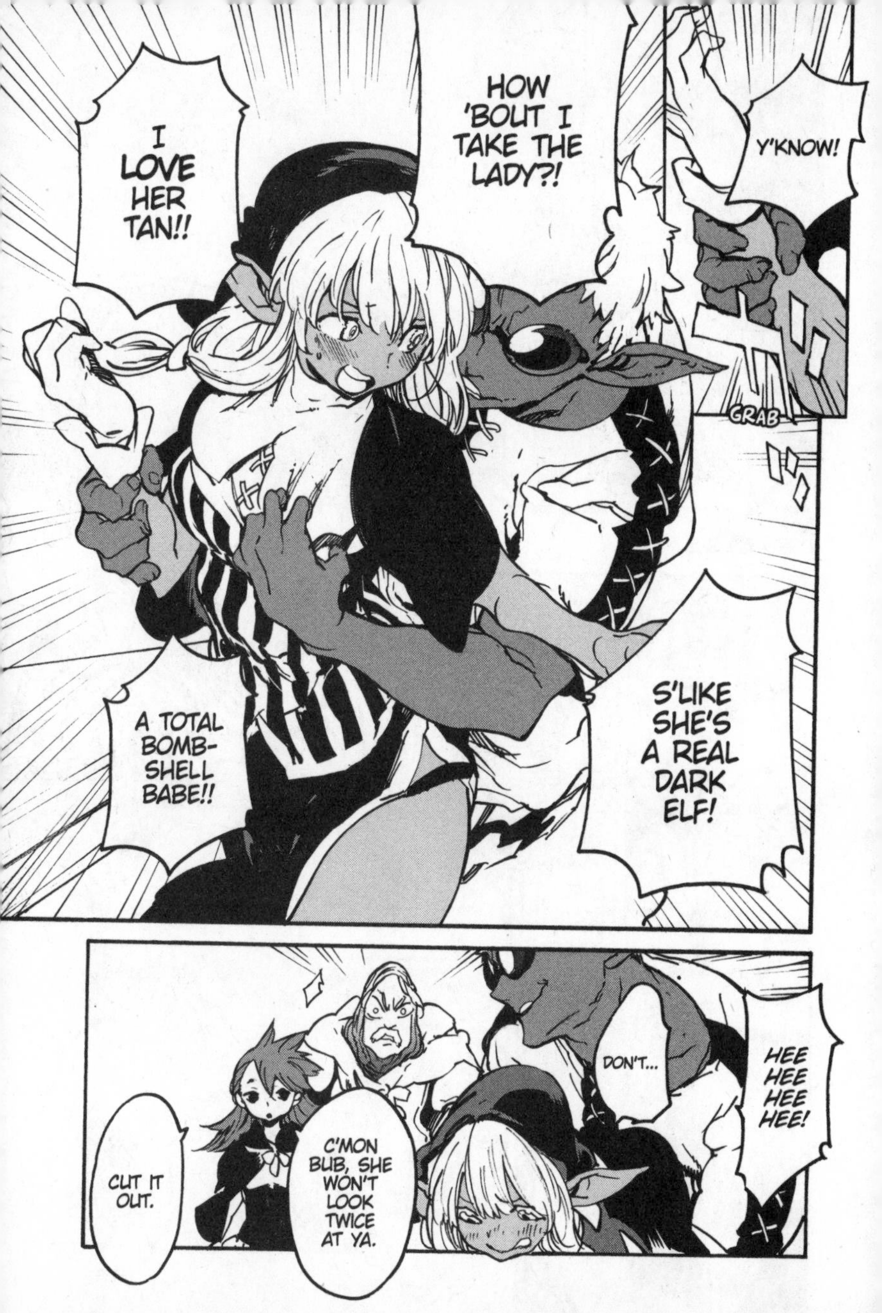
Y'KNOW!
GRAB
HOW 'BOUT I TAKE THE LADY?!
I LOVE HER TAN!!
S'LIKE SHE'S A REAL DARK ELF!
A TOTAL BOMB-SHELL BABE!!
HEE HEE HEE HEE!
DON'T...
C'MON BUB, SHE WON'T LOOK TWICE AT YA.
CUT IT OUT.

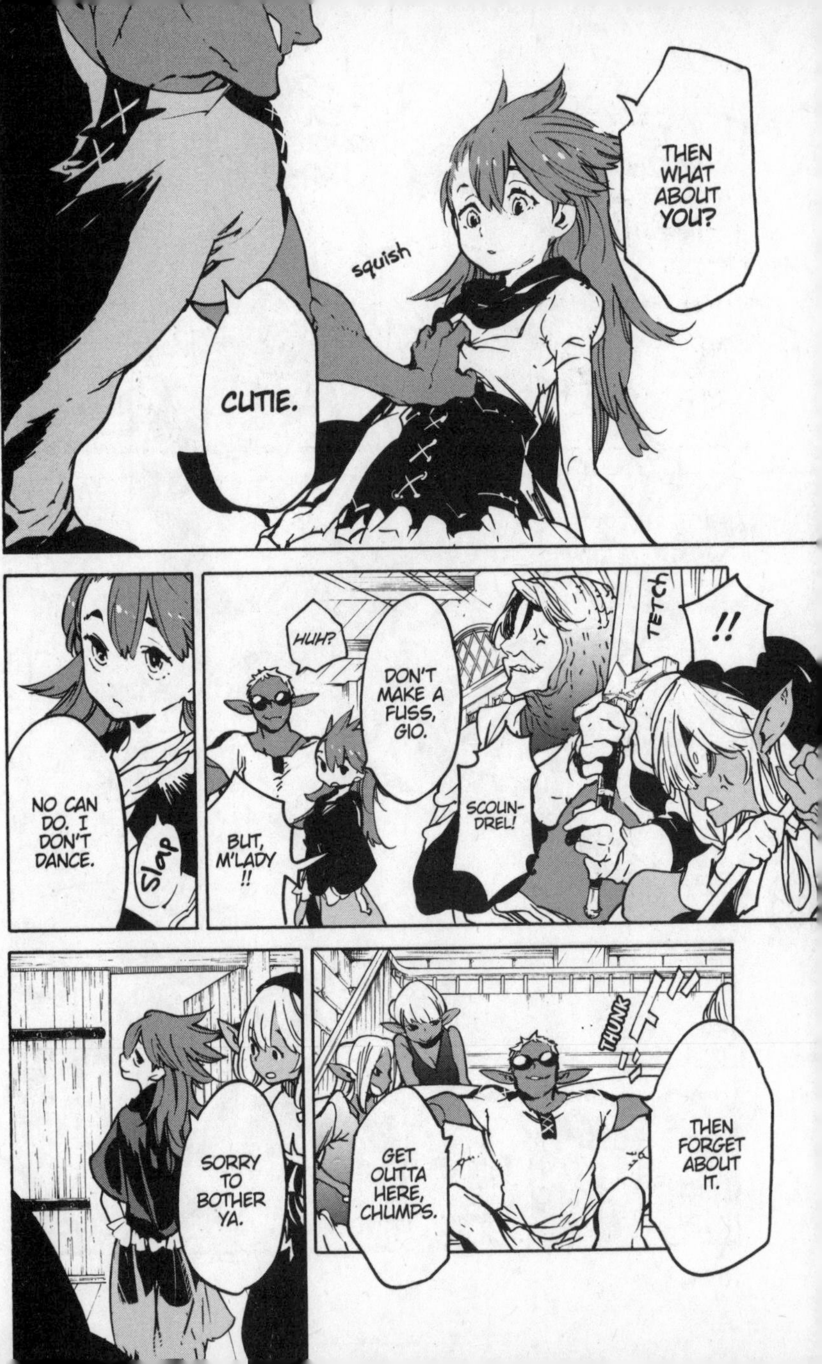
THEN WHAT ABOUT YOU?
squish
CUTIE.
!!
TETCH
HUH?
DON'T MAKE A FUSS, GIO.
SCOUN-DREL!
BUT, M'LADY !!
NO CAN DO. I DON'T DANCE.
Slap
THUNK
THEN FORGET ABOUT IT.
GET OUTTA HERE, CHUMPS.
SORRY TO BOTHER YA.

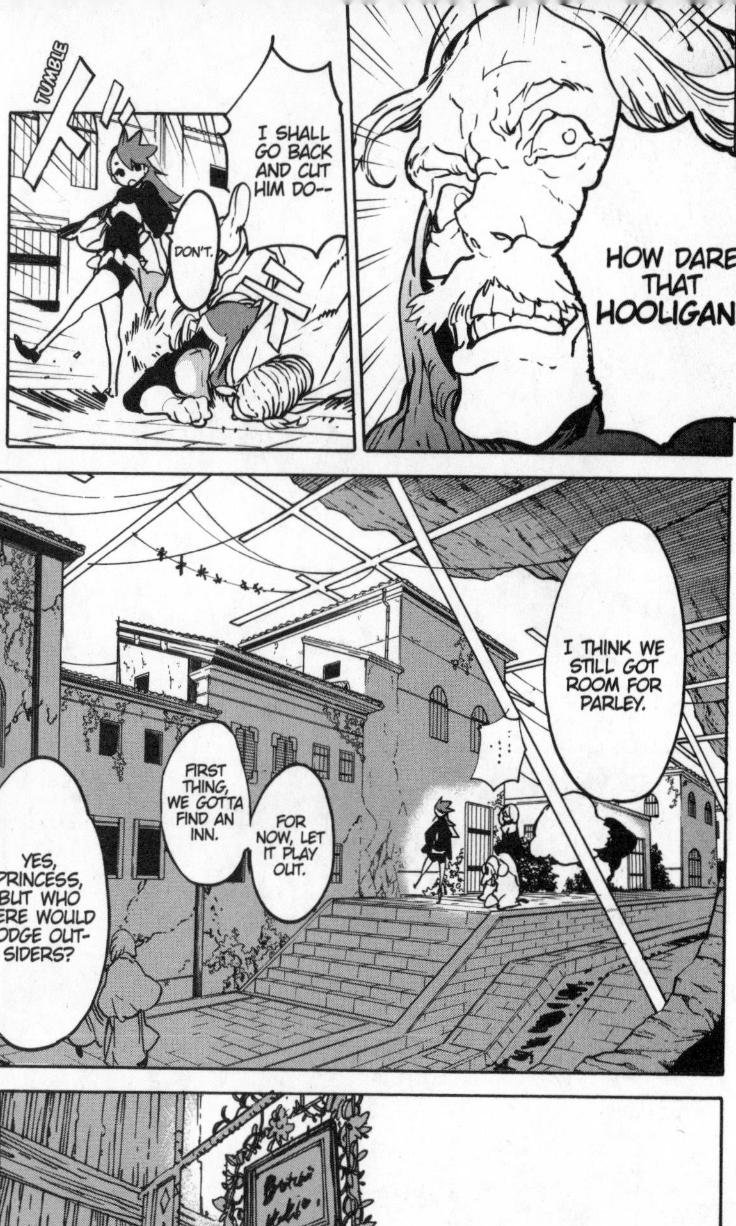
HOW DARE THAT HOOLIGAN!
I SHALL GO BACK AND CUT HIM DO--
DON'T.
TUMBLE
I THINK WE STILL GOT ROOM FOR PARLEY.
FOR NOW, LET IT PLAY OUT.
FIRST THING, WE GOTTA FIND AN INN.
YES, PRINCESS, BUT WHO HERE WOULD LODGE OUT-SIDERS?

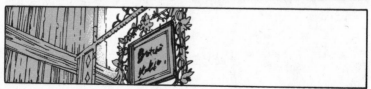

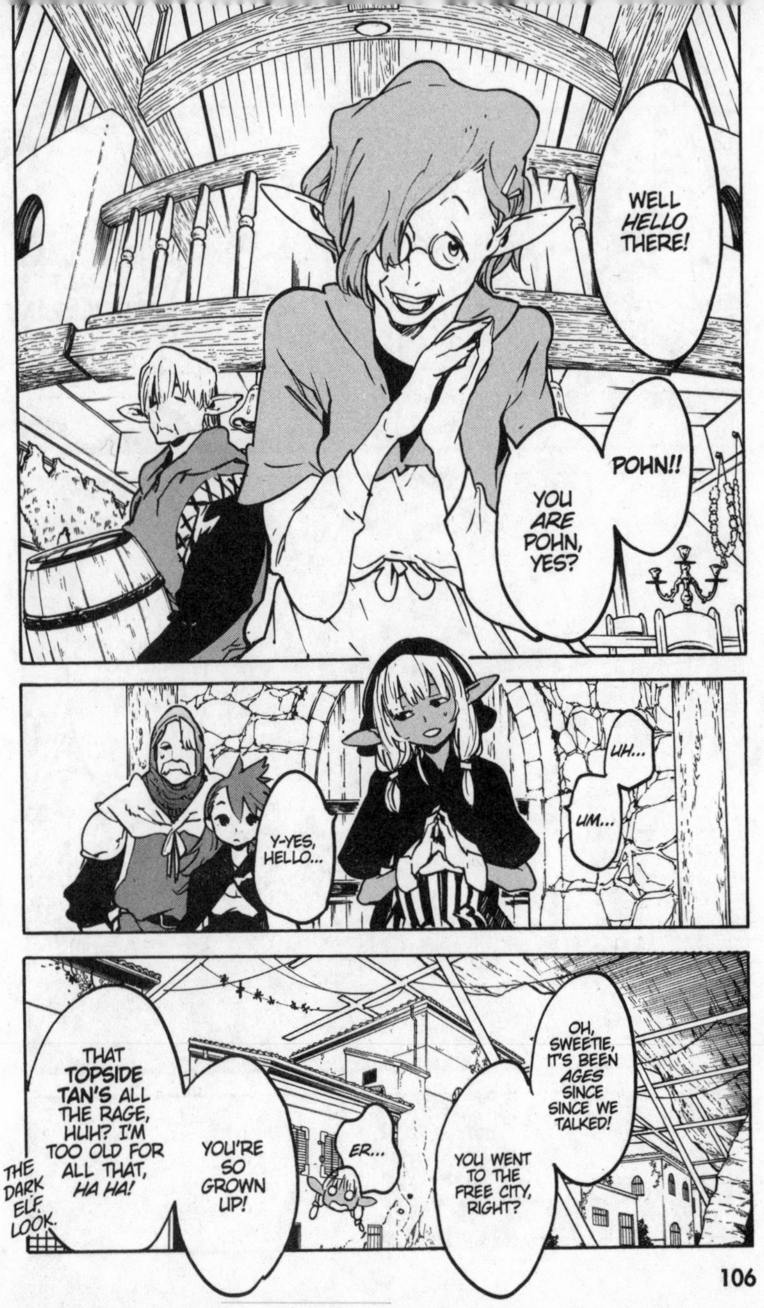
WELL HELLO THERE!
POHN!!
YOU ARE POHN, YES?
UH...
UM...
Y-YES, HELLO...
OH, SWEETIE, IT'S BEEN AGES SINCE SINCE WE TALKED!
YOU WENT TO THE FREE CITY, RIGHT?
ER...
YOU'RE SO GROWN UP!
THAT TOPSIDE TAN'S ALL THE RAGE, HUH? I'M TOO OLD FOR ALL THAT, HA HA!
THE DARK ELF LOOK.

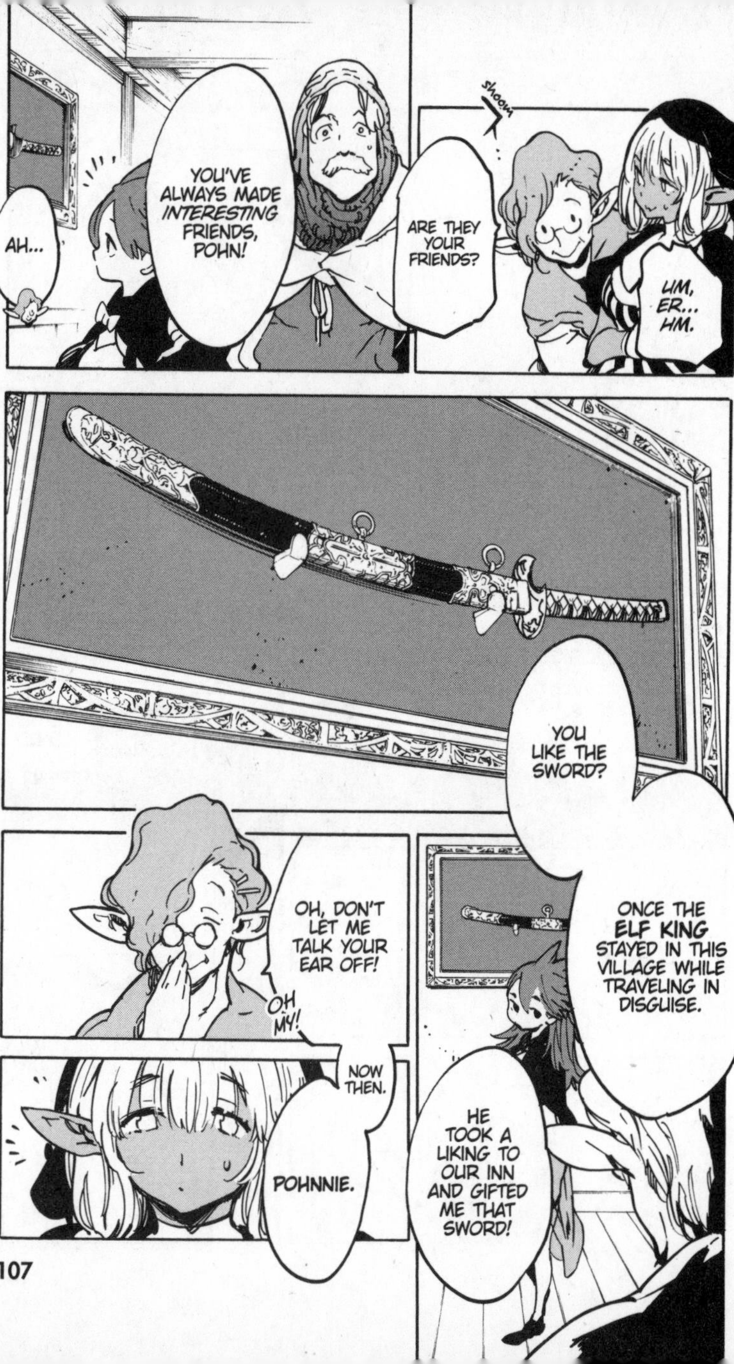
shoom
ARE THEY YOUR FRIENDS?
UM, ER... HM.
YOU'VE ALWAYS MADE INTERESTING FRIENDS, POHN!
AH...
YOU LIKE THE SWORD?
ONCE THE ELF KING STAYED IN THIS VILLAGE WHILE TRAVELING IN DISGUISE.
HE TOOK A LIKING TO OUR INN AND GIFTED ME THAT SWORD!
OH, DON'T LET ME TALK YOUR EAR OFF!
OH MY!
NOW THEN.
POHNNIE.

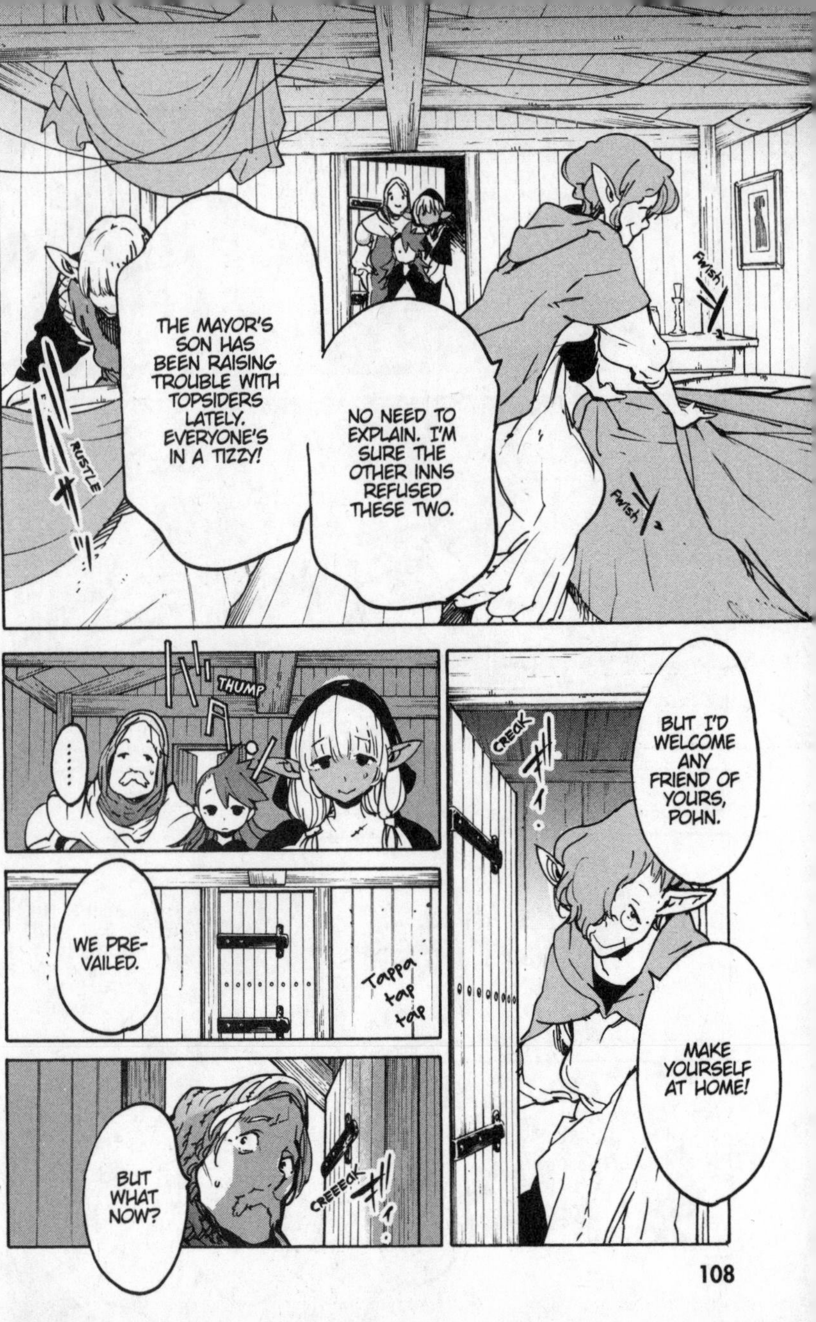
Fwish
NO NEED TO EXPLAIN. I'M SURE THE OTHER INNS REFUSED THESE TWO.
Fwish
THE MAYOR'S SON HAS BEEN RAISING TROUBLE WITH TOPSIDERS LATELY. EVERYONE'S IN A TIZZY!
RUSTLE
BUT I'D WELCOME ANY FRIEND OF YOURS, POHN.
CREAK
MAKE YOURSELF AT HOME!
THUMP
......
Tappa tap tap
WE PRE-VAILED.
CREEEAK
BUT WHAT NOW?

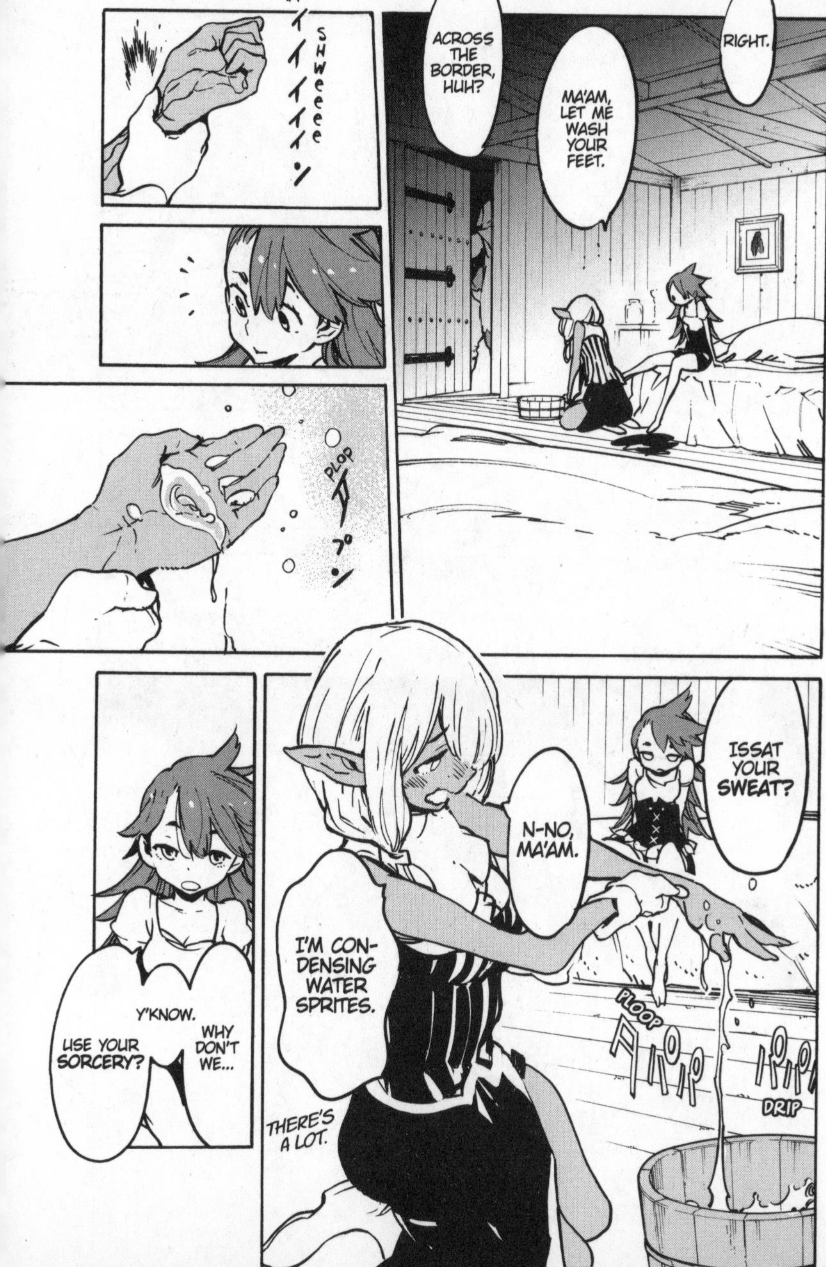

RIGHT.
ACROSS THE BORDER, HUH?
MA'AM, LET ME WASH YOUR FEET.
SHWeeee
イイイイン
PLOP
ISSAT YOUR SWEAT?
N-NO, MA'AM.
I'M CON-DENSING WATER SPRITES.
PLOOP
DRIP
THERE'S A LOT.
WHY DON'T WE...
Y'KNOW.
USE YOUR SORCERY?

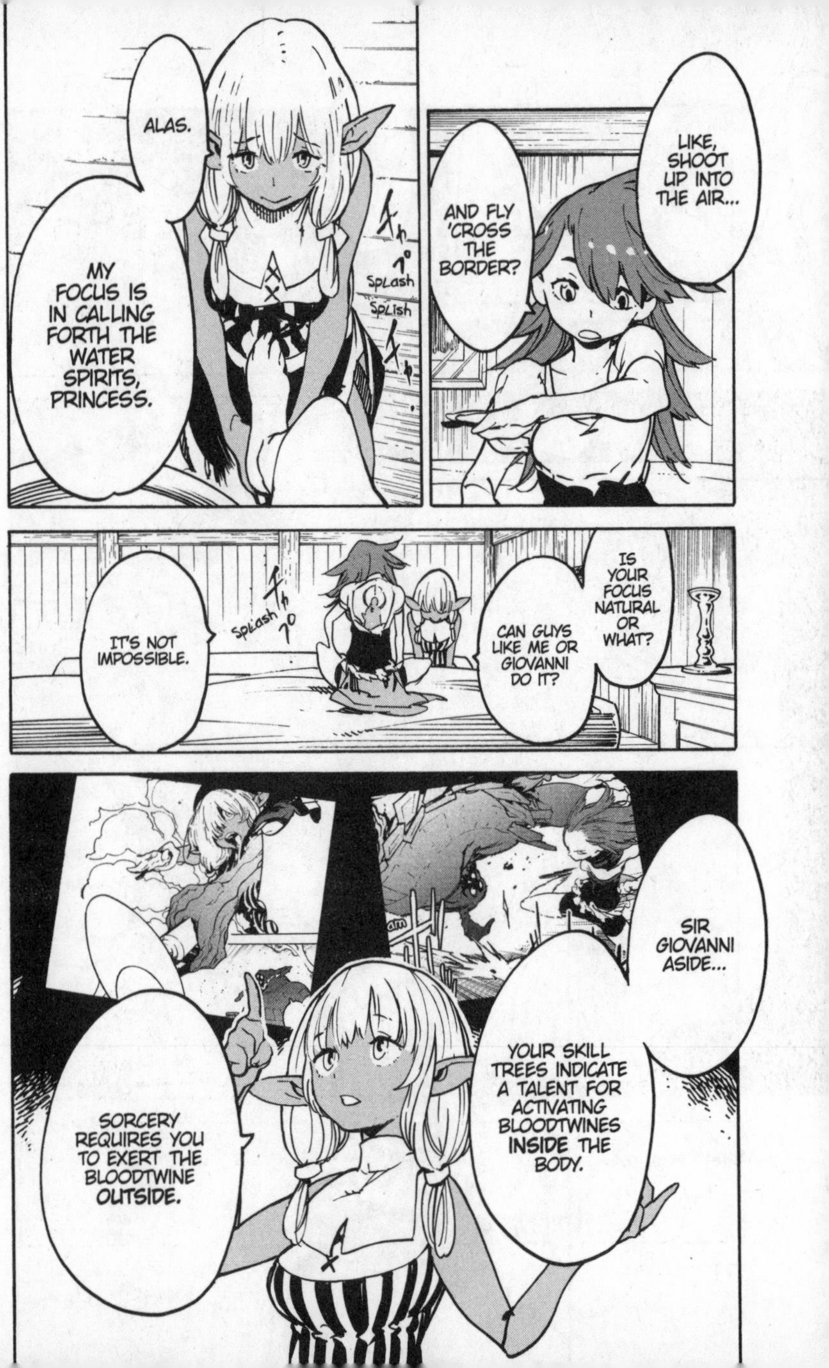
LIKE, SHOOT UP INTO THE AIR...
AND FLY 'CROSS THE BORDER?
ALAS.
Splash
Splish
MY FOCUS IS IN CALLING FORTH THE WATER SPIRITS, PRINCESS.
IS YOUR FOCUS NATURAL OR WHAT?
CAN GUYS LIKE ME OR GIOVANNI DO IT?
Splash
IT'S NOT IMPOSSIBLE.
SIR GIOVANNI ASIDE...
YOUR SKILL TREES INDICATE A TALENT FOR ACTIVATING BLOODTWINES INSIDE THE BODY.
SORCERY REQUIRES YOU TO EXERT THE BLOODTWINE OUTSIDE.

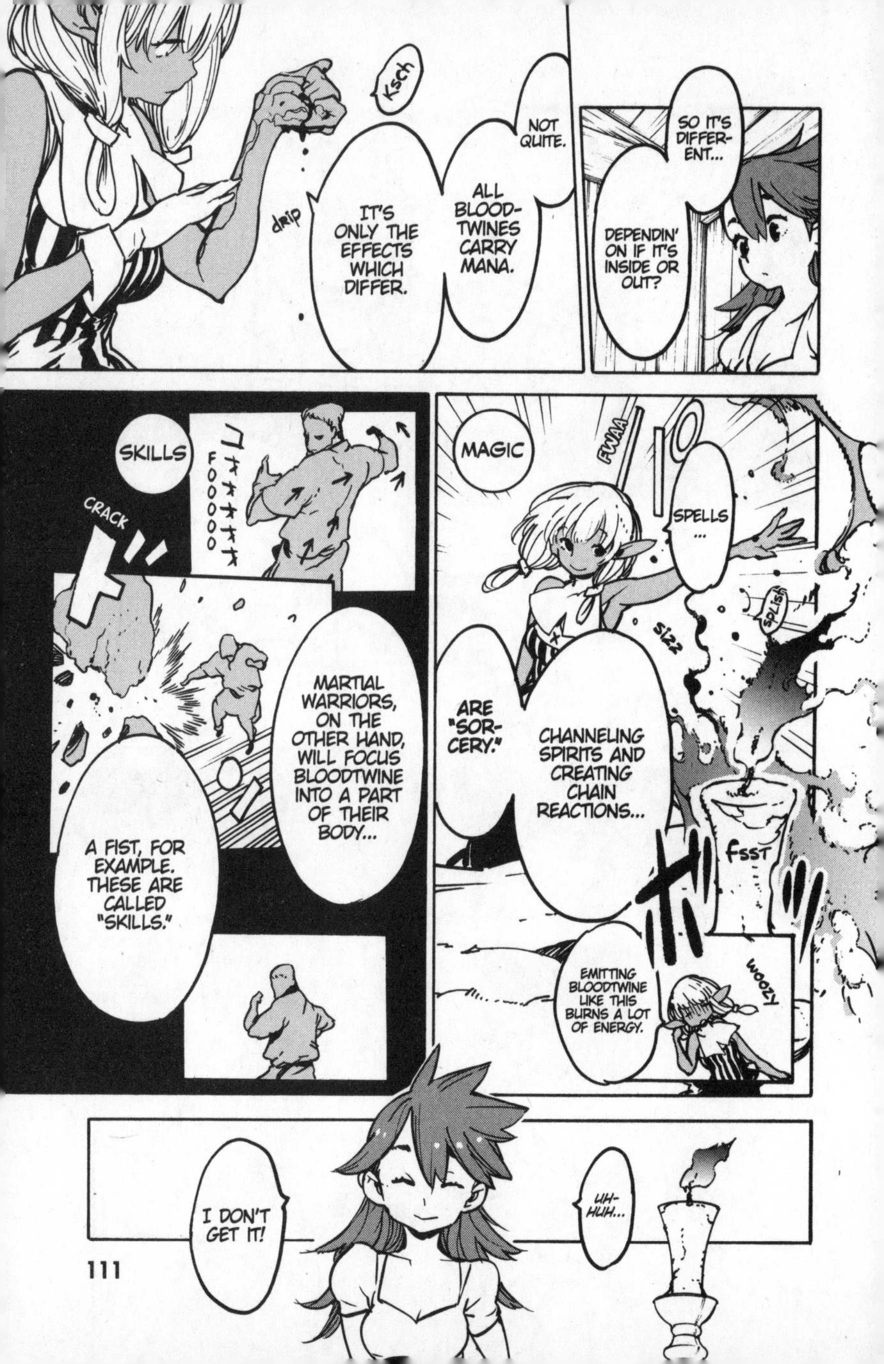
SO IT'S DIFFER-ENT...
DEPENDIN' ON IF IT'S INSIDE OR OUT?
NOT QUITE.
ALL BLOOD-TWINES CARRY MANA.
IT'S ONLY THE EFFECTS WHICH DIFFER.
Ksch
drip
MAGIC
FWAA
SPELLS ...
SPLISH
sizz
CHANNELING SPIRITS AND CREATING CHAIN REACTIONS...
ARE "SOR-CERY."
fSST
EMITTING BLOODTWINE LIKE THIS BURNS A LOT OF ENERGY.
woozy
SKILLS
FOOOOO
CRACK
MARTIAL WARRIORS, ON THE OTHER HAND, WILL FOCUS BLOODTWINE INTO A PART OF THEIR BODY...
A FIST, FOR EXAMPLE. THESE ARE CALLED "SKILLS."
UH-HUH...
I DON'T GET IT!

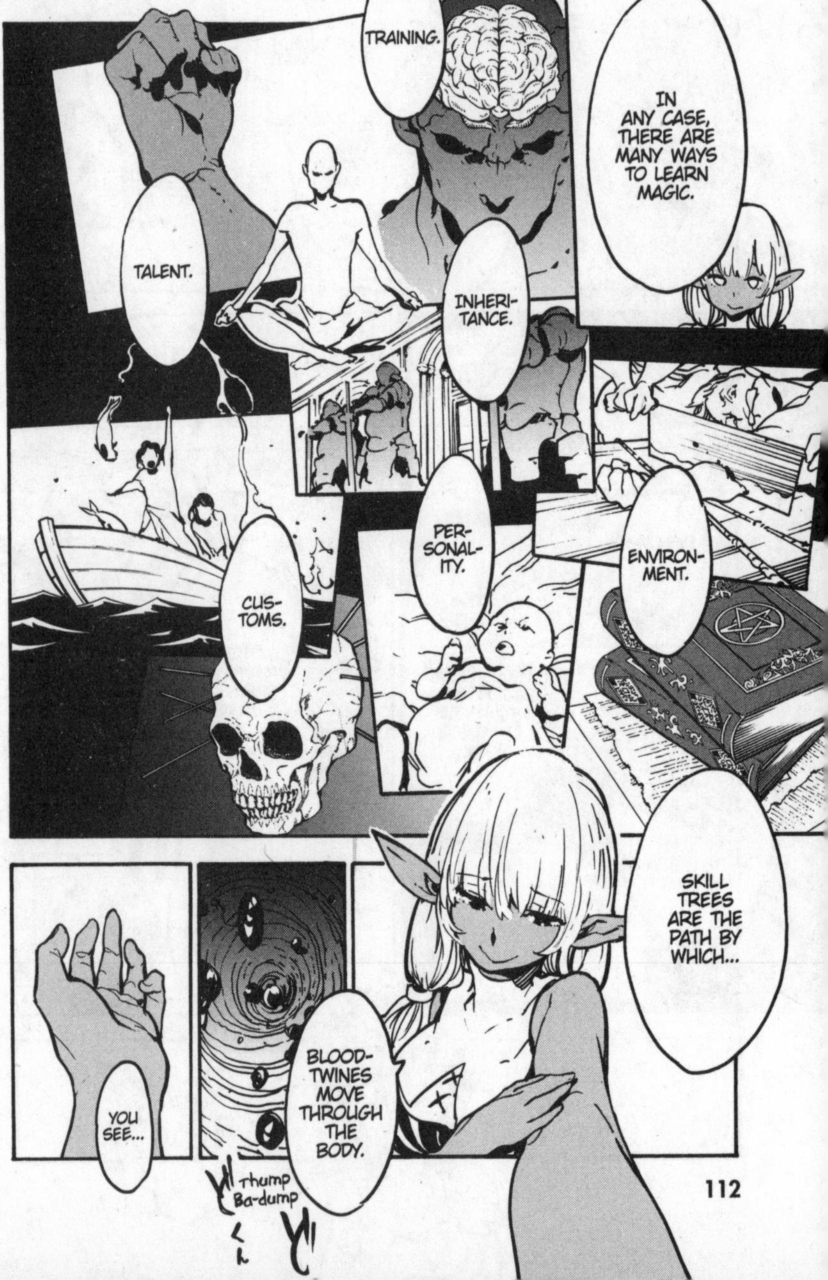
IN ANY CASE, THERE ARE MANY WAYS TO LEARN MAGIC.
TRAINING.
INHERITANCE.
TALENT.
ENVIRONMENT.
PERSONALITY.
CUSTOMS.
SKILL TREES ARE THE PATH BY WHICH...
BLOOD-TWINES MOVE THROUGH THE BODY.
Thump Ba-dump
YOU SEE...

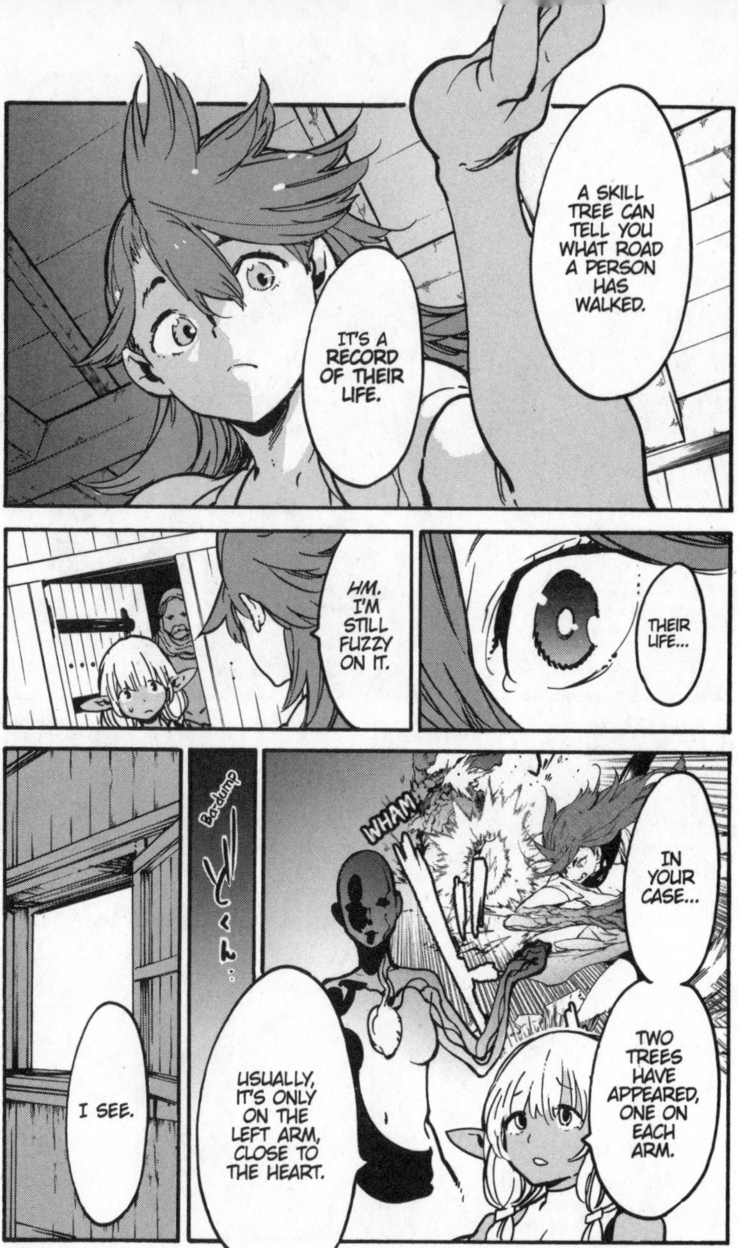
A SKILL TREE CAN TELL YOU WHAT ROAD A PERSON HAS WALKED.
IT'S A RECORD OF THEIR LIFE.
THEIR LIFE...
HM. I'M STILL FUZZY ON IT.
IN YOUR CASE...
TWO TREES HAVE APPEARED, ONE ON EACH ARM.
WHAM
USUALLY, IT'S ONLY ON THE LEFT ARM, CLOSE TO THE HEART.
Ba-dump
どくん‥
I SEE.

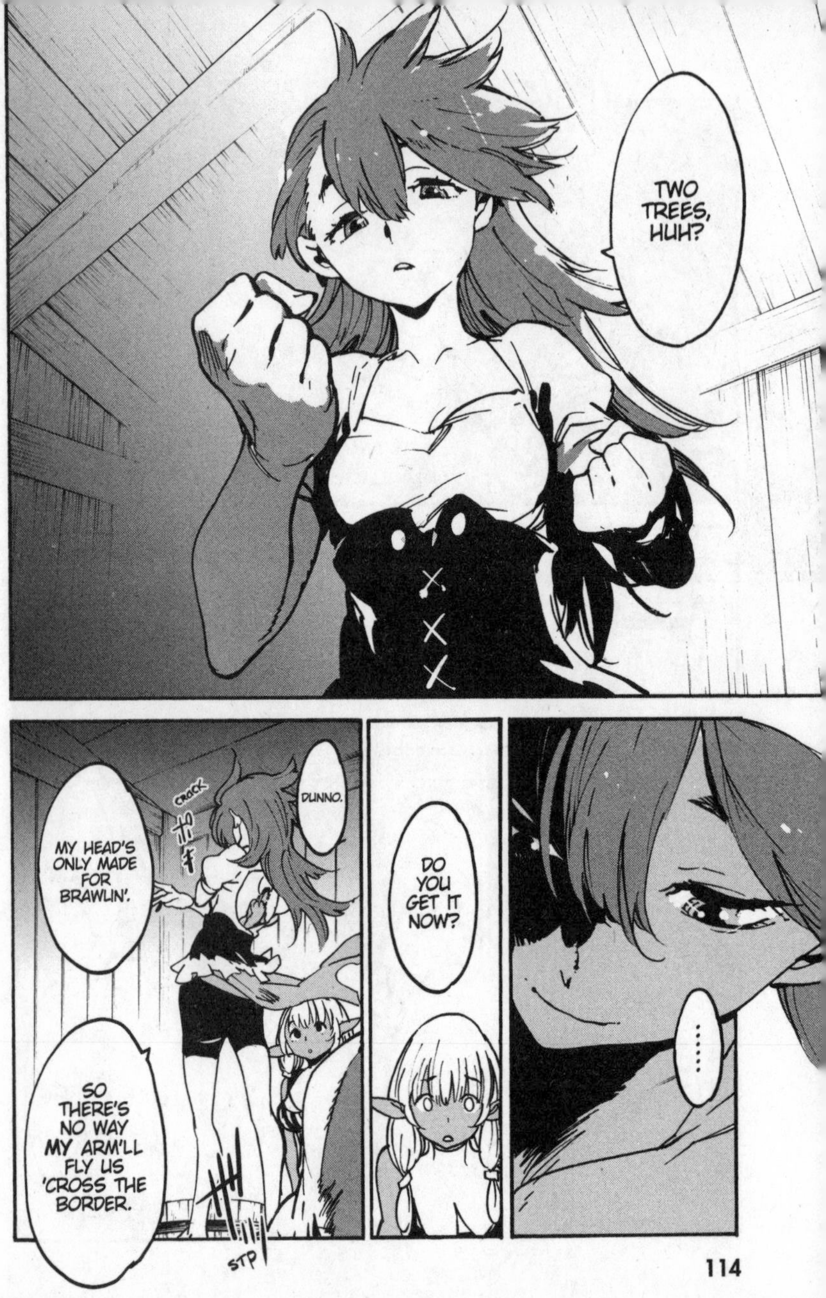
TWO TREES, HUH?
......
DO YOU GET IT NOW?
DUNNO.
CRACK
MY HEAD'S ONLY MADE FOR BRAWLIN'.
SO THERE'S NO WAY MY ARM'LL FLY US 'CROSS THE BORDER.
STP

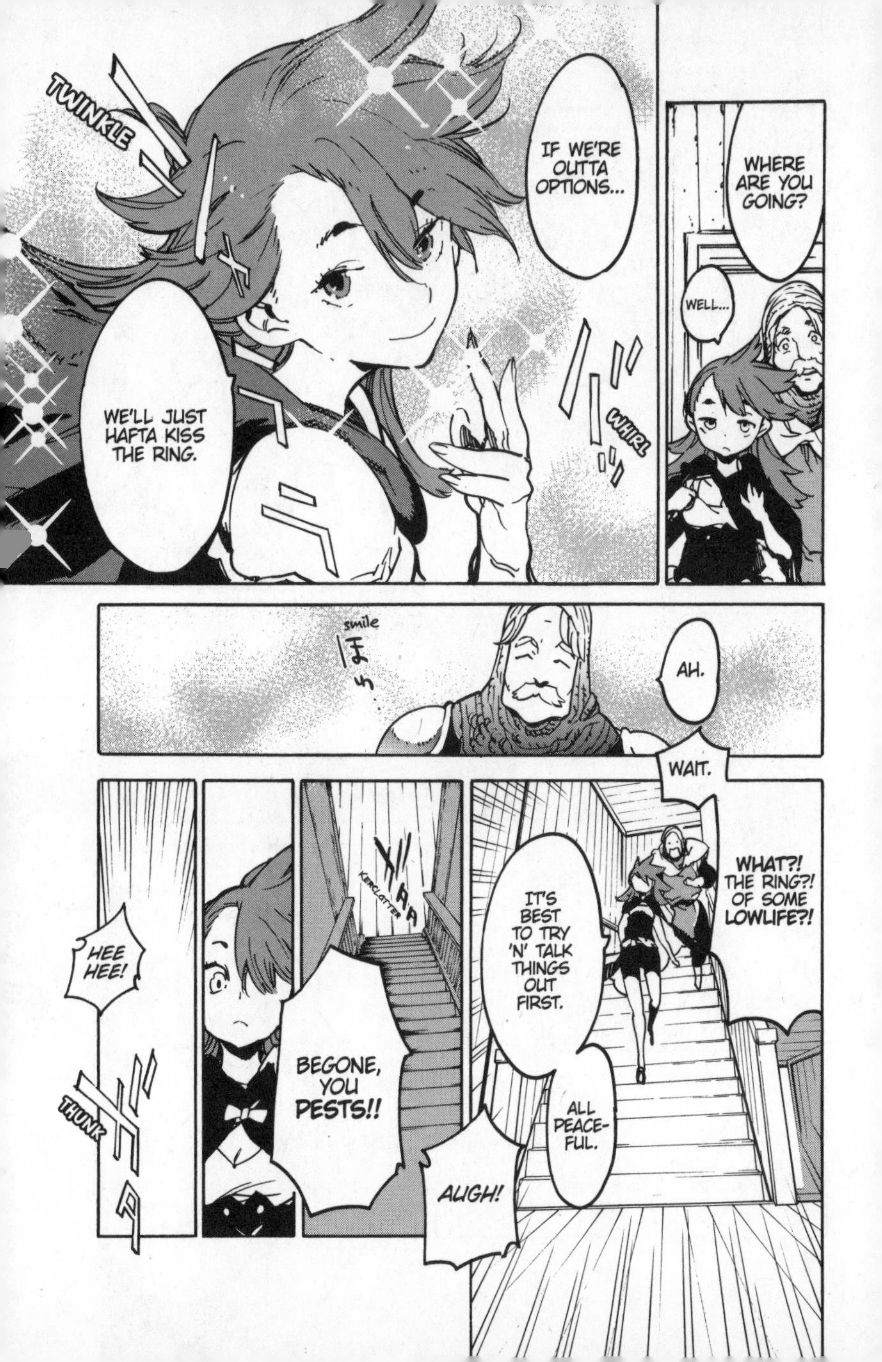
WHERE ARE YOU GOING?
WELL...
IF WE'RE OUTTA OPTIONS...
TWINKLE
WHIRL
WE'LL JUST HAFTA KISS THE RING.
AH.
smile
ほわ
WAIT.
WHAT?! THE RING?! OF SOME LOWLIFE?!
IT'S BEST TO TRY 'N' TALK THINGS OUT FIRST.
ALL PEACE-FUL.
KERCLATTER
BEGONE, YOU PESTS!!
AUGH!
HEE HEE!
THUNK

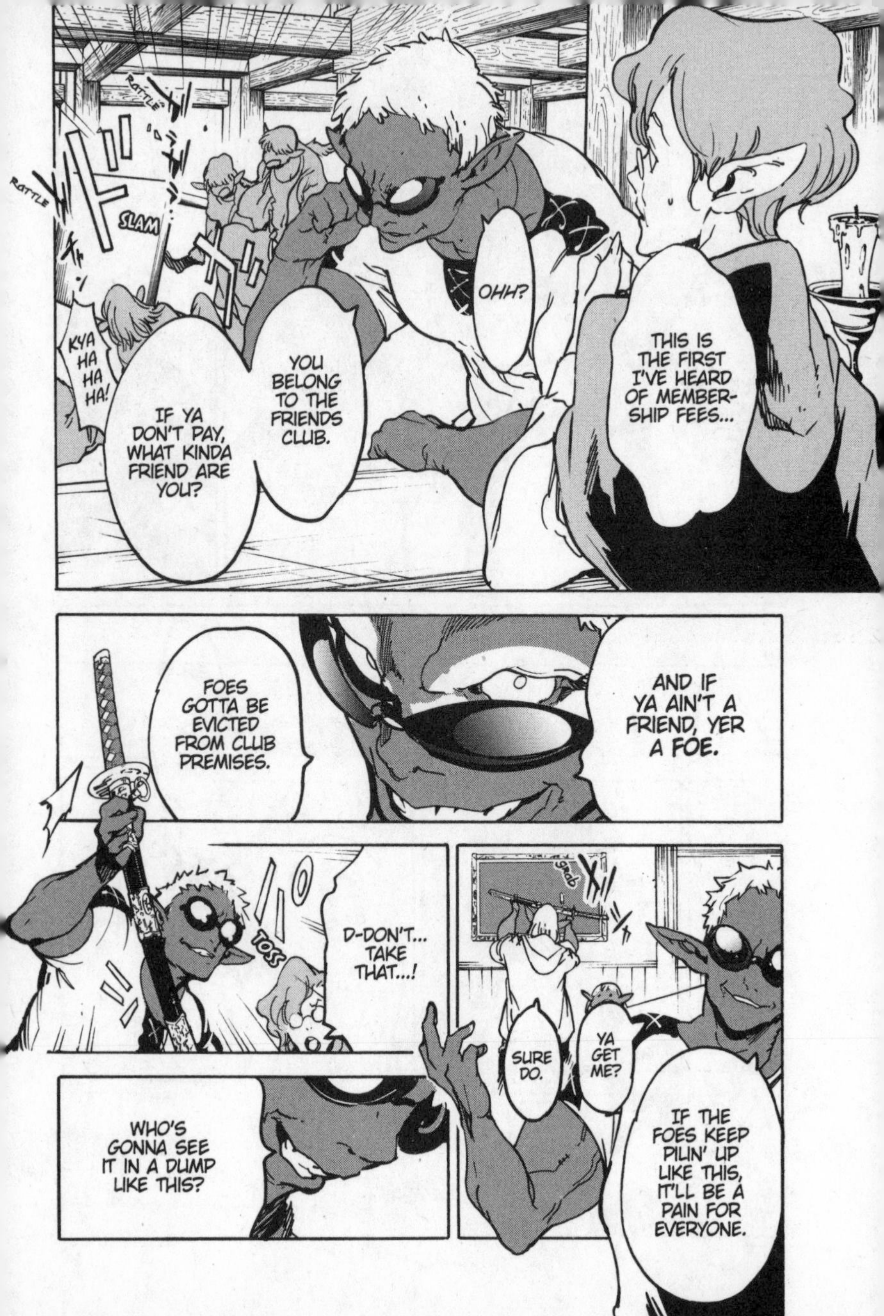
THIS IS THE FIRST I'VE HEARD OF MEMBERSHIP FEES...
OHH?
YOU BELONG TO THE FRIENDS CLUB.
IF YA DON'T PAY, WHAT KINDA FRIEND ARE YOU?
RATTLE
RATTLE
SLAM
KYA HA HA HA!
AND IF YA AIN'T A FRIEND, YER A FOE.
FOES GOTTA BE EVICTED FROM CLUB PREMISES.
grab
YA GET ME?
SURE DO.
IF THE FOES KEEP PILIN' UP LIKE THIS, IT'LL BE A PAIN FOR EVERYONE.
TOSS
D-DON'T... TAKE THAT...!
WHO'S GONNA SEE IT IN A DUMP LIKE THIS?

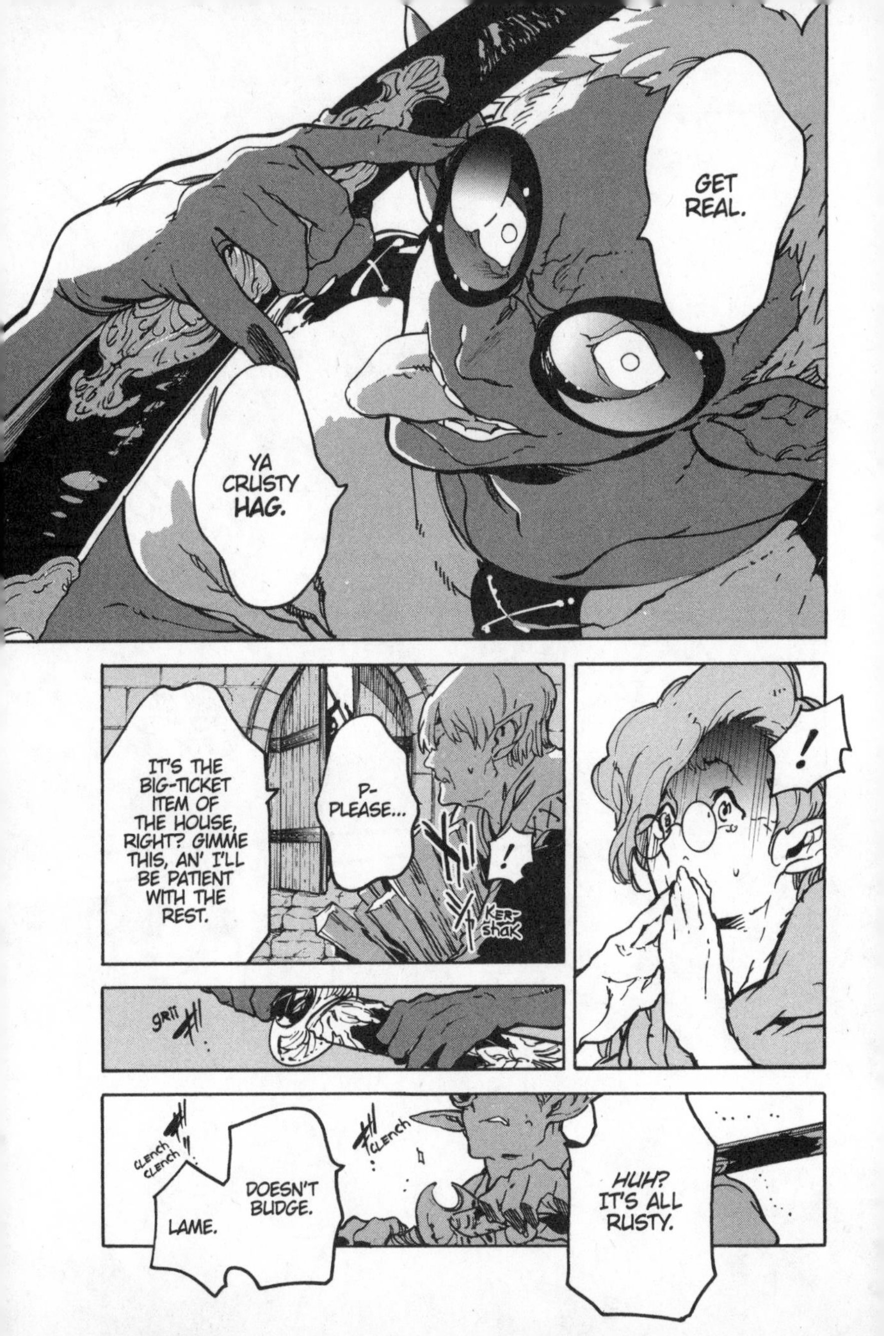
GET REAL.
YA CRUSTY HAG.
!
P-PLEASE...
!
KER-SHAK
IT'S THE BIG-TICKET ITEM OF THE HOUSE, RIGHT? GIMME THIS, AN' I'LL BE PATIENT WITH THE REST.
GRII
...
HUH? IT'S ALL RUSTY.
CLENCH
DOESN'T BUDGE.
LAME.
CLENCH CLENCH

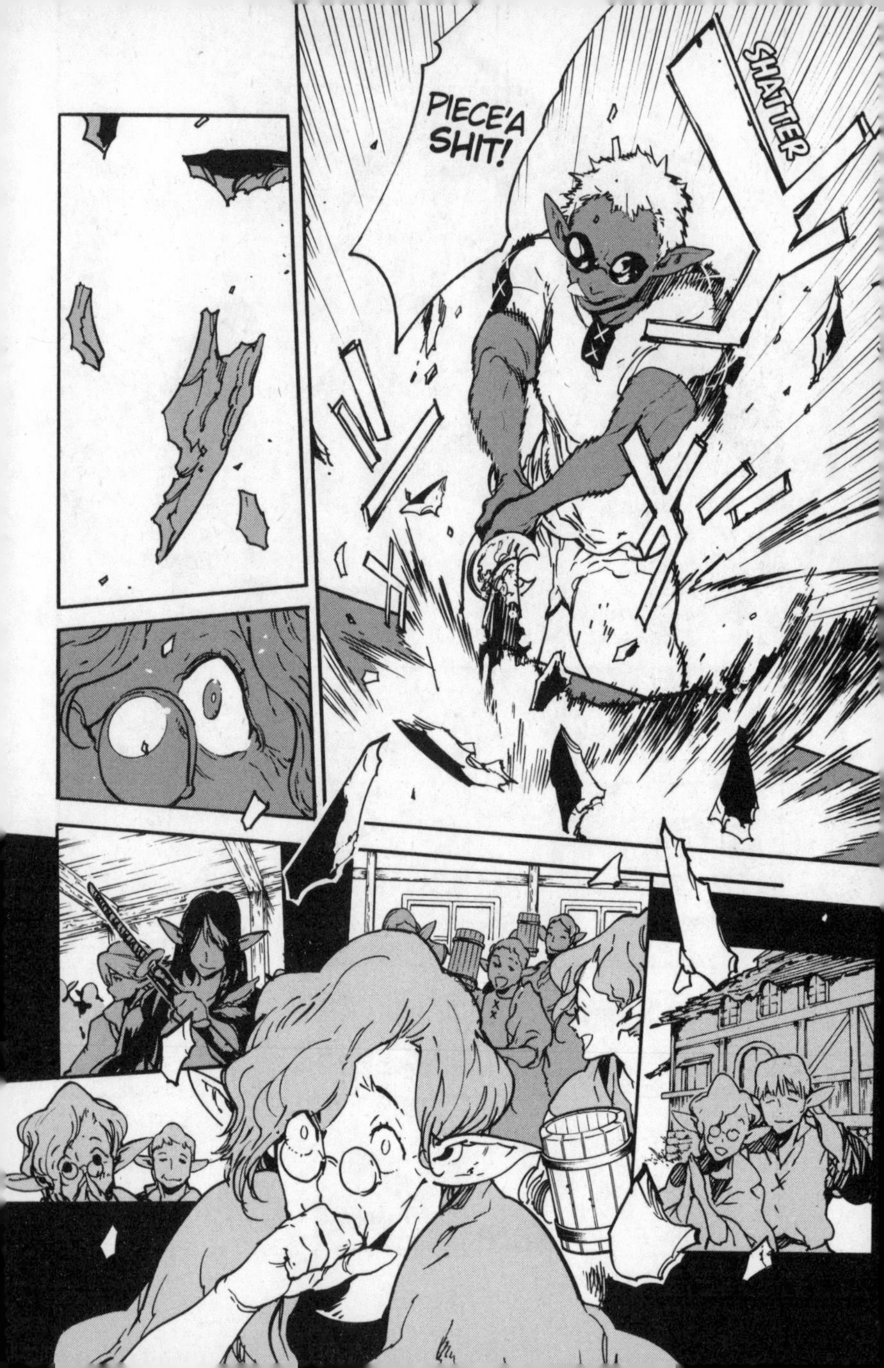
SHATTER
PIECE'A SHIT!

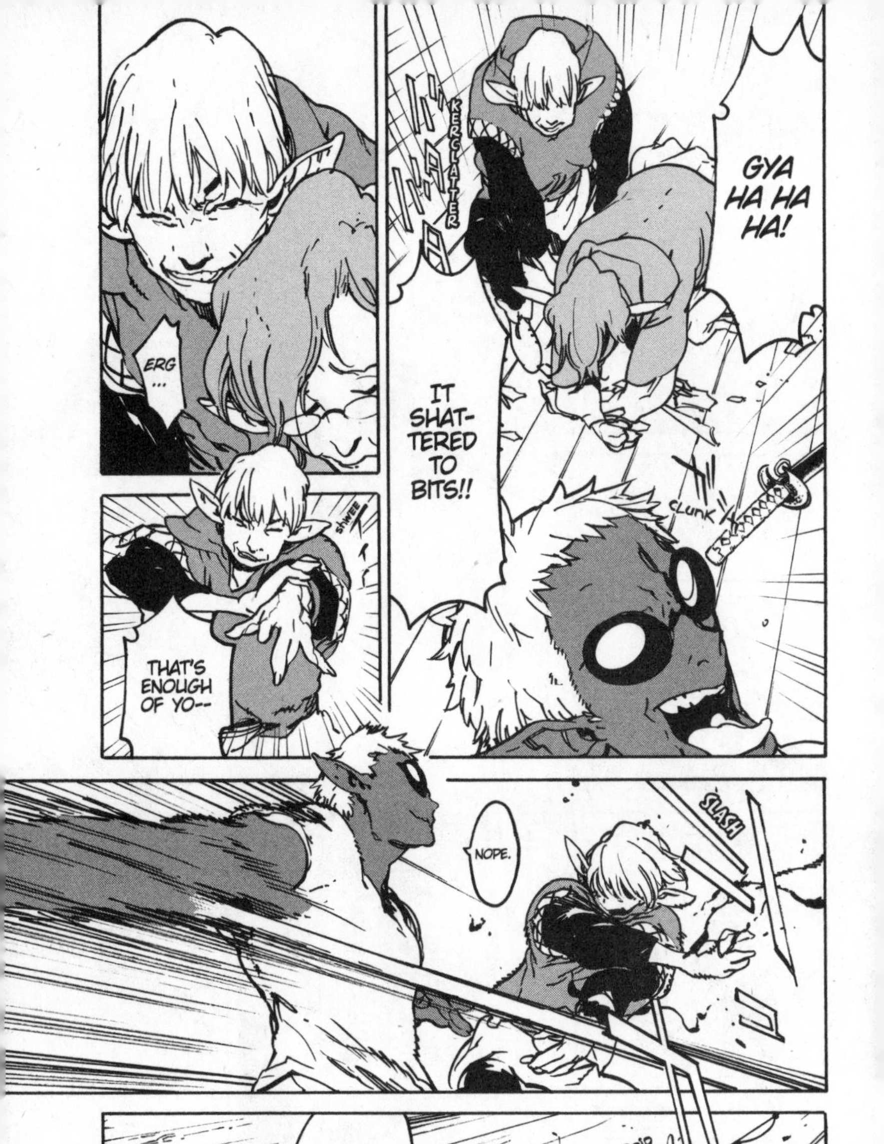
GYA HA HA HA!
KERGLATTER
IT SHAT-TERED TO BITS!!
CLUNK
ERG ...
SHWEE
THAT'S ENOUGH OF YO--
SLASH
NOPE.
Drip
TEE HEE, BYE-BYE SKILL TREE.
Drip

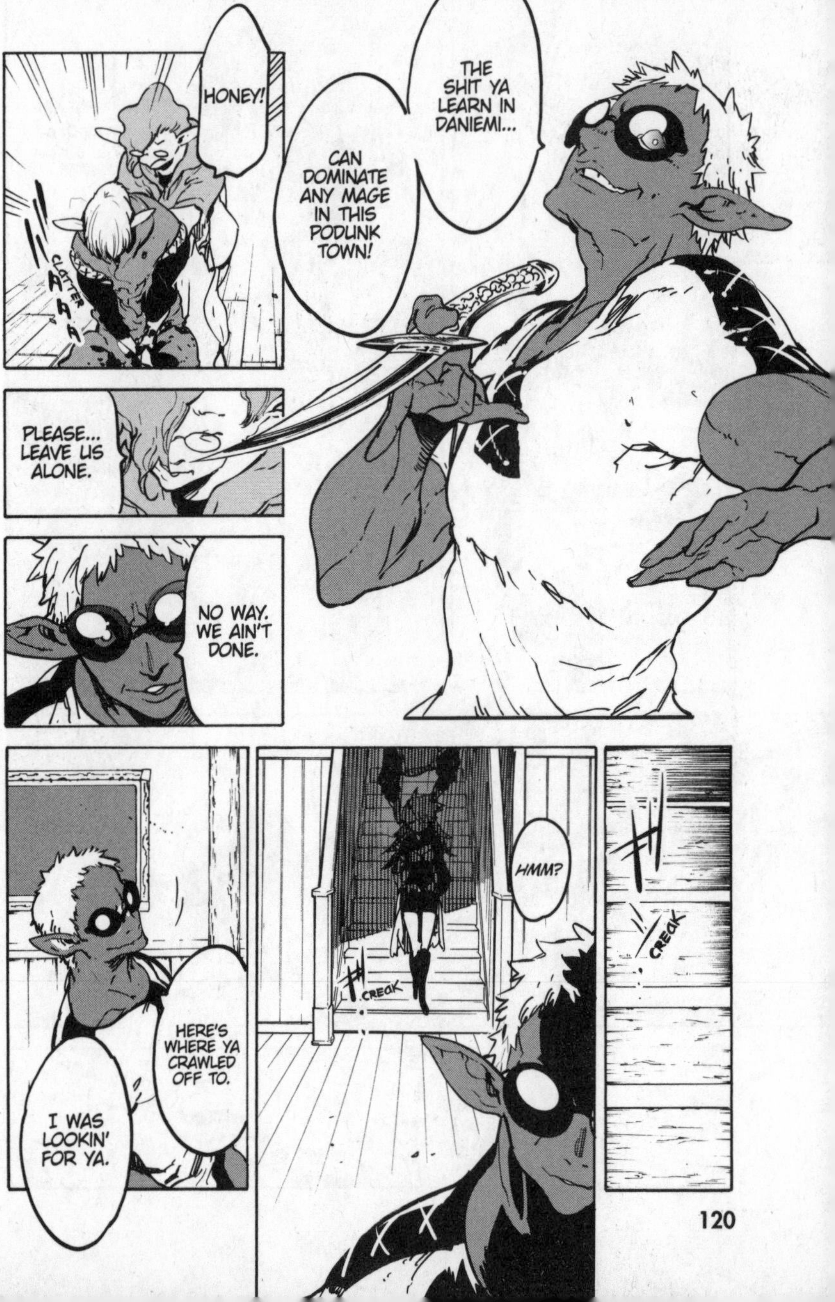
THE SHIT YA LEARN IN DANIEMI...
CAN DOMINATE ANY MAGE IN THIS PODUNK TOWN!
HONEY!
CLATTER
PLEASE... LEAVE US ALONE.
NO WAY. WE AIN'T DONE.
CREAK
HMM?
CREAK
HERE'S WHERE YA CRAWLED OFF TO.
I WAS LOOKIN' FOR YA.

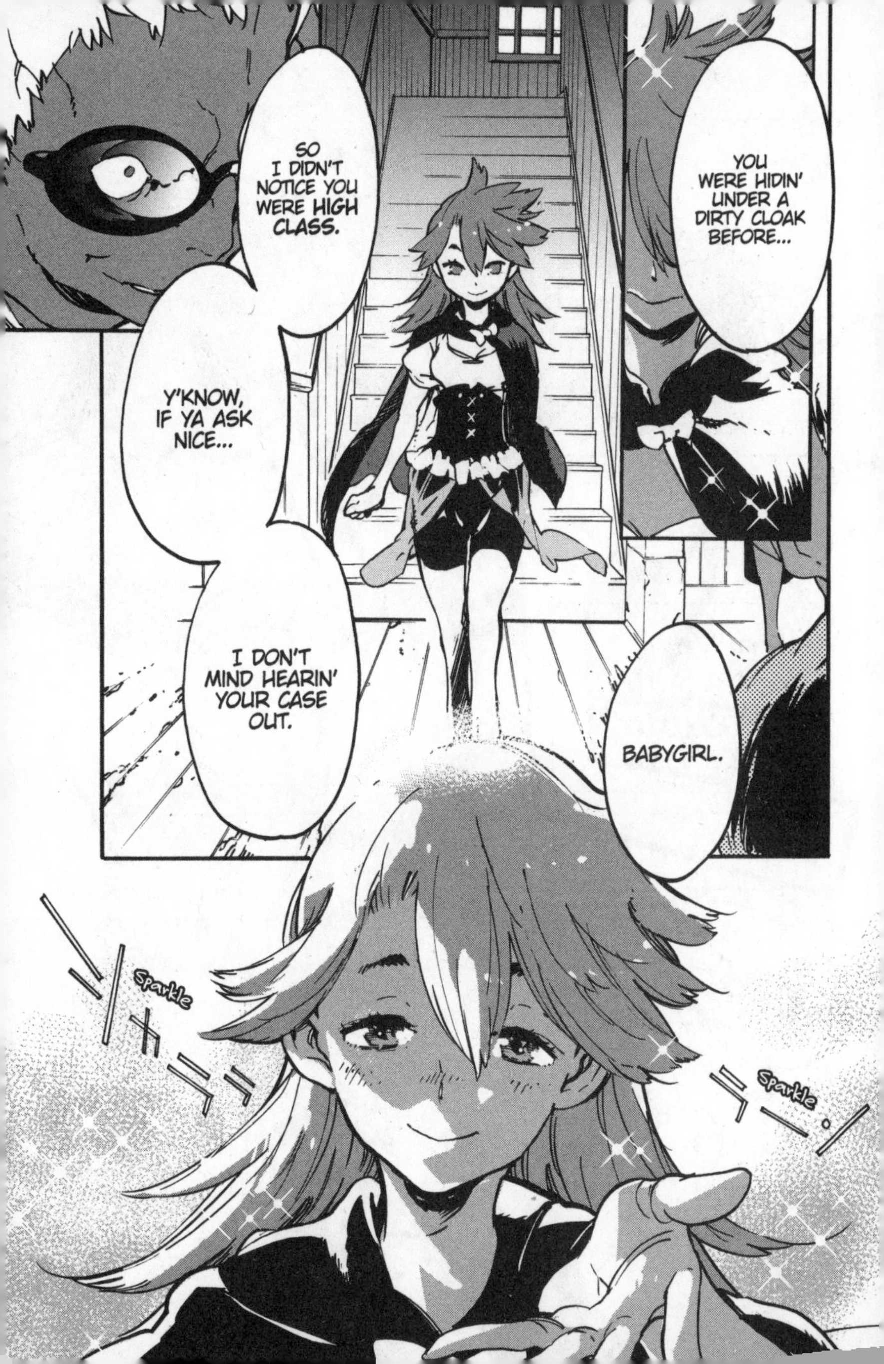
YOU WERE HIDIN' UNDER A DIRTY CLOAK BEFORE...
SO I DIDN'T NOTICE YOU WERE HIGH CLASS.
Y'KNOW, IF YA ASK NICE...
I DON'T MIND HEARIN' YOUR CASE OUT.
BABYGIRL.
Sparkle
Sparkle

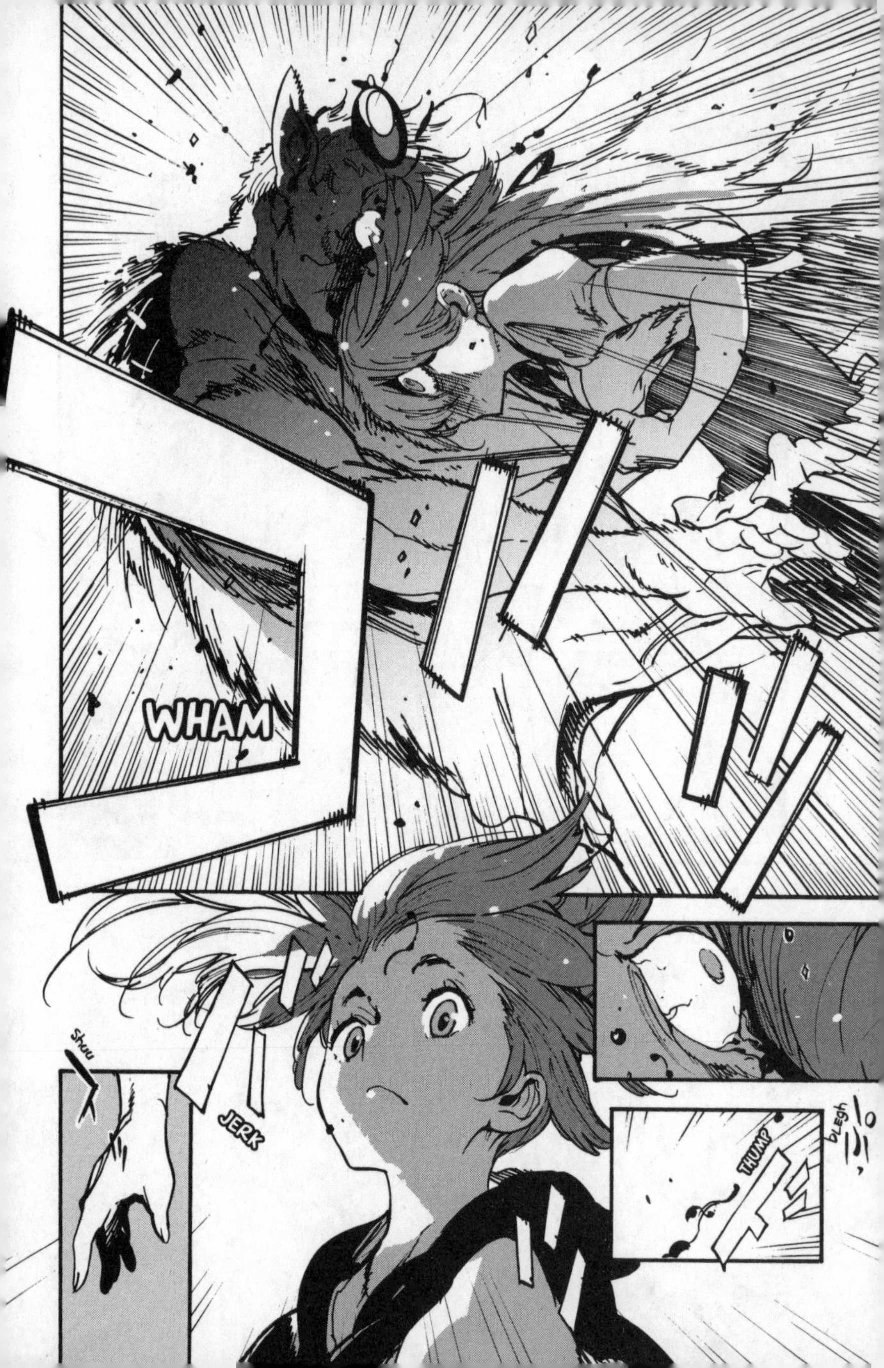
WHAM
blegh
THUMP
JERK
Shuu

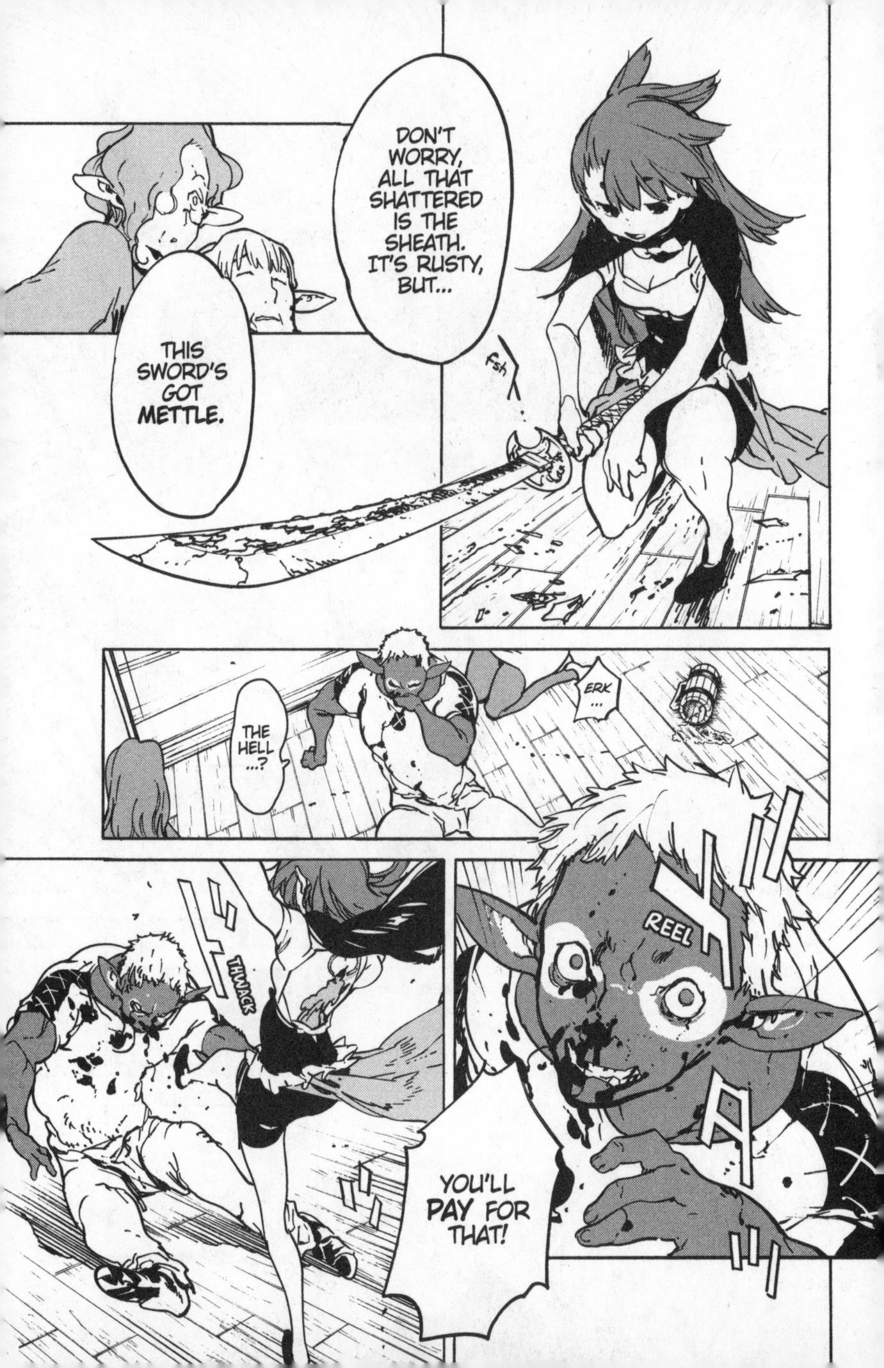
DON'T WORRY, ALL THAT SHATTERED IS THE SHEATH. IT'S RUSTY, BUT...
fsh
THIS SWORD'S GOT METTLE.
ERK...
THE HELL...?
REEL
YOU'LL PAY FOR THAT!
THWACK

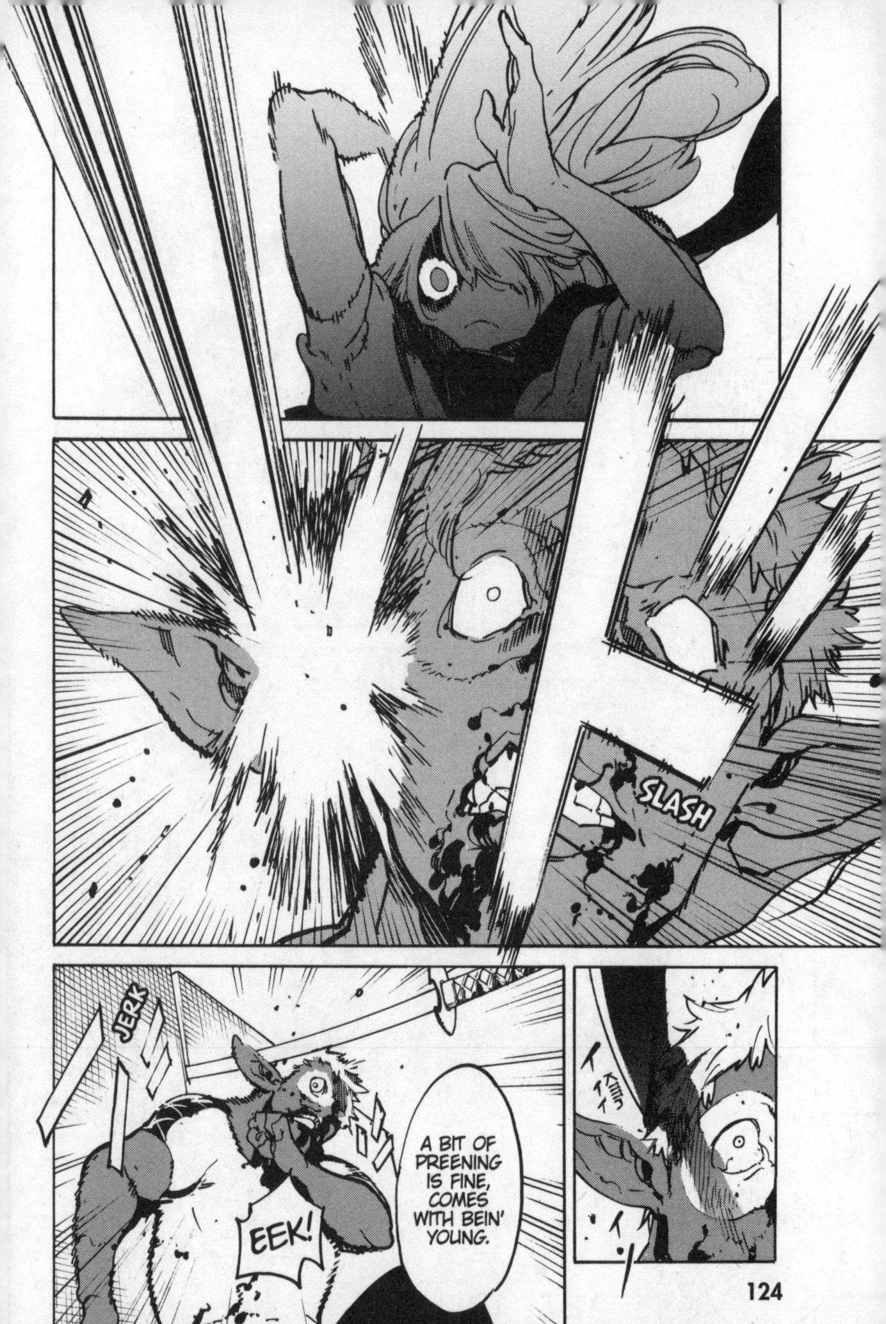
SLASH
A BIT OF PREENING IS FINE, COMES WITH BEIN' YOUNG.
JERK
EEK!

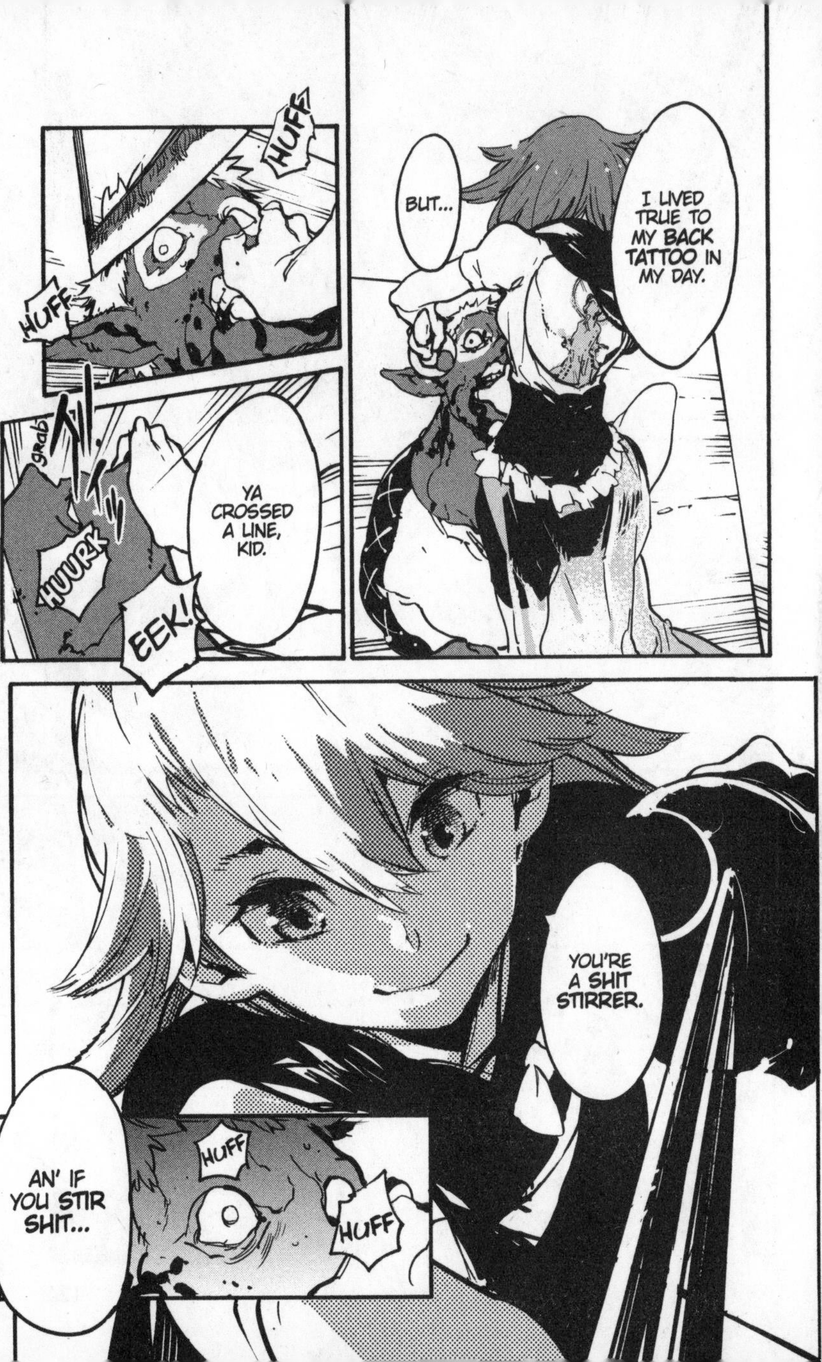
I LIVED TRUE TO MY BACK TATTOO IN MY DAY.
BUT...
HUFF
HUFF
YA CROSSED A LINE, KID.
grab
HUUURK
EEK!
YOU'RE A SHIT STIRRER.
HUFF
HUFF
AN' IF YOU STIR SHIT...

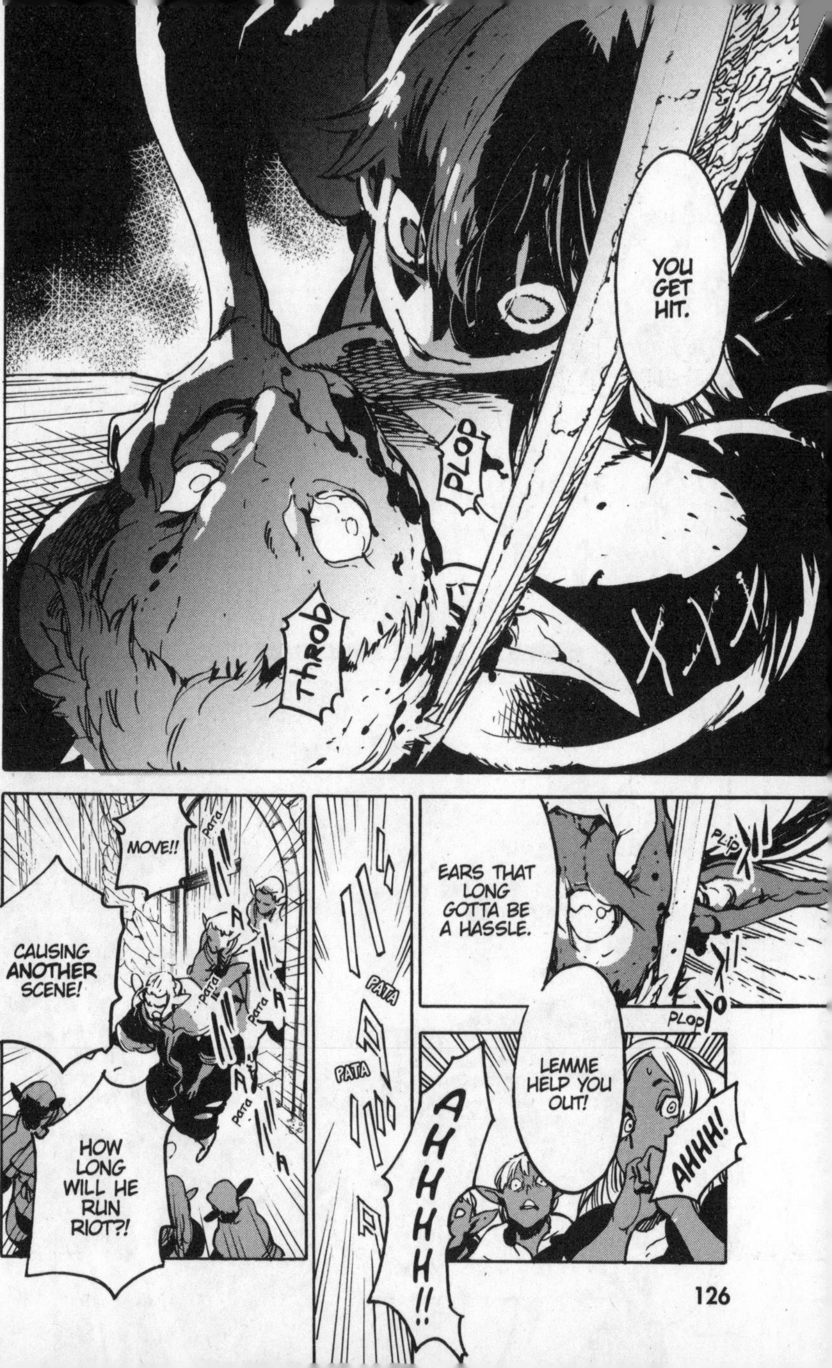
YOU GET HIT.
PLOP
THROB
EARS THAT LONG GOTTA BE A HASSLE.
PLIP
PLOP
LEMME HELP YOU OUT!
AHHH!
AHHHHH!!
PATA
PATA
MOVE!!
CAUSING ANOTHER SCENE!
HOW LONG WILL HE RUN RIOT?!

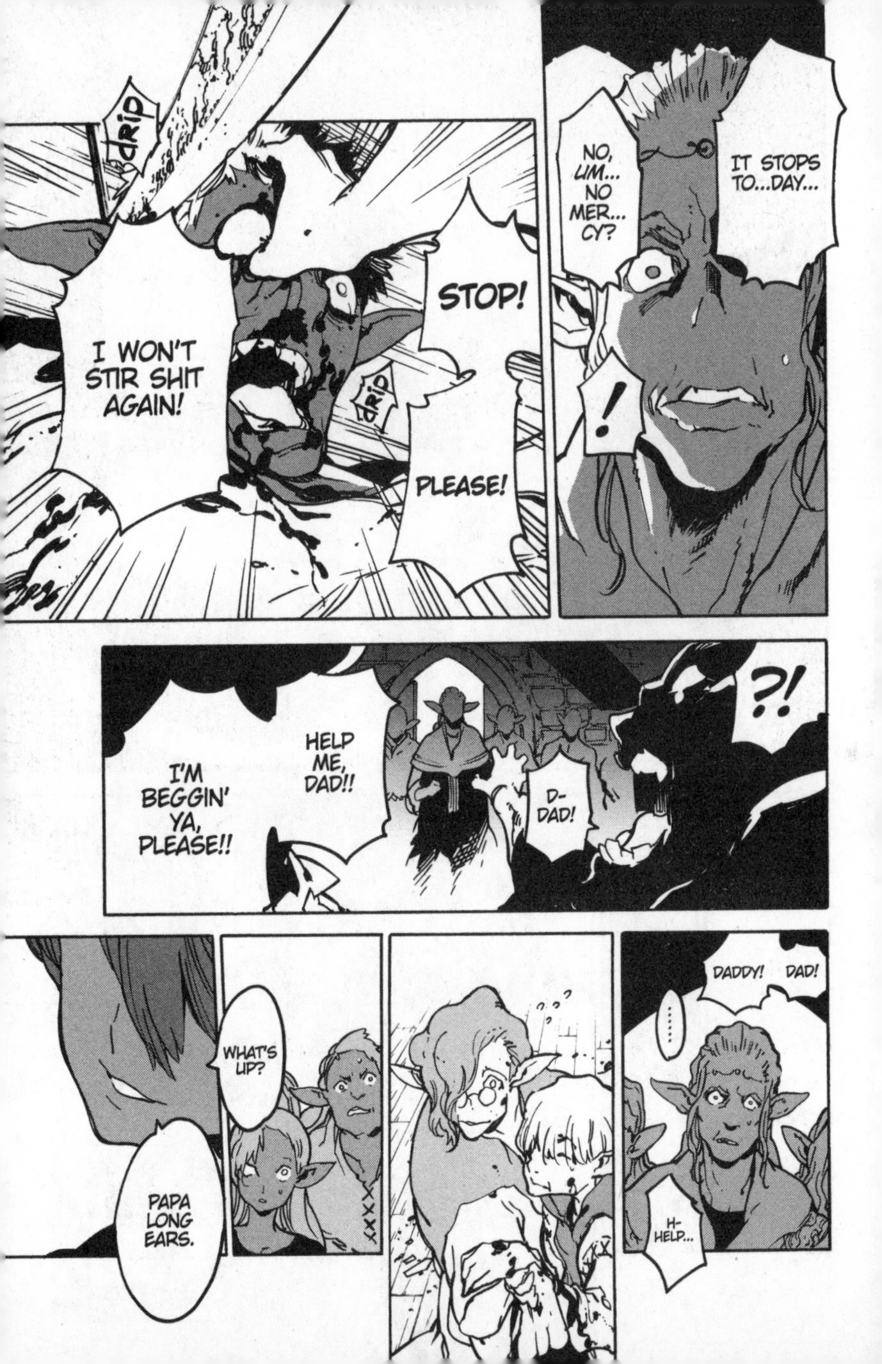
IT STOPS TO...DAY...
NO, UM... NO MER... CY?
!
STOP!
drip
PLEASE!
I WON'T STIR SHIT AGAIN!
drip
?!
D-DAD!
HELP ME, DAD!!
I'M BEGGIN' YA, PLEASE!!
DAD!
DADDY!
......
H-HELP...
WHAT'S UP?
PAPA LONG EARS.

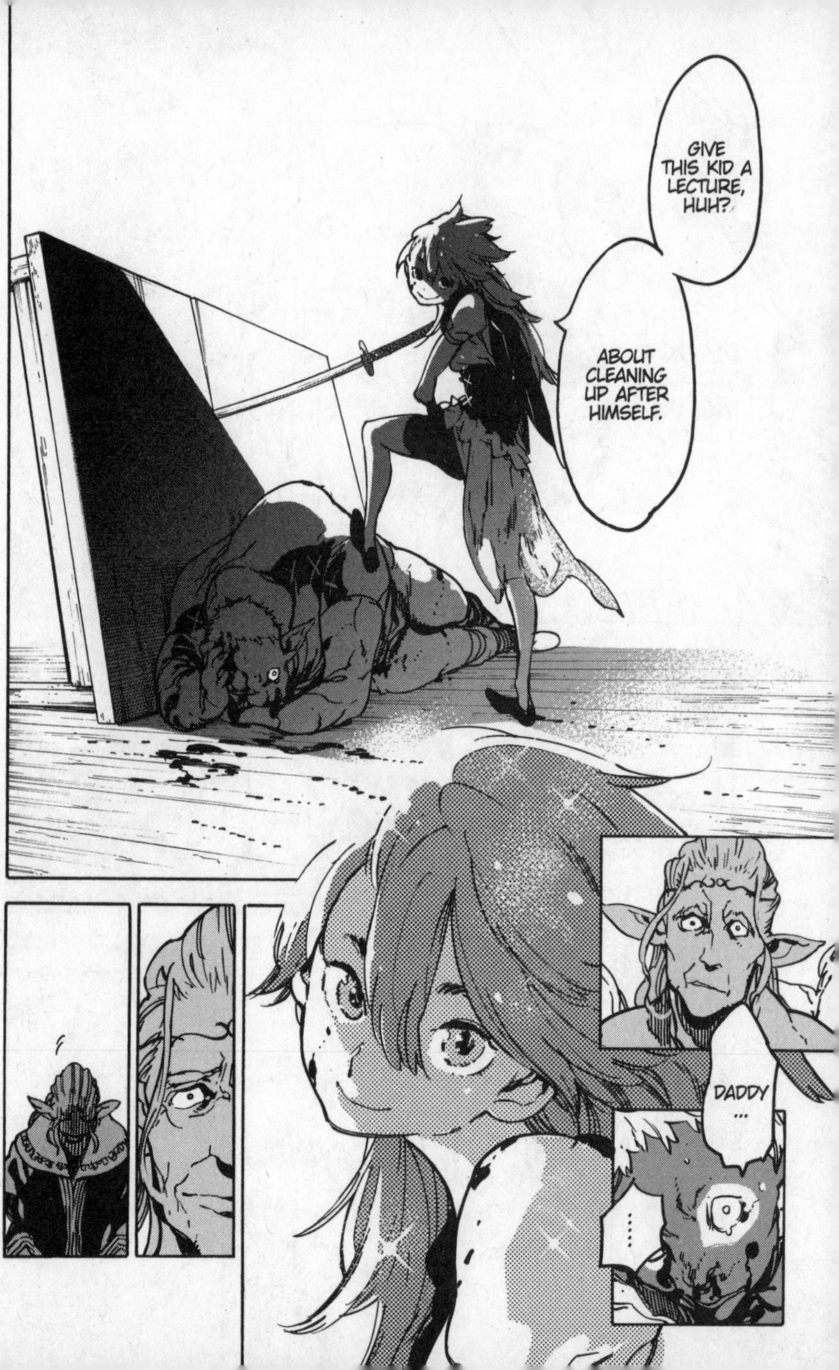
GIVE THIS KID A LECTURE, HUH?
ABOUT CLEANING UP AFTER HIMSELF.
DADDY ...
......

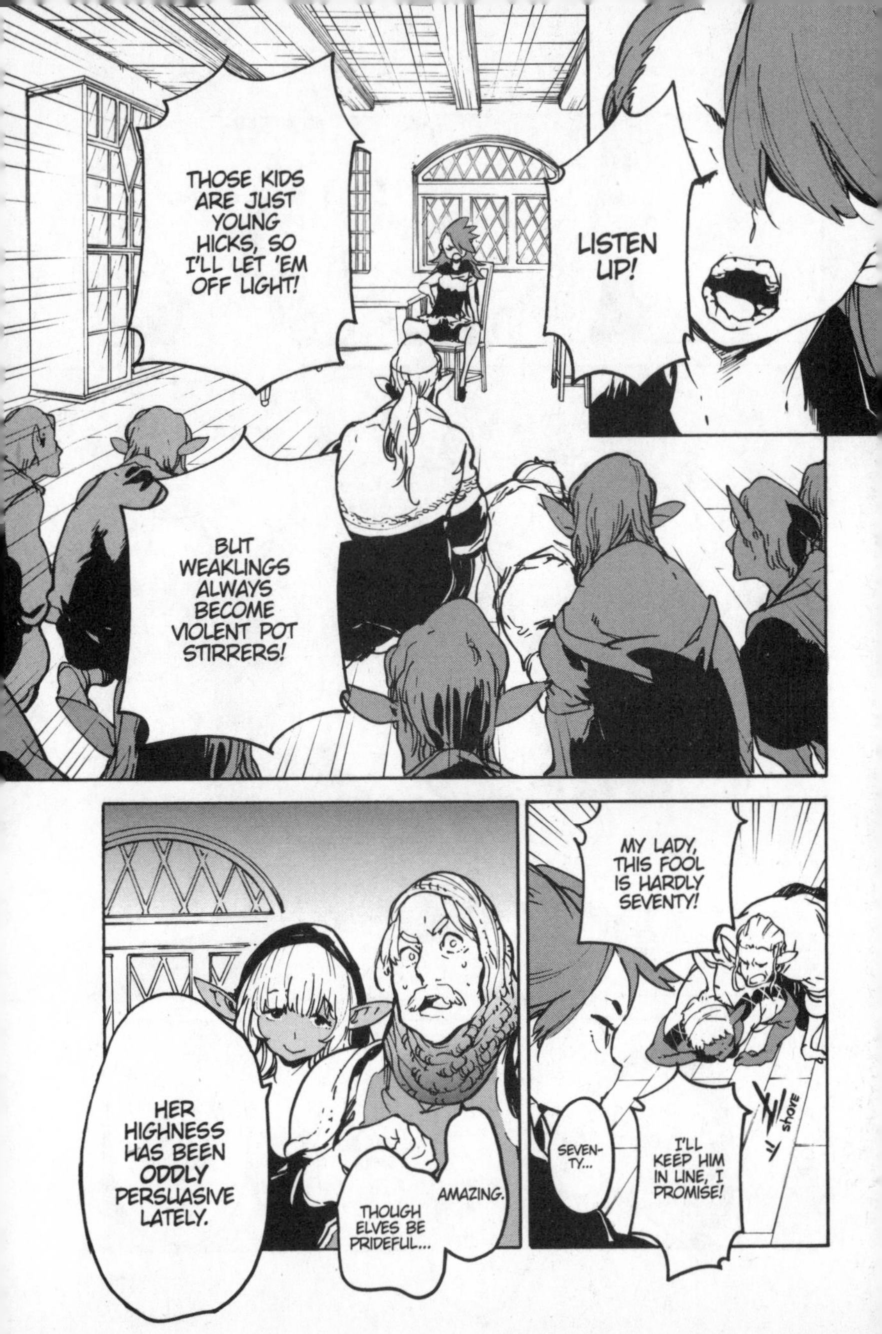
LISTEN UP!
THOSE KIDS ARE JUST YOUNG HICKS, SO I'LL LET 'EM OFF LIGHT!
BUT WEAKLINGS ALWAYS BECOME VIOLENT POT STIRRERS!
MY LADY, THIS FOOL IS HARDLY SEVENTY!
SHOVE
I'LL KEEP HIM IN LINE, I PROMISE!
SEVENTY...
AMAZING.
THOUGH ELVES BE PRIDEFUL...
HER HIGHNESS HAS BEEN ODDLY PERSUASIVE LATELY.

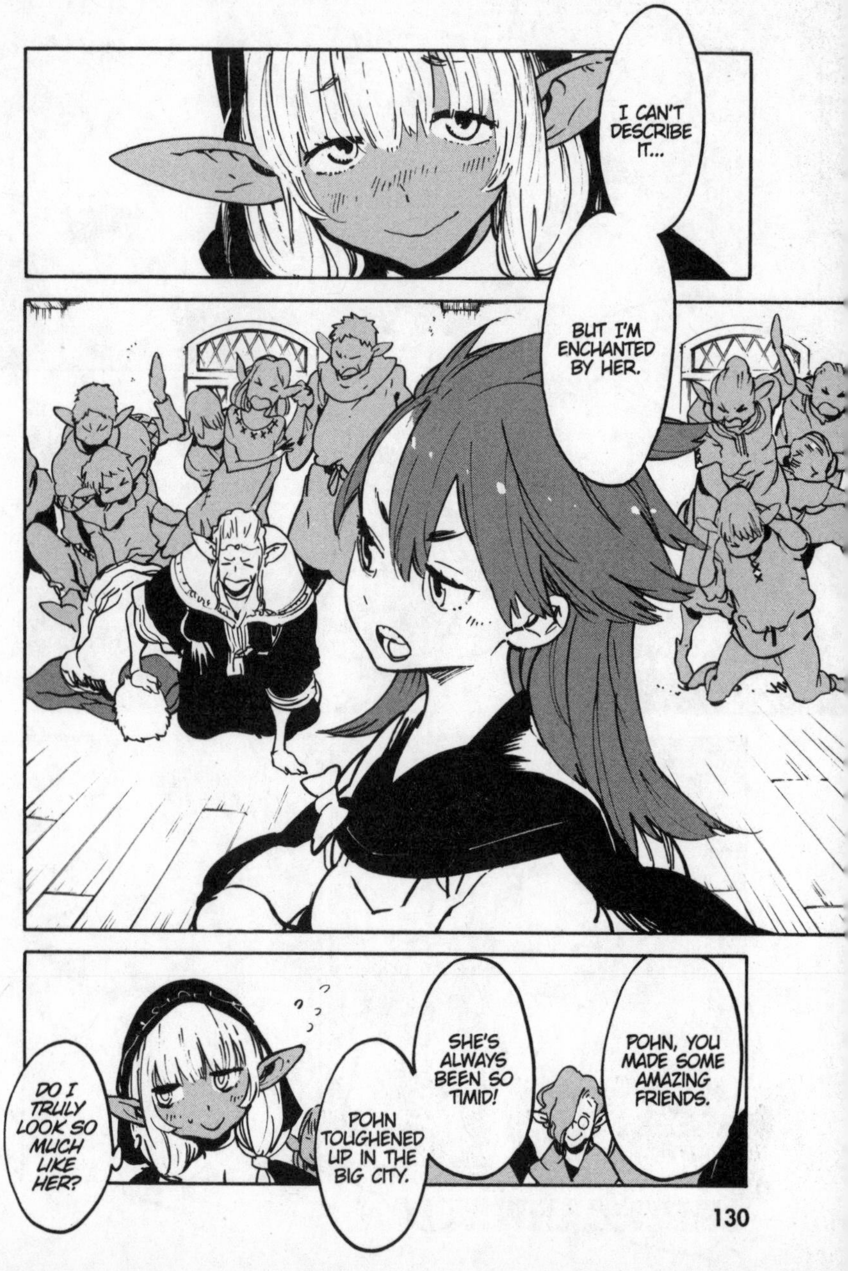
I CAN'T DESCRIBE IT...
BUT I'M ENCHANTED BY HER.
POHN, YOU MADE SOME AMAZING FRIENDS.
SHE'S ALWAYS BEEN SO TIMID!
POHN TOUGHENED UP IN THE BIG CITY.
DO I TRULY LOOK SO MUCH LIKE HER?

YAKUZA
REINCARNATION

YAKUZA

REINCARNATION

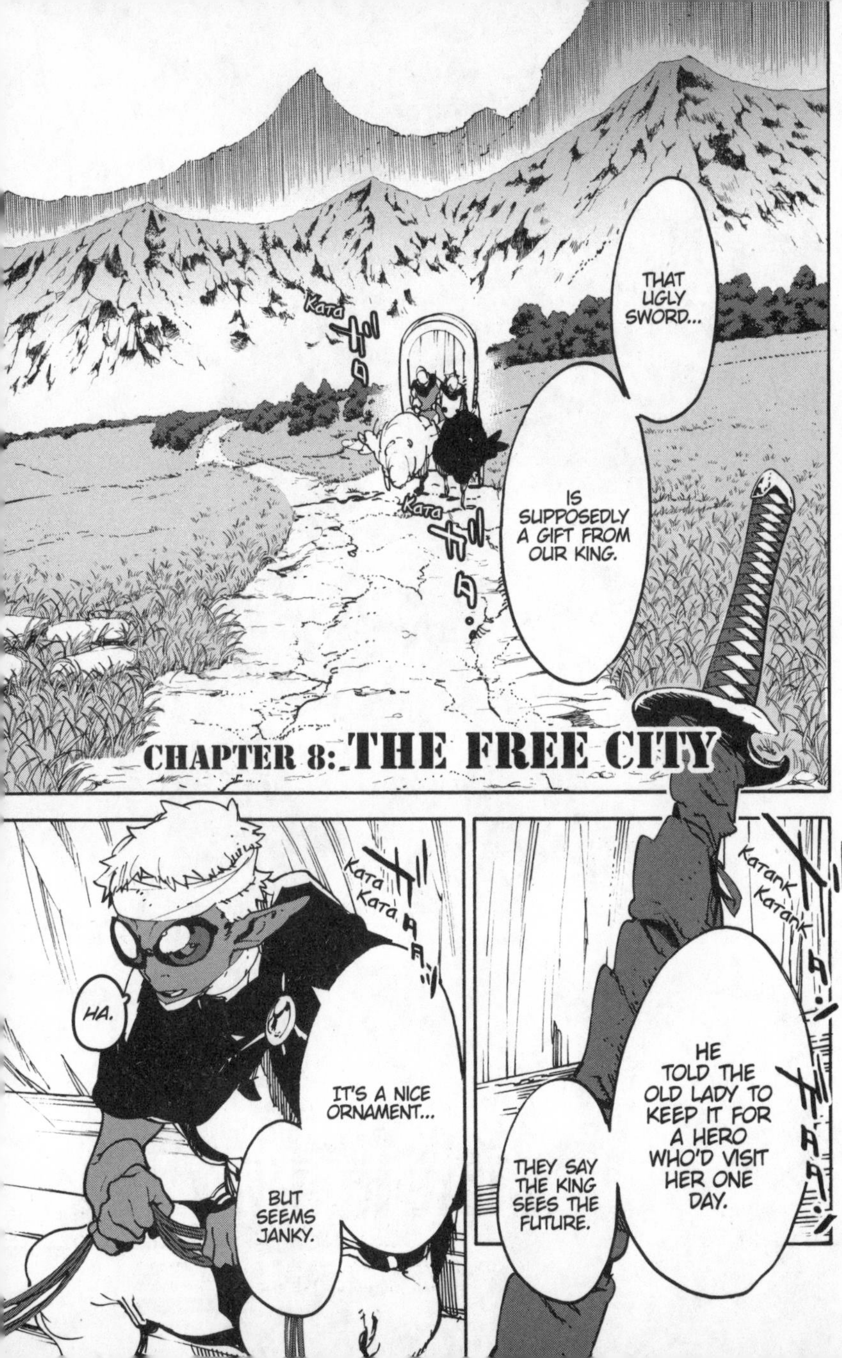
THAT UGLY SWORD...
IS SUPPOSEDLY A GIFT FROM OUR KING.
Kata
Kata
CHAPTER 8: THE FREE CITY
Katank Katank
HE TOLD THE OLD LADY TO KEEP IT FOR A HERO WHO'D VISIT HER ONE DAY.
THEY SAY THE KING SEES THE FUTURE.
Kata Kata
IT'S A NICE ORNAMENT...
BUT SEEMS JANKY.
HA.

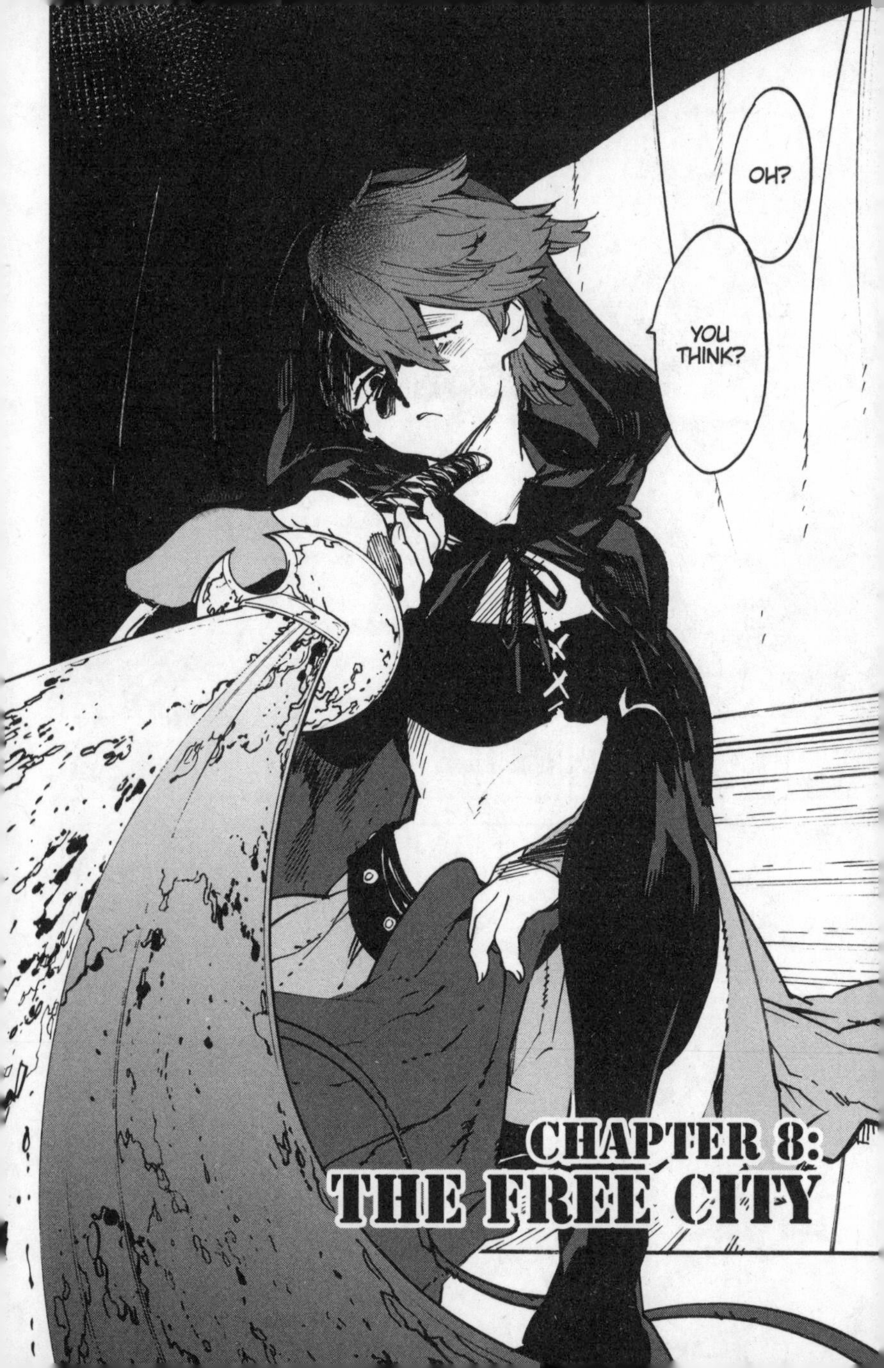
OH?
YOU THINK?
CHAPTER 8:
THE FREE CITY

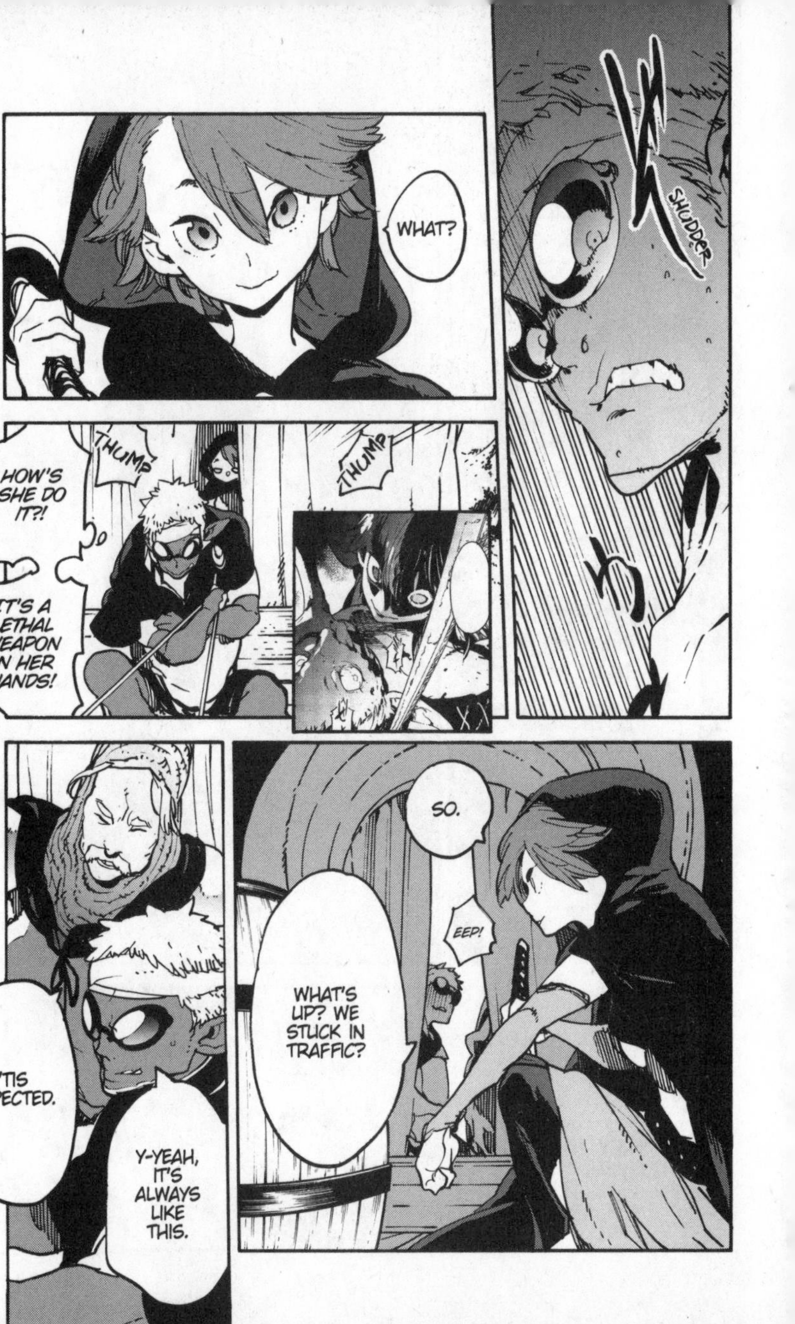
SHUDDER
WHAT?
THUMP
THUMP
HOW'S SHE DO IT?!
IT'S A LETHAL WEAPON IN HER HANDS!
SO.
EEP!
WHAT'S UP? WE STUCK IN TRAFFIC?
Y-YEAH, IT'S ALWAYS LIKE THIS.
'TIS EXPECTED.

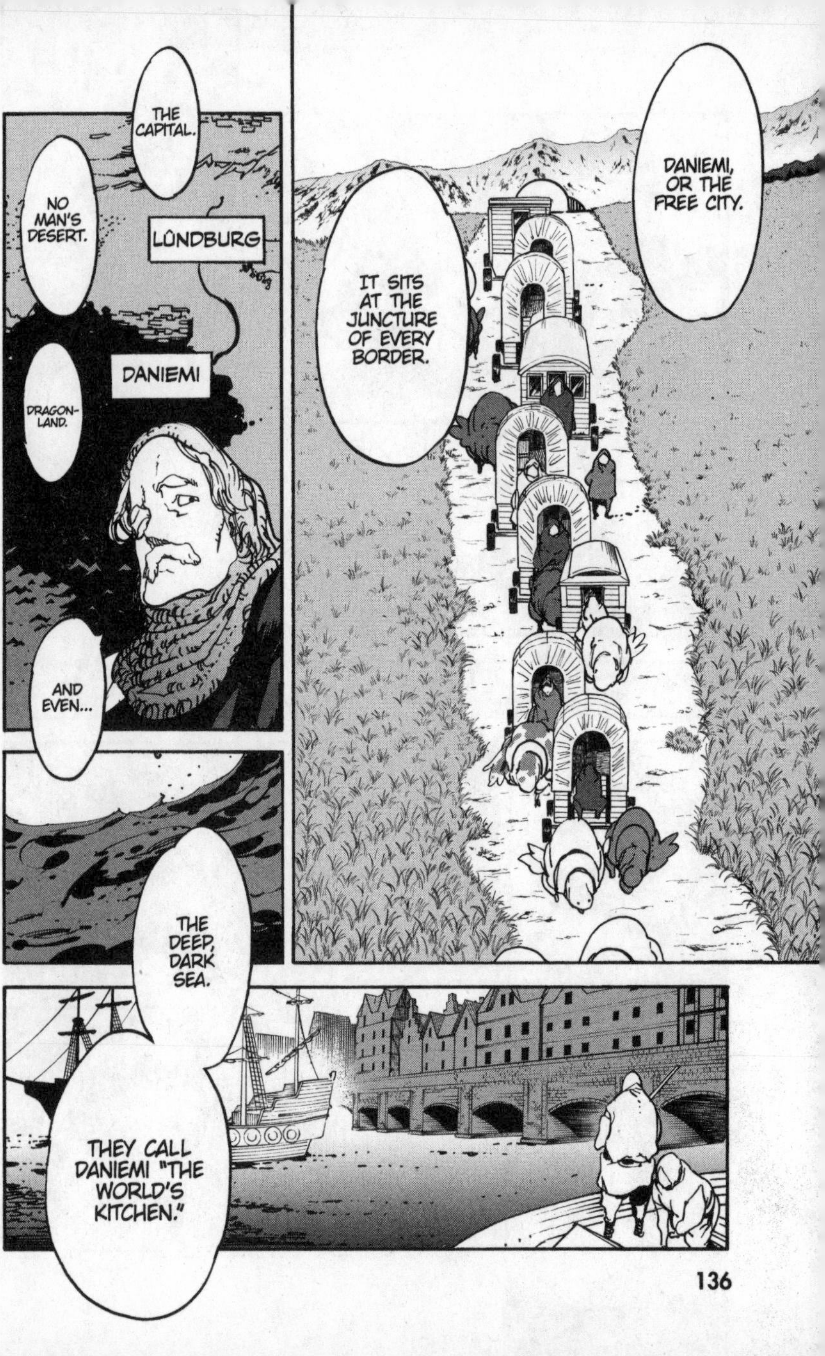
DANIEMI, OR THE FREE CITY.
IT SITS AT THE JUNCTURE OF EVERY BORDER.
THE CAPITAL.
LÛNDBURG
NO MAN'S DESERT.
DANIEMI
DRAGON-LAND.
AND EVEN...
THE DEEP, DARK SEA.
THEY CALL DANIEMI "THE WORLD'S KITCHEN."

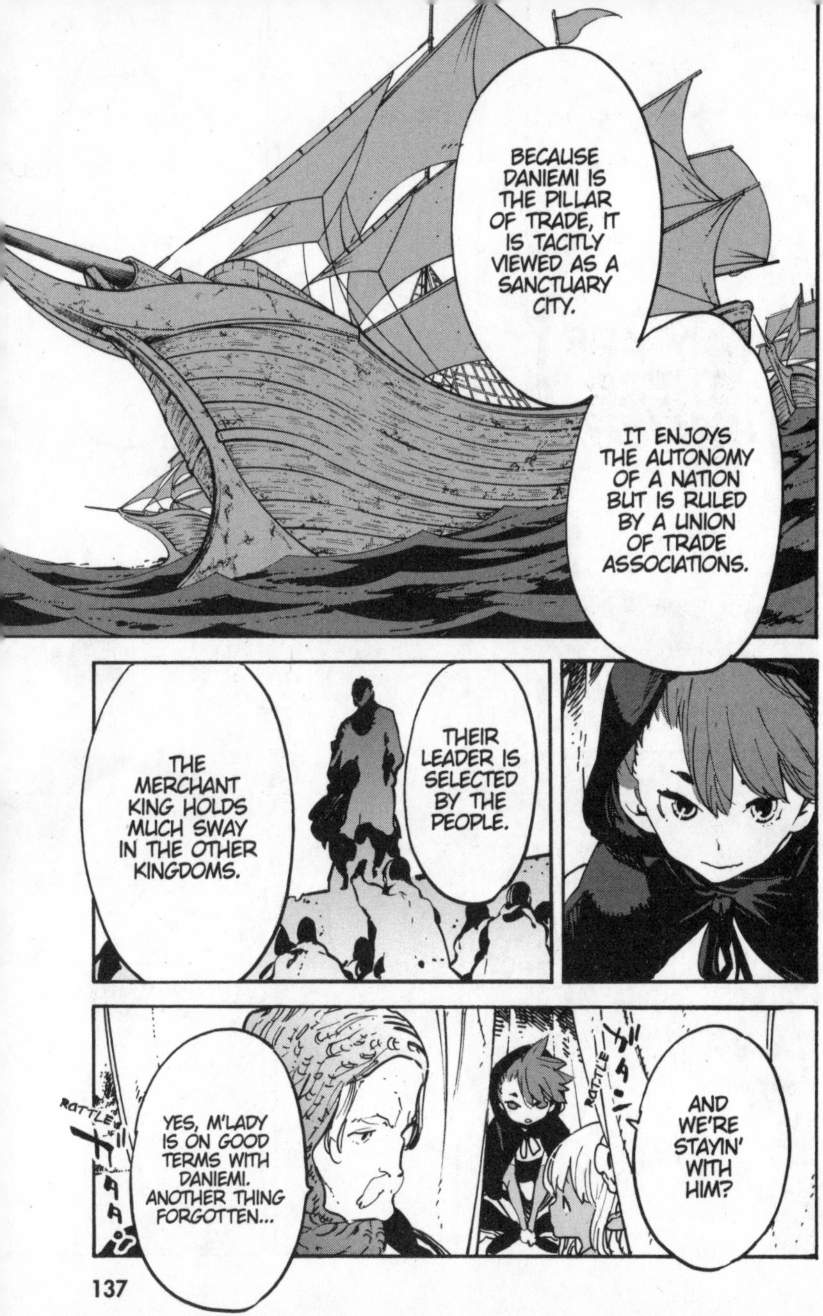
BECAUSE DANIEMI IS THE PILLAR OF TRADE, IT IS TACITLY VIEWED AS A SANCTUARY CITY.
IT ENJOYS THE AUTONOMY OF A NATION BUT IS RULED BY A UNION OF TRADE ASSOCIATIONS.
THEIR LEADER IS SELECTED BY THE PEOPLE.
THE MERCHANT KING HOLDS MUCH SWAY IN THE OTHER KINGDOMS.
AND WE'RE STAYIN' WITH HIM?
RATTLE
YES, M'LADY IS ON GOOD TERMS WITH DANIEMI. ANOTHER THING FORGOTTEN...
RATTLE

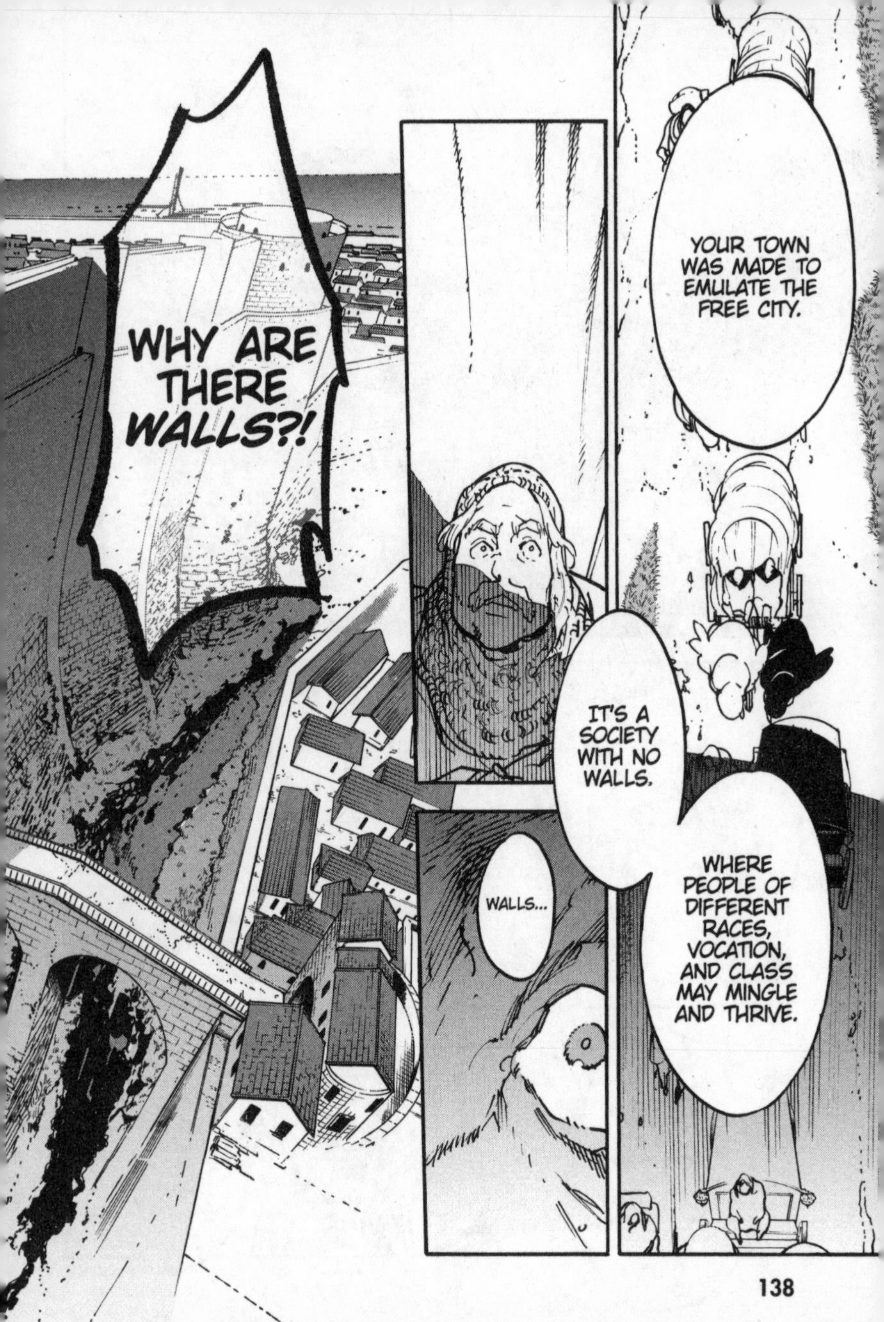
YOUR TOWN WAS MADE TO EMULATE THE FREE CITY.
IT'S A SOCIETY WITH NO WALLS.
WHERE PEOPLE OF DIFFERENT RACES, VOCATION, AND CLASS MAY MINGLE AND THRIVE.
WALLS...
WHY ARE THERE *WALLS*?!

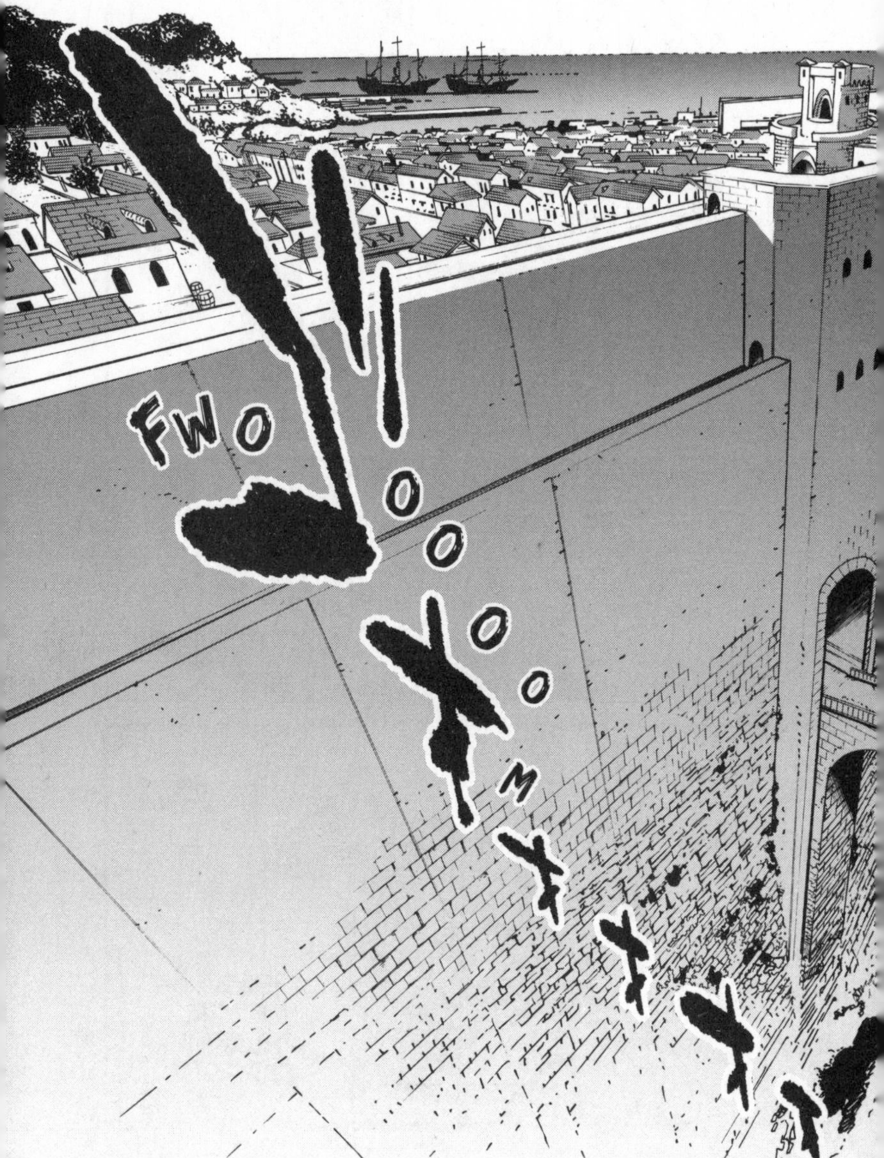
FWOOOOOM

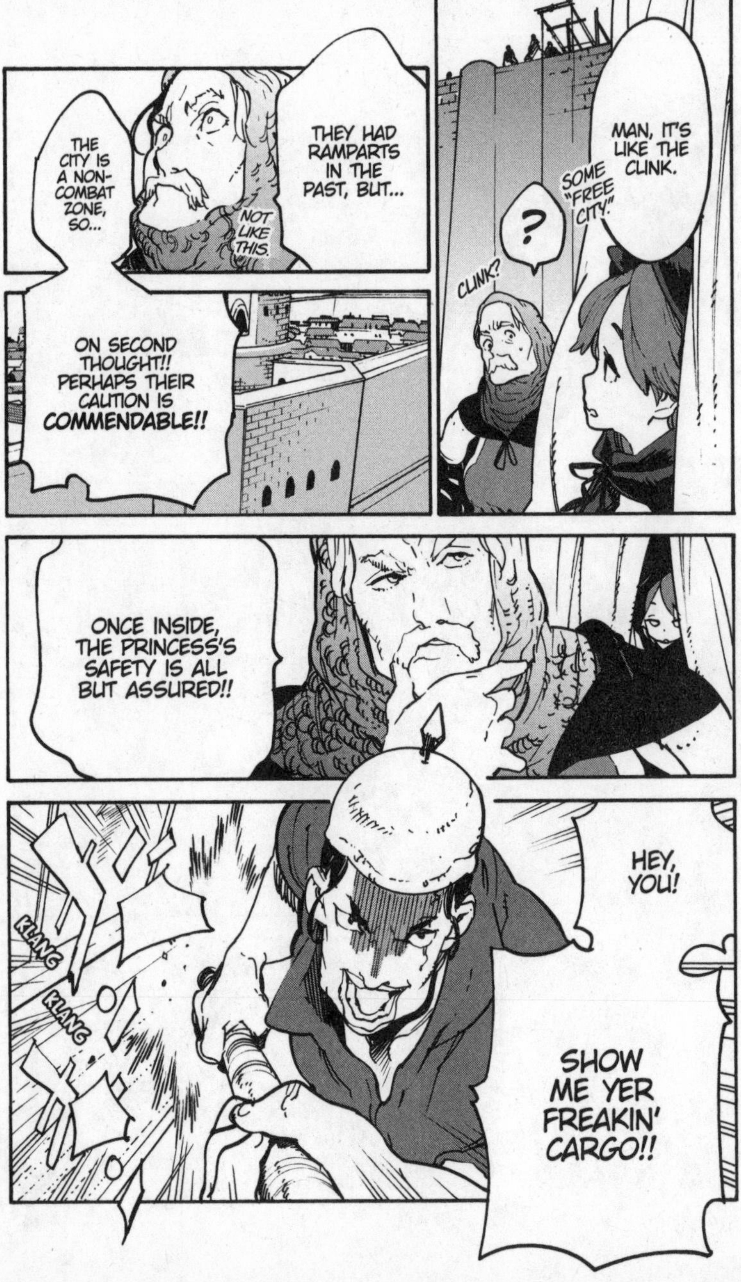
MAN, IT'S LIKE THE CLINK.
SOME "FREE CITY."
?
CLINK?
THEY HAD RAMPARTS IN THE PAST, BUT...
THE CITY IS A NON-COMBAT ZONE, SO...
NOT LIKE THIS.
ON SECOND THOUGHT!! PERHAPS THEIR CAUTION IS COMMENDABLE!!
ONCE INSIDE, THE PRINCESS'S SAFETY IS ALL BUT ASSURED!!
HEY, YOU!
SHOW ME YER FREAKIN' CARGO!!
KLANG
KLANG

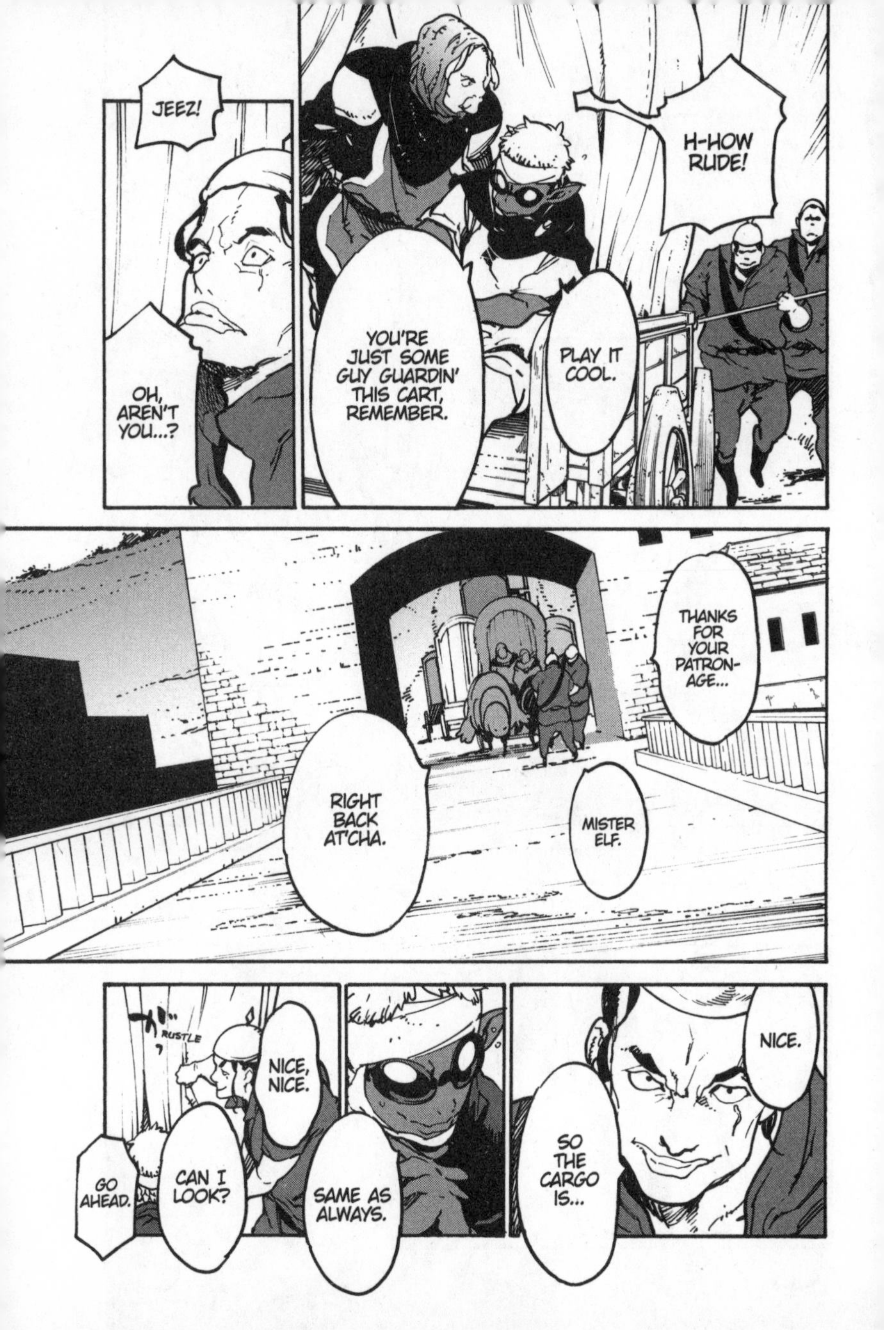
H-HOW RUDE!
PLAY IT COOL.
YOU'RE JUST SOME GUY GUARDIN' THIS CART, REMEMBER.
JEEZ!
OH, AREN'T YOU...?
THANKS FOR YOUR PATRON-AGE...
MISTER ELF.
RIGHT BACK AT'CHA.
NICE.
SO THE CARGO IS...
SAME AS ALWAYS.
NICE, NICE.
RUSTLE
CAN I LOOK?
GO AHEAD.

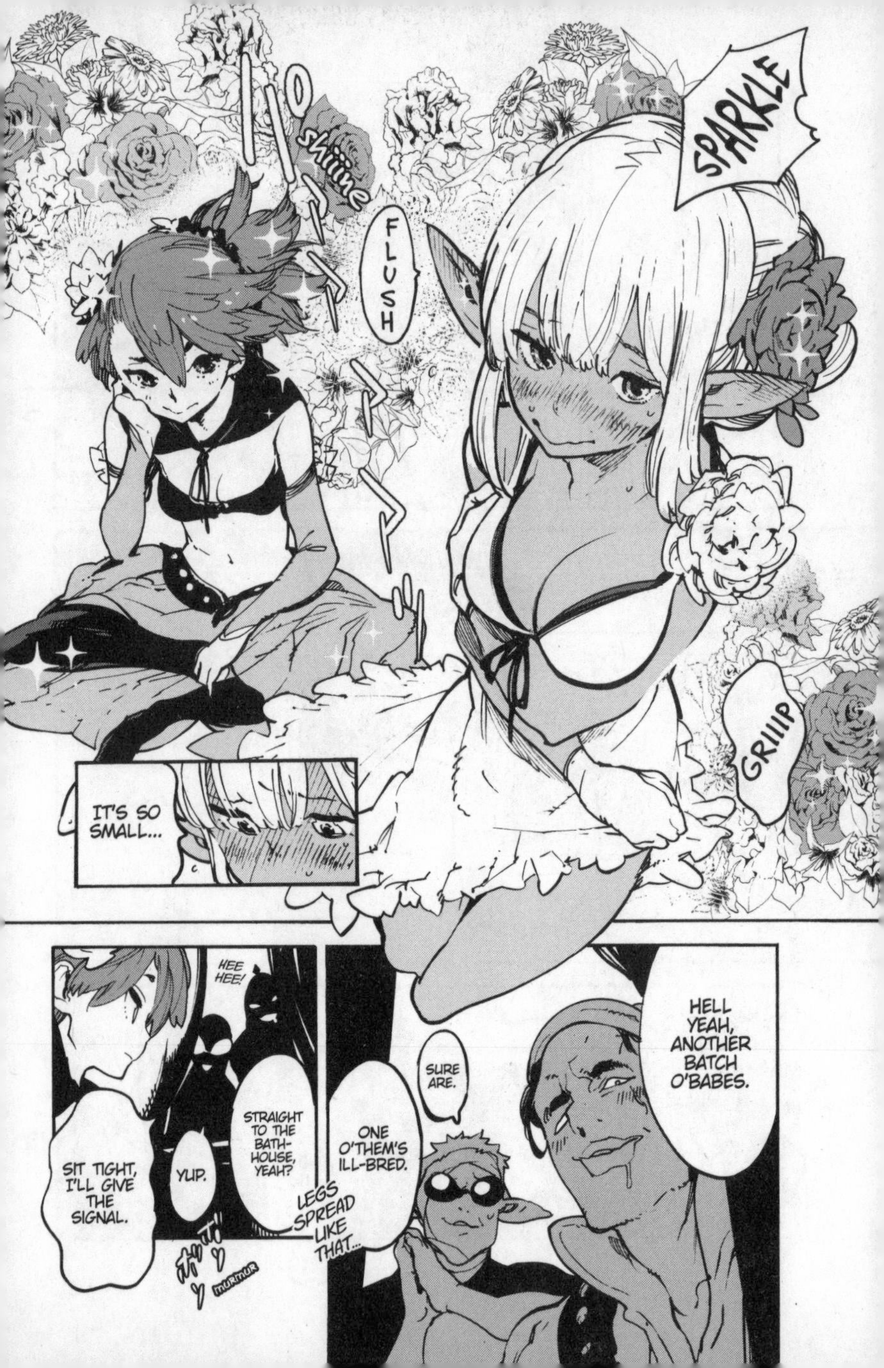
SPARKLE
shiiine
FLUSH
GRIIIP
IT'S SO SMALL...
HELL YEAH, ANOTHER BATCH O'BABES.
SURE ARE.
ONE O'THEM'S ILL-BRED.
LEGS SPREAD LIKE THAT...
HEE HEE!
STRAIGHT TO THE BATH-HOUSE, YEAH?
YUP.
SIT TIGHT, I'LL GIVE THE SIGNAL.
murmur

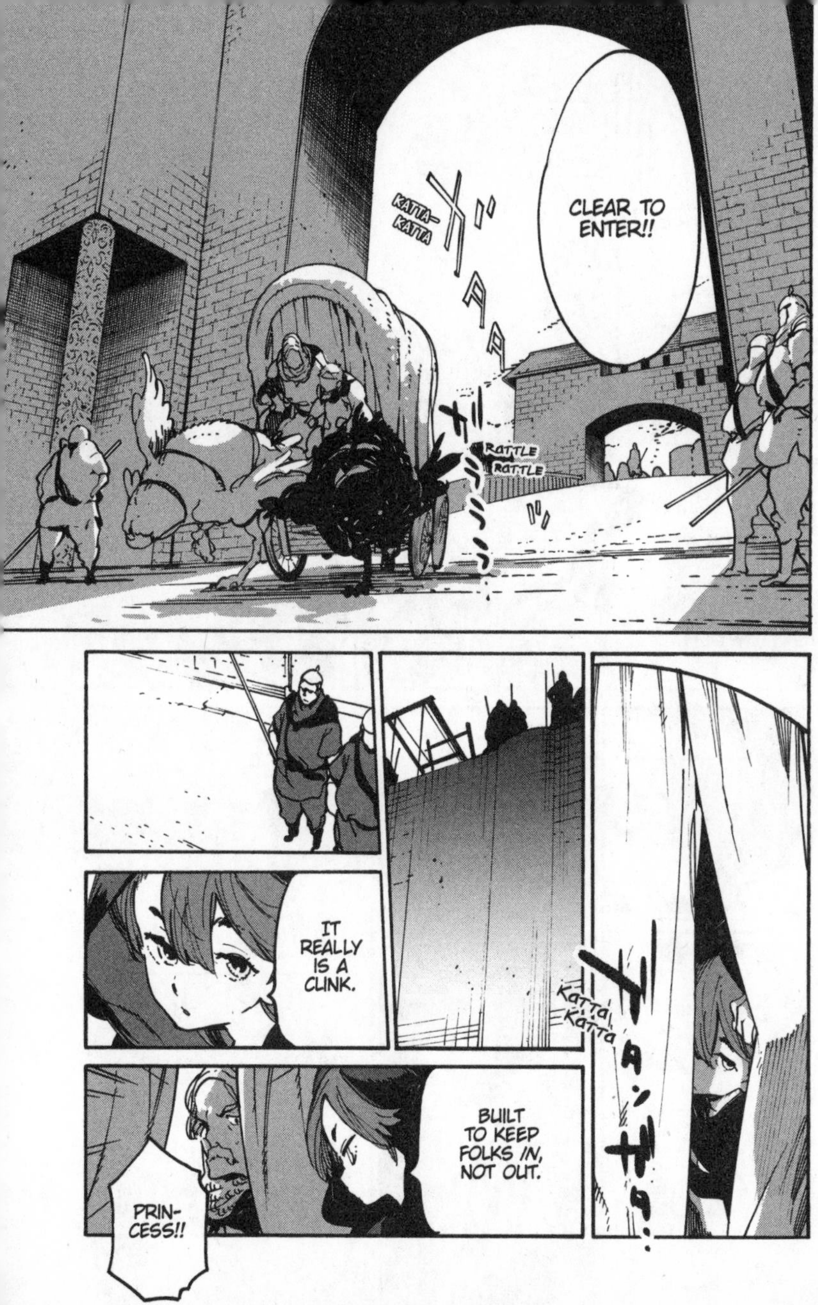
CLEAR TO ENTER!!
KATTA-KATTA
RATTLE RATTLE
Katta Katta
IT REALLY IS A CLINK.
BUILT TO KEEP FOLKS *IN*, NOT OUT.
PRIN-CESS!!

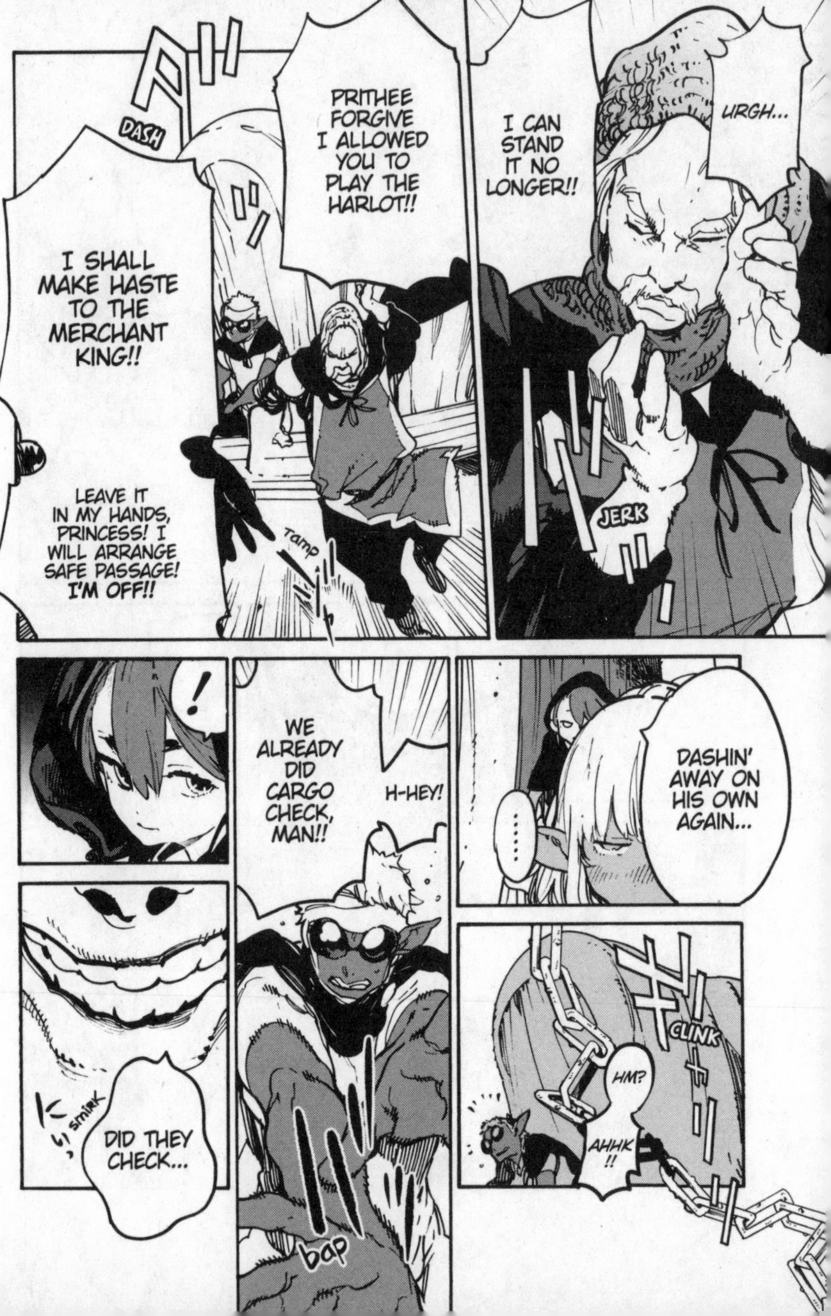
URGH...
I CAN STAND IT NO LONGER!!
JERK
PRITHEE FORGIVE I ALLOWED YOU TO PLAY THE HARLOT!!
DASH
I SHALL MAKE HASTE TO THE MERCHANT KING!!
Tamp
LEAVE IT IN MY HANDS, PRINCESS! I WILL ARRANGE SAFE PASSAGE! I'M OFF!!
DASHIN' AWAY ON HIS OWN AGAIN...
......
CLINK
HM?
AHHK!!
H-HEY!
WE ALREADY DID CARGO CHECK, MAN!!
bap
!
smirk
DID THEY CHECK...

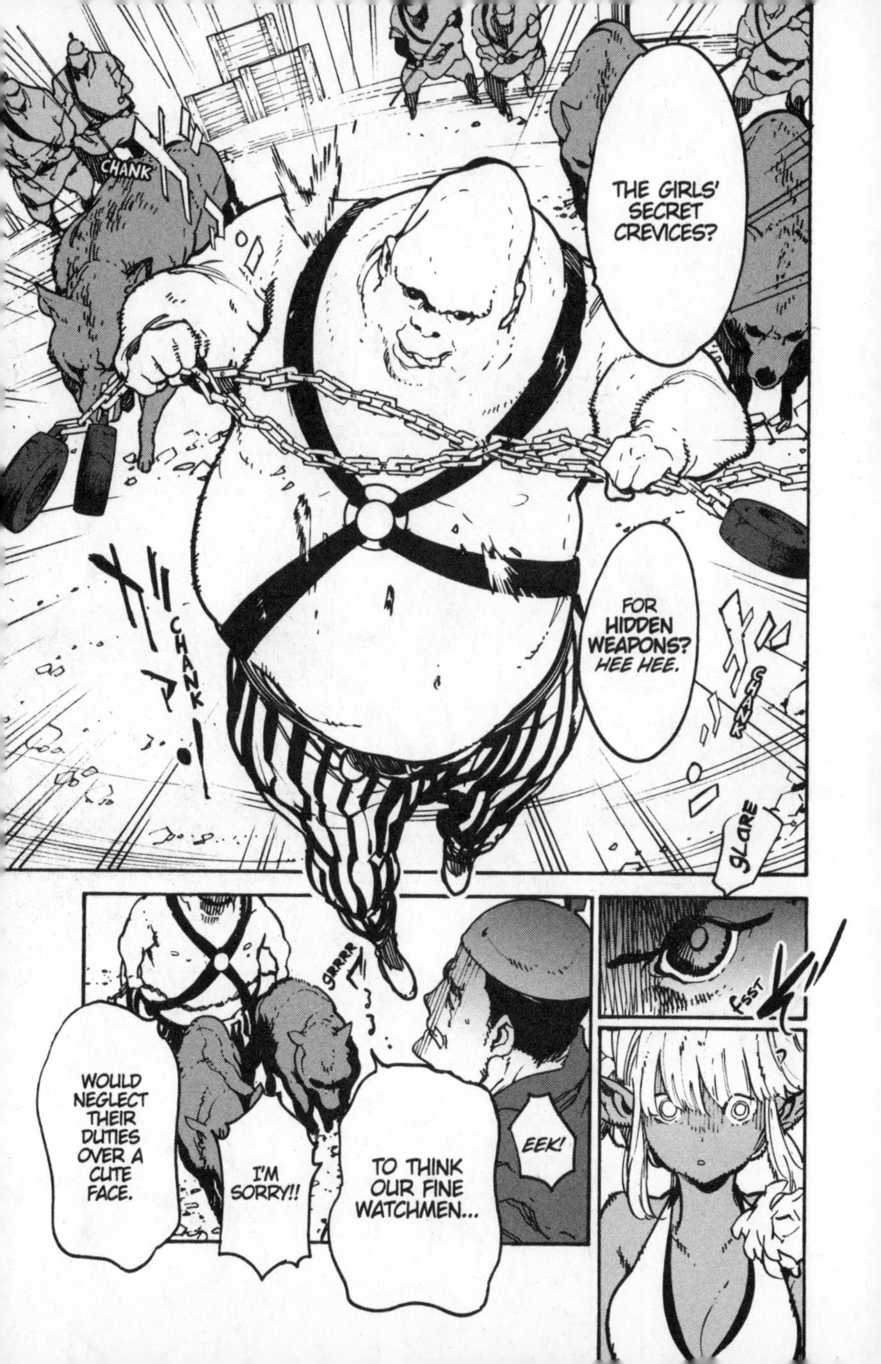
THE GIRLS' SECRET CREVICES?
CHANK
FOR HIDDEN WEAPONS? HEE HEE.
CHANK
CHANK!
GLARE
FSST
EEK!
GRRRR
TO THINK OUR FINE WATCHMEN...
I'M SORRY!!
WOULD NEGLECT THEIR DUTIES OVER A CUTE FACE.

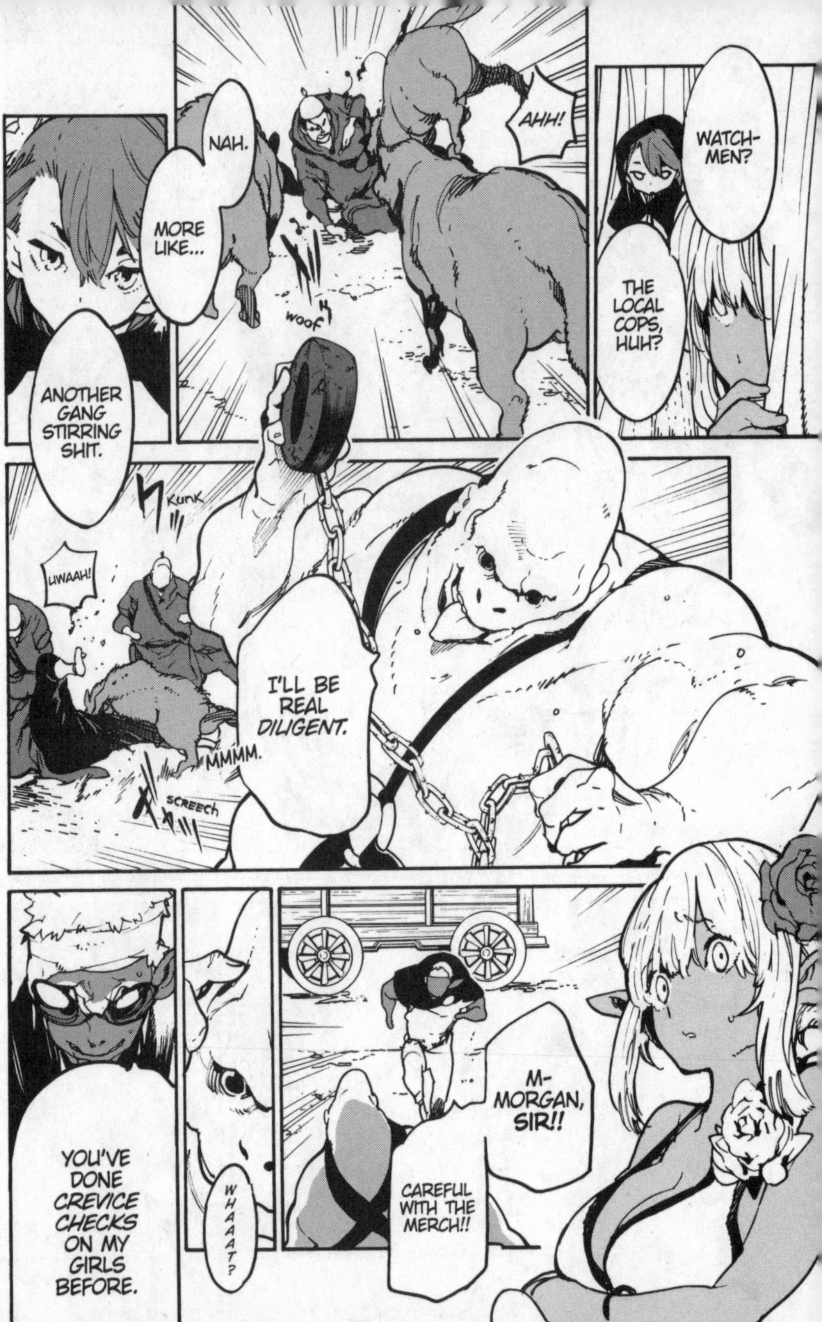
WATCH-MEN?
THE LOCAL COPS, HUH?
AHH!
woof
NAH.
MORE LIKE...
ANOTHER GANG STIRRING SHIT.
I'LL BE REAL DILIGENT.
MMMM.
Kunk
UWAAH!
SCREECH
M-MORGAN, SIR!!
CAREFUL WITH THE MERCH!!
WHAAAT?
YOU'VE DONE CREVICE CHECKS ON MY GIRLS BEFORE.

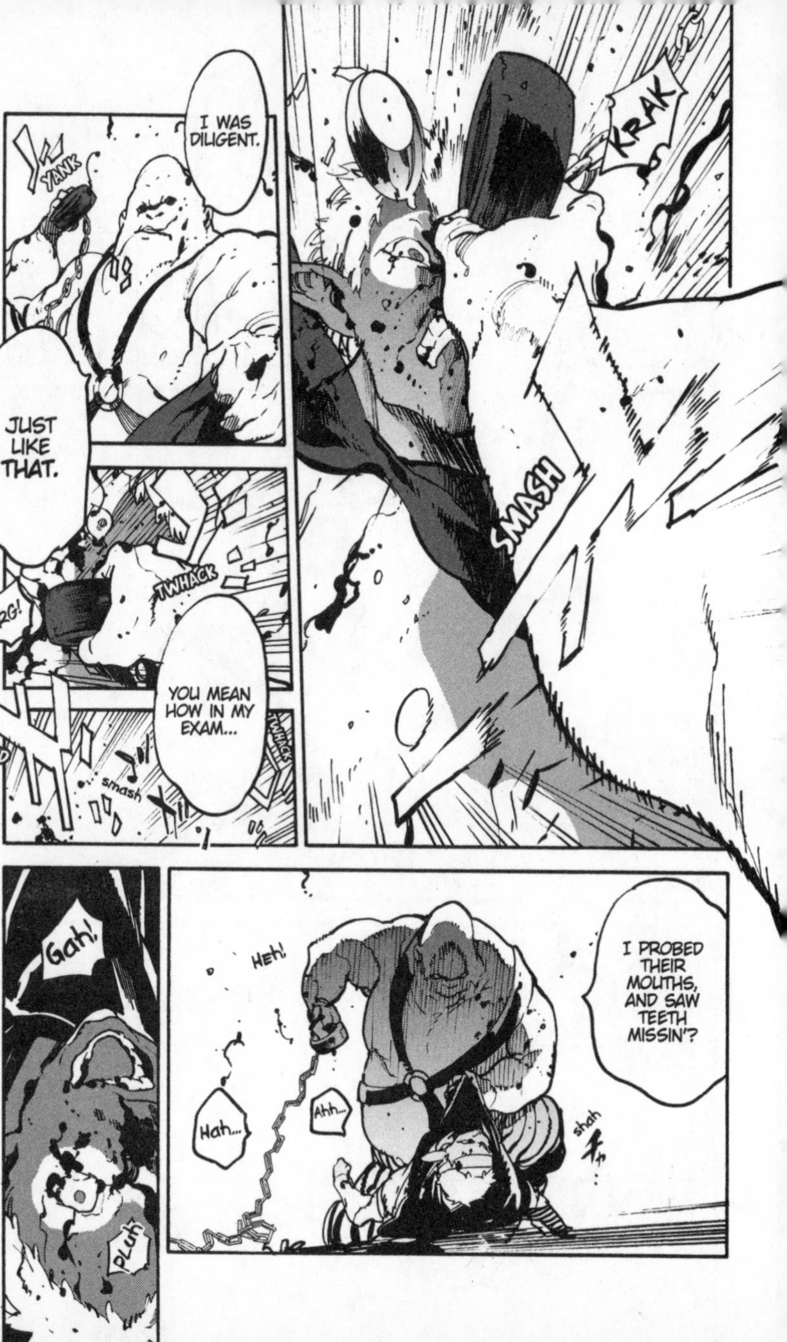
KRAK
SMASH
I WAS DILIGENT.
YANK
JUST LIKE THAT.
TWHACK
YOU MEAN HOW IN MY EXAM...
TWHACK
GRG!
GRIND
smash
I PROBED THEIR MOUTHS, AND SAW TEETH MISSIN'?
Heh!
shah
Ahh...
Hah...
Gah!
Pluh

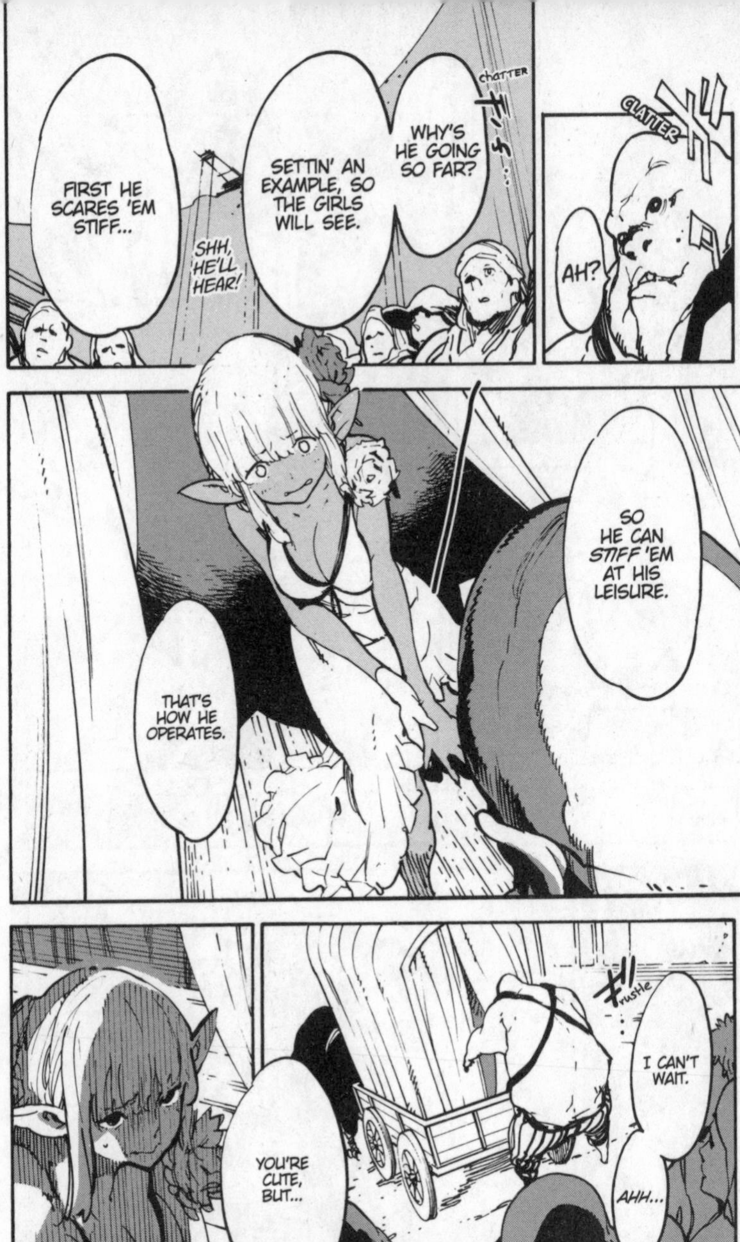
CLATTER
AH?
chatter
WHY'S HE GOING SO FAR?
SETTIN' AN EXAMPLE, SO THE GIRLS WILL SEE.
SHH, HE'LL HEAR!
FIRST HE SCARES 'EM STIFF...
SO HE CAN STIFF 'EM AT HIS LEISURE.
THAT'S HOW HE OPERATES.
rustle
I CAN'T WAIT.
AHH...
YOU'RE CUTE, BUT...

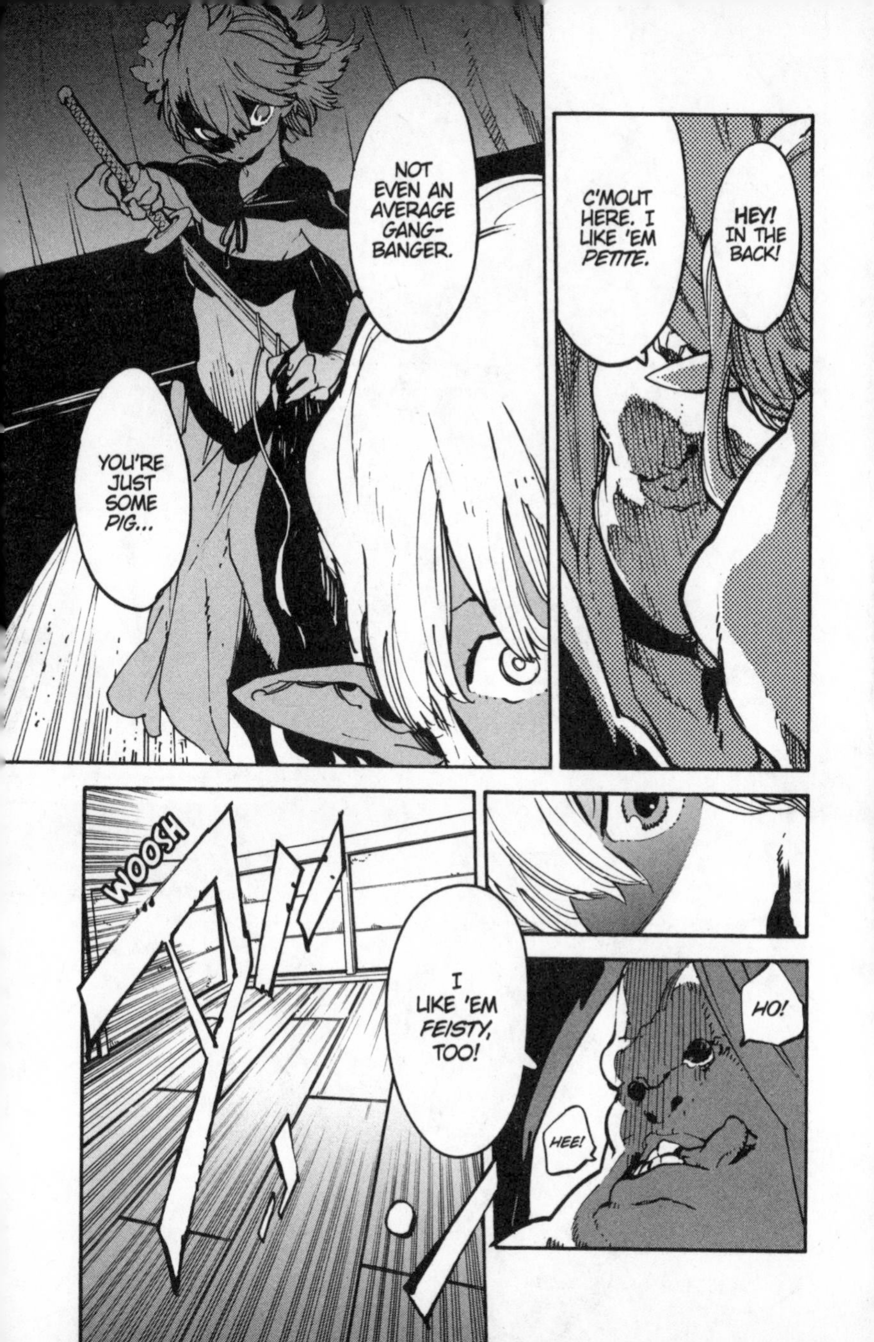
HEY! IN THE BACK!
C'MOUT HERE. I LIKE 'EM *PETITE.*
NOT EVEN AN AVERAGE GANG-BANGER.
YOU'RE JUST SOME *PIG*...
HO!
HEE!
WOOSH
I LIKE 'EM *FEISTY,* TOO!

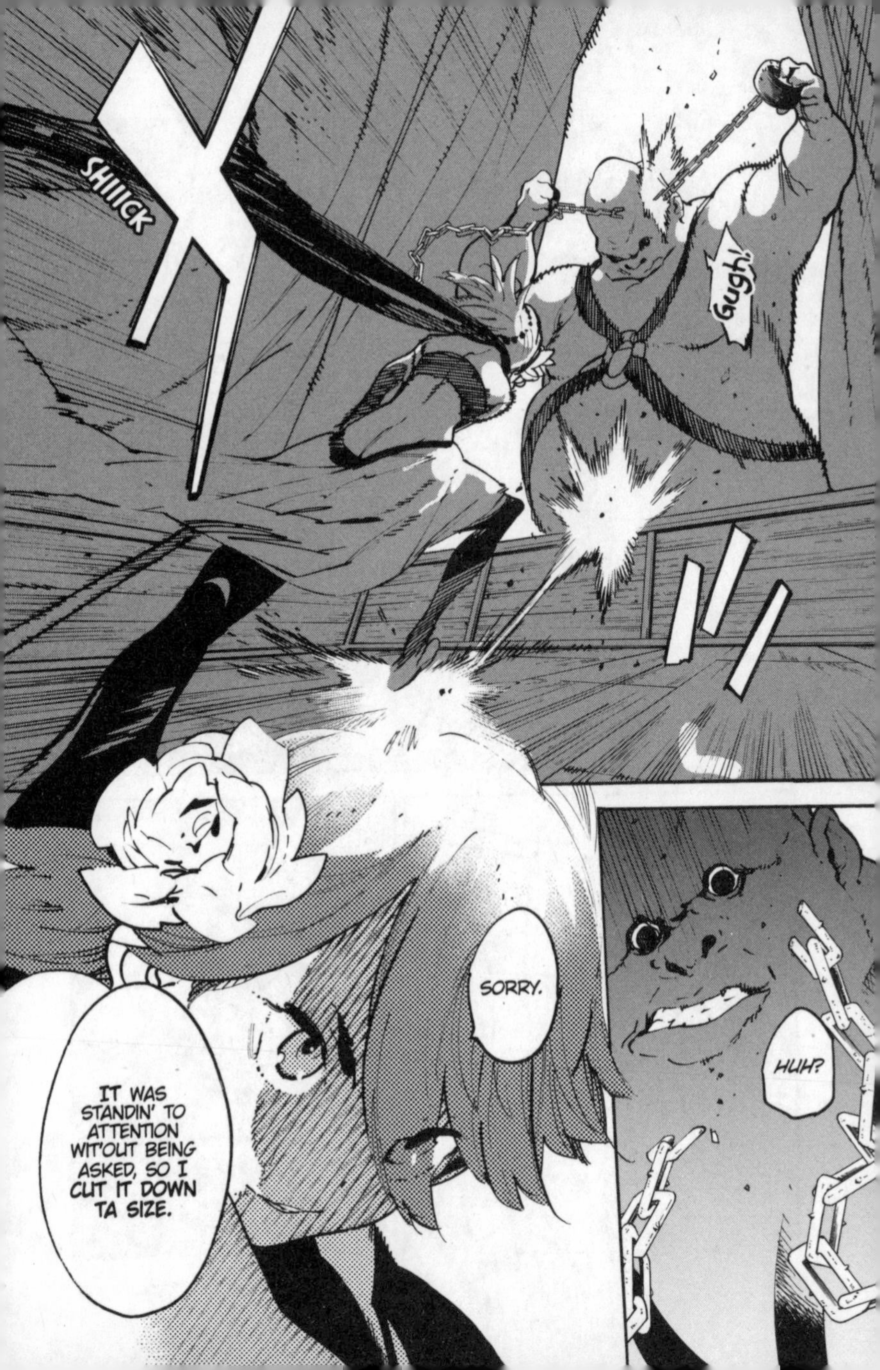
Gugh!
SHIIICK
HUH?
SORRY.
IT WAS STANDIN' TO ATTENTION WIT'OUT BEING ASKED, SO I CUT IT DOWN TA SIZE.

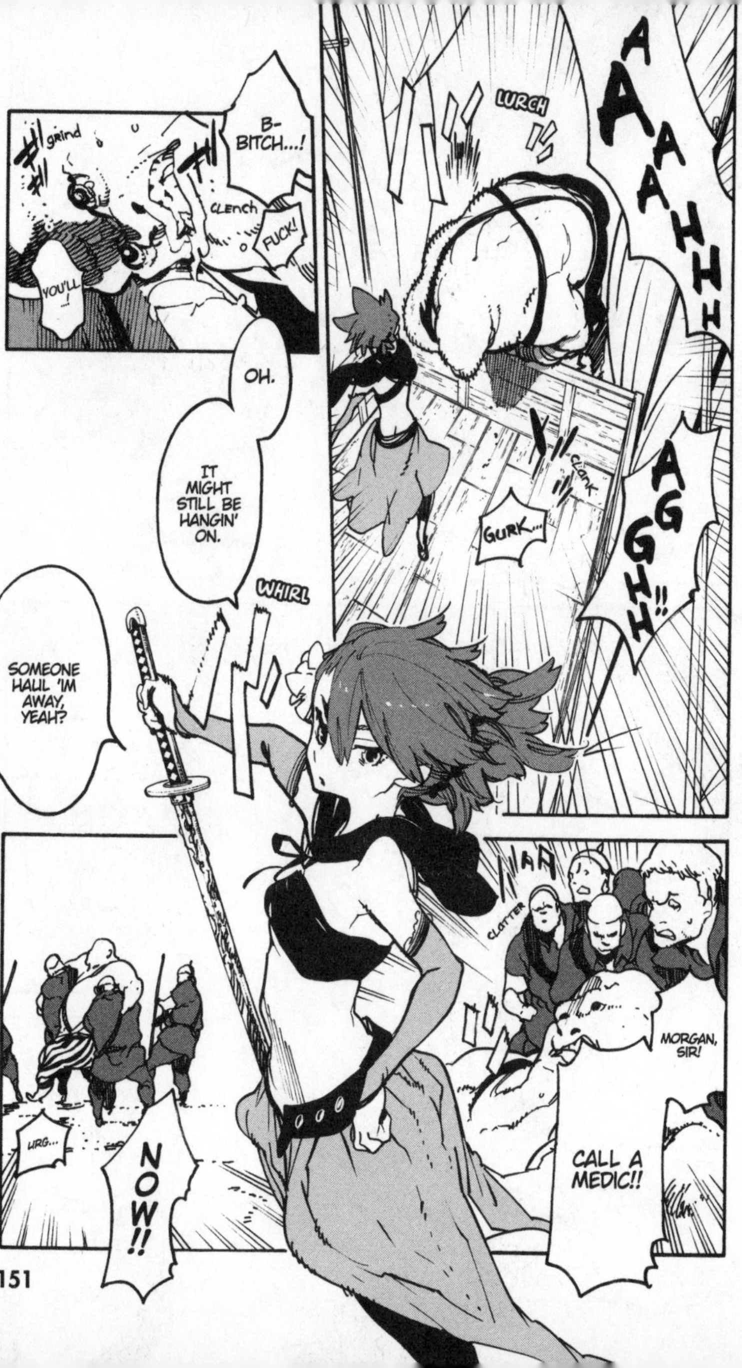
AAAHHH!
LURCH
CLANK
GURK...
AGGHH!!
grind
B-BITCH...!
CLENCH
FUCK!
YOU'LL...!
OH.
IT MIGHT STILL BE HANGIN' ON.
WHIRL
SOMEONE HAUL 'IM AWAY, YEAH?
AA
CLATTER
MORGAN, SIR!
CALL A MEDIC!!
URG...
NOW!!

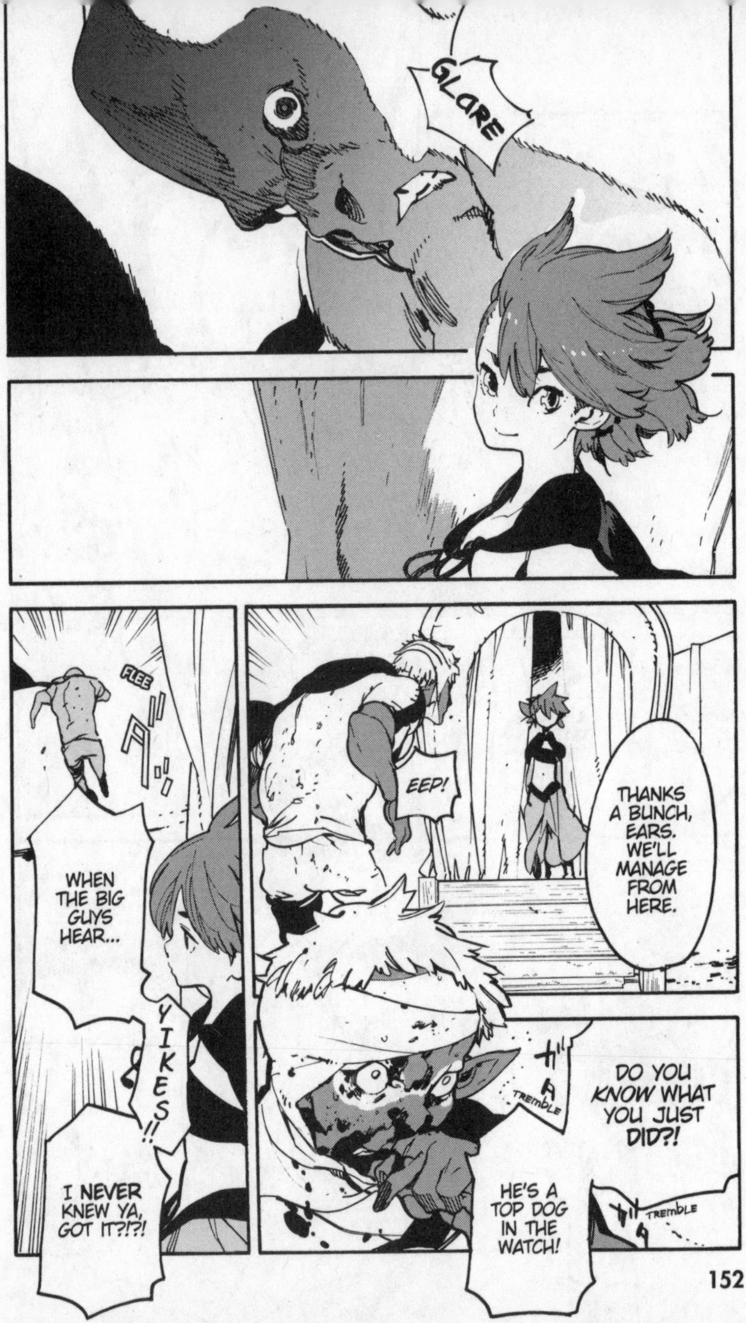
GLARE
THANKS A BUNCH, EARS. WE'LL MANAGE FROM HERE.
EEP!
DO YOU KNOW WHAT YOU JUST DID?!
TREMBLE
TREMBLE
HE'S A TOP DOG IN THE WATCH!
FLEE
WHEN THE BIG GUYS HEAR...
YIKES!!
I NEVER KNEW YA, GOT IT?!?!

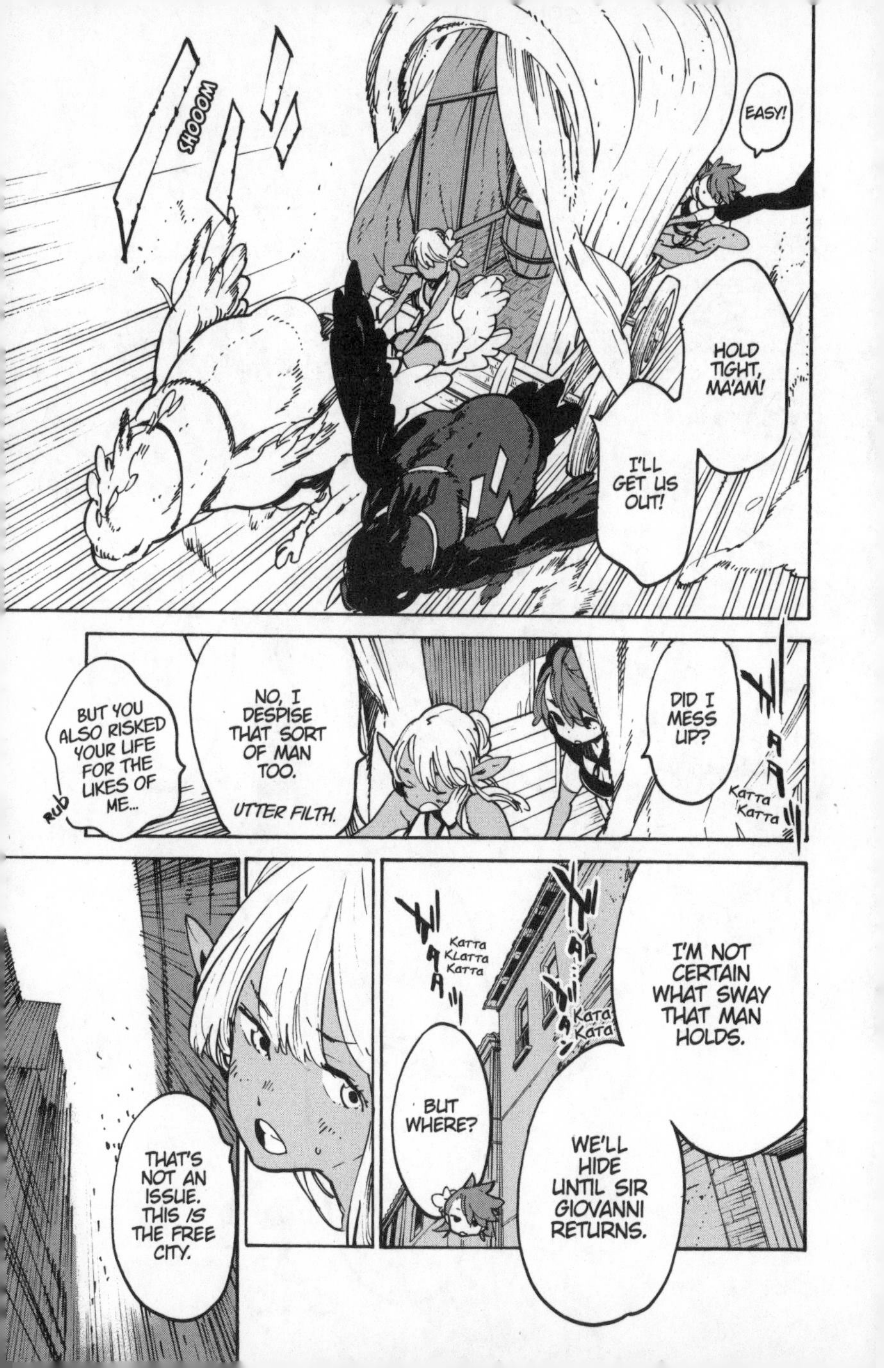
EASY!
HOLD TIGHT, MA'AM!
I'LL GET US OUT!
SHOOOM
Katta Katta
DID I MESS UP?
NO, I DESPISE THAT SORT OF MAN TOO.
UTTER FILTH.
BUT YOU ALSO RISKED YOUR LIFE FOR THE LIKES OF ME...
RUB
I'M NOT CERTAIN WHAT SWAY THAT MAN HOLDS.
WE'LL HIDE UNTIL SIR GIOVANNI RETURNS.
Kata Kata
BUT WHERE?
Katta Klatta Katta
THAT'S NOT AN ISSUE. THIS IS THE FREE CITY.

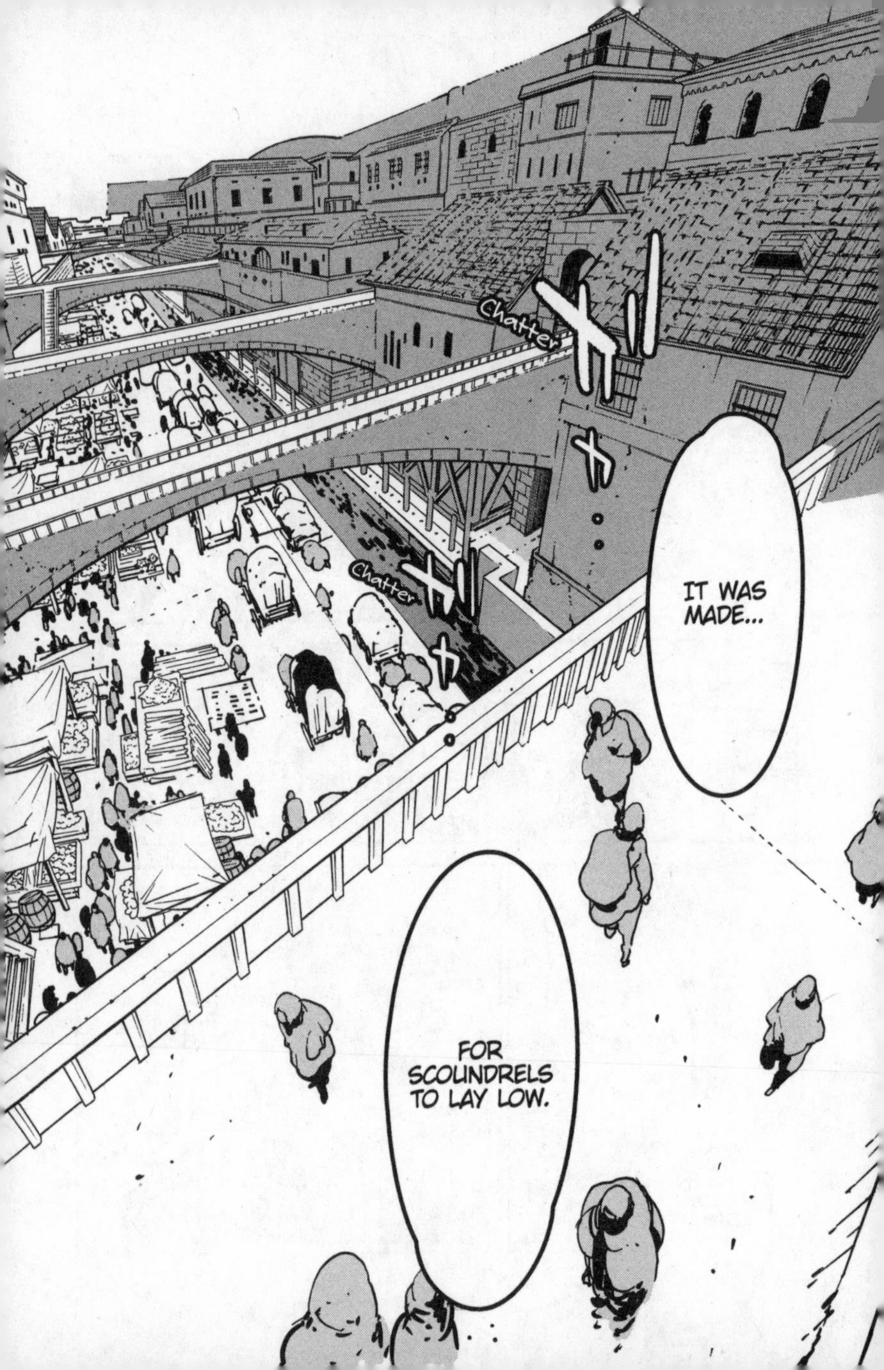
Chatter
Chatter
IT WAS MADE...
FOR SCOUNDRELS TO LAY LOW.

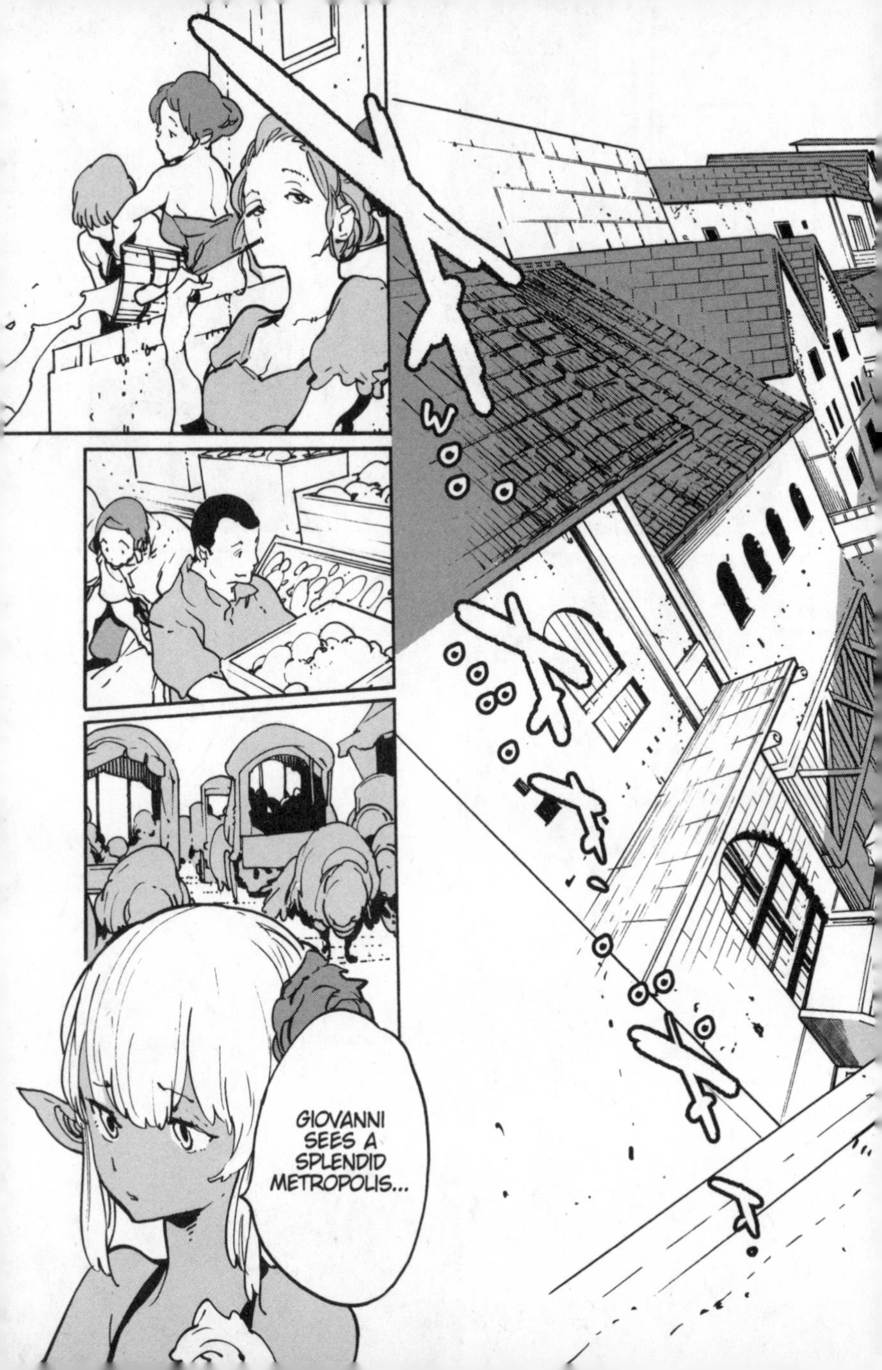
GIOVANNI SEES A SPLENDID METROPOLIS...

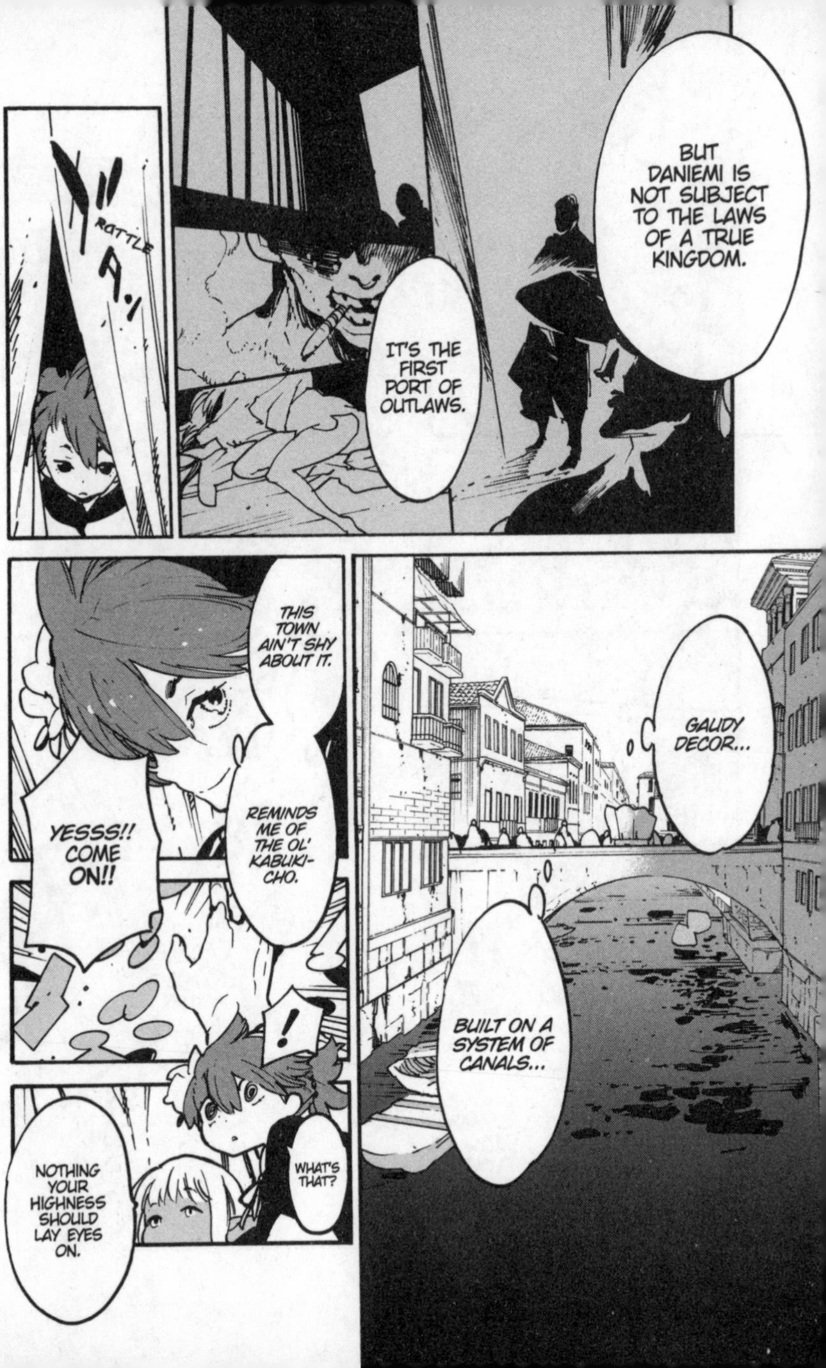
BUT DANIEMI IS NOT SUBJECT TO THE LAWS OF A TRUE KINGDOM.
IT'S THE FIRST PORT OF OUTLAWS.
RATTLE
GAUDY DECOR...
BUILT ON A SYSTEM OF CANALS...
THIS TOWN AIN'T SHY ABOUT IT.
REMINDS ME OF THE OL' KABUKI-CHO.
YESSS!! COME ON!!
!
WHAT'S THAT?
NOTHING YOUR HIGHNESS SHOULD LAY EYES ON.

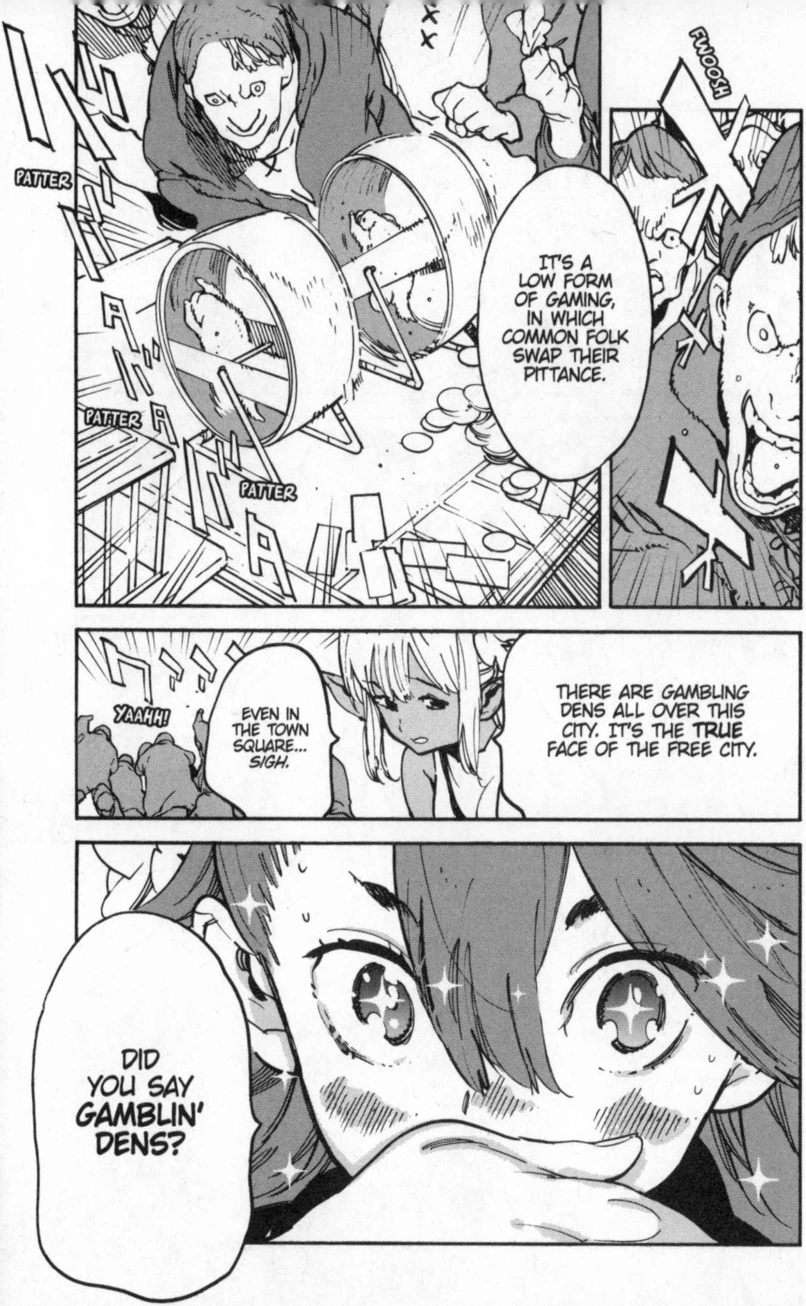
FWOOSH
IT'S A LOW FORM OF GAMING, IN WHICH COMMON FOLK SWAP THEIR PITTANCE.
PATTER
PATTER
PATTER
THERE ARE GAMBLING DENS ALL OVER THIS CITY. IT'S THE TRUE FACE OF THE FREE CITY.
EVEN IN THE TOWN SQUARE... SIGH.
YAAHH!
DID YOU SAY GAMBLIN' DENS?

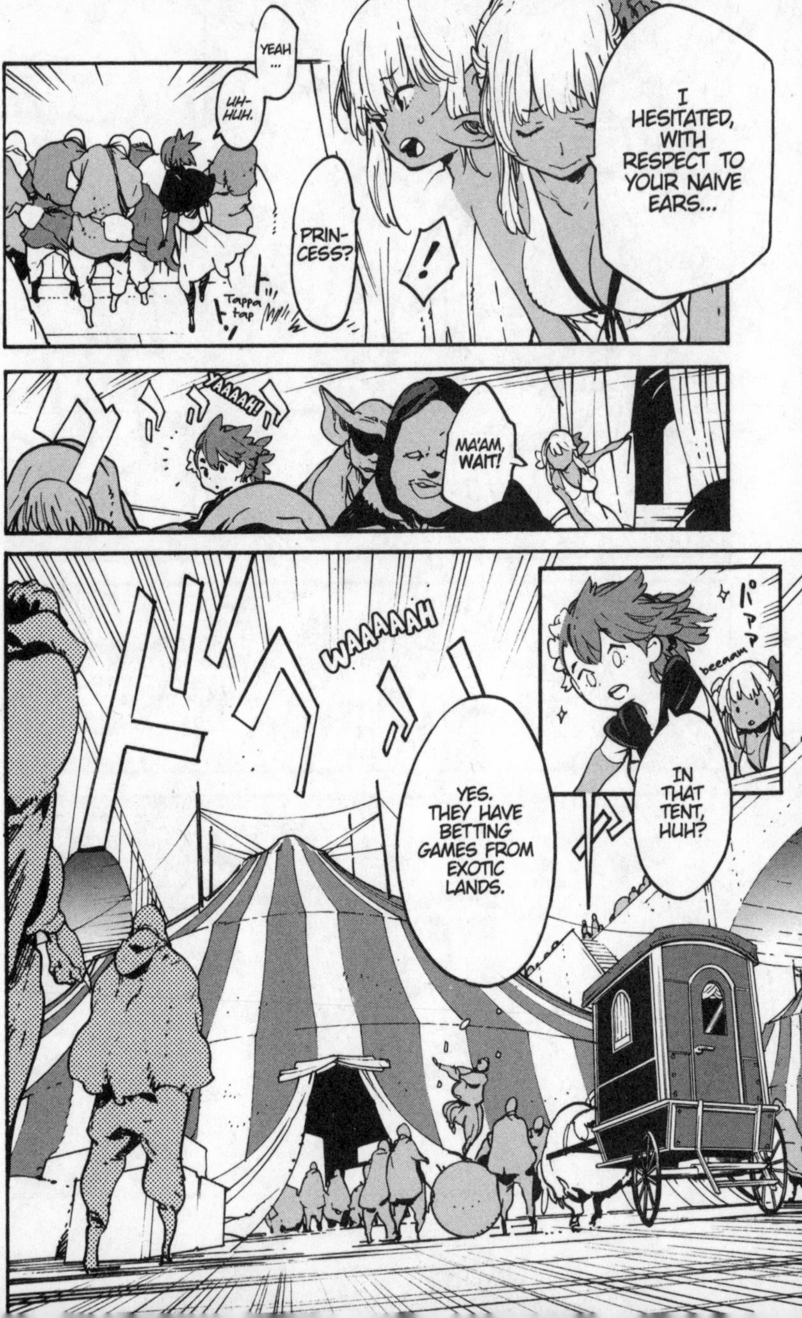
I HESITATED, WITH RESPECT TO YOUR NAIVE EARS...
!
PRINCESS?
YEAH ...
UH-HUH.
Tappa tap
MA'AM, WAIT!
YAAAAH!
beeaam
IN THAT TENT, HUH?
YES. THEY HAVE BETTING GAMES FROM EXOTIC LANDS.
WAAAAAH

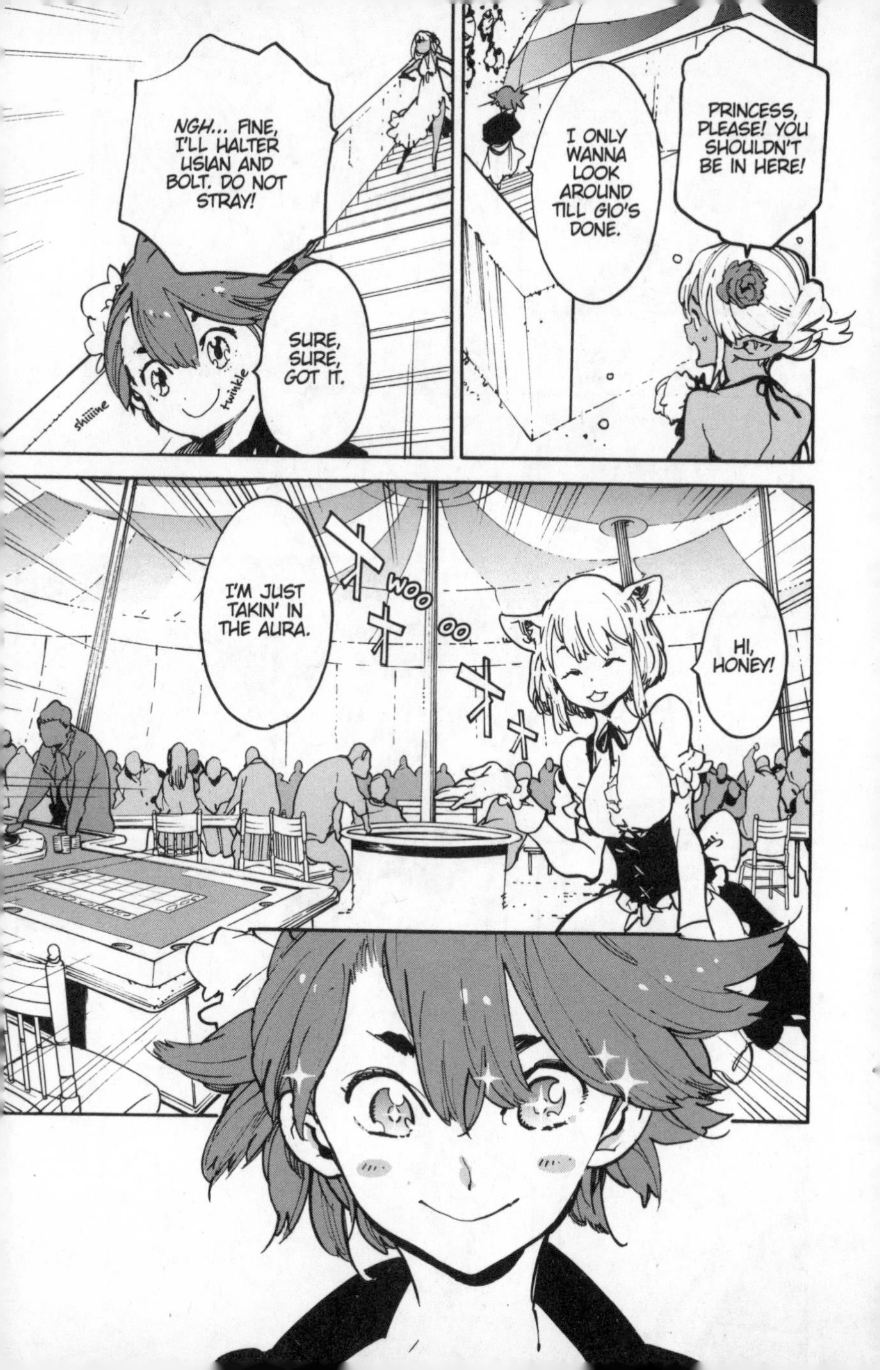
PRINCESS, PLEASE! YOU SHOULDN'T BE IN HERE!
I ONLY WANNA LOOK AROUND TILL GIO'S DONE.
NGH... FINE, I'LL HALTER USIAN AND BOLT. DO NOT STRAY!
SURE, SURE, GOT IT.
twinkle
shiiiine
HI, HONEY!
WOO OO
I'M JUST TAKIN' IN THE AURA.

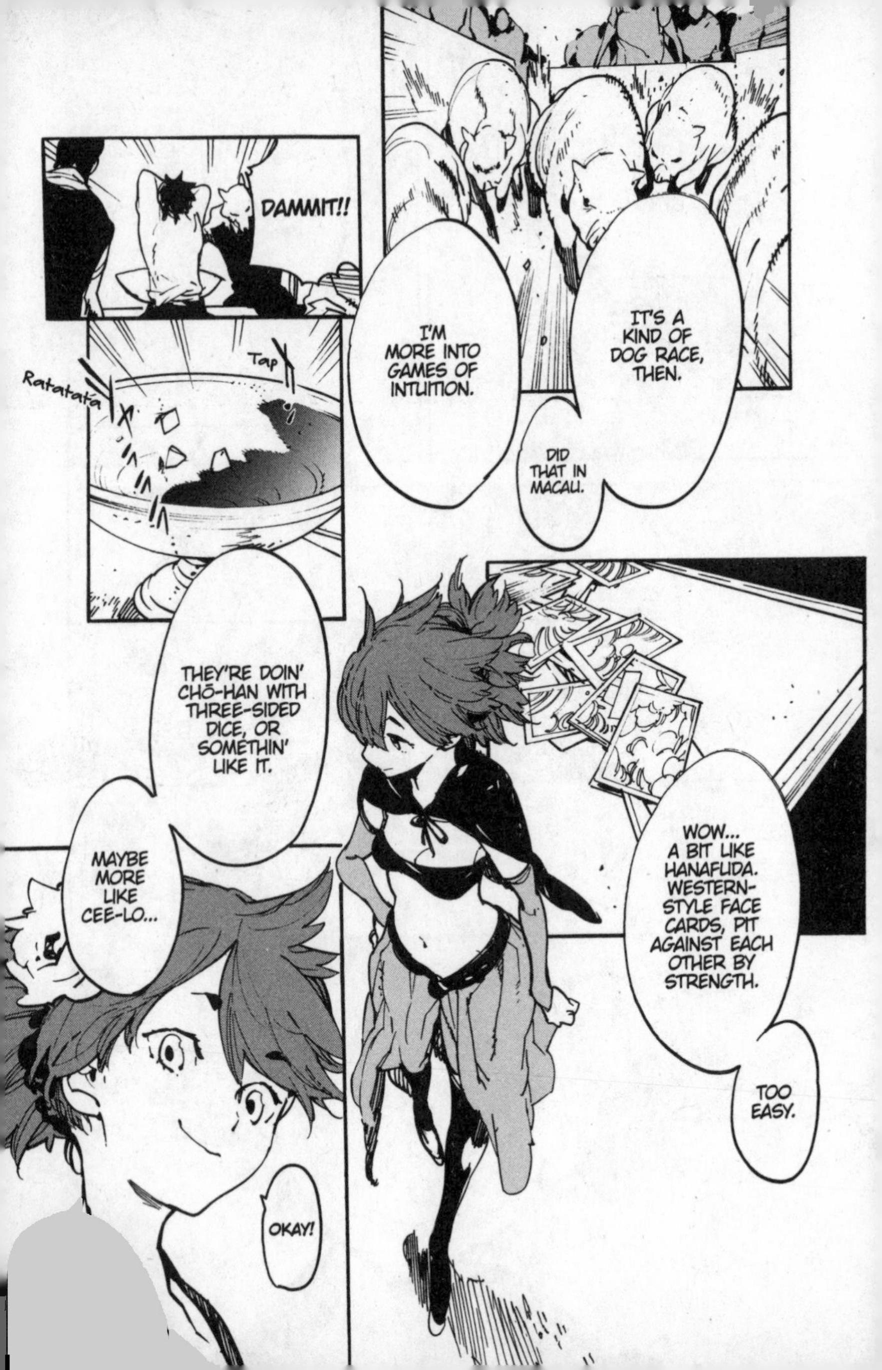
IT'S A KIND OF DOG RACE, THEN.
DID THAT IN MACAU.
I'M MORE INTO GAMES OF INTUITION.
DAMMIT!!
Tap
Ratatatá
THEY'RE DOIN' CHŌ-HAN WITH THREE-SIDED DICE, OR SOMETHIN' LIKE IT.
MAYBE MORE LIKE CEE-LO...
WOW... A BIT LIKE HANAFUDA. WESTERN-STYLE FACE CARDS, PIT AGAINST EACH OTHER BY STRENGTH.
TOO EASY.
OKAY!

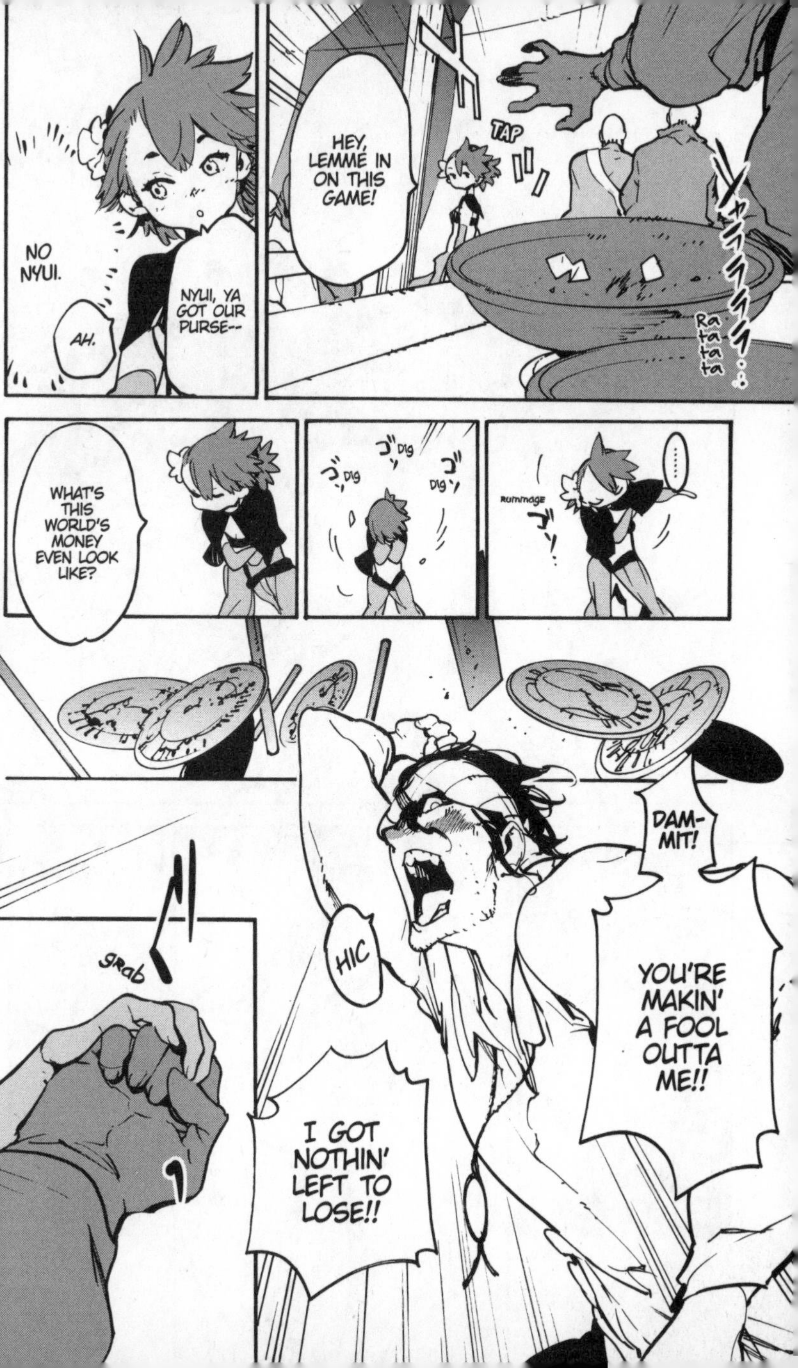
TAP
Ra ta ta ta
HEY, LEMME IN ON THIS GAME!
NYUI, YA GOT OUR PURSE--
NO NYUI.
AH.
......
rummage
Dig
Dig
Dig
WHAT'S THIS WORLD'S MONEY EVEN LOOK LIKE?
DAM-MIT!
YOU'RE MAKIN' A FOOL OUTTA ME!!
HIC
I GOT NOTHIN' LEFT TO LOSE!!
grab

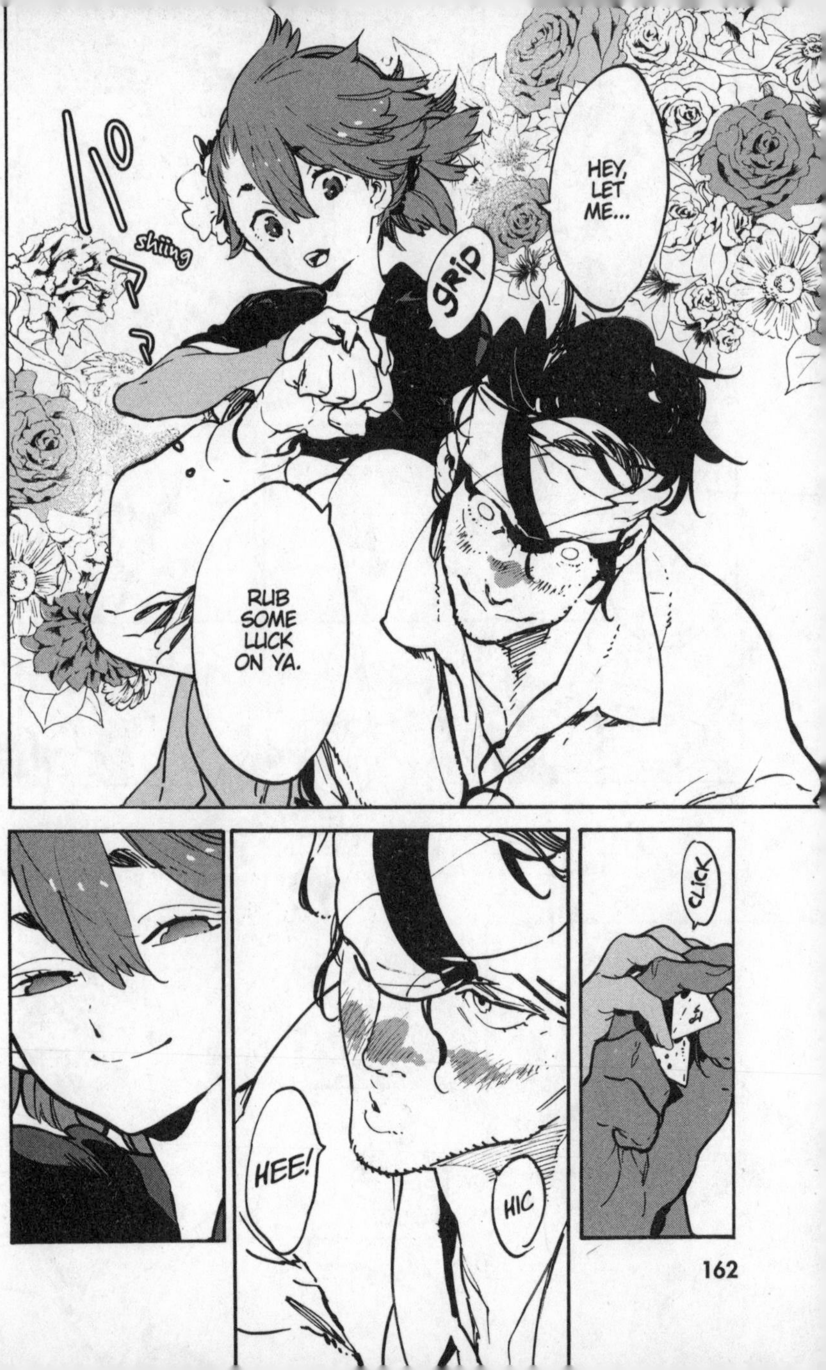
HEY, LET ME...
GRIP
shiing
RUB SOME LUCK ON YA.
CLICK
HEE!
HIC

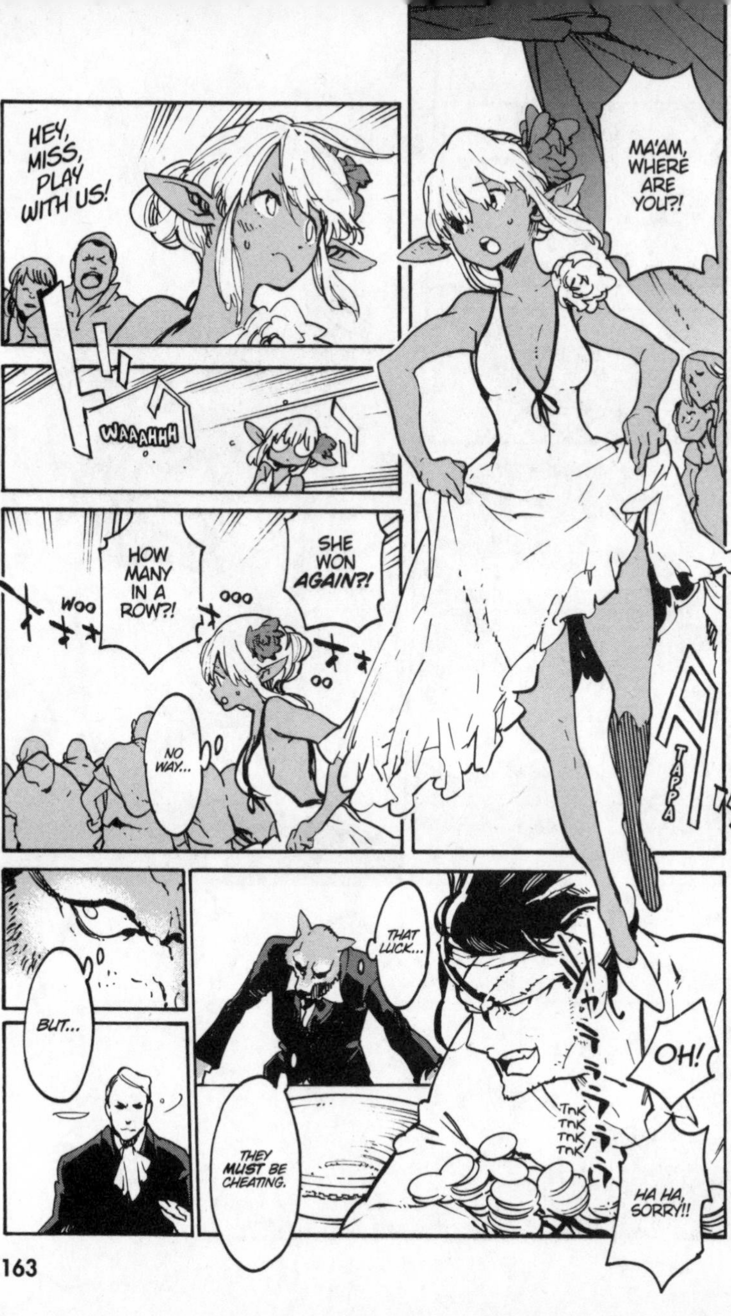
MA'AM, WHERE ARE YOU?!
TAPPA
HEY, MISS, PLAY WITH US!
WAAAHHH
SHE WON AGAIN?!
HOW MANY IN A ROW?!
WOO
NO WAY...
OH!
THAT LUCK...
TNK TNK TNK TNK
HA HA, SORRY!!
THEY MUST BE CHEATING.
BUT...

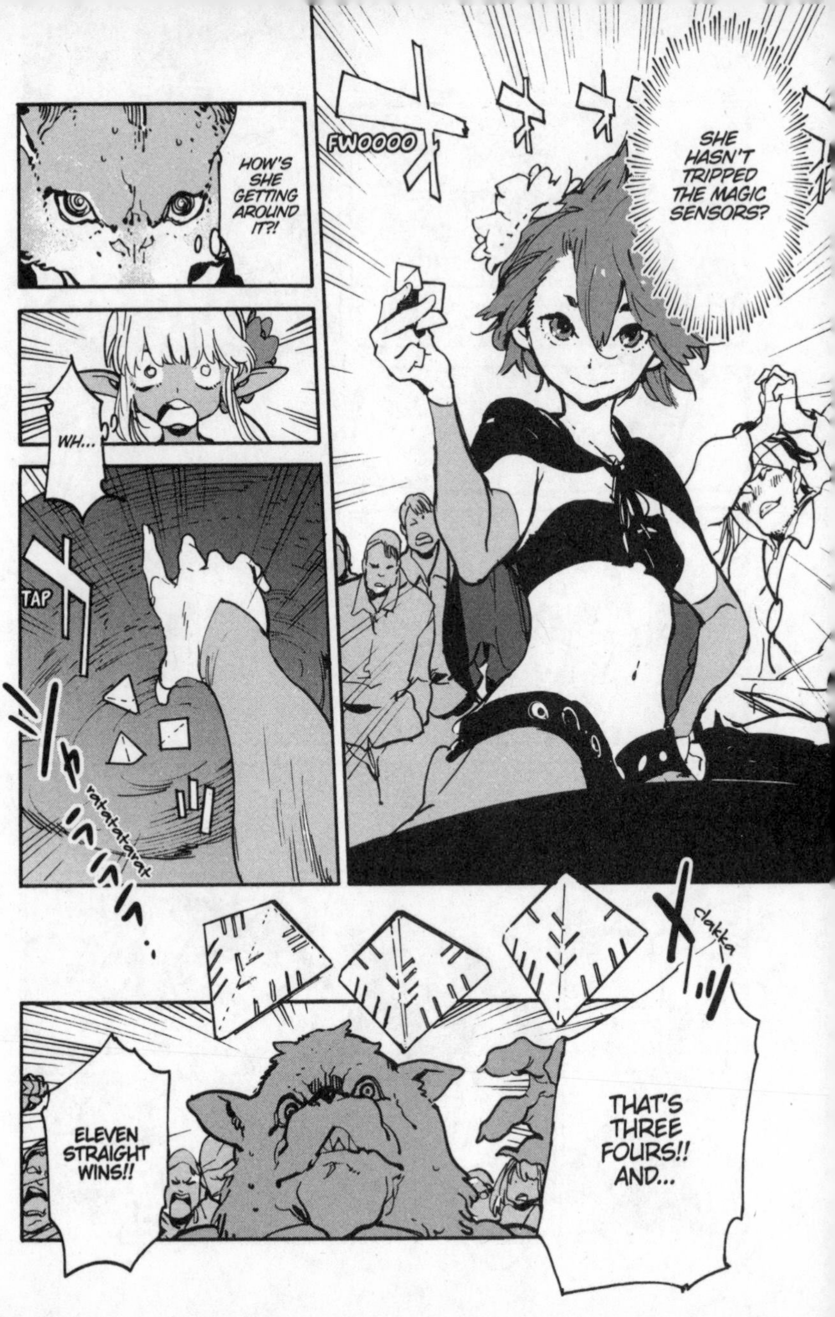
FWOOOO
SHE HASN'T TRIPPED THE MAGIC SENSORS?
HOW'S SHE GETTING AROUND IT?!
WH...
TAP
ratatatarat
clakka
THAT'S THREE FOURS!! AND...
ELEVEN STRAIGHT WINS!!

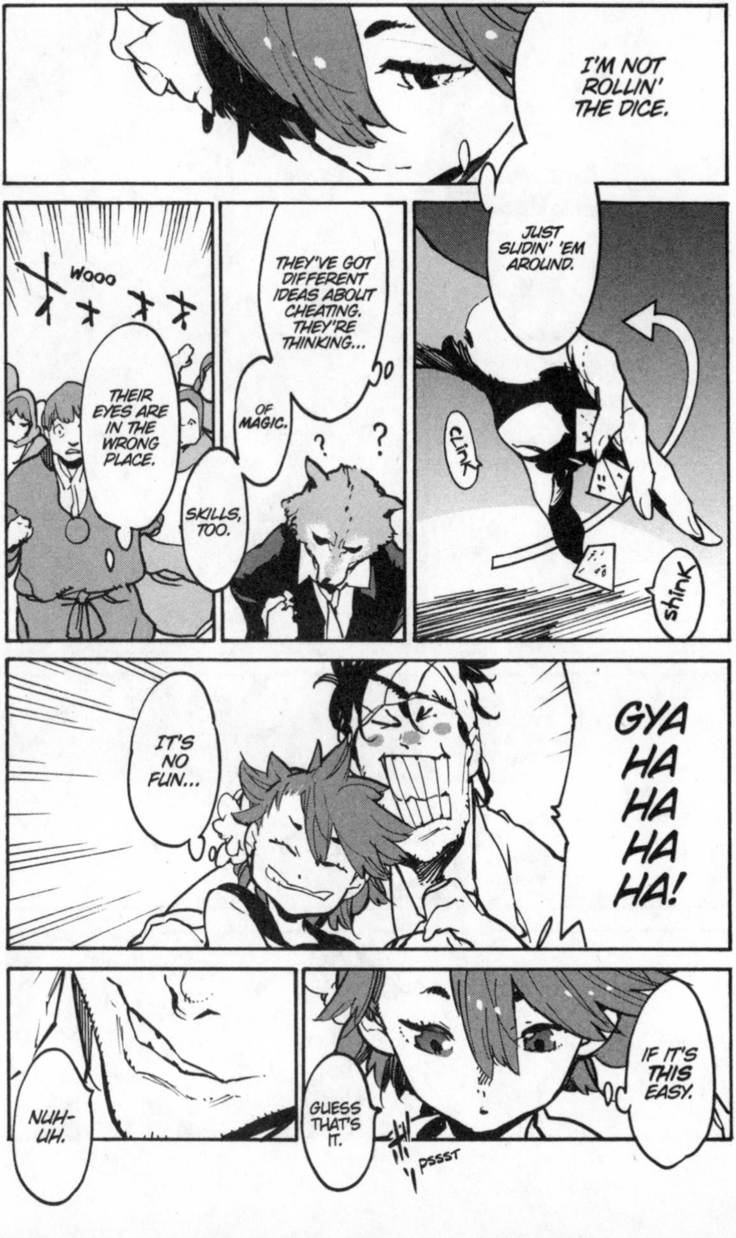
I'M NOT ROLLIN' THE DICE.
JUST SLIDIN' 'EM AROUND.
clink
shink
THEY'VE GOT DIFFERENT IDEAS ABOUT CHEATING. THEY'RE THINKING...
OF MAGIC.
SKILLS, TOO.
WOOO
THEIR EYES ARE IN THE WRONG PLACE.
GYA HA HA HA HA HA!
IT'S NO FUN...
IF IT'S THIS EASY.
GUESS THAT'S IT.
PSSST
NUH-UH.

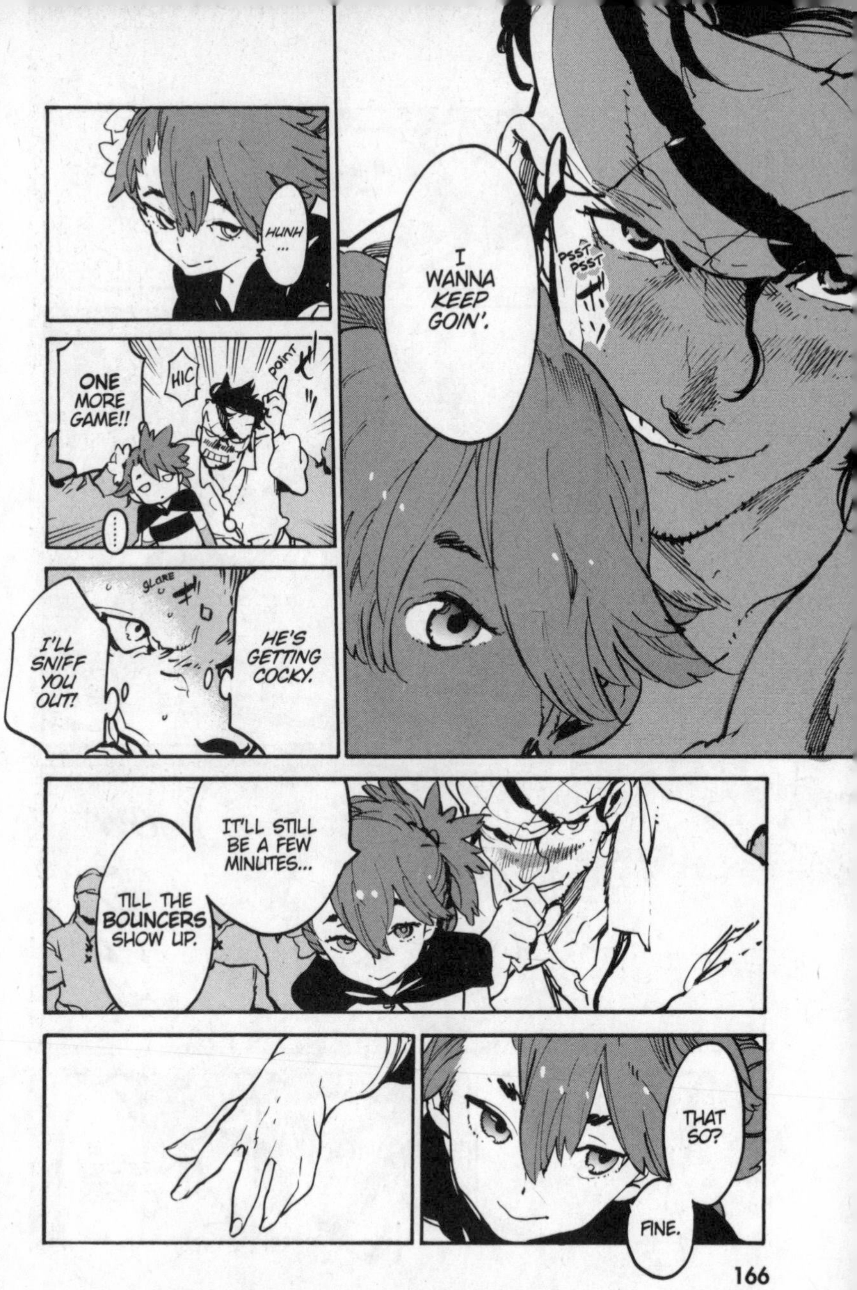
I WANNA KEEP GOIN'.
PSST PSST
HUNH...
ONE MORE GAME!!
point
HIC
...
GLARE
HE'S GETTING COCKY.
I'LL SNIFF YOU OUT!
IT'LL STILL BE A FEW MINUTES...
TILL THE BOUNCERS SHOW UP.
THAT SO?
FINE.

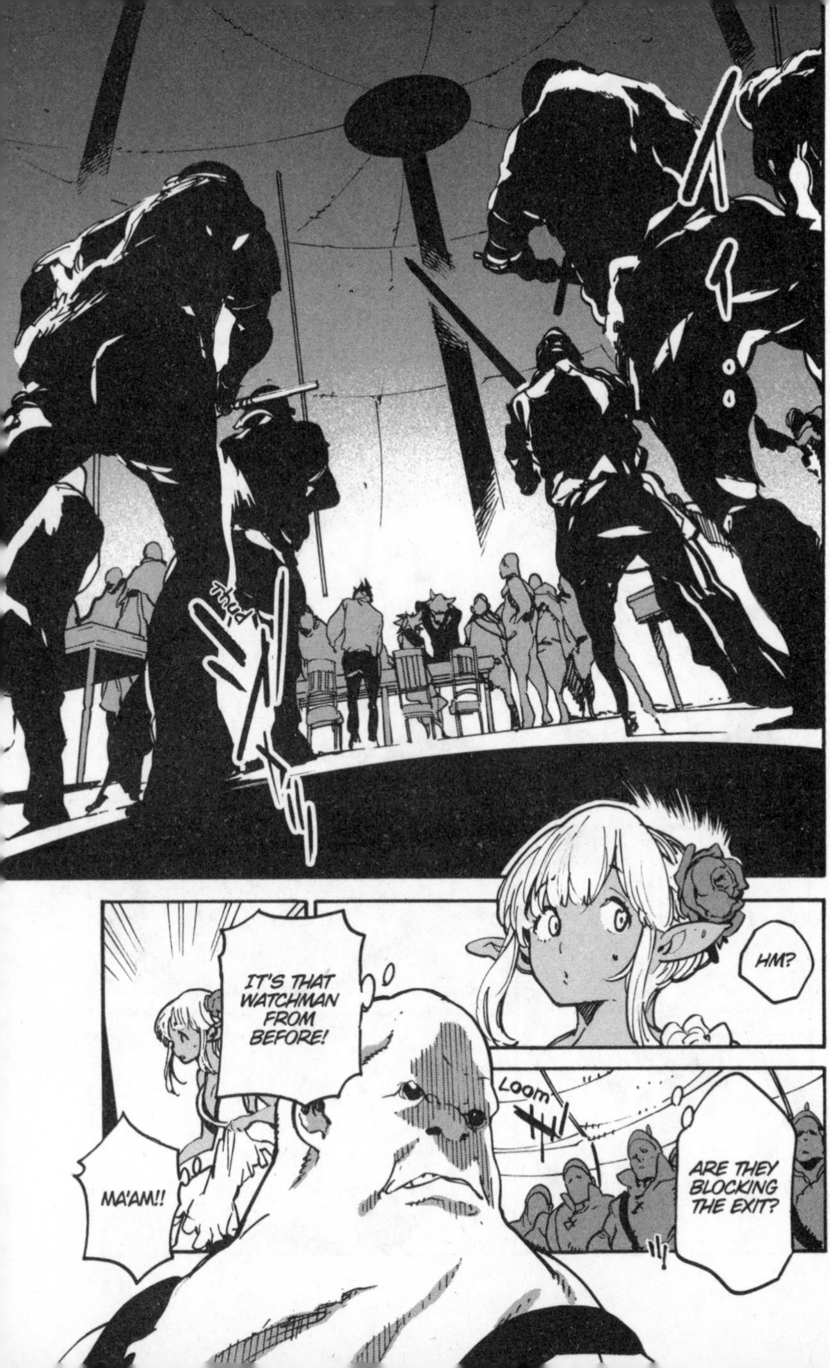
thud
HM?
Loom
ARE THEY BLOCKING THE EXIT?
IT'S THAT WATCHMAN FROM BEFORE!
MA'AM!!

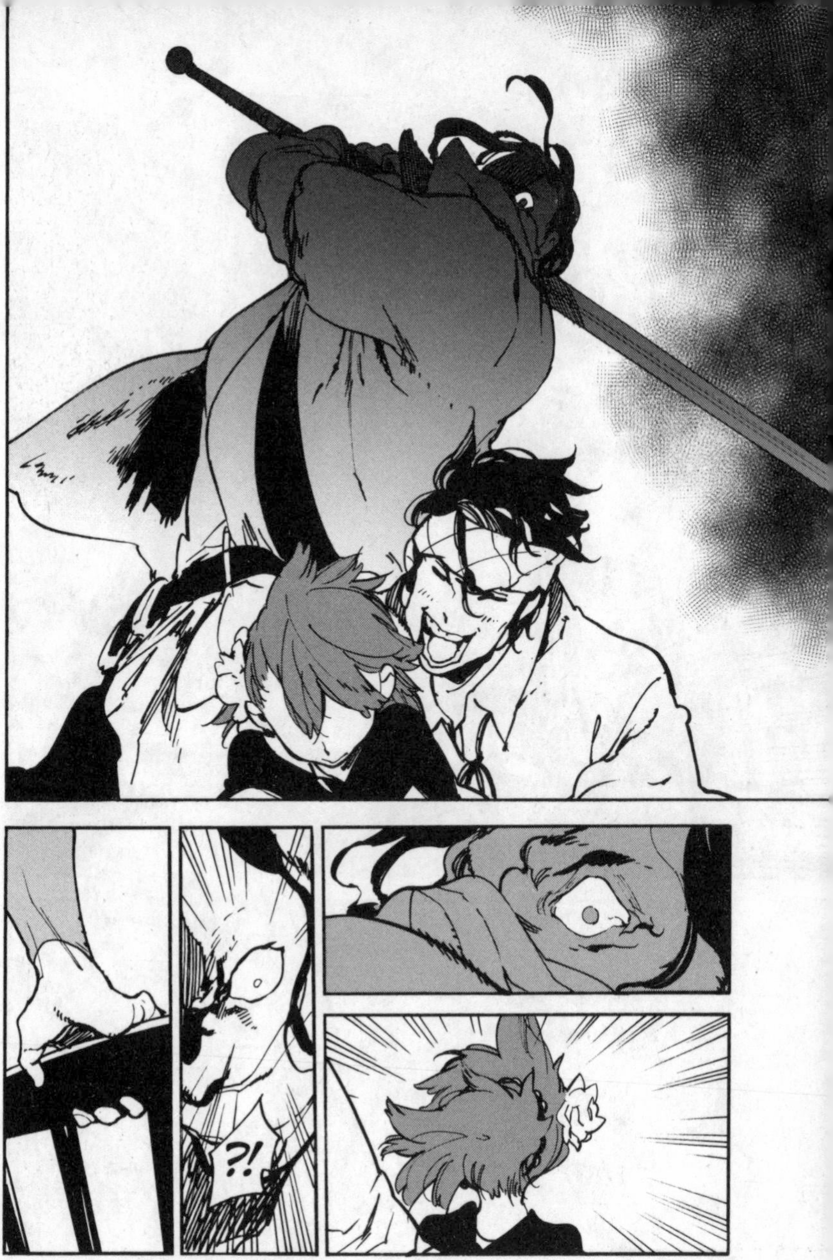
?!

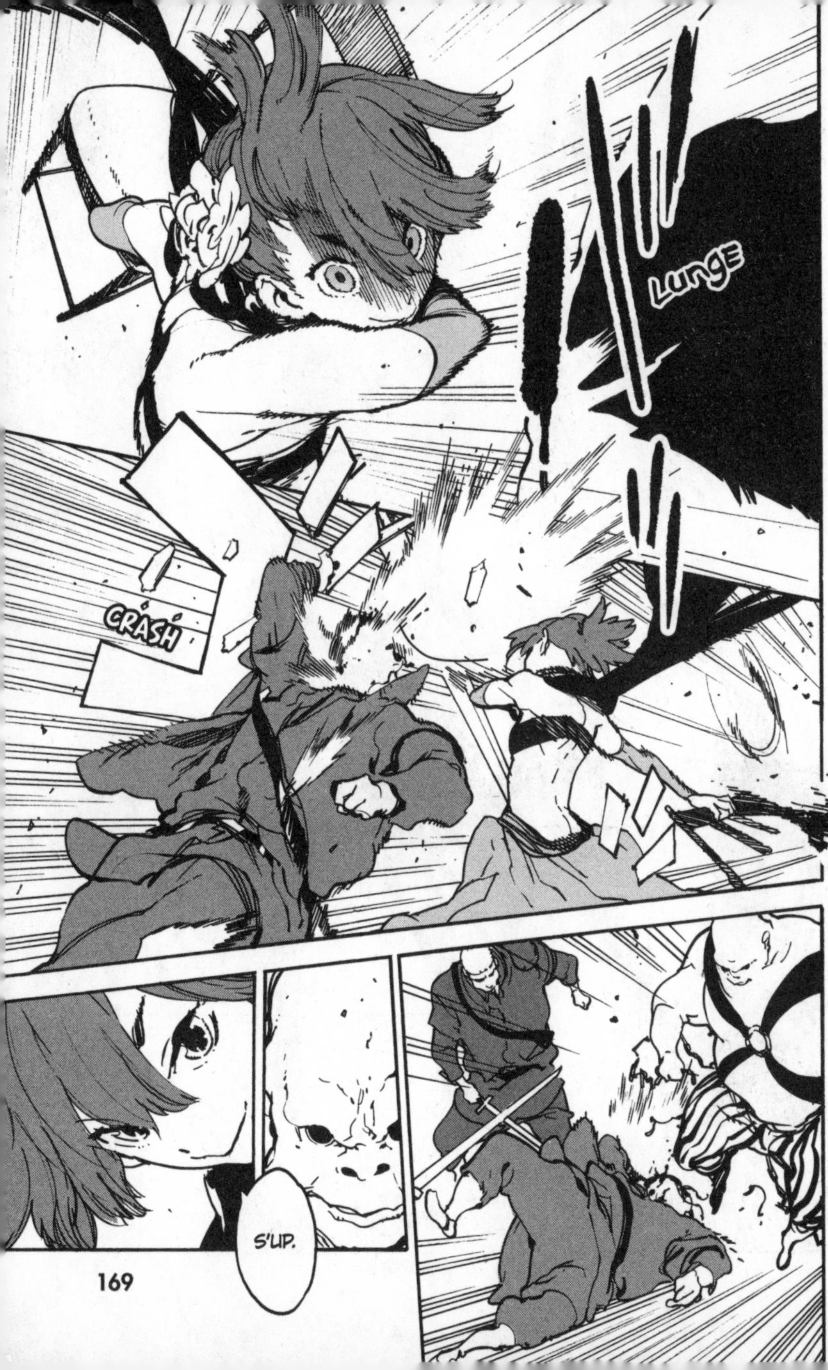
LUNGE
CRASH
S'UP.

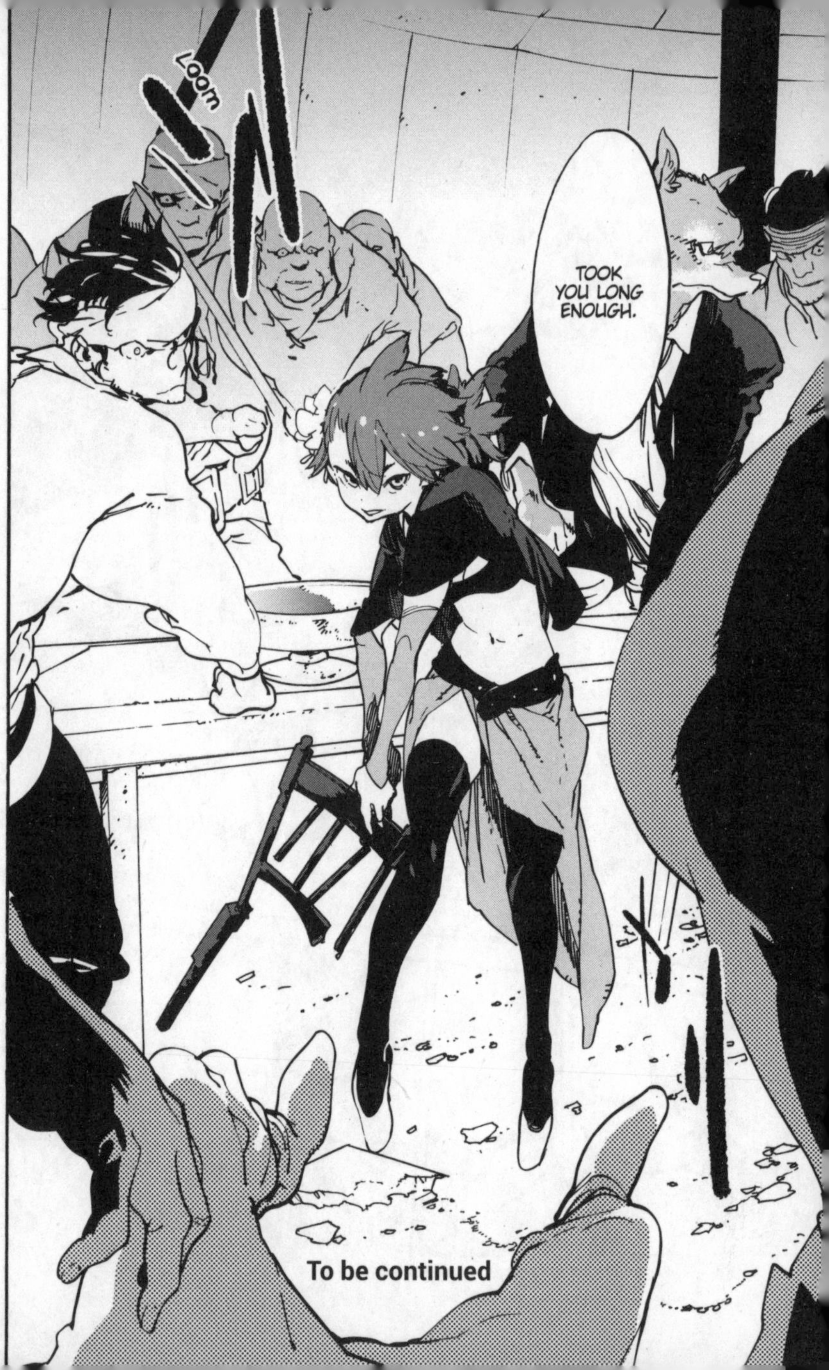
LOOM
TOOK YOU LONG ENOUGH.
To be continued

YAKUZA
REINCARNATION

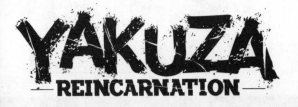

YAKUZA REINCARNATION
SPECIAL COLUMN

Takeshi Natsuhara explains the drug scene in Lûndburg!
Read this to enhance your experience with *Yakuza Reincarnation!*

What is witchin?

Witchin is a fictional drug. It's taken like cocaine, but the effect on the psyche is closer to PCP. It negates fear and pain, and so can embolden some pretty extreme stuff. A wilder beast than your average stimulant, for sure.

The Japanese have a long history with stimulants. The first boom was after the war, when soldiers came home addicted to Philopon, called "cat's eye pills," because it enhanced their night vision. The methamphetamine spread to epidemic levels. Even respectable members of society, such as novelist and essayist Ango Sakaguchi, became frequent users. Naturally, it turned into a giant money tree for the yakuza the moment it was banned.

The second boom came during the rapid growth period, when workers doing long hours—like night laborers and truck drivers—needed frequent pick-me-ups. By then the yakuza had degenerated into gangs, with the Yamaguchi-gumi's ranks swelling. Every syndicate was involved in the stimulant trade and getting filthy rich off it.

The third boom was in 1998, when stims smuggled in from China and Korea hit it big with the youth culture. The new ingestion method was smoking, which had far less social stigma than injection. Paired with the rise of MDMA and drugs with trendy names like "speed" and "angel dust," amphetamines were cool again.

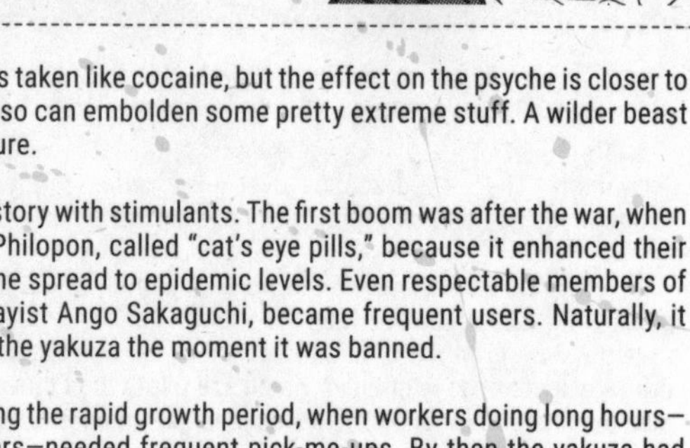

AN INFERNAL PLAGUE THAT DELUDES MEN INTO ACTS OF FALSE GRANDEUR.

WHERE ARE THEY?!

THE PUNKS WHO PUSHED JUNK IN MY TOWN!

The popular drugs of the west, like opium, cocaine and heroin, hold little appeal in Japan. Stimulants are king because of their utility: they prevent fatigue, amp up productivity and increase sexual pleasure. The name "Philopon" is derived from the Greek *philos ponos* (love, labor).

Although drugs have been one of the most reliable sources of income for yakuza, there are still some who refuse to deal in them. It's unheard of for a syndicate to wash their hands of it, but many individuals hold the belief that prostitution and stims are a vulgar form of income. They'll say "There's a drugstore over there," when referring to peers who act as pimps and pushers. It's as good as calling a guy a scammer. This is the sort of man our Ryumatsu is.

I conducted several interviews with people who had experience with stimulants. They explained that the gap between the euphoria and self-confidence of the *kikime* (the stretch of time the drug is working) and the sense of emptiness that comes with the *kireme* (when the drug's effects end) is intense. Kamikaze pilots didn't just use them to improve eyesight, but also to kill their fear and strengthen their self-images as heroes.

Lately, celebrities have been getting arrested for cocaine possession. Cocaine is similar to stims, but the *kikime* is short. In the west, it's common to snort a line before giving a corporate presentation. The popularity of the drug is due to the ease of consumption. There's a stereotype that cocaine users love Jack Daniels, and call their favorite drink combo "Jack and Coke." And we're not talking about Coca Cola.

The *kikime* of witchin is like turbo-charged cocaine. Overuse mutates the user's body and can even lead to a total collapse of the ego. The military has attempted to create superhumans with the drug, but has only succeeded in making more addicts.

-Written by Takeshi Natsuhara

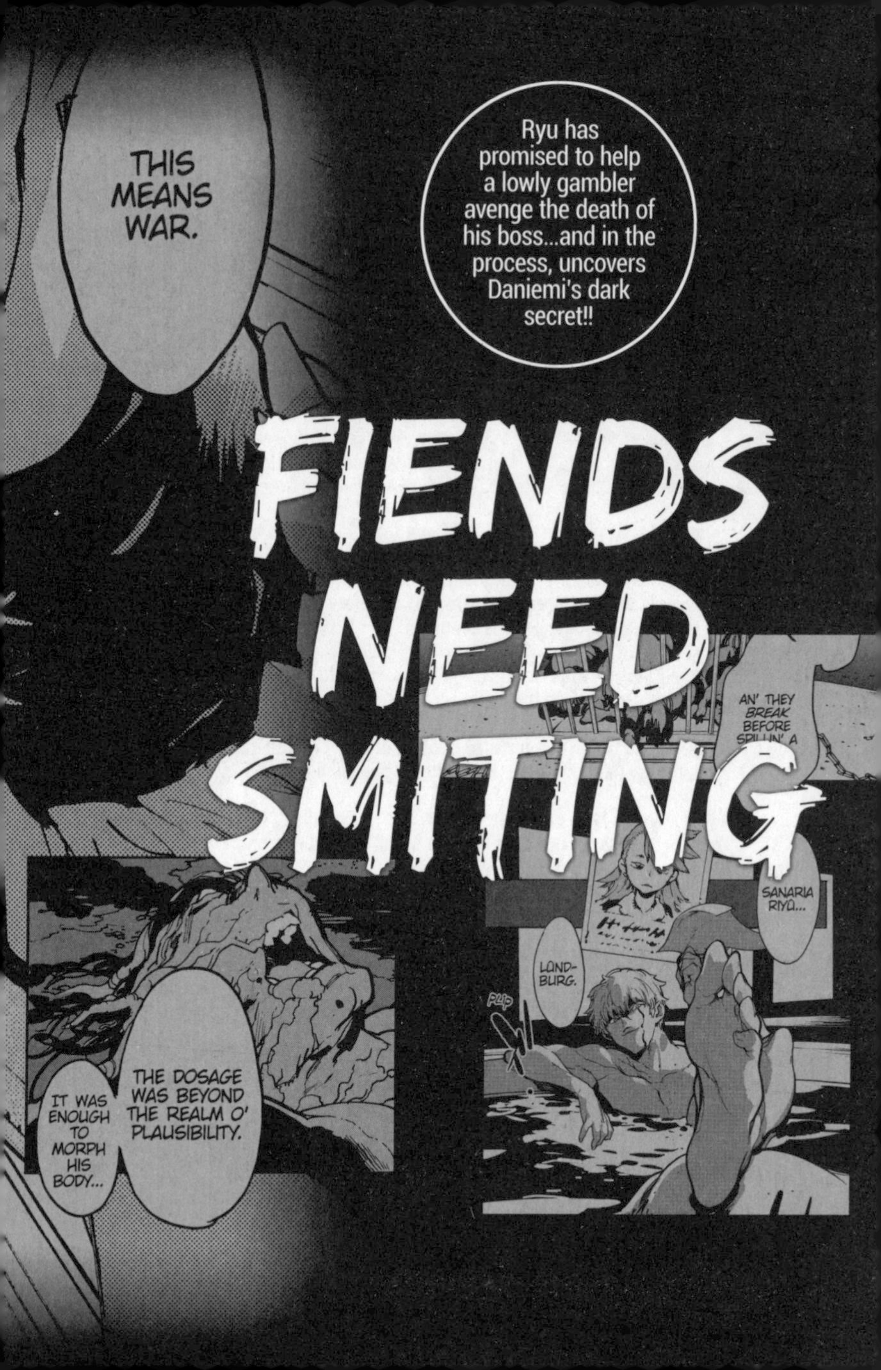
Ryu has promised to help a lowly gambler avenge the death of his boss...and in the process, uncovers Daniemi's dark secret!!
THIS MEANS WAR.
FIENDS NEED SMITING
AN' THEY BREAK BEFORE SPILLIN' A
SANARIA RIYŪ...
LAND-BURG.
PLIP
THE DOSAGE WAS BEYOND THE REALM O' PLAUSIBILITY.
IT WAS ENOUGH TO MORPH HIS BODY...

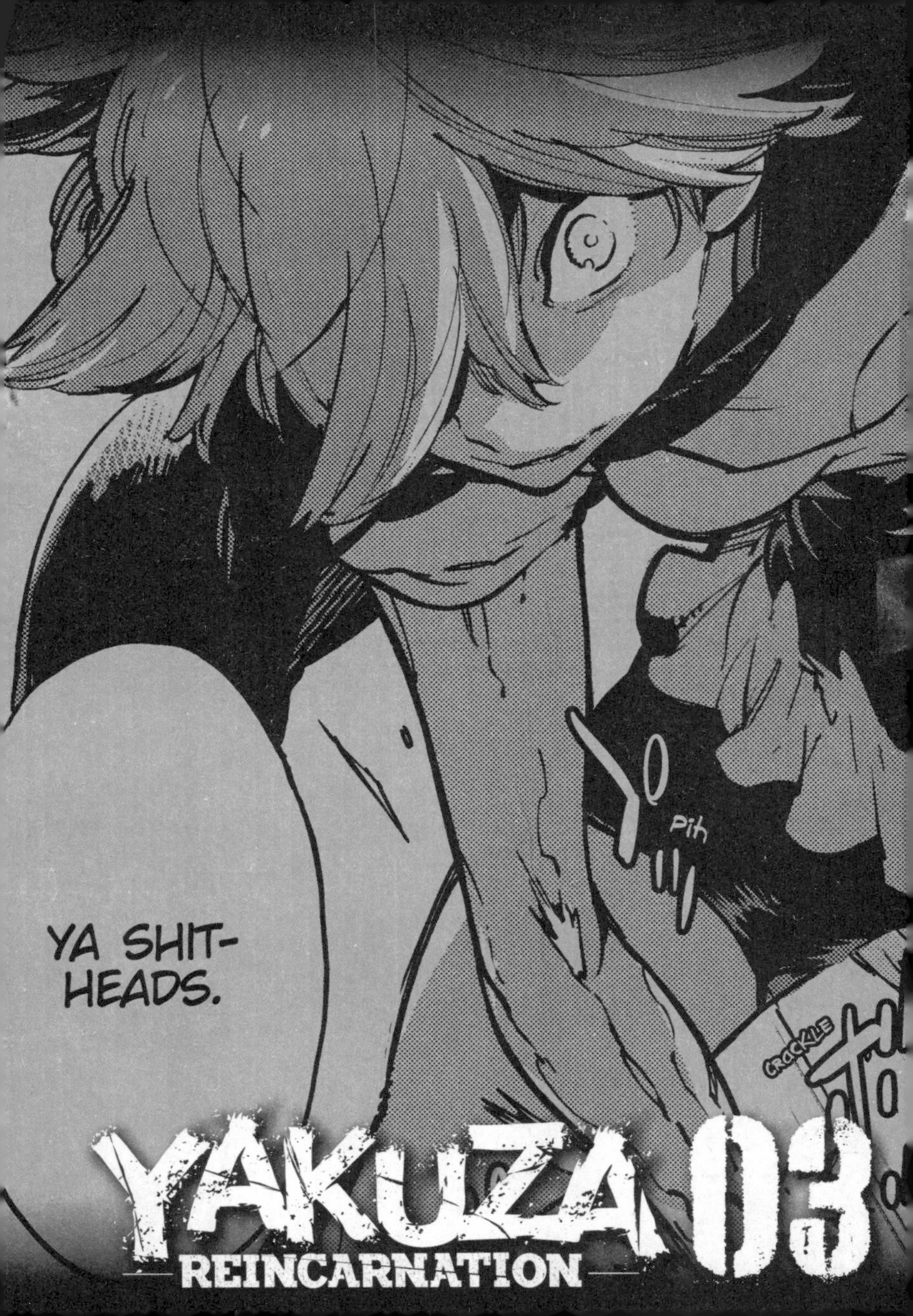
Pih
YA SHIT-
HEADS.
CRACKLE
YAKUZA
REINCARNATION
03

SEVEN SEAS ENTERTAINMENT PRESENTS

YAKUZA REINCARNATION

VOLUME 2

story by **TAKESHI NATSUHARA**   art by **HIROKI MIYASHITA**

TRANSLATION
Giuseppe di Martino

ADAPTATION
Jennifer Geisbrecht

LETTERING
Carl Vanstiphout

ORIGINAL COVER DESIGN
**Masato Ishizawa
+ Bay Bridge Studio**

COVER DESIGN
H. Qi

PROOFREADER
Kurestin Armada

COPY EDITOR
Dawn Davis

EDITOR
K. McDonald

PRODUCTION DESIGNER
Christina McKenzie

PRODUCTION MANAGER
Lissa Pattillo

PREPRESS TECHNICIAN
Melanie Ujimori

PRINT MANAGER
Rhiannon Rasmussen-Silverstein

EDITOR-IN-CHIEF
Julie Davis

ASSOCIATE PUBLISHER
Adam Arnold

PUBLISHER
Jason DeAngelis

NINKYO TENSEI -ISEKAI NO YAKUZA HIME- Vol. 2
by Hiroki MIYASHITA, Takeshi NATSUHARA
© 2020 Hiroki MIYASHITA, Takeshi NATSUHARA
All rights reserved.

Original Japanese edition published by SHOGAKUKAN.
English translation rights in the United States of America, Canada, the United Kingdom, Ireland, Australia and New Zealand arranged with SHOGAKUKAN through Tuttle-Mori Agency Inc.

Seven Seas press and purchase enquiries can be sent to Marketing Manager Lianne Sentar at press@gomanga.com. Information regarding the distribution and purchase of digital editions is available from Digital Manager CK Russell at digital@gomanga.com.

Seven Seas and the Seven Seas logo are trademarks of Seven Seas Entertainment. All rights reserved.

ISBN: 978-1-64827-841-9
Printed in Canada
First Printing: June 2022
10 9 8 7 6 5 4 3 2 1

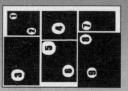

READING DIRECTIONS

This book reads from *right to left*, Japanese style. If this is your first time reading manga, you start reading from the top right panel on each page and take it from there. If you get lost, just follow the numbered diagram here. It may seem backwards at first, but you'll get the hang of it! Have fun!!

Follow us online: www.SevenSeasEntertainment.com